GLOBALIZATION OF INTERNATIONAL FINANCIAL MARKETS

Globalization of International Financial Markets

Causes and Consequences

HAK-MIN KIM
College of Social Sciences
Soonchunhyang University

LONDON AND NEW YORK

First published 1999 by Ashgate Publishing

Reissued 2018 by Routledge
2 Park Square, Milton Park, Abingdon, Oxon, OX14 4RN
52 Vanderbilt Avenue, New York, NY 10017

Routledge is an imprint of the Taylor & Francis Group, an informa business

A Library of Congress record exists under LC control number: 99072239

ISBN 13: 978-0-367-00056-1 (hbk)
ISBN 13: 978-0-429-44475-3 (ebk)

Contents

List of Figures

List of Tables

Acknowledgments

I would like to express my gratitude to my teachers, Dr Brian J.L. Berry, Dr Edward J. Harpham, Dr Euel W. Elliott, and Dr James C. Murdoch for their inspirations on my study at the University of Texas at Dallas. I owe special thanks to the Washington DC economists, Dr Neil Patterson (Deputy Division Chief at the IMF's Statistics Department), Dr Peter J. Wall (Senior Market Analyst at the IFC's Emerging Market Division) and Dr Kwang W. Jr (Senior Financial Economist at the World Bank's Debt and International Finance Division) for sharing their knowledge of international capital flows. Appreciation is also extended to my friends, Dr David S. Kelleher (Hoseo University, Korea) and Dr Chung-Ron Pi (City of Dallas) for their encouragement on this research. My deepest appreciation goes to my parents, Mr Eun-Kyoung Kim and Mrs Soon-Ja Baek for their love and patience.

Preface

This study investigates the causes and consequences of globalization of international financial markets, including all types of private sector capital (portfolio investment, bank capital, FDI, and other private sector capital) for 121 countries for the period 1980–1990. Globalization of international financial markets, a crucial component of the secular process of increasing functional integration of the global economy, while widely recognized and discussed, has not been subject to thorough empirical analysis. In this study, globalization institutions and technologies that lower national financial boundaries, provide improved information and reduce transaction costs are assessed in terms of their qualitative and quantitative impacts on financial globalization. This assessment proceeds within an integrated theoretical framework which draws from the principal theoretical approaches in international finance – flow, portfolio and monetary theories.

Globalization of international financial markets has been accelerated by such specific factors as increasingly open financial markets, participation in international tax treaties, financial instrument innovation and telecommunication network development. The portfolio market has been the greatest beneficiary of these globalization factors and it represents the most rapidly growing financial market during the period studied.

Portfolio and monetary theories appear to be effective in explaining inflows and outflows of most financial items, while the explanatory power of flow theory is limited to bank capital outflow. Portfolio and FDI outflows are driven by investment capacity (national wealth and current account surplus), while bank capital outflows are promoted by domestic financial market performance (lower creditworthiness and lower rate of return). These capital outflows represent capital inflows to countries where higher creditworthiness and more financial instrument options are provided. These processes are accelerated by the globalization institutions and technologies. As a result of globalization of international financial markets, countries with inflow of a certain financial item also promote outflow of that financial item (synchronized intra-item movement); countries with one type of capital inflow also induce inflows of other types of capital (synchronized inflow movement); countries with one type of capital outflow also induce outflows of other types of capital (synchronized outflow movement); and countries with one type of capital inflow reduce outflows of other types of capital or vice-versa (counteractive movement). These synchronized and counteractive movements imply an improvement in the efficiency of capital resource allocation and a phenomenon of agglomeration of international capital among countries with globalization facilities. This pattern is especially pronounced in short-term capital flows.

As a consequence of greater globalization among more developed countries, the external financial resource gap between the capital-rich countries and capital-poor countries has widened. In globalized financial markets, monetary policy plays a limited role in inducing foreign capital; more effective means of stimulating capital inflow include the provision of new financial instruments, advanced telecommunication networks, and improved country risk management. Collective efforts of international organizations to develop underdeveloped countries' financial markets in order to improve global equity of access to international capital are therefore indicated.

1 Introduction

Issues on Globalization

The most significant development in the world economy in recent decades is the increasing globalization[1] of economic activities. The capitalist system now should be understood as global rather than national since the major forces that are restructuring both domestic and international economic systems are globalization processes. The integration[2] of global financial markets, facilitated by regulatory changes and by technological innovations in the information economy is one of the most important factors contributing to this globalization (Ross, 1983; Obstfeld, 1986; Kane, 1988; Walter, 1989; Honeygold, 1989; O'Brien, 1992).

As a result of the globalization process in financial markets, global transactions of total private capital tripled during 1980–1990.[3] The integration of global financial markets has been primarily promoted by increased financial market activities as well as multinational enterprises. Arguing that information technology and regulatory revolution have resulted in the integration of global financial markets, O'Brien (1992) maintains that we have reached the 'end of geography'. This pattern is most marked in the portfolio and non-bank capital markets. Portfolio and non-bank financial institutions' capital transactions increased by approximately five times and four times respectively during 1980–1990. Efficiency-seeking multinational enterprises transfer capital, technology and managerial skills to the most profitable places (Hood and Young, 1979, pp. 2–3) and thus integrate the global economy (Casson, 1986; Dunning, 1988, pp. 43, 258–61). During the same period, the global transactions of foreign direct investment increased more than four times. These three financial products became more important global financial resources, increasing their proportion to total capital transactions from 46 per cent in 1980 to 62 per cent in 1990. Although the traditional bank capital doubled its global transactions, the proportion to total capital transactions decreased.

In this integrated world economy, the developed countries and a small number of developing countries have experienced substantial industrial growth, but other countries have experienced deep financial difficulty, widening the

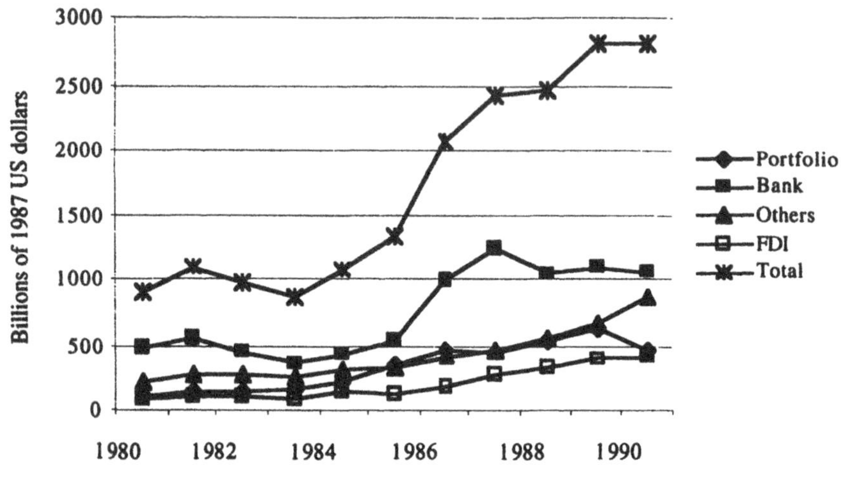

Year

Proportion of total capital (%)

Year	Portfolio	Bank K	Other K	FDI
1980	11.66	54.13	24.55	9.65
1981	13.01	51.13	25.26	10.60
1982	15.30	45.82	28.06	10.82
1983	17.82	42.27	28.98	10.94
1984	19.36	39.48	28.17	12.99
1985	25.60	40.81	24.16	9.44
1986	22.69	48.23	20.13	8.95
1987	18.69	51.07	19.23	11.02
1988	21.70	42.62	22.44	13.24
1989	22.40	39.63	23.93	14.04
1990	16.64	37.82	30.68	14.86
Sum	19.41	44.05	24.53	12.00

Figure 1 Global capital transactions by financial item (121 countries in 1980–1990)

Source: Balance of Payments Statistics Yearbook (IMF).

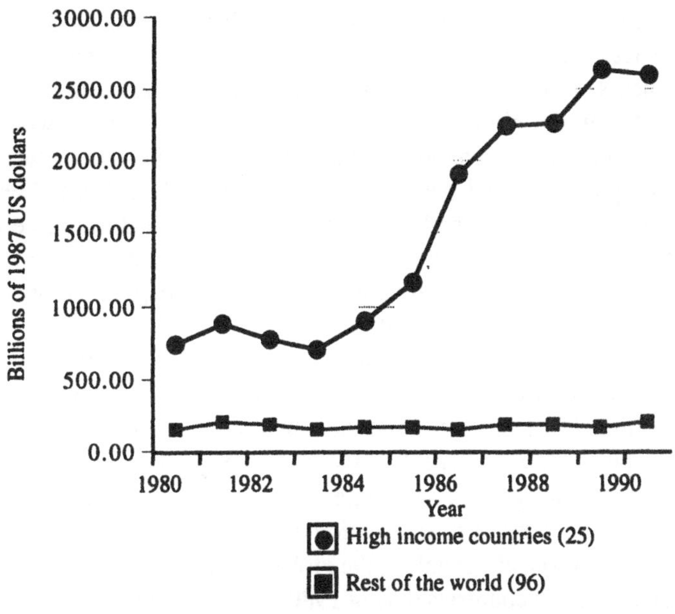

Share of world total (%)

Year	High income	Rest of the world
1980	81.76	18.24
1981	80.42	19.58
1982	80.44	19.56
1983	80.74	19.26
1984	83.68	16.32
1985	86.59	13.41
1986	92.12	7.88
1987	92.28	7.72
1988	92.02	7.98
1989	93.96	6.04
1990	92.60	7.40
Sum	89.28	10.72

Figure 2 Global capital transactions by level of income (high income countries vs rest of the world in 1980–1990)

Source: Balance of Payments Statistics Yearbook (IMF).

development gaps between the rich and poor. During 1980–1990, almost 90 per cent of global capital transactions were carried by 25 high income countries out of 121 countries.[4] The low income countries' share of global capital transactions was less than 1 per cent. As more information technologies and financial instruments were provided by the high income countries in recent years, the gap between the high income countries and the rest of the world became wider; the high income countries' share of global capital transactions increased from 82 per cent to 93 per cent during 1980–1990. Gill and Law (1988, p. 127) see this pattern as the 'transnational stage' in the development of capitalism. Since the capitalist system in the transnational stage separates the production process over space and national boundaries, capital moves in the most efficient way seeking more profits.

The parallel integration of finance and economies, O'Brien (1992, pp. 90–7) argues, is followed by the process of integration at the political level. Persson and Tabellini (1992, pp. 696–700) show that flexible capital mobility creates more competition, which results in similar monetary policy among countries. As a result, the government type, Persson and Tabellini argue, becomes similar as voters react to international competition. Indicative of financial market integration, about half of the global capital transactions were conducted by the European countries during 1980–1990. What has happened in Europe in recent decades is the future of the rest of the world as further globalization of international financial markets occur.

Omae (1985) sees the resultant global economy consisting of the 'triad of economic powers' of three regional blocs: North America, the European Community, and a Japan-dominated Asian bloc. These three regional leaders together contributed 43 per cent to global capital transactions and 56 per cent to global portfolio transactions during 1980–1990. The US and Japan were leaders in their regions while the UK was accompanied by neighbours as the European countries moved to the stage of regional integration. The same process is now under way in North America and Asia.

What has happened in the world economy in the last decade is a revolutionary change – a change in fundamental ways. It raises many research questions about the causes and consequences of globalization. Effects of ideological and environmental changes in world politics and institutional and technological innovations in the world economy should be analyzed, as should the impacts of the integrated world economy on political and economic activities. Social scientists and policy makers need to understand this new stage of transnational capitalism to prepare for a new global order. As a first step to providing this understanding, this study explores global capital flows,

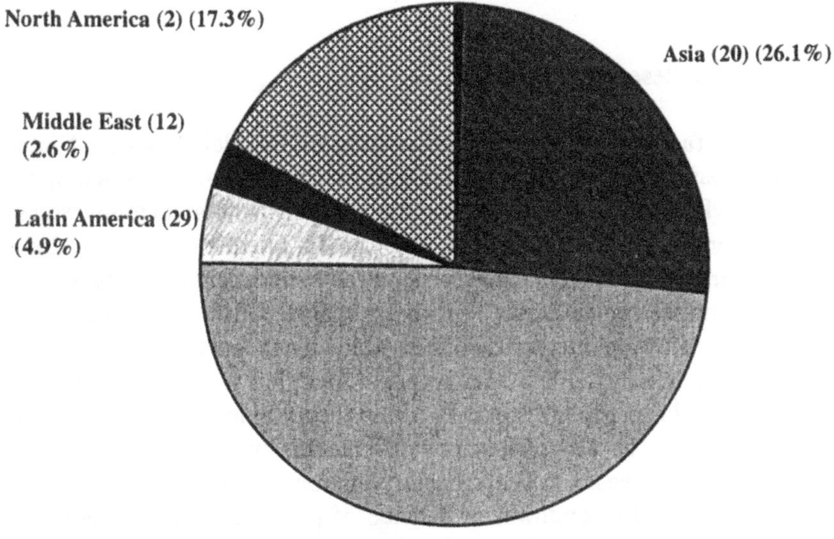

Major three countries vs rest of the world

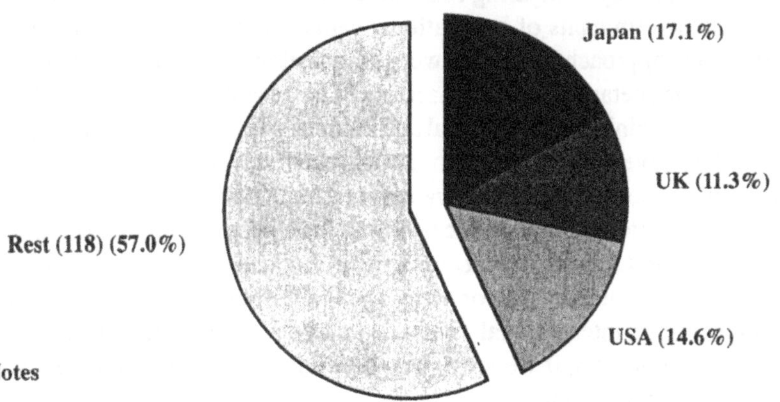

Notes

1 First (): number of countries
2 Second (): % share of the world total

Figure 3 Global capital transactions by region and major countries: sum of 11 years (1980–1990)

Source: Balance of Payments Statistics Yearbook (IMF).

one of the key contributors to the integration of global financial markets and thus to the integration of global economic activities.

Statement of Research Problem

Despite the fact that the theoretical literature on the globalization of international financial markets has grown rapidly in recent years, it has not properly answered what has caused this globalization. It is also important to investigate what the consequences of this globalization are for international capital flows. Since the first question has not been properly answered, neither has the second.

International capital flows have been analyzed from three theoretical perspectives: flow theory, portfolio theory, and the monetary approach to the balance of payments. Flow theory postulates that a given interest rate differential induces capital flows. Portfolio theory asserts that capital flows are dependent not only on interest rate differentials but also on risk estimates and capacity of investors. The monetary approach claims that a monetary policy based on the condition of balance of payments and the control of domestic credit determines international capital flows. The portfolio balance model incorporates portfolio theory and the monetary approach.

Since flow theory tries to measure the degree of integration of international financial markets by comparing real interest rates across countries, it cannot address the determinants of international capital flows. Portfolio theory and the monetary approach partly answer the question by examining portfolio factors and monetary factors separately. The portfolio balance model is effective in explaining both financial and monetary factors together. However, most studies have neglected the impact of recent developments in financial markets such as technological innovations and regulatory changes. In addition, the impacts of international political factors have been ignored in explaining international capital flows. It is necessary to investigate not only the traditional financial and monetary factors but also technological and regulatory developments in international financial markets along with international political environments, if we are to see the whole picture of globalization of international financial markets.

Most empirical studies have focused at best on small groups of countries, with the result that the determinants of international capital flows at a global level have not been illuminated. It is necessary to include a large number of countries to understand the globalization process. In addition, each empirical study has analyzed one financial product, focusing on portfolio flows, foreign direct investment flows, and bank loan flows separately. In doing so, interactions of these financial products cannot be examined in the context of total capital inflows to a country or total capital outflows from a country. It is necessary to analyze all of these financial products together in one system to investigate these interactions. This procedure will provide a more complete picture of global capital flows.

Purposes of the Study

This study includes international portfolio flows, bank capital flows, foreign direct investment flows, and other private sector capital flows of 121 countries for the period of 1980–1990 and draws flow, portfolio and monetary theories into a single framework. The purposes are:

- to investigate causes of the globalization of international financial markets;
- to examine consequences of this globalization for international capital flows; and
- to explore interactions among all private capital flows in the globalized financial markets.

From these analyses, the study develops policy options for developing countries needing external financial resources. Thus it may suggest more focused, efficacious strategies for international development organizations which seek to assist these developing countries in their economic development efforts.

Research Questions

The specific research questions that are examined are as follows:

I What are the causes of the globalization of international financial markets?

1 Do instrumental innovations in financial markets accelerate globalization?
2 Do technological innovations in telecommunication accelerate globalization?
3 Do relaxed monetary regulations accelerate globalization?

4 Do increased international economic relations accelerate globalization?

II What are the consequences of the globalization of international financial markets for international capital flows?

1 What types of capital flow (inflow or outflow) and which type of capital (portfolio, bank, foreign direct investment or other sector capital) are influenced by instrumental innovations in financial markets?
2 What types of capital flow or type of capital are influenced by technological innovations in telecommunication?
3 What types of capital flow or type of capital are influenced by regulatory changes?
4 What types of capital flow or type of capital are influenced by international economic relations?

III What are the interactions among different financial items as a result of globalized financial markets?

1 What types of capital flow or type of capital are closely related?
2 What types of capital flow or type of capital are sensitive to interest rate differentials?
3 What types of capital flow or type of capital are sensitive to risk differentials?
4 What types of capital flow or type of capital are sensitive to the current account balance?

Notes

1 We use the term 'globalization' as defined by Dicken (1992, p. 1). According to Dicken, 'internationalization' refers to the increasing geographical spread of economic activities across national boundaries while 'globalization' is a more advanced and complex form of internationalization which implies a degree of functional integration between internationally dispersed economic activities.
2 Integration of financial markets is interchangeably used with globalization of financial markets in this study since we view the both terms imply processes that allow the free flow of capital and permit all firms to compete in all international financial markets.
3 See Figure 1 and Appendix C.2 for global capital transactions. (Unless otherwise noted, in this study 'transaction' refers tothe total ovlume of trasnactions.)
4 See Figure 2 for global capital transactions by level of income, Figure 3 for global capital transactions by region, and Appendix C.1 for individual countries information.

2 Review of Literature

A Brief Review of the Conceptual Approaches

Most economists have been concerned with capital, but international capital flows did not become a major concern until relatively recently. Theories of capital flows developed in response to the internationalization of economic activities. There were four stages in this theoretical development.

In *the first stage*, it was thought that international capital flows are unnecessary or disadvantageous. In *The Wealth of Nations* (1776), Adam Smith argued that capitalists prefer to invest their funds at home because of the uncertainty of foreign countries.[1] He warned that international capital transfer involves monopolistic behaviour by capitalists to eliminate the import of goods and to control local markets by producing the same goods in the foreign country.[2] He has little to say, however, about the determinants of international capital flows.

In *Money, Credit and Commerce* (1923) Alfred Marshall supported Smith's position that it is easier and safer to invest capital in the home country since it is easier to obtain information and to deal with legal conditions at home. He showed that domestic investments have 'a great balance of pecuniary advantage as well as of sentimental attractiveness' under conditions of 'equal intrinsic merits' of domestic and foreign capital investments. Marshall concluded that higher profit advantages by transferring capital to foreign countries and disadvantages of risks and difficulties in doing business in foreign countries are equal; thus, 'net profits are kept nearly uniform throughout the country' (ibid., pp. 9–11). Interpreting his argument, the major obstacle to international capital flows is the real cost of risk due to the lack of information on foreign markets and legal systems.

The second stage in conceptual development concerning international capital flows involves the one-way movement of capital from capital-rich to capital-poor countries so as to gain a higher marginal return on capital. David Ricardo explained in *Principles of Political Economy and Taxation* (1817) that there is an incentive for capital to move from England to foreign countries based on the law of comparative advantage.[3] This can be interpreted as capital flowing from a country with a lower marginal product of capital to a country with a higher marginal product of capital since the capital transfer would be advantageous to the capitalists and the consumers in both countries. Ricardo, unlike Smith, supported international capital transfers arguing that excessive taxation of capital should be removed in order to induce capitalists to carry their capital to another country (ibid., ch. XVII).

John Stuart Mill in *Principles of Political Economy* (1848) argued that the international mobility of capital and labour was more popular among 'the more civilized countries' whose economic systems were becoming similar in the way that those countries exported capital and labour to colonial countries (ibid., Bk III, ch. XVII). He claimed that one of the major causes of international capital flows is the level of comparative costs. He observed that the determinant of capital outflow from England to her colonies and foreign countries is the decline of profits in England compared to the foreign countries due to higher costs in England.[4] This implied that capital outflows will occur from the country with higher marginal costs to the country with lower marginal costs since higher marginal costs will reduce the level of profit.

John E. Cairnes in his *Some Leading Principles of Political Economy* (1874) supported the theories of international trade in which the comparative cost of production leads to international capital flows. Unlike Ricardo and Mill who did not necessarily assume an absolute impossibility of moving capital and labour, however, Cairnes specifically pointed to factors that disturb the international movements of capital and labour. The obstacles are, in order, difference in political institutions, difference in cultures, and geographical distance (ibid., Pt III, ch. 1, pp. 305–6).

Walter Bagehot in his *Economic Studies* (1880, edited by Richard Holt Hutton) began to see the differences between international flows of capital and labour. He was the first scholar to mention interest rates as a cause of international capital flows. According to Bagehot, capital in the 'old country' is cheaper than that in the 'new country' since the 'old country' has accumulated capital and the 'new country' has saved little. Thus he argued that 'a cosmopolitan loan fund' is spread out everywhere 'as the rate of interest tempts it'. Bagehot concluded that capital will be diffused throughout the all countries attracted by different interest rates (Bagehot, 1976, St John-Stevas edition, Vol. 11, pp. 276–7).

John H. Williams (1929) pointed out that capital flows depend on differences in countries' levels of development. He assumed that under conditions of uniform development of all nations, there is no incentive for the transnational capital flow. He argued, however, that there is a strong incentive for capital outflow from the more developed countries to the less developed countries since the more developed countries take advantage of economic opportunities in the less developed countries where there is inferior domestic banking and inferior internal means of communication (Williams, 1929). Williams' theory thus confirms that capital moves from 'capital abundant' (Ricardo), 'more civilized' (Mill), or 'old' (Bagehot) countries to less developed countries.

The third stage of conceptual development involves the recognition that international capital flows are multidirectional in order to reduce risk, or as a result of different preferences for capital in international loan markets. Bertil Ohlin in his PhD dissertation, *Handelns Teori* (1924), saw two types of endogenous capital flows, summarized in his concept of factor mobility equalization and in his balance of payments model.[5] In the factor equalization model, capital flow is induced by higher returns on capital as discussed in the second stage. The higher returns on capital are generated by interest rate differentials in international loan markets and by the large profits of foreign direct investments. In the case of different interest rates, Ohlin argued that capital mobility equalizes interest rates like labour mobility equalizes wage rates. This is factor price equalization. In the case of foreign direct investment, Ohlin argued that the characteristics of the asset or the preferences of particular investors who are willing to take risky investments determine the direction and volume of the capital flows even if there is no interest rate differential (Heckscher and Ohlin, 1991, pp. 122–5)[6] or even if the general level of interest rate is low (Ohlin, 1933, pp. 364–5).

Karin Kock (1929) developed Ohlin's idea of different types of assets, introducing the different types of capital in life insurance companies, savings banks and public institutions of the Swedish loan market in 1925–1927. He argued that the marginal international mobility for the different types of capital may not be the same since the preferences of individual investors differ because of their different techniques and organizations (Kock, 1929, pp. 60–90). This is why a country may both import and export capital at the same time.

Harry D. White (1933) extended Ohlin's idea of different preferences of investors, arguing that international capital flows also are affected by an inclination to spread capital over several investments in order to minimize the risk. In his *The French International Accounts 1880–1914,* White showed that the geographical distribution of French foreign bond holdings before the First World War tended to increase rather than to decrease the risk of loss, however. A quarter of the French holdings were concentrated in Russia, and the rest consisted of loans to countries of very doubtful political economic stability (White, 1933, p. 289).

Fritz Machlup (1932) showed that the Williams' theory is not always the case by arguing that capital may move in an opposite direction from the less developed country with higher interest rates to the more advanced country with lower interest rates. Machlup introduced 'Kapitalflucht' – capital flight– the motive of which is to avoid risk in the home country rather than to obtain a higher rate of return from foreign countries (Machlup, 1932, p. 512). For the country whose domestic conditions are unstable, Marshall's assumption that the home country is safer than foreign countries is no longer guaranteed. If it is true that the less developed countries are politically less stable than the more developed countries, capital may move from the less developed countries to the more developed countries. Even though Machlup did not distinguish capital flight from capital exporting, his theory suggests that political insecurity or instability of the currency of the home country may induce capital outflow.

Carl Iversen in his *International Capital Movements* (1936) summarized these studies, arguing that 'a reduction in the cost of capital transfer or an increase in the interest rate differentials' induce international capital flows (Iversen, 1936, p. 117). A reduction in the cost of capital transfer can be obtained by political security and economic stability (ibid., p. 126). International interest rate differentials are affected by changes in such factors as consumption behaviour, level of income, supply of productive factors, and methods of production (ibid., p. 127). He also suggested that other factors contributing to international capital flows be considered such as an inclination to diversify the portfolio, political considerations in which friendly countries use capital for diplomatic purposes,[7] and purely personal preferences (ibid., pp. 143-51).

The fourth stage of conceptual development involves the realization that capital flows emerge as a result of the balance of payments. The theory of balance of payments has a long history from David Hume (1752) to Frank Taussig (1918) to Bertil Ohlin (1929) even before the Keynesian revolution in the 1930s. In the analysis of the price-specie-flow mechanism, Hume saw that international trade is automatically balanced (Hume, 1752, Rotwein edition 1955). Taussig argued that the balance of trade is not automatically determined, but is a result of changes in the relative price of exportables and importables (Taussig, 1918, p. 411). However, theory was not focused on capital flows until Ohlin introduced the concept of 'buying power'. According to Ohlin, changes in 'buying power' lead through trade imbalance to changes in the demand and supply functions of domestic money, which eventually induces international capital flows. A country with a trade deficit, thus, needs to import capital to maintain the same level of consumption or income even though there is a reduction in exports (Ohlin, 1991, pp. 140–6, 154–5; Ohlin, 1929, pp. 400–4). In this sense, he believed that the trade balance would be always in equilibrium if there were no international capital movements (Ohlin, 1991, p. 125).

The balance of payments approach that Ohlin introduced was further advanced by Keynes and his followers. The Keynesian revolution in the 1930s opened a new approach to the study of balance of payments. The Keynesian approach saw that international adjustments of the balance of payments result from government policies that influence the balance of trade and capital accounts in separate ways. In terms of the balance of trade, Keynes argued that the major factor in international capital flow ('the volume of foreign investment') depends on government policies which affect the balance of trade. With this understanding, Keynes said in his analysis of the transfer problem of German reparations that the gold-rate of efficiency-earnings of the German factors of production should be reduced sufficiently to enable them to increase their exports so as to pay reparations (capital outflow) through trade surplus and improved reserves. Thus, Keynes concluded that the transfer problem could be solved when the German industries were in a competitive position in the international markets (Keynes, 1929, pp. 4–6), which implied the current account balance as a solution.

In *The General Theory of Employment, Interest and Money* (1936), he emphasized the mechanism of 'effective demand' in which the level of output and employment at a given wage rate and population depends on the marginal propensity to consume,[8] the marginal efficiency of capital,[9] and the quantity of money and liquidity preference.[10] Although the *General Theory* assumed a closed economy, the basic idea of multiplier analysis was applied to balance of payments theory for an open economy by Machlup (1943) and Roy F. Harrod (1951), who incorporated the income effects and price effects.[11]

Modern Theories of Determinants of International Capital Flows

From these conceptual beginnings, three major theories of the determinants of international capital flows have emerged: flow theory in the late 1950s and early 1960s, portfolio theory in the late 1960s and the 1970s, and the monetary approach in the 1970s and the 1980s. Flow theory suggests that a given interest differential induces a permanent inflow or outflow of capital. Portfolio theory emphasizes the capacity of investors and creditworthiness of importers as well as interest rate differentials. The monetary approach claims that a monetary policy based on the condition of balance of payments and the control of domestic credit determines international capital flows.

Flow Theory

According to flow theory, an increase of foreign interest rates will increase the outflow (or reduce the inflow) of capital to foreign countries, and as long as foreign interest rates remain high relative to domestic interest rates, the increased outflow of capital will continue. Conversely, an increase of domestic interest rates will induce the inflow (or reduce the outflow) of capital from foreign countries, and as long as domestic interest rates remain high relative to foreign interest rates, the increased inflow of capital will continue. This is called flow theory because it postulates a relationship between the flow of capital and the level of interest rates.

The relationship of capital flows to level of interest rates was widely accepted until the mid-1960s by the Keynesian economists. The Keynesian approach to the balance of payments is developed by James E. Meade (1951) in the analysis of the orthodox current account as shown below.

Trade Balance: $T = T(Y^{-}, e/P^{+})$
where T = trade balance, Y = output, *e* = exchange rate, P = price level; thus, *e*/P = competitiveness.

Capital Inflow: $F = F(i^{+}, i^{*-})$
where F = net inflow of capital, *i*=interest rate, and * indicates foreign variable.

Balance of payment identity: $\Delta R = PT+F$

Balance of payment equation: $\Delta R = PT(Y^{-}, e/P^{+}) + F(i^{+})$
where R = reserves.

The balance of payments equation of the Keynesian approach is similar to the discussion of the German transfer problem (Keynes, 1929) as introduced earlier. In Meade's analysis of the Keynesian approach to the balance of payments, the balance of payments deteriorates when output increases for a given price and interest rate because an increase in income will induce imports. The balance of payments also deteriorates when price increases for a given output and interest rate, because an increase in price will erode competitiveness and so worsen the balance of trade. The balance of payments, however, improves when interest rates increase for a given output and price because an increase in domestic interest rates will attract foreign capital. The balance of payments also improves when exchange rates increase (devaluation) for a given output, price, and interest rate because an increase in the exchange rate will improve the competitiveness of prices.

In the framework of the Keynesian approach to the balance of payments, Mundell and Fleming explain that capital flow is determined by interest rate level. Mundell assumes that at high rates of domestic interest the net inflow of capital will be large or the net outflow of capital will be small (Mundell, 1960, p. 230; 1962, p. 72). Fleming adds that international capital flows are more sensitive to the rate of interest under a flexible exchange rate system than under a fixed exchange rate system (Fleming, 1962, pp. 373–4). In the equation of change in reserves of the Keynesian approach, the price level or exchange rate affects only the balance of trade, and the interest rate affects only the rate of capital imports or exports. Mundell, however, implies that the interest rate corrects the balance of payments because when reserves are below or above the desired level, the interest rate changes and, thus, capital is attracted from abroad or moves abroad (Mundell, 1960, pp. 230–7). Similarly, Fleming assumes that the balance of payments on capital account varies directly with the interest rate under a flexible exchange rate (Fleming, 1962, pp. 369–70). That is, the exchange rate depreciates to the point at which the balance of trade becomes favourable under the assumption that international capital flows are infinitely elastic with respect to the interest rate (ibid., p. 274).

Jorgenson (1963) and Bischoff (1971) develop flow theory from the framework of the neoclassical theory of the demand for investment goods rather than from the framework of the balance of payments. The neoclassical theory of the demand for investment goods is derived from the same position of flow theory in a sense that the desired capital stock is related to the interest rate level and expected output. More precisely, this theory explains that the capital stock depends on the user cost of owned capital goods and returns on the capital. In this view of investment behaviour, it is changes in interest rates, other things held constant, that cause changes in the desired capital stock. These generate investment flows, which are, after all, simply changes in asset and liability positions.

Since flow theory explains that interest rate differentials induce international capital flows, comparison of interest rate differentials across countries has been used to evaluate the mobility of international capital. Martin

Feldstein and Charles Horioka (1980) set up a strong assumption that the real interest rates of all countries are the same under perfect capital mobility. Thus exogenous changes in national saving rates have no effect on investment rates. They correlate saving and investment shares to measure the extent of capital mobility by the following equation:

$$(I/Y)i = \alpha + \beta\ (S/Y)i$$

with the ratio of gross domestic investment (I) to gross domestic product (Y) in country *i* on the left hand side and the corresponding ratio of gross domestic saving (S) to gross domestic product (Y) on the right hand side. If there is a perfect capital mobility, saving and investment shares should be uncorrelated ($\beta = 0$) while if there is a low degree of capital mobility, a coefficient will be close to or equal to one.

Jeffrey Frankel (1989, 1992) argues that it is better to examine differences in rates of return across countries rather than saving-investment correlations in order to measure the degree of integration of international capital markets. Frankel assumes, like Feldstein and Horioka, that the real interest rate should be the same across countries under the perfect capital mobility. However, the Feldstein-Horioka hypothesis requires that all determinants of a country's rate of investments other than its real interest rate be uncorrelated with its rate of national saving (Frankel, 1992, pp. 192–7). From this argument, Frankel asserts that international capital mobility should be measured directly by real interest rate differentials rather than by the savings-investment ratio.

As portfolio theory[12] indicates that investors' decision-making is based on their expected rate of return differentials, Frankel defines expected rate of return differentials by real interest rate differentials:[13]

$$r - r^* = (i - \Delta p^e) - (i^* - \Delta p^{e*})$$

where r = real interest rate, i = nominal interest rate, p^e = expected inflation, and * indicates foreign variable.

This can be broken down as follows:

$$r - r^* = (i - i^* - fd) + (fd - \Delta s^e) + (\Delta s^e - \Delta p^e - \Delta p^{e*})$$

where fd = forward discount on the domestic currency and s^e = expected depreciation of the domestic currency.

The first term (i - i* - fd) is the covered interest rate differential, the second term (fd $-\Delta s^e$) the risk premium, and the third term ($\Delta s^e - \Delta p^e - \Delta p^{e*}$) expected real depreciation. Frankel calls the covered interest rate differential the political or country premium because it captures all barriers to integration of financial markets across national boundaries. These barriers are transaction costs, information costs, capital controls, tax laws, and risk of future capital controls. The second and third terms together constitute the currency premium because they pertain to differences in assets according to the currency in which they are denominated, rather than in terms of the political jurisdiction in which they are issued (Frankel, 1992, pp. 199–200). From this understanding, Frankel asserts that the degree of integration of international capital markets should be measured by comparing real interest rates among countries.

Portfolio Theory

In the late 1960s, economists began to argue that the notion that international capital flows respond to interest rate differentials is an improper generalization, suggesting that international capital flows (total foreign assets) are determined not only by the level of interest rates but also by the level of risk both at home and abroad and the capacity of lenders or potential lenders. Portfolio theory for international capital flows originally stems from the theory of domestic portfolio distribution which was developed by Markowitz (1952) and Tobin (1958). In the analysis of portfolio selection, Markowitz (1952, pp. 81–7) argues that investors would want to choose the most efficient combination of the expected return and variance of return[14] – a variety of investments not simply for the highest yields but also for their preferences of risk avoidance. Tobin (1958, p. 85) criticizes the Keynesian assumption of the inverse relationship between the demand for cash and the rate of interest, which implies that each investor holds only one asset. Analyzing the behaviour of different types of investors based on their preferences,[15] Tobin argues that there is a trade-off between the higher expectation of return and additional risk over a whole range of assets. The Markowitz-Tobin model of portfolio distribution concludes that distribution of assets depends on the rate of return and estimates of risk for the alternative assets.

Applied the Markowitz-Tobin model to international capital movements, Branson developed the stock-adjustment model to explain the allocation of wealth between domestic and foreign assets. He initially shows that short-term financial capital flows are determined by imports, exports, interest rates, and exchange rates, while long-term financial capital and bank loans are determined by domestic and foreign income and interest rates (Branson, 1968, pp. 162–6).[16] Incorporating this framework within the Markowitz-Tobin model, he then argues that the proportion of foreign assets (F) in a given stock of wealth (W) is a function of the domestic and foreign interest rates (i and i^*), a measure of risk (E) and the stock of wealth:

$$F^f/W = f(i, i^*, E, W).$$

An equation explaining capital flows is obtained by taking first differences on both sides:

$$\Delta F^f = f(i, i^*, E, W)\,\Delta W + f_i\, W\,\Delta i + f_{i*}\, W\,\Delta i^* + f_E\, W\,\Delta E + f_W\, W\Delta W + u,$$

where u = error term.

The first component on the right-hand side measures the continuing 'flow effect' of portfolio growth on capital flows. The second component measures the 'stock effects' of portfolio adjustment associated with changes in interest rates and other relevant variables.[17] Most authors have ignored the flow effect and instead use a linear form of the above equation,

$$\Delta F^f = a_0 + a_1\Delta i + a_2\Delta i^* + a_3\Delta E + a_4\Delta W + u.$$

This basic form with a variety of additional explanatory variables has been used to explain individual items on the capital account as well as the net magnitude of capital flows.

In Branson's model, risk estimations are exogenously given and exchange rates are held constant. The model also assumes no barrier to international investment and homogeneous financial instruments across countries. Branson's model has been developed in a series of modifications by both portfolio theorists[18] and monetary theorists[19] using improved assumptions. The parameter uncertainty model analyzes the relationship between the quality of information and risk estimation. Tobin's Q theory explores the effects of marginal efficiency and cost of capital on investment decision-makings. The barrier-to-international investment model investigates the relationship between tax rates and rate of returns. The portfolio balance model examines the impacts of exchange rates on the rate of returns.

The first modification of Branson's model became possible as the quality of information in international financial markets was improved through innovations in telecommunication technology. In Branson's model, information is provided equally to the domestic and foreign portfolios or is provided equally to all investors. It has been known, however, that substantial capital flows arise from better information through innovations in telecommunication technology. The theorists of the parameter uncertainty model have attempted to analyze the effects of changes in the quality of information on international portfolio decisions and levels of risk premium.

In the parameter uncertainty model,[20] investors require parameter values for the expected return vector and the variance/covariance matrix of returns. However, investors generally do not know the true parameters, and they have to use statistical techniques to construct estimates. Although the estimation process provides a set of point estimates for parameters, a band of uncertainty necessarily remains. The parameter uncertainty model illustrates how this estimation risk is properly incorporated in portfolio selection theory. Bawa, Brown and Klein (1979) and Stiglitz (1982) assume that the true information is given by the set $\theta = \{\mu, E\}$, with μ the expected return vector and E the variance/covariance matrix or estimation risk. They calculate the point estimates for the parameter as $\theta^* = \{\mu^*, E^*\}$. The estimation risk E^* can be reduced by the improvement in information quality. They define the number of observations T as a measurement of the quality of information:

$$\theta = \{\mu^*, [1 + (1/T)]E^*\}$$

where $[1 + (1/T)]$ is an adjustment factor which is greater than 1.

In this model, if the number of observations T approaches infinity as information becomes certain, the adjustment factor approaches 1. In this case, the estimates for the expected return and risk become the true information for the expected return and risk: $\theta = \{\mu, E\} \equiv \theta^* = \{\mu^*, E^*\}$. This condition of improved information will reduce the foreign asset risk premium, and the demand for foreign assets will then increase.

Branson and Jaffe (1991) analyze the effects of improving information on portfolio decisions based on the three different conditions of access to information: identical access, asymmetric access, and symmetric but biased access. If all investors have identical access to information for both domestic and foreign assets, there will be an increase in demand for both assets proportionally as they are initially allocated (Branson, 1991, pp. 48–50, 57). If only home country investors have improved information for domestic assets, there will be no change in foreign demand for domestic assets. However, if home country investors have improved information for foreign assets while there is no change in information for home assets, there will be an increase in demand for foreign assets and a decrease in demand for domestic assets as they shift their domestic assets to foreign assets (ibid., pp. 52–3, 57–8). If home country investors have improved information only for their own countries' assets while no change in foreign assets, there will be a decrease in demand for foreign assets and an increase in domestic assets as they shift their assets from foreign to domestic assets (ibid., p. 58).

A second modification of Branson's model has been necessary as financial instruments have been innovated and introduced to selected countries. In Branson's model, homogeneous financial products are provided to all financial markets. It has been known, however, that substantial capital flows arise from innovations in various financial instruments. Innovations in financial instruments have been classified into two groups (Yumoto et al., 1986, pp. 46–9): (1) innovations which result from, and seek to reduce, the shadow cost of regulatory constraints; and (2) innovations which, independent of regulatory constraints, seek to reduce physical transaction costs or to improve allocation of risk. The second type of innovation may have the same effect as innovation in telecommunications. Anderson and Harris (1986) argue that innovations in financial instruments provide improved information to investors who then reduce the cost of investments through risk management.

The first type of innovation, involving the shadow cost of regulatory constraints, can be analyzed using Tobin's Q theory (Tobin, 1969) since Q depends on the marginal efficiency of capital and cost of capital. Tobin's Q theory of investment has been developed in the framework of investment theory (Mussa, 1977; Abel, 1979; Fischer and Merton, 1984; Chirinko, 1987) as follows: a competitive firm invests (I) so as to maximize its own value (V) subject to the constants imposed by technology (f), the capital stock adjustment cost [C (I/K)], and financial costs (ρ). That is,

$$\max V_t = E_t\{\sum_{j=0}^{\infty}\beta^j I f_{t+j}(K_{t+j}) - C_{t+j}(I_{t+j}/K_{t+j}) - I_{t+j}]\} \text{ subject to}$$

$$K_{t+j} = (1-\delta)K_{t+j-1} + I_{t+j},$$

where E_t = expectational operator conditional on information available at time t,

δ = rate of depreciation of the capital stock, and

$\beta^j = \pi^j_{s=1}(1+\rho)^{-1}$ = discounting factor dependent on real financial cost of capital (ρ) to the firm (π being the product operator).

The Q variable mathematically corresponds to the multiplier associated with the capital accumulation constraint. When solving the first order conditions of the maximization problem, the firm's Q (shadow price associated with the capital accumulation restriction) is calculated as below:

$$Q_t = E_t[\sum_{j=0}^{\infty} \beta^j \frac{\delta Z_{t+1}}{\delta K_{t+1}} (1\text{-}\delta)^j],$$

where $Z_{t+j} = f_{t+j}(K_{t+j}) - C_{t+j}(I_{t+j}/K_{t+j}) - I_{t+j}$.

Therefore, Q will be higher when the financial cost of capital is lower (β higher), when the net income (Z_{t+j}) coming from the addition to the capital stock is higher and when the rate of depreciation of capital stock (δ) is lower.

In short, investment depends positively on Q (shadow price associated with the capital accumulation restriction). In turn, Q will be larger when the marginal efficiency of capital is higher, and when the financial cost of capital is lower. As a result, investment decisions of a firm will be determined by the evolution of Q dictated by the behaviour of the marginal efficiency of capital and the cost of capital. Here, innovations in the first type of financial instrument provides a cheaper cost of capital by reducing regulatory constraints. This will lower the financial cost (ρ) of capital in the β equation, and thus will increase β. The increased β consequently increases Q. Thus the first type of financial innovation will eventually increase international investment, and thus international capital flows.

In addition to these modifications in response to innovations in telecommunication technology and financial instruments, one more modification of Branson's model has been necessary as barriers to international portfolio investments have been differentially enforced across countries. In Branson's model, barriers to international portfolio investments are assumed to be zero or enforced equally by all countries. It has been known, however, that substantial capital flows arise from lowered barriers through competition in regulatory changes. The barrier-to-international-investment theorists[21] assume imperfect capital markets where there are barriers to international financial markets and these barriers are different across countries. The barrier models have attempted to analyze the effects of changes in regulations on international portfolio decisions and rate of returns.

In the barrier model, transaction costs and taxes on the rate of return to foreign investment are treated as barriers. Lowering these barriers to international investments thus raises the level of expected rate of returns for investors since a cost associated with holding foreign investments declines. Black (1974) and Stulz (1981) treat taxes as barriers to international investments, and Huizinga (1991) explicitly treats them as costs.

Black shows that if a tax is imposed on borrowing and lending abroad, it is possible that neither borrowing or lending occurs between countries (Black, 1974, pp. 349–50). In Stulz's model, taxes on absolute values of the investors' holdings of foreign assets are treated as a barrier. Stulz assumes that domestic investors have to pay taxes on their foreign assets while foreign investors do not have to pay taxes on any foreign investments. Thus the return to domestic investors on foreign assets (μ) is calculated by the return of foreign investors on foreign assets (μ^*) minus tax rate (t) $\mu = \mu^* - t$. From this assumption Stulz argues that the yield differential between domestic and foreign stocks for foreign investors is simply computed by the interest rate differential between foreign and domestic stocks. But yield differentials for domestic investors are significantly different because of the barrier (Stulz, 1981, pp. 927–33).

In Huizinga's model, different tax rates and different costs apply to domestic and foreign investments. Tax rates can be higher or lower on domestic capital than on foreign capital. The cost of domestic investment, which includes transaction costs, difficulties in foreign legal systems, and so on, is assumed to be zero while that of foreign investment is positive. He also assumes that yield (r) on investment is universal. He argues the net proceeds of an investor's capital, N, are given by the sum of net-of-tax (t = tax on domestic and t* = tax on foreign assets) investment income from domestic (i) and foreign (i*) investments minus the costs (c) associated with foreign investment:

$$N = [(1 - t)\, r\, (k - i^*)] + [(1 - t^*)\, r\, i^* - c\, (i^*)]$$

where k = total capital available to invest in both domestic and foreign portfolios.

By differentiating this equation with respect to I* : $r(t - t^*) = c''\,(I^*)$. In this equation, the cost function will be reduced when the foreign tax rate is reduced, and will be increased when the foreign tax rate is increased (Huizinga, 1991, pp. 712–3). All of the barrier models show that reducing barriers to international investments will increase yields on foreign asset, and that this condition will increase the demand for foreign assets.

Critics of portfolio theory argue that interest rate differentials contribute not only to a portfolio shift between domestic and foreign bonds but also to a shift between bonds, money and other assets (Kouri and Porter, 1974, pp. 445–6). It is also important, for the whole picture of international capital flows, to consider other categories of equity and direct investment which are likely to be controlled more by profit prospects associated with the level of income than by the interest rates available on financial claims (Gilman, 1981, pp. 33-5, 38–42). Moreover, portfolio theory cannot be used to analyze macro-economic problems such as the effect of income fluctuations on the capital account, the link between the current account and capital flows, and the effect of changes in investment and saving behaviour on the capital account. Portfolio and monetary theorists extend their models to account for these criticisms by incorporating portfolio theory and the monetary approach to the balance of payments.

The Monetary Approach to the Balance of Payments

The monetary approach to the balance of payments implies that international capital flows are essentially a monetary phenomenon that is determined by reserve changes and monetary policies based on the control of domestic credit. Those who advocate the monetary approach to the balance of payments argue that it is a mistaken strategy to try and predict the balance of payments on the basis of the sum of separately determined current and capital accounts.[22] The overall balance of payments is, monetarists argue, an inflow or outflow of money (Mussa, 1974; Frenkel and Johnson, 1976, pp. 21–3). This monetary approach has been developed by modifying the Keynesian approach to the balance of payments (Johnson, 1972; Mussa, 1974; Frenkel and Johnson, 1976; Frenkel et al., 1980) and by incorporating portfolio theory (Kouri and Porter, 1974; Adler and Dumas, 1983; Marwah, 1984; Marwah et al., 1985; Stockman and Svensson, 1987).

Johnson argues that variation in the supply of money relative to the demand for money associated with international capital flows must work toward an equilibrium between money demand and money supply with a corresponding equilibrium of the balance of payments. In his view, deficits and surpluses represent phases of stock adjustment in the money market and not equilibrium flows, and should not be treated within an analytical framework that treats them as equilibrium phenomena. In order to obtain flow-equilibrium deficits or surpluses on the basis of stock adjustments in the money market, he argues, it is necessary to construct a model in which the need for stock adjustments is being continuously recreated by economic change (Johnson, 1976, pp. 152–3). His version of the monetary approach to the balance of payments can be summarized as follows:

$\mathbf{H_d = H(P^+, Y^+, i^-)}$ – a demand for money function
$\mathbf{H_s = H(1/\Phi)(R + D)}$ – a supply of money function

where P = price level, Y = output, *i* = interest rate, R = reserves, D = domestic credit, and Φ = reserve ratio of commercial banks (thus $1/\Phi$ = money multiplier = *m*).

Let $\mathbf{H_d = H_s}$, then $\mathbf{R + D = \Phi H(P, Y, \mathit{i})}$ for equilibrium.
Thus, $\mathbf{dR = Hd\Phi + \Phi H_1 dP + \Phi H_2 dY + \Phi H_3 di - dD}$ – monetary balance of payments equation.

The monetary balance of payments equation implies that reserve changes are the consequences of changes in the reserve ratio, price level, the rate of interest and domestic credit expansion. This equation is a fundamental challenge to the Keynesian approach to the balance of payments, showing exactly opposite arguments.[23] The monetary approach argues that an increase in income or prices will increase the demand for money and so improve reserves, while an increase in interest rates will decrease the demand for money and so cause a payments deficit.

Applied to international capital flows, the monetary approach thus is at odds with the Keynesian approach to the balance of payments. The question is whether incomes, prices and interest rates are exogenously determined. If they are all exogenous like global monetarists have argued,[24] the Keynesian approach cannot determine the balance of payments. In case of perfect capital mobility under unequal prices and incomes between countries, the balance of payments would be determined by the monetary approach equation rather than the Keynesian approach; the Keynesian approach cannot explain the change in reserves since domestic and foreign interest rates are the same under the perfect capital mobility.

When they are endogenous, the questions about the effects of incomes, prices, and interest rates on the balance of payments all depend on the causes of the increases in these factors. An increase in domestic interest rates due to foreign interest rates leads to outflows of capital as the Keynesian approach argues, while an increase in domestic interest rates due to the monetary policy leads to inflows of capital because the monetary approach equation has a negative coefficients for domestic credit. An increase in price due to the domestic forces, the Keynesian approach argues, leads to outflows of capital, while an increase in prices due to foreign inflation, as the monetary approach suggests, leads to inflows of capital. An increase in incomes due to an increase in supply capacity may lead to outflows of capital as the Keynesian approach argues, while an increase in incomes due to an increase in demand capacity may lead to inflows of capital as the monetary approach argues.

It is wrong to conclude that the Keynesian and monetary approaches imply different conclusions, however. A general equilibrium model needs to contain both equations. Frenkel, Gylfason and Helliwell (1980) present a general short-run model including the Keynesian and monetary approaches.[25] In their general equilibrium model, balance-of-payments deficits lead to a decrease in the demand side (K-schedule), and this movement leads automatically to an increase in the supply side (M-schedule). The changes in reserves, they hypothesize, keep taking place until the stock of reserves is depleted, or some policy is instituted (ibid., pp. 589–91). From their analysis, capital flows in the short run depend on interest rate levels, while capital flows in the long run depend on the demand for money function and/or policy variables. In this sense, the Keynesian approach is good for short-run capital flows since interest rates are the only factor that affects capital flows, while the monetary approach is good for long-run capital flows since the adjustment of money stock and domestic credit policy altogether affect capital flows. Thus, the monetary approach to the balance of payments becomes a useful tool for predicting the overall inflows and outflows of capital.

Portfolio theorists have incorporated their models into the framework of monetary approach to the balance of payments. Unlike portfolio selection theory that considers only portfolio shift between domestic and foreign countries, theorists of portfolio balance models have attempted to analyze portfolio and money shifts between domestic and foreign countries based on macroeconomic theory- demand function for domestic and foreign financial assets and demand functions for domestic and foreign money. By proceeding in this way, they have attempted to establish their financial asset demand functions by portfolio selection theory and money demand functions by monetary theory.

According to this approach, equilibrium in financial markets occurs when the available stock of national money and other financial assets is equal to the stock demands for these assets based on current wealth, and wealth accumulation continues only until current wealth is equal to desired wealth. This is the so called portfolio balance model because it explains that continuous capital flows induced by interest rate differentials cannot be permanent; capital flows are adjusted by the resulting wealth accumulation and other monetary conditions. Thus the portfolio balance model employs a balance of payments condition with the asset market equilibrium conditions to jointly determine interest rates, exchange rates, and rates of wealth transfer between home and foreign countries. This model was widely accepted during the 1970s and 1980s because foreign financial asset growth is determined not only by rates of return but also by monetary policy (i.e., interest rates and/or exchange rates), fiscal policy (i.e., tax and/or subsidy), and reserve conditions (i.e., current account balances).

In Kouri and Porter's portfolio balance model (1974), three kinds of financial assets such as base money, domestic bonds, and foreign bonds are included, and income, wealth, and the expected yield variables (interest rates and risk estimates) enter all demand function for these assets.[26] They assume that money supply is the sum of the domestic (NDA) and foreign assets (NFA) of the central bank, where domestic money supply depends on changes in monetary policy instruments in open market operations and foreign money supply depends on net capital inflow (TC) and current account balance (CAB).[27]

Under these assumptions, they argue that equilibrium can be obtained when demand for money base (L function) equals total money supply:

$$\mathbf{L\,(Y, W, i, i^*, E) = \Delta NDA + CAB + TC}$$

where * indicates foreign variable.

Net capital inflows can be identified by net foreign demand for domestic bonds (F function) minus domestic demand for foreign bonds (J function):

$$\mathbf{TC = \Delta F\,(Y^*, W^*, \mathit{i}, \mathit{i}^*, E) - \Delta J\,(Y, W, \mathit{i}, \mathit{i}^*, E).}$$

Invoking the wealth constraint, that is,

$$\mathbf{L_W + H_W + J_W = 1}, \text{ and } \mathbf{L_n + H_n + J_n = 0}, \text{ where } \mathbf{n = Y, i, i^*}.$$

They obtain the reduced form equation for total net capital inflow:

$$\begin{aligned} TC = \frac{\mathbf{-1}}{\boldsymbol{H_i + F_i}} \{ & [(J_i + F_i)\, L_{i*} + L_i(F_{i*} - J_{i*})]\, \Delta i^* \\ & + [(J_i - F_i)\, L_Y - L_i J_Y] \Delta\, Y + (F_i - J_i) \Delta NDA \\ & + (F_i - J_i)\, CAB + [\,(F_i - J_i)\, L_w - J_w L_i\,] \Delta W \\ & + L_i\, F_{i*} \Delta Y^* + L_i\, F_{w*} \Delta W^* \}. \end{aligned}$$

In the limiting case of perfect capital market integration, they assume perfect substitution and equivalent risk between domestic and foreign bonds. Total net capital inflows can be rewritten under conditions of perfect capital mobility:

$$\mathbf{TC = -\Delta NDA - CAB + [\,L_i^* - (\,J_i^*\,L_i\,)/J_i]\Delta i^* + L_Y\Delta Y + L_w\Delta W}$$

which is Kouri and Porter's portfolio balance equation.

This equation contains the monetary policy instrument (ΔNDA), the current account balance (CAB), change in foreign interest rate (Δi^*), change in domestic income (ΔY), and change in domestic wealth (ΔW). Total net capital inflows are increased when net domestic assets of central bank and/or current account balances are reduced. The extent to which monetary policy is offset by capital flows is estimated by the coefficients on ΔNDA and CAB. Changes in foreign interest rates affect net capital inflows. The coefficient on the foreign interest rate $[L_i^* - (J_i^*\,L_i)/J_i]$ measures the interest elasticity of demand for money. As long as the domestic interest rate is allowed to adjust under perfect capital mobility, foreign interest rate changes need not be a major source for capital flows; however, indirectly, changes in the foreign interest rate can have a much bigger effect on the capital account through the effect on income and the current account as the coefficient indicates. Total net capital inflow is increased when domestic income is increased. The coefficient for a source of capital flows due to the fluctuation in money demand caused by income is L_Y, the inverse of the marginal income velocity of base money. The changes in domestic wealth is another source for capital flows with coefficient of L_W (ibid., pp. 470–52).

$\mathbf{[L_i^* - (\,J_i^*\,L_i)/J_i]\Delta i^* + L_Y\Delta Y + L_w\,\Delta W - \Delta NDA}$ in Kouri and Porter's model is simply a restatement of the Johnson's monetary balance of payments equation, $\mathbf{dR = Hd\Phi + \Phi H_1 dP + \Phi H_2 dY + \Phi H_3 di - dD}$. And **CAB** in Kouri and Porter's model is the Keynesian current account balance of payments, **T (Y, *ep**/p)**. Thus Kouri and Porter's portfolio equation is equivalent to the monetary approach balance of payment model plus the Keynesian current account model as rewritten below:

$$\mathbf{dTC = dR\,(d\Phi\,, dP, dY, di, dD) - T(Y, eP^*/P)},$$

where TC = total net capital inflow R = reserves, **Φ** = reserve ratio of commercial bank, P = price level, Y = output, *i* = interest rate, D = domestic credits, and *e* = exchange rate.

The equation Kouri and Porter develop says that capital inflows are that part of the shortfall of money supply below money demand that is not made good by the current account surplus, whereas the latter is determined by the usual Keynesian variables, which can be considered predetermined in the short-run period necessary for adjustment of the financial markets. Most of the key variables – P, Y, D, *e*, and P* in the above equation – can be taken as predetermined in the short run under perfect capital mobility. That leaves only the interest rate *i*. As Kouri and Porter suggest, however, the interest elasticity of demand for money is not so high as to cause massive capital flows under the perfect capital mobility. Thus, the monetary approach to the balance of payments is good to short-run capital flow forecasting under conditions of high capital mobility.

In Kouri and Porter's model, risk and exchange rates are assumed to be held constant across countries under a perfect capital market assumption. The model has been extended by portfolio theorists as discussed earlier in the modification of Branson's model. The parameter uncertainty model has been applied to Kouri and Porter's model to analyze the effects of changes in the quality of information on international portfolio decisions and levels of risk premium. The barrier to international investment model has been applied to Kouri and Porter's model to show the effects of changes in tax rates on international portfolio decision and expected rate of returns. In addition to these modifications, the monetarists have also developed Kouri and Porter's model by introducing flexible exchange rate systems. Since the breakdown of the Bretton Woods system in 1971 and the adoption by many countries of a managed float in 1973, it has been known that substantial capital flows arise from expectations of movements in exchange rates.

The theorists of the portfolio balance model[28] have analyzed the determinants of exchange rates and the effect of exchange rates on capital flows. Following the monetary approach to the balance of payments (capital flows are a sum of the current account and capital account) and portfolio adjustment theory (capital flow depends on the yield and risk differentials between domestic and foreign securities), they argue that a change in capital accounts is influenced not only by interest rate differentials but also by exchange rates. Their portfolio balance models regard the exchange rate as the mechanism in a floating regime for equilibrating the external balances on both current and capital accounts.

In the analysis of expected rate of return from domestic and foreign assets, Marwah and Klein (1983) argues that the expected yield depends on the exchange rates:

$$\mu_* = (1 + i)\frac{e_f}{e_s} - 1$$

where μ = yield on securities, i = interest rate, e_f = forward exchange rate, and e_s = spot exchange rate, and * indicates foreign variable.

In the above equation, if the forward exchange rate is larger than the spot exchange rate, the yield on foreign securities will become larger. If we estimate the yield on domestic securities where there is no difference between forward and spot exchange rates, the yield on domestic securities will purely depend on the domestic interest rate:

$$\mu = (1 + i)1/1 - 1 = i.$$

Then, the yield differential between domestic and foreign securities ($\mu - \mu_*$) depends on changes in interest rates and exchange rates:

$$(\mu - \mu_*) = (i - i_*\frac{e_f}{e_s}) + (1 - \frac{e_f}{e_s}).$$

In the above equation for yield differentials, the first component measures covered interest arbitrage and the second measures the speculative element in terms of the forward premium (Marwah et al., 1985, pp. 94–5). If the exchange rate is held constant, say $e_f/e_s = 1$, then the yield differential will be purely dependent on the interest rate differential, as in Kouri and Porter's model and other studies that use the monetary approach.[29]

Using combined monetary and portfolio theories, a number of studies have attempted to understand international capital flows. Adler and Dumas (1983) incorporated international capital flows into a 'true stochastic theory of the balance of payments' based on optimizing behaviour and rational expectations in the portfolio selection process. Branson and Henderson (1985) developed the portfolio balance model by introducing four assets: domestic money, foreign money, domestic securities, and foreign securities under a flexible exchange rate system. Their analysis is very similar to Kouri and Porter's model, except it considers exchange rates. Floyd (1985) and Frankel and Razin (1987) analyzed an equilibrium model under flexible exchange rates with an imperfect capital mobility condition. Stockman and Svensson (1987) showed that international capital flows reflected changes in the level and location of world wealth.

More conceptual studies have been conducted in recent years to explore the effects of economic and political integration on international capital flows. Webb (1982; 1990) analyzed the effect of economic integration among developing countries on capital inflows. In his analysis, two developing countries are under a customs union through mutual reduction of tariffs[30] and a third country is not a member of this customs union. The unionized countries, he argues, increase their exports and so do their rates of return on capital while those of the ununionized country remain constant. Under this condition, capital of the ununionized country will flow to the unionized countries in order to get higher rates of return (Webb, 1982, pp. 355–6). Webb also applied this idea to the international allocation of capital, subject to changes in tariff policies and subsequent price adjustments. He concludes that preferential trading agreements accelerate capital flows (Webb, 1990).

Although Persson and Tabellini (1992) analyzed international allocation of physical capital rather than financial capital, their study raised some important questions regarding the impact of high capital mobility on economic equilibrium and political equilibrium. They assume that higher capital mobility due to lower mobility cost leads to competition by lowering tax rates among countries in order to attract foreign capital since rates of return solely depend on tax rates under zero mobility costs in their model. Thus, the process of European integration should bring about lower equilibrium tax rates everywhere. However, they hypothesize that there are two types of government; more left-wing governments with initially higher tax rates and more right-wing governments with initially lower tax rates. Because voters in different countries find it optimal to react to this tax competition by electing a government less sensitive to these strategic aspects of tax policy, Persson and Tabellini (1992, pp. 696–700) argue that more left-wing countries will reduce tax rates, shifting their political equilibrium to the right while more right-wing countries will not cut taxes further, moving to the left. Hence, they conclude that the European economic integration can bring about political convergence.

Previous Empirical Analyses

Empirical Findings of Flow Theory

Empirical studies of the Keynesian version of flow theory have had great difficulty in demonstrating that interest rate differentials determine international capital flows, although it is one of the most accepted paradigms in international finance. One reason is in the model specification. Since international capital flows are composed of portfolio investment, direct investment, and bank lending, empirical studies that include only interest rate differentials can produce biased estimates, due to the effect of the omission of other important variables. Another reason is statistical. Capital flows and interest rate differentials may introduce a simultaneity bias. As a result, most empirical studies have been conducted in the framework of portfolio theory to see the effects of interest rate differentials on capital flows. Before the portfolio-centred studies are reviewed, the empirical studies that do use flow theory will be discussed.

Miller and Whitman (1973) attempted to analyze capital flows within a simultaneous equations framework under a fixed exchange rate system. Bryant (1975) presented a survey of the effects of interest rate differentials on international capital movements. Haynes and Pippenger (1979) attempted to examine the effects of observed interest rate differentials and autarky interest rate differentials between the US and Canada on the capital inflows to Canada from the US in a simple version of the portfolio balance model. Later they used cross spectral analysis to investigate the interest rate interdependence resulting from capital flows (Haynes and Pippenger, 1982). All of these studies found that high interest rate differentials induce capital flows.

In another study, Haynes (1988) applied a simultaneous equation system to monthly and quarterly data for the US–Canada long-term portfolio bond flows in 1960–1970 under fixed exchange rates. He hypothesized that capital flows depend on interest rate differentials and that capital flows simultaneously affect interest rates.[31] For both OLS and instrumental variables[32] estimates in the monthly data, all coefficients on the interest rate differentials are positive. The significant time periods in the OLS estimates were (t-1), (t-3), and (t-6), and those in the instrument variables are (t), (t-1), (t-3) and (t-6). The cumulative coefficients for both estimates are all significant except the contemporaneous OLS one (Haynes, 1988: 106–107). In the same procedure with the quarterly data, none of the time period coefficients is significant, however (ibid., pp. 109–10). One of the reasons why his model with monthly data supports flow theory, but the one with quarterly data does not can be found in the Keynesian approach to the balance of payments. Interest rate differentials are short term effects. It is necessary to include risk and other policy variables for the long term effect, as the monetary approach to the balance of payments suggests.

Feldstein and Horioka's version of flow theory has been tested empirically and has been criticized in several studies since the mid-1980s. Feldstein and Horioka (1980) solved the model $(I/Y)i = \alpha + \beta(S/Y)i$ for 16 OECD countries for the period 1960–1974. Their results show that there is a low degree of capital mobility ($\beta = 0.85$–0.95). This can be interpreted as resulting from the fact that the domestic investment share is affected by other exogenous factors. Subsequent empirical studies by Feldstein (1983) and Feldstein and Bachetta (1991) accept this close correlation (β is close to one) as a robust empirical regularity. Tesar (1991) finds a different pattern of saving and investment shares using different time periods, however. She includes 16 to 24 OECD countries for the different time periods, using the pooled data, and shows that there is a relatively uncorrelated relation for 24 countries for the most recent period (β = 0.20 for the period of 1975–1986 and β = 0.35 for the period of 1960–1986), while other models of different sample countries and different time periods show a closer correlation (β = 0.71–0.87). Sinn (1992) estimates the coefficient based on annual data (1960–1988) for 23 OECD countries, and finds that the coefficient varies considerably from year to year (β coefficients from 1976 to 1986 are lower than rest of the years). He also attempts to compare the coefficients between international capital mobility and internal capital mobility for the US and finds that internal capital mobility is much higher than international capital mobility.

Dooley and associates (1987) show that the coefficients for LDCs are lower than for industrialized countries (ICs). This implies that the capital mobility is higher among LDCs than among ICs, which is problematic. Vos (1988) estimated three different data sets for all countries, LDCs and ICs. In the model for all countries, the coefficients declines over time; 1960–1965 (0.60), 1980–1984 (0.20). The same pattern is shown for ICs; the coefficients are 0.84 and 0.55 for the corresponding time periods. However, the coefficients for LDCs do not show the same pattern; 0.68 in 1960–1965, 0.83 in 1966–1972, 0.91 in 1973–1984, and 0.68 in 1980–1984. This result is similar that of Dooley and associates (1987) in suggesting that capital mobility was higher in LDCs than in ICs for the period 1960–1965.

Even though the empirical studies of the Feldstein-Horioka model have shown conflicting results, researchers deny that it is evidence for less than perfect capital mobility. Obstfeld (1986) argues that the growth rate of income may simultaneously affect saving and investment. Murphy (1986) and Wong (1990) point out that a non-traded consumption good simultaneously affects saving and investment. Dooley and associates (1987) address the potential simultaneity of saving and investment shares by instrumental variable analysis. Other than the simultaneity problem, some researchers attribute the high correlation of saving and investment to government policy. Bayoumi (1990) evaluates the correlation between private saving and private investment and finds that the correlation coefficient in private saving and investment is lower than in national savings and investment. Even though his evidence supports the 'policy-reaction' argument, there is a sample selection bias since he includes only 10 OECD countries.

Frankel's version of flow theory (that real interest rate differentials across national boundaries under perfect capital mobility should be the same) has been tested several times. Hordick (1979), Howard (1979), Cumby and Obstfeld (1984), and Cumby and Obstfeld (1985) all have rejected the null hypothesis. However, the later studies have accepted the null hypothesis for the samples of advanced countries.

Frankel (1989) selected 25 countries from various groups, including five closed LDCs, three liberalizing Pacific LDCs, three liberalizing Pacific ICs, nine closed European ICs, and five open Atlantic ICs, using three month data for the period 1982–1988. In his reports of the mean real interest rate differential and the standard deviation, the five closed LDCs constitute the group with the highest variability, and the five open Atlantic ICs the group with the lowest (Frankel, 1989, pp. 25–7). This result confirms that capital controls and other barriers to international capital flows remained for many countries, except some Atlantic ICs, in the period of the study. From annual changes in the real interest differentials among countries, he concludes that real interest rate differentials have been getting closer among the European countries and Japan (ibid., pp. 38–9).

Haque and Montiel (1990; 1991) selected the 15 LDCs with annual data for the period 1969–1987. Since data for the market-clearing interest rate are not available in most developing countries, the degree of capital mobility is defined by the estimation of money demand, where the demand for money is a function of the interest rate, income, and the lagged money stock. Thus, unobservable closed economy interest rates can be calculated as a function of income, lagged money, and the closed economy money supply.[33] Their results support the finding of high capital mobility among 10 liberalized LDCs.

Empirical Findings of Portfolio Theory

Most of the empirical studies that rely on portfolio theory have shown that an increase in yields on foreign assets has a positive impact on capital flows while an increase in estimated risk of foreign assets has a negative impact on capital flows. In many studies, interest rate differentials have been defined as yield differentials. Earlier studies do not include any specific risk estimation variable. One of the important findings in the empirical studies is that net capital flow as a dependent variable is not captured appropriately in a portfolio theory framework.

An investigation of US capital inflows and outflows conducted by Branson (1968) is one of the earlier pieces of empirical research using portfolio theory. He estimates the changes in short-term and long-term portfolio liabilities to foreigners in the inflow model and the changes in short-term and long-term portfolio claims on foreigners in the outflow model using monthly and quarterly data for the period 1959–1964. He assumes that short-term capital flows are mainly import and export finance respectively and long-term capital flows are portfolio investments.[34] Thus, he includes imports and exports in the short-term capital flow model and GNP in the long-term capital flow model along with domestic and foreign interest rates as explanatory variables.[35] The relationship of short-term capital flows to trade flow of the previous years and the relationship of the long-term capital flows to GNP growth of both current and previous periods are shown to be significant. In both short-term and long-term capital flows, interest rates of both current and previous periods and policy variable of interest equalization tax play a powerful role in determining capital flows.

The explanatory power of the above test was slightly enhanced when Branson and Hill (1971) introduced domestic wealth assets[36] along with series of time lagged value of foreign GNP. They conducted a very similar study to Branson's 1968 model using quarterly data for the period 1961–1969. Among their statistically significant explanatory variables in the model of long-term capital outflows, foreign interest rates show a positive sign while domestic wealth[37] and dummy variables for credit tightening years show negative signs. In the long-term capital inflow estimation, foreign treasury bill rates of the previous period and foreign GNPs of three previous time periods are statistically significant with negative signs while US interest rates or credit rationing index are not significant. Most variables except risk are validated empirically, with high R-squared scores ranging from 0.68 to 0.81.

There have been a limited number of empirical studies on capital flows of bank loans and foreign direct investments using portfolio theory. Bryant and Hendershott (1970) estimated borrowings by Japanese banks from American banks using annual data for the period 1959–1967. Their model expresses short-term borrowing from American banks by Japanese banks as a function of the Japanese banks' net worth, Japanese imports, government policy, cost of borrowing, and several borrowing and lending rates. Among significant variables in their model, lagged values of rates of return show positive signs while government restriction policies and cost variables negative signs. Prachowny (1972) estimated capital flows of foreign direct investment by US firms and foreign firms for the period 1953–1964. In his outflow model (i.e., US foreign direct investment in foreign countries), only rates of return are significant. In the model for capital inflows (i.e., foreign firms' direct investment in the US), however, earning differentials, time dummies, and balance of payments are significant. Gilman (1981) investigated capital flows in financing foreign direct investment from parent countries to foreign affiliate countries. He included the US, Canada, and European countries in the 1960s and 1970s. In the most of the sample countries, the results show that total assets invested in the foreign affiliates are positively related to capital flows from home to foreign affiliate. Depreciation provisions of foreign affiliate and profits of foreign affiliate are negatively related to these capital flows.

Several investigations have attempted to diversify the dependent variables. Stevens (1984) endogenized net capital flow for 24 OECD countries for the period 1975–1980. Exogenous variables are covered interest rate differentials, risk estimation, and asset values. Stekler (1988) also used net capital flow as a dependent variable using the same OECD countries for the period of 1975–1985. His multi-country model includes real interest rate differentials and asset values in the country as exogenous variables. The result of these studies do not support portfolio theory. The cause of the poor statistical power in their models may, however, lie in the net capital flows effect because the separated risks associated with inflows and outflows are confounded when they are treated together.

Unfortunately the parameter uncertainty model has not, thus far, been tested empirically in an appropriate way. The most difficult problem is in the definition of information in capital flows. Although Garbade and Silber (1978) did not apply the uncertainty parameter model, their empirical research on the impacts of communications technology innovations on US domestic financial markets is useful in helping us understand how these innovations are affecting on financial markets. In their model, three different types of telecommunication innovations in the US domestic financial markets for the period 1840–1975 (the domestic telegraph in the 1840s, the trans-Atlantic cable in 1866, and the consolidated tape in 1975) are analyzed. They find that the first two innovations led to significant and rapid narrowing of inter-market price differentials. This effect was captured immediately after the innovations, without any learning period. However, the third innovation, the consolidated tape, has not had the same effect. They argue that the first two technologies sped the flow of information and also provided a quicker mechanism for transmitting an order to execute a trade. On the other hand, the consolidated tape only accelerated the flow of information (ibid., pp. 830–1). This is very valuable, verifying the parameter uncertainty model's assumption in the sense that improved information reduces the cost of transactions, since the study shows the integration of inter-markets.

Tobin's Q theory has been tested to find the effect of Q (shadow price associated with capital accumulation restriction) on a firm's investments. Some studies have found it significant but most studies conclude that the effect of Q is relatively weak.[38] Abel and Blanchard (1986) attempted to examine the marginal efficiency of capital and cost of capital separately. Their results show that the marginal efficiency of capital has larger and more significant effects than costs of capital on investments. Mairesse and Dermont (1985) and Bruno (1986) argue that expected profits have significant effects but costs of capital have no significant effect on investments. Chirinko (1987, p. 86) concludes that Q theory is unlikely to provide the basis for a satisfactory investment model due to slow adjustment processes, significant lagged variables, and serially correlated residuals. The empirical findings in investment theory, however, are based on the firms' behaviour in domestic markets rather than individual investors' behaviour in international financial markets. The effects of innovations in financial instruments on costs of investments and thus on capital flows in international financial markets may provide different results since reduced costs of financial investments will directly influence profits (i.e., rate of returns), and individual investors in financial markets may adjust quickly as Garbade and Silber (1978) found in their empirical study of telecommunication innovations.

Empirical Findings of Monetary Approach

Empirical studies of the monetary approach to the balance of payments initially focused on reserve inflows. Genberg (1973) estimated the Swedish reserve flows for the period 1950–1968 using quarterly data. In his model, international reserves are dependent on money supply, domestic money stock, changes in domestic prices, changes in domestic income, and changes in domestic interest rates. The only significant variable in the Swedish case is money supply which is negatively related to reserve inflows. Zecher (1976) estimated the international reserve inflows to Australia for the period 1951–1071 using quarterly and annual data. His results reveal that Australian reserves are well-explained by the monetary approach framework compared to the Swedish case. Among significant variables for both quarterly and annual data, income and price are positively related and the money multiplier and money supply are negatively related to reserve inflows. However, interest rates do not affect reserve inflows in both quarterly and annual data. Results similar to Zecher's findings have been presented by Bean (1978) for the Japanese case. Guiltian (1976) investigated the effects of central bank's credit controls on reserve inflows to Spain along with GDP, domestic and foreign prices. His results show that credit control variables are significant, but not in GDP, domestic and foreign prices. The empirical results of these studies show that different countries have different patterns of reserve inflows. However, these studies support the basic argument that reserve inflows are stemmed by domestic monetary policy.

Kouri and Porter (1974) incorporated monetary theory with portfolio theory to investigate net capital flows. Their model was constructed to test net capital flows as a function of wealth of the country, interest rates, domestic credit, and current account balance. They used monthly data for four European countries (Germany, Australia, Italy and the Netherlands) for the period 1960–1970. Among the statistically significant variables, income has a positive sign while net domestic assets and current account balance show a negative sign for all countries. Their results support the monetary approach to the balance of payments, confirming that the behaviour of the overall balance of payments is dominated by factors that influence capital flow (ibid., pp. 452–64). However, changes in Eurodollar rate are not significant. In addition, Germany's parameter is positive while others are all negative. This indicates that endogenizing net capital flows cannot easily capture the effect of interest rate changes since it cannot measure the extent to which capital inflows and capital outflows are driven by the effect of interest rate changes in a separate manner. When Herring and Marston (1977) present the model[39] with capital inflows to and outflow from Germany as the dependent variables, the interest rate differential of time lagged values between the German interbank rate and Eurodollar rate becomes significant in both inflows and outflows. In their model for capital inflows, all monetary factors, including dummy variables for years a ban was introduced and for speculative disturbances are significant.

Applying the portfolio balance model, Marwah et al. (1985) estimated US capital inflows from four countries (Canada, and France, West Germany, and the UK) and US capital outflows to the four countries in two different models. They used pooled cross-section and time-series data for the period 1972–1979. In their inflow model, a change in US liabilities to country *i* divided by net foreign assets is defined as the dependent variable, which implies an inflow of capital from country *i* to the USA In their outflow model, a change in US claims on country *i* divided by net foreign asset is defined as dependent variable which, implies an outflow of capital from the USA to country *i*. They find that the yield differential variable, which is defined by differentials divided by the exchange rate, is an important determinant of both inflows and outflows. The price parity deviations are found to be important in explaining inflows but have no impact on outflows. Surprisingly, the balance of payments on the current account has no impact on the bilateral flows of these countries (Marwah, Klein, and Bodkin, 1985, pp. 102–7). Their empirical test reveals that there are important differences in the nature and magnitude of the structural responses of capital inflows and capital outflows, which differences have been lost in the analysis of net capital flows.

Several studies have attempted to investigate the relationship between capital inflows and changes in exchange rates alone. Johnson, McKibbin and Trever (1982) examined this relationship using a simulation model. Their empirical results show that changes in exchange rates quickly induce capital mobility. Thus they argue that a floating exchange rate reduces the variance of prices by helping to produce monetary control with lower interest rates in the case of the inflationary foreign stocks (ibid., p. 681). However, they do not specify under what condition capital flows are highly mobile or immobile. This must be answered by investigating the effect of exchange rate changes on capital flows. Froot and Stein (1991) analyzed the connection between exchange rates and capital inflows to the USA for the period 1973–1987 with both quarterly and annual data. Their dependent variables are total assets, foreign official assets, foreign private assets, direct investment, US treasury securities, and corporate and other bonds in the different models. Their findings show several surprising results. The general expectation is that all types of capital inflows should be negatively correlated with the value of the dollar. However, foreign direct investment is the only type of capital inflow which is statistically significant and negatively correlated. Foreign private assets and portfolio inflows are positively correlated but not statistically significant. They argue that portfolio investments are not passive investments, which are usually uncorrelated with exchange rates (ibid., p. 1209). Their model emphasizes that it is necessary to look at the different types of capital flows since some assets could be influenced differently by the same fiscal factor.

Ruffin and Rassekh (1986) used an eclectic model to investigate the effect of portfolio and monetary factors on US capital outflows with quarterly data of 1970–1983. In their model, portfolio investment to foreign countries is a function of domestic monetary factors (such as inflation rates, money supply, the real gold price, and capital control policy) and portfolio factors (such as income, foreign interest rates, capital inflows, financial wealth, and direct investment). Among the significant variables, money supply and capital inflows show a positive sign while direct investment has a negative sign.

Regarding the impact of capital inflows on capital outflows, they conclude that there is the mutual dependence between outflows and inflows arising from the institutional features of the international capital market. Regarding the foreign direct investment impact on foreign portfolio investment, they suggest that foreign direct investment displaces an equal amount of portfolio investment and, thus, multinational corporations may have no significant impact on net capital flows (Ruffin and Rassekh, 1986, pp. 1128–9).

Most of the empirical studies that examine LDC capital inflows have used the monetary framework. Eaton and Gersovitz (1980) investigated the effects of the balance of payments on the public debt and on international reserve holdings for 45 LDCs for the period 1970–1974. Their results show that import ratio and population are significant to the public debt and that income and exports to international reserve holdings. Nunnenkamp (1990) examined the relationship between private loans and monetary factors in 20 LDCs for the period 1983–1986. The result shows that inflows of private loans to LDCs depend on capital self-formation capacity and stable exchange rates. Lesink and Van Vergeijk (1991) analyzed the determinants of developing countries' access[40] to international capital markets in the period 1985–1987. Using a logit model that investigates the probability of participation in international financial markets as a function of economic performance variables and creditworthiness indicators, the results show that the combination of economic performance variables such as GDP per capita, the net-debt-to-GDP ratio, and the investment share predicts correctly in 75 per cent of the cases whether a country will have access to the international capital market. Traditional creditworthiness indicators such as inflation, the debt-export ratio, debt-service ratio and use of IMF credits prove to be insignificant determinants, however. Thus they conclude that there is a positive relation between good economic performance and lending, which is contrary to Krugman's statement in 1989 (Lesink and Van Vergeijk, 1991, p. 97).

Overview of Literature

What might we conclude from the foregoing? A summary of the key findings and unresolved issues from the accumulated body of theoretical and empirical studies is a necessary first step in the attempt to find an improved explanation of the causes of the globalization of international financial markets and the consequences of globalization for international capital flows. Tables 1 and 2 summarize the major theories and principal empirical findings.

Table 1 Summary of theoretical literature

Theories	Model names	Major theorists	Key propositions	Hypotheses ^1
Flow theory	Keynesian Balance of Payment	Meade (1951), Mundell (1960, 1962) Fleming (1962)	K flow depends on i differentials (+) in capital account balances.	F = f(i+, i*-)
	Investment Flow	Jorgenson (1963), Bischoff (1971)	Demand for investment depends on i differentials (+).	Kd = f(i+, i*-)
	Saving-Invstment Ratio	Feldstein and Horioka (1980) Feldstein (1983)	Saving-investment ratio is uncorrelated under perfect K market condition.	(I/Y) = a+b(s/Y): b = 0
	Real Interest Rate Differential	Obstfeld (1986), Frankel (1989)	Real interest rates are the same in all countries under perfect K market condition.	r-r* = (i-e)-(i-e*) = 0
Portfolio theory	Portfolio Selection	Markowitz (1952), Tobin (1958)	Investment depends on rate of return (+) and risk estimation(-).	F = f(i-i*, E-)
	Portfolio Adjustment	Branson (1968)	K flow depends on rate of return (+) risk estimation(-), and wealth of investor (+)	FF = f(i-i*, E-, W+)
	Parameter Uncertainty	Bawa et al (1979), Stigliz (1982) Branson and Jaffee (1991)	K flow depends on quality of inormation (+) on foreign stock.	F = f(i-i*, info+)
	Tobin's Q Theory	Tobin (1969) Fischer and Merton (1984)	Investment depends on marginal efficiency of capital (+) and cost of capital (-)	Q = o/c(K)+c' (i/K)
	Barrier to investment	Black (1971), Stulz (1981) Huizinga (1991)	K flow depends on tax rate (-) on foreign investment.	F = f(i-i*, t-)
Monetary approach	Monetary Balance of Payment	Johnson (1972), Mussa (1974) Frenkel et al. (1980)	K flow is a monetary phenomenon, depending on overall balance of payment.	dR = f(X-M, Fi-Fo)
	Portfolio Equilibrium	Kouri and Porter (1974) Herring and Marston (1977)	K flow depends on both portfolio and monetary factors.	F = f(i-i*, W, E, CAB)
	Portfolio Balance	Dornbusch (1975), Diskill (1981) Marwah et al. (1982, 1985)	Rate of returen (u) depends on exchange rate (ef/es).	u* = (1-i*)/ef/es)-1

Notes

1 * indicates foreign variable.

a) Dependent variables: F = capital flow, I/Y = national invetsment rate, Kd = demand for capital, r = real interest rate, Q = present value of extra unit of capital, dR = change in reserve, u = rate of return

b) Independent variables: a = intercept, b = coefficient, CAB = current account balance, c(K) = cost of capital, Fi = capital inflow, Fo = capital outflow, i = interest rate, info = information, o = output, S/Y = national saving rate, W = wealth of stock

Table 2 Summary of major empirical findings

Theories	Model names	Empiricists (year)	Basic models ^1	Methods ^2	Data sets Country (year)	Results: S = support, N = not, M = mixed
Flow theory	Nominal interest rate differential	Haynes and Pippenger (1979)	F i= f(i, i*, Fo)	SEM	US–Canada (60–65)	(S): significant in i*
		Haynes (1988)	Fo = f(i-i*, Fi)	SEM	US–Canada (60–75)	(S): significant in (i-i*)
	Saving-investment ratio	Feldstein and Horioka (1980)	(I/Y) = a+b(S/Y)	OLS	16 OECD (60–74)	(N): b> 0.85
		Vos (1988)	(I/Y) = a+b(S/Y)	OLS	48 LDC & IC (60–84)	(N): LDC's b < IC's b
		Tesar (1991)	(I/Y) = a+b(S/Y)	OLS	24 OECD (60–80)	(S): b getting smaller
	Real interest rate differential	Mishkin (1984)	(r-r*) comparison	MAD	20 IC (77–80)	(N): large in r-r*
		Frankel (1989)	(r-r*) comparison	MAD	25 LDC & IC (82–88)	(S): small r-r* in IC
		Haque and Montiel (1990)	(r-r*) comparison	MAD	15 LDC (69–87)	(S): small r-r* in 10/15 LDC
Portfolio theory	Portfolio adjustment	Branson (1968)	Fi(o) = f(i-i*, Y, D)	OLS	US-4 Euro (59–64)	(S): all significant
		Branson and Hill (1968)	Fi(o) = f(i-i*, Y, D)	OLS	US-UK (61–69)	(S): all significant
		Stevenson (1984)	Fn = f(i-i*, E, W)	OLS	24 OECD (75–80)	(N): due to net flow effect
		Stelker (1988)	Fn = f(i-i*, E, W)	MCM	24 OECD (75–80)	(N): due to net flow effect
	Parameter uncertainty	Garbade and Sibler (1978) (US domestic market only)	stock price comparison	MAD	US mkt (1840–1975)	(S): significant in telecomm
	Tobin's Q theory	Chirinko (1987)	I/K = f(profit, K cost)	OLS	US firms (50–81)	(N): not significant in K cost
	Barrier to investment	No study for international markets				
Monetary approach	Monetary balance of payment	Zwcher (1976)	R = f(Y, i, p, m, Ms)	OLS	Australia (51-71)	(S): all significant except i
		Guiltian (1976)	R = f(Y, p, p*, D)	OLS	Spain (55–71)	(S): all siginificant except p
	LDC capital inflow	Nunnenkamp (1990)	Fi = f(I, export, Infl, I, Def)	OLS	45 LDC (83–86)	(M): not significant in Inf.l & Def
		Lesink and Vergeijk (1991)	Fi = f(Y, Infl, I, Debt, R)	LOGIT	95 LDC (85–87)	(M): not significant in Infl. & R
	Portfolio balance	Kouri and Porter (1974)	Fn = f(Y, i*, DA, CAB)	OLS	4 EC (60–70)	(S): all significant except i
		Herring and Marston (1977)	Fi(o) = f(Y, i-i*, Cont)	OLS	Germany (64–69)	(S): all significant
		Marwah et al. (1985)	Fi(o) = f(u-u*, p-p*, W, CAB)	GLS	US-4 IC (72–79)	(S): all significant except CAB
		Ruffin and Rassekh (1986)	Fi(o) = f(F, Ms, i-i*, W)	OLS	US-3 IC (70–83)	(M) not significant in i-i*. & W

Notes

1 * indicates foreign variable: a) dependent variables: Fi = K inflow, Fo = K outflow, Fn = K net flow, I/K = investment rate, R = reserve, I/Y = national investment rate; b) Independent variables: a = intercept, b = coefficient, CAB = current account balance, Cont = credit control, DA = domestic asset, Dt = dummy for tax policy, def = gov't deficit, E = risk, i = interest rate, I = investment, Infl. = inflation, m = money multiplier, S/Y = national saving rate, p = price, r = real i rate, u = rate of return, W = wealth

2 Method techniques: GLS = generalized least squares, MCM = multicountry model, MAD = mean absolute value difference, LOGIT = logistic model, OLS = ordinary least squares, SEM = simultaneous equation model

Key findings

Although flow theory does not capture the whole picture of international capital flows due to the elimination of current account balances, it provides a useful empirical tool to measure the degree of globalization of international financial markets. Empirical studies on saving-investment ratios have presented conflicting results because of methodological problems;[41] however, several studies have shown that the degree of capital mobility has increased in recent years compared to earlier years.[42] The same pattern has been reported by empirical analyses of real interest rate differentials.[43] These studies have shown implicitly that there are barriers to international capital flows since the correlation coefficients of saving-investment ratios and real interest rate differentials across countries are not close to zero. Flow theory does not spell out what these barriers to international capital flows are or what the factors contributing to higher capital mobility in recent years have been.

Portfolio theory and the monetary approach to the balance of payments have partly answered these questions. Empirical results of portfolio theory show that expected rates of return, risk estimates and wealth of investors are important variables in determining international capital flows.[44] Empirical research using the monetary approach finds that monetary factors such as international reserves, domestic money supply, domestic credit controls, and current account balances are significant variables in influencing international capital flows.[45] Since portfolio theory alone cannot analyze the linkage between macroeconomic problems and capital flows and the monetary approach alone cannot capture the portfolio effects on capital flows, a more complete picture of international capital flows has been provided by the portfolio balance model.[46]

When portfolio and monetary factors are embedded together in the framework of the portfolio balance model, empirical research shows that determinants of international capital flows differ by country and time span. Capital flows of some countries are more influenced by portfolio factors while those of other countries are more influenced by monetary factors.[47] International capital flows also are shown to have been induced by developments of financial markets and monetary policies, which are differently implemented across countries and time. Portfolio theory explores how improved information[48] and lowered barriers[49] reduce costs of international capital investment and thus increase international capital flows. Monetary theory asserts that fiscal policy[50] and international trading agreements[51] accelerate international capital flows. Heretofore, these theoretical suggestions have not been tested empirically.

There have been several empirical suggestions regarding modelling strategy. Models that endogenize net capital flows are inefficient in capturing the determinants of capital flows. When inflows and outflows are treated together, a model cannot measure the extent to which capital inflows and outflows are driven by interest rate differentials and risk estimates because of confounded effects.[52] When capital inflows and outflows are investigated separately, different responses of portfolio and monetary factors to capital inflows and outflows are evident.[53]

It has been suggested that portfolio flows, direct investment flows, and bank loans should be tested in different models since the determinants of capital flows of each item can be different.[54] However, earlier studies have failed to specify models with distinctive explanatory variables for each financial item. This problem may not be solved since the fundamental motivation of capital flow is the earning differentials. The most important variables emerging from these studies have been portfolio related variables such as rates of return, earning differentials, profits, and costs of transfer or regulatory variables in their results.[55]

Unsolved Issues

One of the most important unanswered questions is why the globalization of international financial markets has accelerated in recent years. Despite the fact that the parameter uncertainty and barrier-to-international-investment models suggest that reduced costs of capital investments accelerate this integration through improvements in the quality of information and reduction of barriers, there has been little empirical analysis on this matter.

Another important question that has not been answered is what the consequences of globalization are for international capital flows. This can be addressed only after answering the first question, by analyzing as large a number of countries as possible.

Most empirical studies have focused on one financial product in each model. But it is not possible to see the whole picture of international capital flows if foreign direct investments, portfolio investments, and bank loans are examined separately. Only when these financial products are considered together will a better picture of the patterns of global capital flows emerge.

Most theoretical and empirical studies have emphasized analysis of financial and monetary factors. International capital flows also can be affected by political variables and economic stability, since political and economic risk can reduce profits and economic cooperation can secure international investment. Thus it is desirable to include variables that account for economic and political risk factors.

One of the methodological problems in previous studies is that inflows and outflows have been separately estimated. Even though flow theorists found simultaneous effects of capital flows, this simultaneity has not been incorporated into portfolio and monetary studies. This is due to the identification problems in constructing a simultaneous equation system. However, inflows and outflows should be estimated in one system to get rid of simultaneity bias.

Modelling Strategies

From the findings and unsolved issues in the previous studies, we are encouraged to develop three models to promote a better understanding of international capital flows: a globalization model to find causes of globalization of international financial markets; a single financial item's simultaneous equation inflow-outflow model to examine the consequences of this globalization for specific types of inflows and outflows; and a simultaneous equation inflow-outflow model with eight equations in one system to examine the interactions among the four different types of capital inflows and outflows.

In the globalization model, gross capital flow will be used as a dependent variable rather than real interest rates or saving-investment ratios since the actual amount of capital transaction is one of the key phenomena of globalization of international financial markets. Independent variables suggested by the studies are factors that reduce the cost of investments, improve the quality of information, and lower investment barriers.

These non-financial variables also will be included in the simultaneous equation inflow-outflow model, along with traditional financial and monetary variables. The dependent variable in the inflow equation will be the amount of capital inflow from the rest of the world to the domestic country. In the outflow equation it will be the amount of capital outflows from the domestic country to the rest of the world. Financial capital includes portfolio, bank capital, foreign direct investment, and other private sector capital. The models will employ a balance of payments framework so as to link macroeconomic and portfolio effects along with technological innovations, regulatory changes, and political and economic stability factors. A simultaneous equation model for a given type of capital will explore the determinants of that type of capital flow while a model for four financial items will reveal the interactions among them. This will provide a more complete picture of international capital flows than has been heretofore.

Notes

1 Smith explains that 'in the home trade his capital is never so long out of his sight as it frequently is in the foreign trade of consumption'. Capitalists 'can know better the character and situation of the persons whom he trusts'; a capitalist 'knows better laws of the country from which he must seek redress'. Thus, 'upon equal or only nearly equal profits, ... every individual naturally inclines to employ his capital ... in domestic industry, and to give revenue and employment to ... his own country' (Smith, 1776, Campbell edition 1991, Bk IV, ch. II. pp. 398–9).

2 Smith mentions that capital movements from England to colonial countries are driven by the advantage of high rate of profits. If the invested capital returns from the colonial countries to England as higher profits in a short period, it is advantageous to England (ibid., Vol. 2, Bk IV, ch. IV, pp. 92–9). But Smith argues that capital movement from England to America by English capitalists who reside in England gives a monopoly to Americans. In this case, capital is employed to produce the goods to stop the importation of European manufactures. This obstructs European economic growth (ibid., Bk II, ch. V, pp. 327–8).

3 In Ricardo's famous example of the English-Portuguese trade in cloth and wine, England exports cloth and Portugal exports wine based on the law of comparative advantage. Since England has more capital than Portugal and Portugal has more labour than England, Ricardo argues that English capital can move to Portugal to get a higher revenue. Ricardo argues that capital will be carried abroad to get greater net revenue by improving machinery in the foreign country. This will diminish the demand for labour at home but increase the demand for labour at foreign countries. But the cost of production of commodities is reduced and the commodities can be sold at a cheaper price. Otherwise, domestic consumers should pay a higher price for the commodities (Ricardo, 1817, Winch edition, 1973, ch. XXXI. pp. 270–1).

4 Mills states that 'it is the emigration of English capital that we have chiefly to look for keeping up a supply of cheap food and cheap materials of clothing, proportional to the increase of our population; thus enabling an increasing capital to find employment in the country, without reduction of profit, in producing manufactured articles with which to pay for this supply of raw produce'. Therefore, Mills concludes that 'the exportation of capital is an agent of great efficacy' and that 'the more capital we send away, the more we shall posses and be able to retain at home' (Mills, 1848, Ashley edition. 1909, Bk IV, ch. IV, p. 739).

5 The balance of payments model of Ohlin was not fully developed in his work of 1924, and will be discussed under the fourth stage of conceptual approach.

6 Cited from 'The Theory of Trade' in *The Heckscher-Ohlin Trade Theory* (Heckscher and Ohlin, 1991) which is a translated version of *The Effect of Foreign Trade on the Distribution of Income* (Heckscher, 1919) and *The Theory of Trade* (Ohlin, 1924), translated and edited by H. Flam and M.J. Flanders.

7 Viner (1929, p. 157) also pointed out the closeness with which new Russian loan issues on the London market followed the variations in British diplomatic relations with Russia.

8 The concept of the marginal propensity to consume is that an increment of income (ΔY_w) depends on an increment of aggregate investment (ΔI_w) and consumption (ΔC_w): $\Delta Y_w = \Delta C_w + \Delta I_w$. The increment of income also depends on an amount of investment multiplier(k) times the increment of investment: $\Delta Y_w = k\,\Delta I_w$ (Keynes, 1936, pp. 113–5).

9 The marginal efficiency of capital, defined as expectation of yield and the current supply price of capital – which is essentially the marginal cost of production, involves the idea that an inducement to investment depends partly on the investment demand-schedule and partly on the rate of interest. That is, the rate of investment reaches the point on the investment demand-schedule where the marginal efficiency of capital is equal to the market rate of interest (ibid., pp. 136–7).

10 The quantity of money (M) determines the actual rate of interest (r). Liquidity preference (L) is a potentiality or functional tendency, which fixes the quantity of money. Thus quantity of money depends on the relationship between the liquidity preference and interest rate: $M = L(r)$ (ibid., pp. 166–8).

11 Their analysis can be summarized as below:

Income identity: $Y = C + I + G + X - M$, where Y = income, C = consumption, I = investment, G = government expenditure, X = export, and M = import.

Consumption function: $C = c_0 + cY$, where c = marginal propensity to consume.

Import function: $M = m_0 + mY$, where m = marginal propensity to import. The basic multiplier formula is derived by substituting the consumption and import functions into the income identity:

$$Y = (c_0 + cY) + I + G + X - (m_0 + mY)(1 - c + m)$$
$$Y = c_0 + I + G + X - m_0$$
$$Y = \frac{1}{s+m}(c_0 + I + G + X - m_0)$$

The formula for the trade balance, T:

$$T = X - M = X - m_0 - \frac{m}{s+m}(c_0 + I + G + X - m_0).$$

12 This position is from the portfolio uncertainty model developed by Bawa (1979), Bawa, Brown, and Klein (1979), and Barry and Brown (1985), and the portfolio balance model developed by Branson, Halttunen, and Masson (1977), Farber, Roll and Solnik (1977), Diskill (1981), Marwah and Klein (1983), Marwah and Bodkin (1984), and Marwah, Klein and Bodkin (1985). This will be discussed in the portfolio theory section in detail.

13 Previous attempts to measure rates of return used uncovered interest rate differentials which assumes zero exchange risk (Hodrick, 1980, 1983: Hodrick and Srivastava, 1984, 1985). The uncovered interest rate differentials can be used only in model with cash-in-advance constraints in which financial items have identical risk characteristics (Obstfeld, 1986, pp. 60–3).

14 Variance is a measure of dispersion about the expected (Markowitz, 1952, p. 89).

15 Tobin classifies the investors into two types; 'risk-lovers' and 'risk-averters' in response to the change in the interest rate and risk. The latter again is classified into two; 'diversifiers' and 'plungers'.

16 For short-term financial capital flows:

$$L_s = f(M, i_s, i_s^*, e), C_s = f(X, i_s, i_s^*, e).$$

For long-term financial capital flows:

L_l (or C_l or B) = f (GNP,GNP* i_l, I_l*) where L = liabilities to foreigners, C = claims on private foreigners, M = import, X = export, i = interest rate, e = expected exchange rate B = long-term bank claims on foreigners, and GNP = gross national product (subscript s = short-term, l = long term and * = foreign country).

17 Flow effect refers an equilibrium portfolio flow into foreign assets from total portfolio growth due to wealth growth and stock effect is a stock shift in the equilibrium distribution of the portfolio toward foreign assets due to changes in interest rates. Branson and Willet (1972, p. 295) argue that flow effect is small relative to stock effect.

18 The parameter uncertainty model, Tobin's Q theory, and the barriers-to-international investment model have been developed in the framework of portfolio theory.

19 The portfolio balance model incorporates portfolio theory and the monetary approach to balance of payments. Since it has been developed in the framework of balance of payments, we will discuss this in the monetary approach section.

20 The parameter uncertainty model has been developed since Stiglitz introduced private returns to information acquisition (1971, 1982). See Bawa (1979), Bawa, Brown, and Klein (1979), Stiglitz (1982) and Barry and Brown (1985).

21 The barriers-to-international-investment model has been developed by Black (1974), Stulz (1981), Adler and Dumas (1983), and Huizinga (1991).

22 Michael Mussa (1974) argues that analysis of the money market should be furnished by a monetary theory of the balance of payments rather than the balance of trade or the balance on current account. See Meade (1951), Mundell (1962), and Fleming (1968) to recall the Keynesian approach to the balance of payments.

23 See the Keynesian approach.

24 Global monetarists, who are labelled by their assumption that domestic factors are determined by the world market, have argued that income, price and interest rate are exogenous. In their view, income is determined at its full employment level by wage flexibility, while price and interest rate are treated as determined from the world market by perfect arbitrage in goods and securities respectively. The extreme version of global monetarists assumption is summarized as below:

$$Y = Y_{fe}$$
$$P = e\,P^*$$
$$i = i^*,$$

where fe = exchange rate by foreign currency, and e = exchange rate by domestic currency.

25 It is necessary to endogenize interest rate (i), price (P), income (Y), reserves (R) and money supply (M), and to exogenize domestic output (E), government expenditure (G) and net export (T). Then, a general equilibrium model for the Keynesian and monetary approaches can be incorporated by the following developments (Frankel, Gylfason, and Helliwell, 1980, pp. 587–90):

$$R = \dot{P}T\,(Y^-, e/P^+) + F(i^+) \text{ – Keynesian approach equation}$$
$$M = \dot{L}\,(P^+, Y^+, i^-) \text{ – LM equation}$$
$$M \equiv m\,(D + R) \text{ – identity}$$
$$\Delta R = \Delta 1/m\, L\,(P^+, Y^+, i^-) - \Delta D \text{ – monetary approach equation}$$
$$Y = E\,(Y^+, i^-) + G + T\,(Y^-, e/P^+) \text{ – IS equation}$$
$$Y = Y\,(P^+) \text{ – aggregate supply equation.}$$

To focus the analysis on output and the balance of payments, the aggregate supply equation is solved for P:

$P = P(Y^{+})$.

Then using $P = P(Y^{+})$, the IS equation is solved for i by writing:

$i = i(Y^{-}, G^{+}, e^{+})$.

Substituting equations of $Y = Y(P^{+})$ and $i = i(Y^{-}, G^{+}, e^{+})$ into equations of the Keynesian approach (K-schedule) and the monetary approach (M-schedule):

$R = k_1^{-}Y + k_2^{+}G + k_3^{+}e + R_{-1}$ – K-schedule,

$R = m_1^{+}Y + m_2^{-}G + m_3^{-}e - D$ – M-schedule, where $R - R_{-1} = \Delta R$ and R_{-1} = the stock of international reserves held at the beginning of the period.

26 Kouri and Porter's demand functions are

$M_D = L(Y, W, i, i^*, E)$ – Demand for base money

$B_D = H(Y, W, i, i^*, E)$ – Net domestic demand for domestic bonds

$B_F = J(Y, W, i, i^*, E)$ – Domestic demand for foreign bonds, and

$B_{D^*} = F(Y^*, W^*, i, i^*, E)$ – Net foreign demand for domestic bonds.

27 Kouri and Porter's supply functions are:

$M_S = NFA + NDA$ – Total money supply, where NF(D)A = net foreign (domestic) asset of central bank;

$\Delta NDA = -\Delta B_G$ – Domestic component of money supply, where B_G = stock of government bonds held by private sector;

$\Delta NFA = TC + CAB$ – Foreign component of money supply, where TC = total net capital inflow and CAB = current account balance.

28 The portfolio balance model which focuses on exchange rates has been developed by Dornbusch (1975, 1980), Branson, Halttunen, and Masson (1977), Farber, Roll and Solnik (1977), Diskill (1981), Marwah and Klein (1983), Marwah and Bodkin (1984), and Marwah, Klein and Bodkin (1985).

29 See Branson (1968), Frankel (1971, 1976), Kouri and Porter (1974) and Levich (1975).

30 MacDougall (1960) and Deardorff (1984) also discussed that reduced tariffs might attract foreign investment.

31 Capital flows depend on interest rate differential and other variable:

$F(t) = \theta(L)R(t) + z(t)$, where F(t) = bond flows in t period, i = observed interest rate in the t period, $\theta(L)$ = a polynomial in the lag operator L, z = other determinants of capital flow besides i, and R (t) is defined as interest differential between the US and Canada, $R(t) = i_{US}(t) - i_{CAN}(t)$.

Interest rates depend on autarky interest rate and capital flows:

$i_{US}(t) = r_{US}(t) + \zeta_{US}(L)F(t)$ for the US interest rate, and

$i_{CAN}(t) = r_{CAN}(t) + \zeta_{CAN}(L)F(t)$ for the Canadian interest rate, where r = autarky i in t period, $\zeta_{US\,(CAN)}$ and (L) = a polynomial of lag distribution of US (Canada).

32 Instrument variables in his model are lagged values of capital flows, F(t), and interest rate differential, R(t).

33 The closed economy money supply is defined by the money stock net of the monetary effects of the private capital flows.

34 Branson defined short-term liabilities as foreign holdings of deposits and money market paper in the US government bonds and notes and other short-term liabilities, short-term claims as banking claims on foreigners and US deposits abroad, long-term liabilities as foreign holdings of US corporate stocks and bonds, and long-term claims as US holdings of all foreign long-term securities.

35 After the elimination of insignificant variables, Branson presented the preferred models (Branson, 1968, pp. 162–87).

Short-term K inflows: $\Delta L_s = a1 + \Delta M(t\text{-}1) + \Delta^{Uk}(t\text{-}1) - \Delta I^{CAN}(t) + \Delta r^{UK}(t) - \Delta r^{UK}(t - 1) - D$

Short-term K outflows: $\Delta C_s = a2 + \Delta X(t) + \Delta X(t - 1) - \Delta I^{US}(t - 1) + \Delta I^{UK}(t) + \Delta I^{CAN}(t) + \Delta I^{CAN}t - 1)$

Long-term K inflows: $L_l = a3\Delta GNP^{US}(t) - \Delta GNP^{US}(t - 1) - \Delta GNP^{US}(t - 2) + \Delta GNP^{EEC}(t) + \Delta I^{US}(t) + \Delta I^{US}(t - 2)$

Long-term K outflows: $C_l = a4 + T\text{-}D + \Delta GNP^{UK}$(all time lags) $- \Delta GNP^{US}(t - 2) + \Delta GNP^{EEC}(t) - \Delta GNP^{EEC}(t - 1) - \Delta I^{US}(t)$ where L = liabilities to foreigners, C = claims on foreigner, M = imports, X = exports, r^{UK} = expected UK exchange rates, $I^{US\ (UK,\ CAN)}$ = the U.S (U.K Canada) interest rates, $GNP^{Us(UK,\ EEC)}$ = GNP of US (UK, EEC),D = dummy for Interest Equalization Tax (from third quarter to fourth quarter of 1963), and T= a trend term (actual and fitted value from this equation).

36 Defined by US total consumer net worth.

37 They use the Jaffee-Modigliani (1969) credit rationing index multiplied by the sum of sample foreign countries' GNP as a measurement of money supply.

38 Abel (1980 for US), Salinger and Summers (1983 for US), Dinenis (1985 for UK), and Hayashi and Inoue (1987 for Japan) found empirical evidences that confirm the significant effects of Q on investments; however, most of them found that the effects were very weak. Meese (1980 for US) and Chappell and Cheng (1982 for US), Chirinko (1987) found insignificant effects.

39 Their data source is also similar to Kouri and Porter's analysis: Germany and OECDs for 1964–1969.

40 By access to international capital market, they mean, the opportunities to borrow on the international capital market.

41 See Dooley et al (1987), Murphy (1986), Frankel (1989), and Wong (1990).

42 See Tesar (1991) and Sinn (1992).

43 See Frankel (1989, 1992) and Haque and Montiel (1990, 1991).

44 See Branson (1968) and Branson and Hill (1971).

45 See Zecher (1976), Guiltian (1976), Bean (1978), Eaton and Gersovitz (1980), Nunnenkamp (1990), and Lesink and Van Vergeijk (1991).

46 See Kouri and Porter (1974), Herring and Marston (1977), Marwah et al (1985), and Ruffin and Rassekh (1986).

47 For example, Branson (1968) and Branson and Hill (1971) found that interest rate differentials and income were significant for capital flows among the European countries in the 1960s, but Ruffin and Rassekh (1986) found that those variables were not significant in the US outflows to the UK, West Germany, and Canada in the 1970s and early 1980s. Similarly, Kouri and Porter (1974) found that current account balance were significant for net capital flows among the European countries in the 1960s, but Marwah et al. (1985) found that it was not significant for the US capital inflows from or outflows to the UK West Germany, France, and Canada in the 1970s.

48 See parameter uncertainty model developed by Bawa et al (1979), Stgliz (1982), and Branson and Jaffee (1991).

49 See the barrier-to-international-investment model developed by portfolio theorists, Black (1971), Stulz (1981), and Huizinga (1991).

50 See Persson and Tabellini (1992) for the effect of fiscal policy competitions on attracting foreign investments.

51 See the effects of custom unions on international capital flows (Webb, 1982) and the effects of preferential trading agreements on international capital flows (Webb, 1990).

52 Kouri and Porter (1974) did not support the interest rate differentials when they endogenized net capital inflows while Herring and Marston (1977) showed a strong effect of interest rate differentials when they endogenize inflows and outflows separately. Each study used very similar data with the same country and time period. Also see the poor explanatory power of Stevenson (1984) and Stekler (1988) who endogenized net capital flows.

53 Marwah et al. (1985) argued that these differences would not be captured in net capital flows.

54 Different financial items responded differently to changes in exchange rates in Froot and Stein (1991).

55 Significant results for rate of return, cost of transfer, and government policy were found in Bryant and Hendershott (1970), earning differential in Prachowny (1972), and profit in Gilman (1981).

3 Research Methodology

Theoretical Framework

Measurement of Globalization

As discussed earlier, previous attempts to measure the integration of international financial markets have used investment-saving ratios (Feldstein and Horioka, 1980) and real interest rate differentials (Frankel, 1989, 1992). If there are no barriers in financial markets across countries, these studies imply that there will be no difference between domestic and foreign investment-saving ratios or between domestic and foreign interest rates. That is, there will be no yield differentials between domestic and foreign assets under perfect capital mobility. The perfect capital mobility condition can only be obtained when there are zero transaction costs, however, implying a world with no transaction costs, perfect information, and no regulations.

Beyond these conditions, it is implicitly assumed that all investors have homogenous preferences for financial products, and all countries have homogenous financial products. If investors have different preferences regarding certain countries or strong ties with their home country, the Feldstein-Horioka assumption cannot capture the integration of international financial markets even under perfect capital mobility. If each country has different compositions of financial items and each investor has different preferences for certain financial items, real interest rate differentials cannot measure the integration of international financial markets even under perfect capital mobility.

Under the flow theory assumption, if there are neither saving-investment ratio differentials nor real interest rate differentials, there will be no further capital transactions since there will be no higher earning countries. As previous empirical studies have found, several advanced economies are approaching convergent saving-investment ratios and real interest rates. But capital transactions have increased among these countries in recent years, even though interest rate differentials have decreased. This suggests that factors other than interest rate differentials are working.

To complicate matters, the interest rate differential and saving-investment ratio differential measurements used to study globalization of international financial markets do not indicate which factor contributes to the globalization. In place of these measures, the quantity of international capital transactions appears to be a more appropriate measure of global capital investment activities – a measure of the integration of international financial markets since massive international capital transactions reflect progressively more irrelevant national boundaries. It is internationally transacted capital that equilibrates interest rates around the world by increasing outflow countries' interest rates while decreasing those of capital inflow countries.

Causes of Inflows and Outflows of International Capital

In the balance of payments equation, a change in international reserves is a sum of the balances on current account and on capital account.

$$\Delta R_i = CAB_i + KAB_i \qquad \text{eq. 3.1.1}$$

where R_i = international reserve, CAB_i = current account balance, and KAB_i = capital account balance.

The current account balance is determined by country's export and import of goods and services (X), and the capital account by inflow and outflow of capital (F).

$$\Delta R_i = (\Sigma X_{i*} - \Sigma X_{*i}) + (\Sigma F_{*i} - \Sigma F_{i*}) \qquad \text{eq. 3.1.2}$$

where X_{i*} = export of goods and services from i to the rest of the world, X_{*i} = import of goods and services from the rest of the world to i, F_{*i} = capital inflow from the rest of the world to i, and F_{*i} = capital outflow from i to the rest of the world.

$$\text{Thus, } \Sigma F_{i*} = (\Sigma X_{i*} - \Sigma X_{*i}) + \Sigma F_{*i} - \Delta R_i . \qquad \text{eq. 3.1.3}$$

The capital outflow of country (i) to international financial markets is a result of current account surplus, capital inflow, and negative change in the international reserves.

$$\text{Or, } \quad \Sigma F_{*i} = \Sigma F_{i*} - (\Sigma X_{i*} - \Sigma X_{*i}) + \Delta R_i . \qquad \text{eq. 3.1.4}$$

The capital inflow of country is a result of current account deficit, capital outflow, and positive change in the international reserve.

These are the basic monetary approach equations of the balance of payments, which emphasizes that the current account and the capital account should be analyzed in the same equation. Most research using a monetary approach[1] has focused on the demand for money function as a result of balance of payments and domestic credit policy and reserve policy. This basic monetary approach to the balance of payments should be embedded in the capital outflow and capital inflow equations that are discussed in the next section. However, we have to use either current account balance or international reserve, not both of them, in an equation of capital flow. Otherwise, there will be full collinearity problems, as equations 3.1.3 and 3.1.4 indicate. This study selects the current account balance condition rather than the reserve condition since the current account balance provides more information such as trades of goods and services, and other foreign income earnings, while the reserve condition can be arbitrarily manipulated by the governments.

According to portfolio theory, capital inflow is induced when the expected rate of return on domestic investments is larger than foreign investments. By the same logic, capital outflow is induced when the expected rate of return on foreign investments is larger than domestic investments. In portfolio theory, expected rates of return are determined not only by interest rate differentials but also by risk estimates. For convenience, flow theory mathematics will be discussed first, followed by the mathematics of portfolio theory.

In flow theory, under the assumption of perfect capital markets, expected rate of return is determined by real interest rates. Thus, international capital flows are induced by real interest rate differentials between domestic and foreign countries. Consider an investor who has investment income from both domestic and foreign financial markets. The sum of domestic and foreign investment income of this investor is:

$$y_T = y + y^*. \qquad \text{eq. 3.2.1}$$

Here, $y = \mu(k - I^*)$ and $y^* = \mu^*(I^*)$ where y_T = sum of yield income of domestic yield income (y) and foreign yield income (y^*), k = total capital available ($k = I + I^*$), I = amount of capital invested, μ = rate of return, and * indicates foreign variable.

$$\text{Then, } y_T = \mu(k - I^*) + \mu^*(I^*). \qquad \text{eq. 3.2.2}$$

Since $\mu = r$ and $\mu^* = r^*$ in perfect capital markets,

$$y_T = r(k - I^*) + r^*(I^*). \qquad \text{eq. 3.2.3}$$

The marginal income[2] of foreign investment is found by differentiating y_T with respect to I*:

$$dy_T/dI^* = r^* - r. \qquad \text{eq. 3.2.4}$$

This explains that the rate of changes in income with respect to foreign investments is r* - r. There are three cases in determining the direction of capital flows accounting to the real interest rate.

If $r^* > r$, then $dy_T/dI^* > 0$	and	capital outflows.
If $r^* < r$, then $dy_T/dI^* < 0$	and	capital inflows.
If $r^* = r$, then $dy_T/dI^* = 0$	and	no capital flows.

The above calculation is identical to that developed in flow theory.[3] Under the perfect capital market assumption, if there is no real interest differential between domestic and foreign financial markets, there will be no capital flows. As previous empirical studies[4] have found, real interest rates differentials across countries are gradually decreasing. Thus international capital flows, from a flow theory point of view, should decrease because of decreased yield differentials. We are, however, experiencing growth in international capital flows, especially among the industrialized countries where real interest rates are close to each other.[5] If real interest rates in domestic financial markets are greater than in foreign financial markets, there should be no outflow of capital, only inflow. However, inflows and outflows of capital can occur simultaneously because expected rates of return are determined not only by real interest rates but also by transaction costs and preferences of investors in the real world, where each country has different financial products, different risk estimations, and different transaction costs. It is therefore necessary to assume imperfect capital markets to analyze the effects of factors other than real interest rates on international capital flows.

If we assume perfect capital markets, we cannot isolate the causes of the integration of international financial markets because the perfect capital market assumption already requires the full range of integration of international financial markets. This invites us to investigate the causes of the integration of international financial markets from the perspective of imperfect capital markets. The next question therefore is what influences international capital flows without regarding real interest rate differentials. As shown in the survey of literature, portfolio theory has developed its scope by introducing the parameter uncertainty model, Tobin's Q theory, and the barriers-to-international-investment model to investigate this question. These theories postulate that improved information and reduced costs of capital investments accelerate international capital movements.

This study sees transaction costs as important factors that affect international investments as a whole. Following Williamson's concept that 'economic counterpart of friction' is transaction cost (Williamson, 1981, p. 552), transaction costs are defined here as any cost that is incurred during capital transfer. Transaction costs, thus, include transportation cost, financial cost (in other word, capital formation cost), information collection cost, and regulation-related cost. As investors enter uncertain international capital markets, they want to be safeguarded by reducing the friction. This safeguard can be obtained when there are lower transaction costs.

Consider again an investor who has investment income from domestic and foreign financial markets. The sum of domestic and foreign investment income is defined by y_T as in eq. 3.2.3.

$$y_T = \mu(k - I^*) + \mu^*(I^*)$$

where y_T = sum of yield income of domestic yield income (y) and foreign yield income (y^*), k = total capital available ($k = I + I^*$), I = amount of capital invested, and * indicates foreign variable.

Under imperfect capital markets,

$$\mu = r\,(1 - C), \text{ and } \mu^* = r^*(1-C^*).$$

where μ = expected rate of return, r = real interest rate, C = transaction costs estimation, and * indicates foreign variable.

$$\text{Then, } y_T = r(1 - C)\,(k - I^*) + r^*(1 - C^*)I^*. \qquad \text{eq. 3.2.5}$$

The marginal income of foreign investment is found by differentiating y_T with respect to I^*:[6]

$$dy_T/dI^* = r^*\,(1 - C^*) - r\,(1 - C) \text{ or } (r^* - r) - (r^*C^* - rC). \qquad \text{eq. 3.2.6}$$

Thus the rate of change in income with respect to foreign investment is

$[r^* (1-C^*) - r (1-C)]$.

The marginal income of foreign investments is again a measurement of differentials in expected rates of return between foreign and domestic investments:

$$\mu^* - \mu = r^*(1-C^*) - r (1-C).$$

Comparing eq. 3.2.4 and eq. 3.2.6, now we show that the expected yield on international investments is affected not only by interest rate differentials but also by transaction cost differentials between domestic and foreign investment. Under the imperfect capital market assumption, there will be nine cases in determining the direction of capital movements because transaction costs are involved:

if $r^* < r$, and $C^* = C$, then $dy_T/dI^* < 0$: capital inflows case (1)
if $r^* > r$, and $C^* = C$, then $dy_T/dI^* > 0$: capital outflows case (2)
if $r^* = r$, and $C^* > C$, then $dy_T/dI^* < 0$: capital inflows case (3)
if $r^* = r$, and $C^* < C$, then $dy_T/dI^* > 0$: capital outflows case (4)
if $r^* < r$, and $C^* > C$, then $dy_T/dI^* < 0$: capital inflows case (5)
if $r^* > r$, and $C^* < C$, then $dy_T/dI^* > 0$: capital outflows case (6)
if $r^* < r$, and $C^* < C$, then $dy_T/dI^* = ?$: indeterminate case (7)
if $r^* > r$, and $C^* > C$, then $dy_T/dI^* = ?$: indeterminate case (8)
if $r^* = r$, and $C^* = C$, then $dy_T/dI^* = 0$: no capital flow case (9).

Cases (1) and (2) show the same results as in perfect capital mobility although they do not assume zero transaction cost. If transaction costs are the same across countries, the direction of capital flow will depend on the level of interest rates. Cases (3) and (4) explain that the direction of capital flow will depend on the level of transaction cost if interest rates are the same across countries. This is a fundamentally different position from flow theory, which implies no capital movement when interest rate differentials are zero. Cases (3), (5), and (8) advance the reasonable assumption that transaction costs in domestic investment are lower than in international investments because there are no barriers, lower transportation costs and more information available in domestic than foreign financial markets.

Cases (4), (6) and (7) focus on the contemporary instances where transaction costs in international investments are lower than in domestic investments. This may occur due to tax rate differences between foreign investors and domestic investors. In recent years, many countries have lowered their tax rates for foreign investors to attract capital inflows.[7] A second reason is the higher risk in domestic investments due to political and economic instability – we are all aware of capital flight from LDCs due to the uncertainty of political and economic conditions.[8] The third explanation for this case is in the level of development of domestic financial markets. If a country's financial market is less developed than foreign financial markets – which have more financial products and better ways to access information for that country's investors – transaction costs in international investments are lower than domestic investments.

In cases (5) and (6), it is easy to find the direction of capital flows since interest rates and transaction costs favour one market. In case (5), there will be capital inflow since the domestic market has higher interest rates and lower transaction costs. In case (6), there will be capital outflow since the domestic market has lower interest rates and higher transaction costs. Cases (7) and (8) are indeterminate with the given information because the direction of capital flows will be determined by the ratio of differentials between domestic interest rates and domestic transaction costs to differentials between foreign interest rates and foreign transaction costs. When interest rates favour the domestic market and transaction costs favour the foreign counterparts (7) or vice-versa (8), the direction of capital flows depends on the ratio of the equation, $(r^* - r)/(r^*C^* - rC)$. In both cases, there can be inflow, outflow or no-flow of capital in domestic financial markets.

In case (9), investors in both domestic and foreign countries may not have any incentive to export capital in so far as interest rates and transaction costs are concerned. There can be capital flows even in this case if we consider investor's preferences.

So far, we have showed how transaction costs are important in determining capital flows. Transaction costs can be reduced by telecommunication technology development, financial instrument innovation, regulatory relaxation, and favoured treaty relations. An improved telecommunication technology lowers the transportation cost since capital transactions become much cheaper and faster with a better telecommunication system. The telecommunication technologies also contribute to lowering information collection cost since the telecommunication networks provide up-to-date information on foreign capital markets. Financial instrument innovation lowers the financial costs by reducing the shadow cost of investors as well as recipients. The financial instrument innovations also reduce the transportation cost and improve allocation of risk (Yumoto et al., 1986, pp. 46–9). Regulatory relaxation and favoured treaty relations lower regulation-related cost by reducing tax burdens.

In addition to transactions cost, there is another factor that affects the rate of return. Even though investors are well-informed about interest rate and transaction cost, they may not know the exact rate of return. Because of this, investors are very sensitive to the conditions of political and economic stability of the market. Political and economic risk can affect the rate of return in many ways. Unstable economic conditions can affect the rate of return through the change in interest rate in the future unless the interest rate is contracted. Unstable political conditions can affect the rate of return through financial costs or regulation cost (for example, a sudden political turmoil or a regulatory change by a new government can cause financial costs and regulations costs).

If a market is not fully opened or is under a serious monetary control, capital flow will be discouraged even though the rate of return is high in that market after considering interest rate, transaction cost, and risk. If a market does not demand external financial resources due to a current account surplus, capital inflow also will be discouraged while capital outflow will be encouraged. Lastly, wealth of investor country (a broad measure of investment capability) is important in determining capital outflow.

This study assumes that the factors lowering the transaction cost and providing favourable investment conditions such as market openness and removal of monetary control are the contributors to the globalization of financial markets. Inducing low transaction cost and favourable investment conditions is more important than higher interest rates. If transaction cost is higher than interest earning, the rate of return will be negative. If there is no market openness, there will be no capital flows. Since controlling interest rate to attract foreign capital is not a practicable policy, providing low transaction cost and favourable investment condition has been used in the global financial competition. This competition has been more active in recent years. Figure 4 summarizes the determinants of international capital flows.

Data Selection

Data and Sample

This study explores all types of private sector capital (portfolio capital, bank capital, foreign direct investment, and other-sector capital). The unit of analysis is the country. There are 121 countries for the descriptive analyses and 86

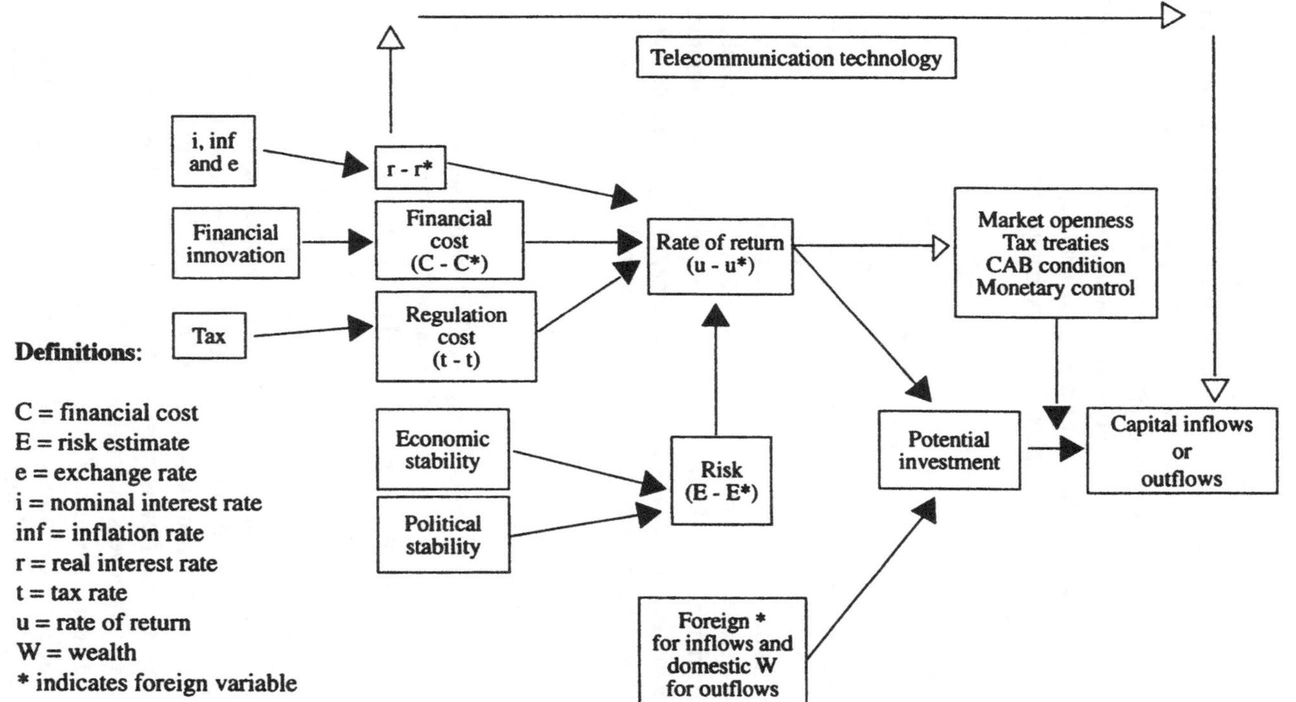

Figure 4 Determinants of international capital flows

countries in the econometric analyses that follow. The time period is 1980–1990.

According to international standards, international capital transactions are composed of private sector capital transactions, official sector capital transactions, and reserve transactions. Portfolio capital, bank capital, foreign direct investment, and other-sector capital are defined as private sector capital. Capital transferred between any level of governments or between governments and international organizations is treated as official capital.[9] Reserves are monetary gold, special drawing rights, foreign exchange assets, etc. The details are presented in Figure 5.

Data availability shapes the structure of empirical models. If there are data for country-by-country capital transfers, we can apply multi-country analysis via a transfer matrix or general equilibrium model. Unfortunately, there are no data on the direction of financial transfers for many countries. The IMF's *Balance of Payments Statistics Yearbook* does, however, provide inward and outward capital flows between a country and the rest of the world. Many countries do not have data for the entire time period of this study, which limits the coverage of countries to 121. Due to the lack of a number of exogenous variables, only 86 of 121 countries are used in the econometric analyses: 19 low income, 27 lower-middle income, 17 upper-middle income, and 23 high income countries. Countries included in the study are reported in Table 3 on pp. 62–3.

Dependent Variables

This study has two basic models; a gross flow model solved by the OLS method to investigate globalization factors, and an inflow-outflow model solved by the simultaneous equation method to explore the consequences of the globalization for capital inflows and outflows, discussed in section on *Model Specifications*. In the simultaneous equation model, the dependent variable of the inflow equation is capital inflow of a country from the rest of the world and the dependent variable of the outflow equation is capital outflow of a country to the rest of the world. In the gross flow model, the sum of capital inflows and outflows is used as the dependent variable. For the descriptive analyses, net flow is calculated by subtracting inflow from outflow.

Since this study covers major financial items, the dependent variable of each financial item is the sum of its components[10] as shown in Figure 5. For example, portfolio inflow is the sum of its inflow components including public bond inflow, private bond inflow, and corporate equity inflow. Portfolio

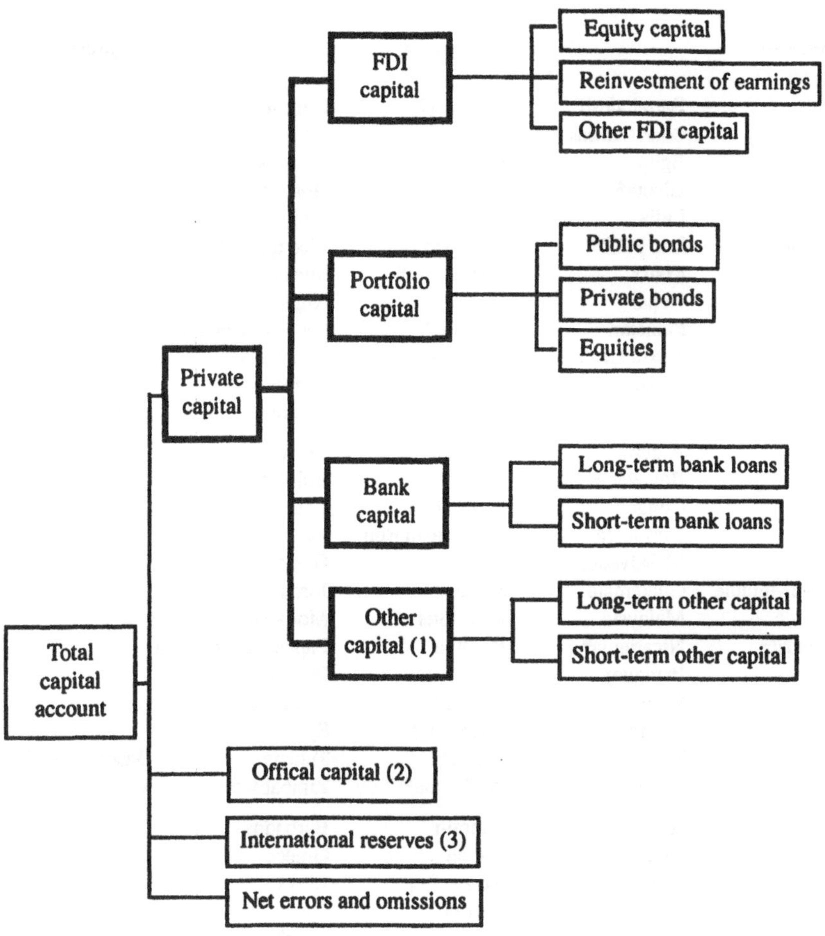

Notes

Thick lines indicate the coverage of the study.

1 Other private sector capital includes non-bank institutions' capital, non-portfolio investment institutions' capital, trade-related credits, etc.
2 Official capital includes borrowing and lending from and to foreign governments or international organizations.
3 International reserves include monetary gold, special drawing rights, reserve position in the Fund, foreign exchange assets, use of Fund credit and loans, etc.

Figure 5 Components of international capital transactions

Table 3 Countries covered in the study

Income level (1)	Country name			Numbers
	Bangladesh	Benin* (2)	Burkina Faso*	
	Central African Rep.*	Chad*	Comoros*	
	Egypt	Ethiopia	Gambia*	
	Ghana*	Haiti	Honduras	
Low income countries	India	Indonesia	Kenya	
	Lao PDR*	Lesotho*	Madagascar	
	Mali*	Mauritania*	Mozambique	
	Nepal	Niger*	Nigeria	
	Pakistan	Rwanda*	Sao Tome & Principe*	
	Sierra Leone	Solomon Islands*	Sri Lanka	
	Sudan	Tanzania	Togo*	Descriptive: 36
	Uganda*	Zaire	Zambia	Model: 19
	Algeria	Argentina	Bolivia	
	Botswana*	Chile	Colombia	
	Congo	Costa Rica	Cote d'Ivoire	
	Dominica*	Dominican Rep.	Ecuador	
	El Salvador	Fiji*	Greneda*	
Lower-middle income countries	Guatemala	Jamaica	Jordan*	
	Malaysia	Mauritius	Morocco	
	Nicaragua*	Panama*	Papua New Guinea	
	Paraguay	Peru	Philippines	
	Romania*	Senegal	St. Lucia*	
	St Vincent*	Swaziland	Syria	
	Thailand	Tonga*	Tunisia	Descriptive: 39
	Turkey	W. Samoa*	Zimbabwe	Model: 27
	Antigua*	Bahrain	Barbados	
	Brazil	Gabon	Greece	
Upper-middle iIncome countries	Hungary*	Korea, Rep.	Libya	
	Malta*	Mexico	Oman	
	Portugal	Saudi Arabia	Seychelles	
	South Africa	Suriname*	Trinidad and Tobago	Descriptive: 21
	Uruguay	Venezuela	Yugoslavia	Model: 17
	Australia	Austria	Bahamas*	
	Belgium-Luxembourg (3)	Canada	Cyprus	
	Denmark	Finland	France	
High income countries	Germany, Federal Rep.	Iceland	Ireland	
	Israel	Italy	Japan	
	Kuwait*	Netherlands	New Zealand	
	Norway	Singapore	Spain	
	Sweden	Switzerland	United Kingdom	Descriptive: 25
	United States			Model: 23
Total	**Descriptive: 121 countries**		**Model: 86 countries**	

Notes

1 The economies are divided according to 1990 GNP per capita, based on the World Bank's Atlas method. The groups are: low income, $610 or less; lower-middle income, $611–$2645; upper-middle income, $2466–$7619; and high income $7620 or more.
2 * denotes countries not covered in the econometric models due to the lack of data for exogenous variables. They are covered only in the descriptive analysis.
3 Belgium and Luxembourg are treated as one unit since IMF reports their capital transaction data as one unit. The exogenous variables of this observation are averaged for the two countries.

outflow, on the other hand, is the sum of its outflow components such as public bond outflow, private bond outflow, and corporate equity outflow. Portfolio gross flow is the sum of inflows and outflows of these three financial components.

This study also investigates short-term capital flows in a separate model. The dependent variable is the sum of short-term bank capital and short-term other-sector capital flows. All currency values, unless specified, are deflated as millions of 1987 US dollar in the descriptive analyses. Since log-linear models are utilized in the econometric analyses, the dependent variables are expressed as the natural logarithm of millions of 1987 US dollars. The variable definitions and their original source are presented in Table 4 and Table 5 on the following pages.

Research Hypotheses and Exogenous Variable Selection

The primary research interest in this study is to investigate the factors that have contributed to recent globalization of international financial markets, and the consequences of globalization for the international capital flows. Thus, this study develops a globalization model and an inflow-outflow model. Utilizing suggestions from the previous studies, capital flows are hypothesized to be determined by flow factors, portfolio factors, monetary factors, and globalization factors. Four major elements are built into the empirical tests: (1) interest rate differential for the flow factors, (2) risk and wealth for the portfolio factors, (3) current account balance condition and regulation for the monetary factors, and (4) international treaty relations, financial instrument innovations, and telecommunication developments for the globalization factors. Table 6 (pp. 96–7) summarizes the definitions of exogenous variables, and Table 7 (pp. 98–9) reports the data sources and calculation methods.

Table 4 Definition of endogenous variables

Flow Type	Variable	Definition (log value of millions of 1987 US dollars)	Components
Inflow	PORTI	Portfolio inflow	PBONDI + RBONDI + EQUITI* (1)
	BANKI	Bank capital inflow	BANKLI + BANKSI* (2)
	OTHI	Other-sector capital inflow	OTHLI + OTHSI* (3)
	FDII	Foreign direct investment inflow	FDII
Outflow	PORTO	Portfolio outflow	PBONDO + RBONDO + EQUITO* (4)
	BANKO	Bank capital outflow	BANKLO + BANKSO* (5)
	OTHO	Other-sector capital outflow	OTHLO + OTHSO* (6)
	FDIO	Foreign direct investment outflow	FDIO
Gross flow	PORTG	Portfolio gross flow	PORTI + PORTO
	BANKG	Bank capital gross flow	BANKI + BANKO
	OTHG	Other-sector capital gross flow	OTHI + OTHO
	FDIG	FDI gross flow	FDII + FDIO
Net flow	PORTN	Portfolio net flow	PORTI - PORTO
	BANKN	Bank capital net flow	BANKI - BANKO
	OTHN	Other-sector capital net flow	OTHI - OTHO
	FDIN	FDI net flow	FDII - FDIO
Total capital	TOTI	Total capital inflow	PORTI + BANKI + OTHI + FDII
	TOTO	Total capital outflow	PORTO + BANKO + OTHO + FDIO
	TOTG	Total capital gross flow	TOTI + TOTO
	TOTN	Total capital net flow	TOTI - TOTO

Flow Type	Variable	Definition (log value of millions of 1987 US dollars)	Components
Short-term capital	STKI	Short-term capital inflow	BANKSI + OTHSI
	STKO	Short-term capital outflow	BANKSO + OTHSO
	STKI1	Short-term capital invested to home from world by foreign investors	BANKSI1 + OTHSI1
	STKI2	Short-term capital withdrawn to home from world by domestic investors	BANKSI2 + OTHSI2
	STKO1	Short-term capital invested to world from home by domestic investors	BANKSO1 + OTHSO1
	STKO2	Short-term capital withdrawn to world from home from by foreign investors	BANKSO2 + OTHSO2

Notes

See Table 5 (Data source of endogenous variables) for the detailed definition of the following components.

1 PBONDI = public bond onflow; RBONDI = private bond inflow; EQUITI = corporate equity inflow.
2 BANKLI = long-term bank capital inflow; BANKS I= short-term bank capital inflow.
3 OTHLI = long-term other-sector capital inflow; OTHSI = short-term other-sector capital inflow.
4 PBONDO = public bond outflow; RBONDO = private bond outflow; EQUITO = corporate equity outflow.
5 BANKLO = long-term bank capital outflow; BANKSO = short-term bank capital outflow.
6 OTHLO = long-term other-sector capital outflow; OTHSO = short-term other-sector capital outflow.

Table 5 Data source of endogenous variables

Variable name			Data source and components *1
PORTG	PORTI	PBONDI	Liabilities constituting foreign authorities' reserves in public sector bonds (54) *2 Other liabilities in public sector bonds (55)
		RBONDI	Liabilities constituting foreign authorities' reserves in non-public sector bonds (57) Other liabilities in non-public sector bonds (58)
		EQUITI	Liabilities constituting foreign authorities' reserves in corporate equities (60) Other liabilities in corporate equities (61)
	PORTO	PBONDO	Assets in public sector bonds (53)
		RBONDO	Assets in non-public sector bonds (56)
		EQUITO	Assets in corporate equities (59)
BANKG	BANKI	BANKLI	Liabilities constituting foreign authorities' reserves denominateded in national currency (72)*3 Liabilities constituting foreign authorities' reserves denominateded in foreign currency (73)*3 Other liabilities in long-term capital of deposit money banks (76) Drawings on loan received in long-term capital of deposit money banks (74) Repayments on loan extended in long-term capital of deposit money banks (70)
		BANKSI	Liabilities constituting foreign authorities' reserves denominated in national currency (90)*4 Liabilities constituting foreign authorities' reserves denominated in foreign currency (91)*4 Other liabilities in short-term capital of deposit money banks (92)
	BANKO	BANKLO	Drawings on loan extended in long-term capital of deposit money banks (69) Repayments on loan received in long-term capital of deposit money banks (75) Other assets in long-term capital of deposit money banks (71)
		BANKSO	Assets in short-term capital of deposit money banks (89)

Variable name			Data source and components *1
OTHG	OTHI	OTHLI	Liabilities constituting foreign authorities' reserves in long-term capital of other sectors (80) Other liabilities in long-term capital of other sectors (83) Drawings on loan received in long-term capital of other sectors (81) Repayments on loan extended in long-term capital of other sectors (78)
		OTHSI	Liabilities constituting foreign authorities' reserves in short-term capital of other sectors (95) Oher liabilities in short-term capital of other sectors (97) Other loan received in short-term capital of other sectors (81)
	OTHO	OTHLO	Drawings on loan extended in long-term capital of other sectors (77) Repayments on loan received in long-term capital of other sectors (82) Other assets in long-term capital of other sectors (79)
		OTHSO	Loan extended in short-term capital of other sectors (93) Other assets in short-term capital of other sectors (94)
FDIG	FDII		Equity capital in inward foreign direct investment (45) Reinvestment of earnings in inward foreign direct investment (46) Other long-term capital in inward foreign direct investment (47)
	FDIO		Other short-term capital in inward foreign direct investment (48) Equity capital in outward foreign direct investment (49) Reinvestment of earnings in outward foreign direct investment (50) Other long-term capital in outward foreign direct investment (51) Other short-term capital in outward foreign direct investment (52)

Notes

1 Capital transactions data from IMF's Balance of Payments Statistics Yearbook (1980–1993)
2 Numbers in brackets are component numbers defined in Balance of Payments Statistics Yearbook
3 Long-term capital of deposit money banks
4 Short-term capital of deposit money banks

Hypotheses Concerning Globalization

As discussed in section on *Measurement of Globalization*, the measurement of globalization of financial markets is quantity of internationally transferred capital. We initially hypothesize that gross capital flow is determined by flow factors, portfolio factors, and monetary factors. We then hypothesize that, at the same level of these three financial and monetary factors, gross capital flow is accelerated by the globalization factors. We develop four gross flow models to investigate which factors have caused the globalization of each financial market, and a total capital gross flow model to explore which factors have accelerated the globalization of the international financial markets as a whole.

Hypotheses to test the effects of flow factors on gross flow Each form of capital has its own profit measurement. Thus, in what follows, government bond yield rates (IGOVT) are used as a representative measurement for the rate of return of portfolio.[11] Deposit interest rates (IDEP) are utilized to measure the rate of return of bank capital. Money market interest rates (IMKT) are used to measure the rate of return of other-sector capital (non-bank financial institution). When the total capital flow model is estimated, we use the average of all three types of interest rate (INT) because the dependent variable is the aggregate value of four financial items.

Since the rate of return of foreign direct investment is not directly involved with interest rates, but rather with price level, we utilize the purchasing power parity ratio (PPPR) in the FDI flow model. The purchasing power parity ratio is calculated by (Ei/Pi) * Pus, where Ei = exchange rate of country i's currency to US dollar, Pi = country i's price index, and Pus = price index of the US. The ratios are standardized as 1979 = 1. Thus PPP ratios provide the information about the purchasing power of the dollar in country i in comparison to that of the US, all expressed as a ratio to the relative purchasing power in 1979. If PPP ratio falls, it means that goods have become relatively more expensive in country i than in the US. Refer Appendix A–1 for calculation method in detail.

Several steps are involved to create the interest rate differentials. Nominal interest rates are deflated by inflation rates to create real interest rates in the first stage, and then the averages of four income groups' (low, lower middle, upper middle, and high income countries) real interest rates are calculated. The interest differential of a country, therefore, is the difference between that country's real interest rate and the average of its income group's real interest rate. Since we assume that level of risk and financial market development is similar in the same income group, this is a reasonable estimate for the rate of return. It postulates that a low income country's interest rate cannot be directly compared with a high income country's interest rate if we are to measure the rate of return.

The interest rate differential provides the relative rate of return in a country's financial markets. Hence, viewed in isolation, a given country's interest rate is not a causal factor in capital flows. For example, a country whose interest rate has not changed from the previous year may have capital inflow if the average of its income group's interest rate decreased. The capital inflow to the country is not due to the increase of its own interest rate, but due to the increase of interest rate differential relative to other countries. Thus it is a reasonable assumption that the interest rate differential captures the flow factors.

Gross flows, like net flows, are confounded by offsetting financial factors. Positive interest rate differentials, for example, attract capital inflows while negative interest rate differentials attract outflows. This condition is also true in the risk differential and the current account balance, which are discussed in the next two sections.

Let us assume two countries, country i and country j. If country i's interest rate is lower than country j's interest rate, then country i will provide capital outflow and country j will experience capital inflow. Both negative (country i) and positive (country j) interest rate differentials can contribute to gross flows. Thus we need to create an absolute value of interest rate differentials to examine the flow factor effect on gross flows.

We hypothesize that gross capital flows are positively affected by the absolute value of the corresponding interest rate differentials.[12]

$$TOTG = a + b(ABINTD) + u \qquad \text{TG-1}$$
$$PORTG = a + b(ABIGOVTD) + u \qquad \text{PG-1}$$
$$BANKG = a + b(ABIDEPD) + u \qquad \text{BG-1}$$
$$OTHG = a + b(ABIMKTD) + u \qquad \text{OG-1}$$
$$FDIG = a + b(ABPPPRC) + u \qquad \text{FG-1}$$

where a = intercept, b = parameter, u = disturbance term, TOTG = total capital gross flow, PORTG = portfolio gross flow, BANKG = bank capital gross flow, OTHG = other-sector capital gross flow, FDIG = foreign direct investment gross flow, ABINTD = average in absolute value of three interest rate differentials from the income group, ABIGOVTD = absolute value of government bond yield rate differentials from the income group, ABIDEPD = absolute value of bank deposit interest rate differentials from the income group, ABIMKTD = absolute value of market interest rate differentials from the income group, and ABPPPRC = absolute value in change of purchasing power parity ratio.

Hypotheses to test the effects of portfolio factors on gross flows To investigate portfolio factors, it is essential to measure risk. However, this is a difficult task. Several institutions such as the World Bank, the International Research Group, *Euromoney*, and *Institutional Investor* attempt to measure country creditworthiness by their own methods. We select the country credit rating index from *Institutional Investor* for a number of reasons.[13] It provides a consistent measurement method for 98 countries for the period of this study. It is sensitive not only to the economic conditions but also to the political conditions of the surveyed countries. The country credit rating is updated every six month on a scale of zero to 100, with zero representing the least creditworthy countries and 100 representing the most creditworthy countries (*Institutional Investor*, every September issue 1980–1990).

Following the same logic as was used with respect to the interest rate differentials, we use the risk differential (RISKD) from the averages of the same income groups. This provides a relative creditworthiness for individual countries within the same income group. This also eliminates a multicollinearity problem: the simple risk estimate causes a serious problem when it is used alongside wealth variables since a country's income is part of the creditworthiness. This will be discussed in the inflow-outflow flow models.

A simple risk estimate is not a causal factor of capital flows. Although a country keeps the same level of creditworthiness, for example, the country can enjoy capital inflows if one or more countries in the income group is in trouble. The capital inflow to the country is not caused by increased creditworthiness of the country, but by its now lower risk relative to other countries (for convenience, hereafter, 'risk' means creditworthiness). This is a more reasonable assumption because sudden political turmoil of country i, for example, decreases country i's own creditworthiness but does not affect country j's creditworthiness. However, country j's risk differential can increase due to country i's political turmoil. Then, capital invested in country i may move to country j, not because of increased creditworthiness of country j, but because of the increased risk differential of country j.

In the gross flow model, the independent risk variable is the absolute value of the risk differential following the same logic applied to the absolute value of interest rate. The country's wealth is estimated by gross national income per capita rather than gross national product or gross domestic income. The capacity for foreign capital investment should include all forms of income of the country.[14] We hypothesize that wealthier countries have more capacity to invest abroad, and they are more attractive to inflow capital as well, considering risk differentials.

We hypothesize that the gross flows of each financial item are positively affected by the absolute value of the risk differential and the wealth of a country. Since the dependent variable is in logarithmic form, we use the logarithm of gross national income per capita for interpretational purposes. This provides the income elasticity of international capital flows.

PORTG = a + b1(ABRISKD) + b2(GNYPC) + u PG-2
BANKG = a + b1(ABRISKD) + b2(GNYPC) + u BG-2
OTHG = a + b1(ABRISKD) + b2(GNYPC) + u OG-2
FDIG = a + b1(ABRISKD) + b2(GNYPC) + u FG-2
TOTG = a + b1(ABRISKD) + b2(GNYPC) + u TG-2

where ABRISKD = absolute value of risk differentials from the income group, and GNYPC = measurement of wealth by log of gross national income per capita.

Hypotheses to test the effects of monetary factors on gross flows Current account balance (CAB) is specifically included in the gross flow models to test the monetary approach to the balance of payments, which argues that international capital flows are a result of balance of payments. An exchange control variable also is tested to see the effect of foreign exchange control policy on capital flows. Current account is composed of goods, services, and income from foreign trades and foreign related businesses.[15]

The absolute value of current account balance (ABCAB) is used in the gross flow model since a negative current account balance demands foreign capital while a positive current account balance induces outflow. Exchange control policy (EXCHCONT) is a dummy variable coded 1 if the country is enforcing exchange control and 0 if the country is not enforcing exchange control. We hypothesize that gross flows of all financial items are positively affected by absolute value of current account balance and negatively affected by exchange control policy.

PORTG = a + b1(ABCAB) + b2(EXCHCONT) + u	PG-3
BANKG = a + b1(ABCAB) + b2(EXCHCONT) + u	BG-3
OTHG = a + b1(ABCAB) + b2(EXCHCONT) + u	OG-3
FDIG = a + b1(ABCAB) + b2(EXCHCONT) + u	FG-3
TOTG = a + b1(ABCAB) + b2(EXCHCONT) + u	TG-3

where ABCAB = absolute value of current account balance, and EXCHCONT = dummy variable for exchange control.

Hypotheses to test the effects of globalization factors on gross flows To examine the causes of globalization, market openness and international political environments should be included. Previous studies have encountered difficulty in operationalizing these factors. This study selects the percentage of share holdings permitted to foreign investors as a representative measurement of financial market openness, and uses evidence of participation in international tax treaties as a representative variable for favoured international economic relations. Since market openness and tax treaties are highly correlated each other, it is not proper to use both of them in a model. Rather, we decide to use an interaction variable (defined as TREATY). Even if we lose some information by using this interaction variable, we may be able to see the trend effect of market openness and international relations.

One of the most important factors that contribute to the globalization of financial markets, as many have argued, is financial innovation. In the sphere of financial innovation, however, it is very difficult to define and isolate its effects. Our primary interest in financial innovations is to investigate the impact of financial instrument innovation and telecommunication technology innovation. There have been hundreds of financial instrument innovations and financial process innovations in recent years.[16] However, there are not comparable data available for financial innovations by country since each country has different financial instruments. One of the most common financial instruments is the certificate of deposit (CD),[17] which this study selects as a representative variable for degree of financial innovation of a country.

The CD is one of the most important financial innovations, with its diffusion and development having been linked closely to other innovations in the financial markets (Podolski, 1986, pp. 119–22). It provides a new means of transaction (Yumoto et al., 1986, p. 47), reduced transaction costs, and increased liquidity (Finnerty, 1988, p. 17). Thus it may serve as a useful proxy for estimating a country's financial instrument availability. It is used in the portfolio, bank capital and other-sector capital flow models, though not in the foreign direct investment model. The variable CD is coded as 1 if a country's financial market provides CDs or 0 if not.

The recent development of telecommunication technologies is another essential part of the globalization process, not only in the financial sector but also in general international business. This study focuses on the innovations of telecommunication network technology and availability of communication circuits: telecommunication network technology provides financial institutions with more efficient ways of gathering information and facilitating fund transfers, while the size of communication circuits determines number of users.

There have been three levels of network development in the time period of this study: CSDN (Circuit Switched Data Network); PSDN (Packet Switched Data Network); and ISDN (Integrated Services Digital Network). These technologies became possible by the concept of VAN (Value Added Network) which was introduced in the 1970s in the US. Public telecommunication operators could provide viewdata or electronic mail in addition to basic telephone services due to the VAN services. When a country established the VAN service, CSDN became available, facilitating more efficient electronic fund transfers (Datapro Information Service Group, 1992).

CSDN service was established in many countries in the late 1970s and early 1980s. PSDN replaced CSDN by deploying to advanced countries in the early 1980s and mid 1980s. PSDN technology has been implemented in worldwide networks as a cost-effective alternative to CSDN. PSDN is totally software-controlled by programs that run multiple processors. It provides a more reliable means of data transmission with high speed[18] and allows operators to lease network capacity to other companies. It reduces operation costs to small financial institutions, enabling them to collect more information. The large financial firms can be more effective in managing their investment through their branch networks without interrupted data transmission.

The most recent development in telecommunication is ISDN. ISDN was developed in the mid-1980s and began to be widely used in the late 1980s. It is a set of internationally standardized interfaces between carrier switching equipment and user premises equipment. It provides a wide range of services since any previous switching systems (circuit or packet) can be sent over ISDN circuits with less cost. It also provides much higher speed (up to two megabytes per second). Due to ISDN, high-quality video conferencing, video telephony, image and graphic applications and broadband data communications are possible. ISDN provides financial markets with a 24 hour monitoring system and practically unlimited multiple uses (ibid.).

The number of international circuit ends is used as a measure of the size of the data transaction network system of a country. This includes the number of terminals on public telephone and telex networks, the number of private leased circuits, and the number of data terminals connected to dedicated public data networks. Even though the size of circuit ends is large, telecommunication efficiency may not be high under less-advanced telecommunication technology. Or even if the size is small, efficiency can be high under more advanced telecommunication technology. Thus the size of data network system is weighted by the level of telecommunication technology.

We quantify the telecommunication technology development level by creating dummy variables. If a country is equipped with CSDN then CSDN is coded as 1, if not CSDN is coded as 0. If country is equipped with PSDN then PSDN is coded as 1, if not PSDN is coded as 0. If a country is equipped with ISDN, then ISDN is coded as 1, if not ISDN is coded as 0. Since most countries have developed their telecommunication network equipment in the sequence CSDN, PSDN, and ISDN, we can add up their dummy variable numbers to measure level of telecommunication development.[19] The size of international circuit ends then is multiplied by the telecommunication development level to complete the measurement of telecommunication development. This variable is defined as TELECOMM.[20]

We hypothesize that gross flows of portfolio, bank capital and other-sector capital are positively influenced by financial market openness and international relations, financial innovations, and telecommunication development.

$$PORTG = a + b1(TREATY) + b2(CD) + b3(TELECOMM) + u \qquad PG\text{-}4$$
$$BANKG = a + b1(TREATY) + b2(CD) + b3(TELECOMM) + u \qquad BG\text{-}4$$
$$OTHG = a + b1(TREATY) + b2(CD) + b3(TELECOMM) + u \qquad OG\text{-}4$$
$$TOTG = a + b1(TREATY) + b2(CD) + b3(TELECOMM) + u \qquad TG\text{-}4$$

where TREATY = interaction between financial market openness and international tax treaties, CD = dummy variable for financial instrument innovation (CD) and TELECOMM = measurement of telecommunication development.

Since CD is not related with foreign investment, we do not include the financial innovation variable in the gross flow model of foreign direct investment. As a counterpart to financial innovation, industrial sector product as a percentage of GDP is utilized in the FDI gross flow model. That is,

$$FDIG = a + b1(TREATY) + b2(INDSTP) + b3(TELECOMM) + u \qquad FG\text{-}4$$

where INDSTP = industrial sector products as a percentage of GDP.

Hypotheses for Capital Inflows and Outflows

We also examine the effects of the flow factors, the portfolio factors, the monetary factors, and the globalization factors on capital inflows and outflows. Since capital inflows and outflows are simultaneously determined by these factors, we utilize a simultaneous equation technique. In the simultaneous equation model, we exogenize one of the endogenous variables in the counterpart flow. That is, we hypothesize that capital inflow is jointly determined by inflow factors and capital outflows while capital outflow is jointly determined by outflow factors and capital inflow.

Hypotheses to test the effects of flow factors on in-outflows Unlike the gross flow model, we use the actual (not absolute) value of interest rate differentials to test the effects of the flow factors on capital inflows and outflows since the sign of the interest rate differentials determine the direction of capital flows. As discussed in the gross flow model, interest rate differentials are matched to the financial items in the inflow and outflow equations; government bond yield rate differential (IGOVTD) for portfolio inflow (PORTI) and outflow (PORTO), deposit interest rate differential (IDEPD) for bank capital inflow (BANKI) and outflow (BANKO), money market interest rate differential (IMKTD) for other-sector capital inflow (OTHI) and outflow (OTHO) and purchasing power parity ratio (PPPR) for FDI inflow (FDII) and outflow (FDIO). When the total capital inflow (TOTI) and outflow (TOTO) are estimated, we use the average of all three types of interest rate differentials (INTD).

We hypothesize that a positive value in interest rate differentials induces capital inflow and discourages capital outflow while a negative value induces capital outflow and discourages capital inflow in a simultaneous system.

Total capital inflow-outflow in one system:

TOTI = a1 + b1(INTD) + b2(TOTO) + u1 TI-1
TOTO = a2 + c1(INTD) + c2(TOTI) + u2 TO-1

where TOTI = total capital inflow, TOTO = total capital outflow, and INTD = average of three interest rate differentials.

Portfolio inflow-outflow in one system:

PORTI = a1 + b1(IGOVTD) + b2(PORTO) + u1 PI-1
PORTO = a2 + c1(IGOVTD) + c2(PORTI) + u2 PO-1

where PORTI = portfolio inflow, PORTO = portfolio outflow, and IGOVTD = government bond yield rate differential.

Bank capital inflow-outflow in one system:

BANKI = a1 + b1(IDEPD) + b2(BANKO) + u1 BI-1
BANKO = a2 + c1(IDEPD) + c2(BANKI) + u2 BO-1

where BANKI = bank capital inflow, BANKO = bank capital outflow, and IDEPD = deposit interest rate differential.

Other-sector capital inflow-outflow in one system:

OTHI = a1 + b1(IMKTD) + b2(OTHO) + u1 OI-1
OTHO = a2 + c1(IMKTD) + c2(OTHI) + u2 OO-1

where OTHI = other-sector capital inflow, OTHO = other-sector capital outflow, and IMKTD = money market interest rate differential.

Foreign direct investment inflow-outflow in one system:

FDII = a1 + b1(PPPR) + b2(FDIO) + u1 FI-1
FDIO = a2 + c1(PPPR) + c2(FDII) + u2 FO-1

where FDII = foreign direct investment inflow, FDIO = foreign direct investment outflow, and PPPR = purchasing power parity ratio.

The above equations face an identification problem since the same variable is used in both the inflow and outflow equations. This problem is solved when the portfolio factors, the monetary factors and the globalization factors are incorporated into a single model. Some of portfolio, monetary, and globalization factor variables will be included only in one equation so as to obviate the identification problem in a complete model.

Hypotheses to test the effects of portfolio factors on in-outflows In the inflow equation, to test the effect of portfolio factors on capital inflow, the risk differential is used because a positive risk differential will induce capital inflow while negative risk differential will discourage capital inflow. In the outflow equation, annual change of the risk differential is used for two reasons. The first reason is a methodological one. By selecting a different variable we can solve the identification problem in the simultaneous equation model. Since the inflow and outflow equations in one system can share the same variables, it is often difficult to find enough omitted variables.

The second reason is theoretical. Outflow is more sensitive to change in risk differentials than to the risk differential itself. In portfolio theory, capital outflow is also determined by wealth. Wealthy countries, however, may have a higher value of risk differential. Thus we assume that capital outflow from the wealthy countries is a result of changes in risk differential. In the case of capital outflow we assume that capital was invested in a country in the previous year due to a positive risk differential; previously-invested capital will leave that country if the country's risk differential drops in the present year. On the other hand, previously-invested capital will stay if the risk differential of the country increases or does not change.

We use the annual change in the risk estimate instead of the annual change in the risk differential in the outflow equation. There are a couple of reasons for using the annual change in the risk differential. As discussed in the gross flow model, a country's risk estimate cannot be as sensitive as the relative value of risk estimate. If the risk estimate of the world in general increased, a small increase in a country's risk estimate may not be attractive as a capital inflow factor of that country. Another reason is to avoid measurement error. Since we use the risk estimate index from *Institutional Investors* as introduced in the gross flow model, this data may not be consistent throughout the years (even though the estimators applied the same measurement method). If we use each year's differential value, we ensure greater consistency.

As the previous literature suggested, the wealth variable is used in the outflow equation only because it is a measurement of capital investment capacity. Thus we hypothesize that capital inflows are determined by risk differential (RISKD) while capital outflows are determined by change in risk differential (RISKDC) and national wealth (GNYPC) in a simultaneous system.

Total capital inflow and outflow in one system:

TOTI = a1 + b1(RISKD) + b2(TOTO) + u1 OI-2
TOTO = a2 + c1(RISKDC) + c2(GNYPC) + c3(TOTI) + u2 OO-2.

Portfolio inflow and outflow in one system:

PORTI = a1 + b1(RISKD) + b2(PORTO) + u1 PI-2
PORTO = a2 + c1(RISKDC) + c2(GNYPC) + c3(PORTI) + u2 PO-2.

Bank capital inflow and outflow in one system:

BANKI = a1 + b1(RISKD) + b2(BANKO) + u BI-2
BANKO = a2 + c1(RISKDC) + c2(GNYPC) + c3(BANKI)
+ u2 BO-2.

Other-sector capital inflow and outflow in one system:

OTHI = a1 + b1(RISKD) + b1(OTHO) + u1 OI-2
OTHO = a2 + c1(RISKDC) + c2(GNYPC) + c2(OTHI) + u2 OO-2.

Foreign direct investment inflow and outflow in one system:

FDII = a1 + b1(RISKD) + b2(FDIO) + u1 OI-2
FDIO = a2 + c1(RISKDC) + c2(GNYPC) + c3(FDII) + u2 OO-2

where RISKD = risk differential from the income group, RISKDC = annual change in RISKD, and GNYPC = measurement of wealth by log of gross national income per capita.

Hypotheses to test the effects of monetary factors on in-outflows Unlike the gross flow model, the actual values of current account balance are used in the inflow and outflow equations as we assume that a negative current account balance demands foreign capital while a positive current account balance induces outflow. We use exchange control policy only in the outflow equation since we assume that the exchange control policy is more effective with respect to capital outflow than to capital inflow. As a counterpart to exchange control policy, we introduce market openness measurement in the capital inflow equation.

In the in-outflow model for monetary factors, we add tax policies on international investments. Since a different tax rate applies to each capital investment, this study selects three different tax rates: tax rate on foreigners' dividends earning (TFDIVD) for the portfolio flow model, tax rate on foreigners' interest earning (TFINTD) for the bank capital and other-sector capital flow models, and tax rate on foreigners' corporate income (TFCORD) for the foreign direct investment flow model. In the total capital flow model, the average of the three tax rates (TAXD) is used as a level of tax rate for a country. All tax rates are calculated by differential terms as discussed with the interest rate differential and risk differential.

To test the effects of monetary factors on capital inflow and outflow, we now hypothesize that capital inflows are negatively affected by current account balance and tax rates while capital outflows are positively affected by current account balance and tax rate, and negatively affected by exchange control policy.

Total capital inflow and outflow in one system:

TOTI = a1 + b1(CAB) + b2(TAXD) + b3(TOTO) + u1 TI-3
TOTO = a2 + c1(CAB) + c2(TAXD) + c3(EXCHCONT) +
c4(TOTI) + u2 TO-3

where CAB = current account balance, TAXD = average of three tax rates differential and EXCHCONT = dummy variable for exchange control.

Portfolio inflow and outflow in one system:

PORTI = a1 + b1(CAB) + b2(TFDIVD) + b3(PORTO) + u1 PI-3
PORTO = a2 + c1(CAB) + c2(TFDIVD) + c3(EXCHCONT) +
c4(PORTI) + u2 PO-3

where TFDIVD = dividend earning tax rate differential from the average of the income group.

Bank capital inflow and outflow in one system:

BANKI = a1 + b1(CAB) + b2(TFINTD) + b3(BANKO) + u1 BI-3
BANKO = a2 + c1(CAB) + c2(TFINTD) + c3(EXCHCONT) +
c4(BANKI) + u2 BO-3

where TFINTD = interest earning tax rate differential from the average of the income group.

Other-sector capital inflow and outflow in one system:

OTHI = a1 + b1(CAB) + b2(TFINTD) + b3(OTHO) + u1 OI-3
OTHO = a2 + c1(CAB) + c2(TFINTD) + c3(EXCHCONT) + c4(OTHI) + u2 OO-3

Foreign direct investment inflow and outflow in one system:

FDII = a1 + b1(CAB) + b2(TFCORD) + b3(FDIO) + u1 FI-3
FDIO = a2 + c1(CAB) + c2(TFCORD) + c3(EXCHCONT) + c4(FDII) + u2 FO-3

where TFCORD = corporate income tax rate differential from the average of the income group.

Hypotheses to test the effects of globalization factors on in-outflows As discussed in the gross flow model, we select the variables that lower national boundaries and lower transaction costs as globalization factors. They are an interaction variable (TREATY) between the financial market openness and international tax treaties, financial instrument innovation (CD), and telecommunication technology innovation (TELECOMM). We initially assume that all of these globalization factors are important to both inflow and outflow. When all variables are included in both equations, a multi-collinearity problem will occur in addition to the identification problem discussed previously. The multi-collinearity problem may increase when portfolio factors and monetary factors are incorporated with the globalization factors in a single model. Thus we select TREATY and CD for the inflow equation, and TELECOMM for the outflow equation.

The selection of TREATY and CD for the inflow equation is theoretically correct since TREATY includes market openness and international tax treaties, which are designed to promote capital inflows. The TREATY variable will be a counterpart to the exchange control policy variable which was introduced in the outflow equation of the monetary factor model. The selection of TELECOMM for the outflow equation is also theoretically appropriate since investment requires an information collection process using the telecommunication networks. Thus we hypothesize that capital inflows are positively influenced by market openness, international tax treaties, and financial instrument innovation while capital outflows are positively affected by telecommunication developments.

Total capital inflow and outflow in one system:

$$TOTI = a1 + b1(TREATY) + b2(CD) + b3(TOTO) + u1 \qquad \text{TI-4}$$
$$TOTO = a2 + c1(TELECOMM) + c2(TOTI) + u2 \qquad \text{TO-4.}$$

Portfolio inflow and outflow in one system:

$$PORTI = a1 + b1(TREATY) + b2(CD) + b3(PORTO) + u1 \qquad \text{PI-4}$$
$$PORTO = a2 + c1(TELECOMM) + c2(PORTI) + u2 \qquad \text{PO-4.}$$

Bank capital inflow and outflow in one system:

$$BANKI = a1 + b1(TREATY) + b2(CD) + b3(BANKO) + u1 \qquad \text{BI-4}$$
$$BANKO = a2 + c1(TELECOMM) + c2(BANKI) + u2 \qquad \text{BO-4.}$$

Other-Sector capital inflow and outflow in one system:

$$OTHI = a1 + b1(TREATY) + b2(CD) + b3(OTHO) + u1 \qquad \text{OI-4}$$
$$OTHO = a2 + c1(TELECOMM) + c2(OTHI) + u2 \qquad \text{OO-4}$$

where TREATY = interaction variable between market openness and tax treaties, CD = dummy variable for certificate of deposit (measurement of financial innovation) and TELECOMM = telecommunication development index. As introduced in the gross flow model for FDI, CD is an irrelevant variable to the FDI inflow equation. Instead, industrial sector products as a percentage of GDP is utilized in the FDI inflow equation.

Foreign direct investment inflow and outflow in one system:

$$FDII = a1 + b1(TREATY) + b2(INDSTP) + b3(FDIO) + u1 \qquad \text{FI-4}$$
$$FDIO = a2 + c1(TELECOMM) + c2(FDII) + u2 \qquad \text{FO-4}$$

where INDSTP = industrial sector products as percentage of GDP.

Model Specifications

Model Specification for Gross Flows

The gross flow model investigates causes of gross capital flows by drawing the flow, portfolio, monetary and globalization factors into a single framework. Thus models TG-1 (the flow factor hypothesis for total gross flow), TG-2 (the portfolio factor hypothesis for total gross flow), TG-3 (the monetary factor hypothesis for total gross flow) and TG-4 (the globalization factor hypothesis for total gross flow) are combined together to specify the total capital gross flow model. By the same logic, PG-1, PG-2, PG-3, and PG-4 are combined together to specify the portfolio gross flow model. BG-1, BG-2, BG-3, and BG-4 are combined together to specify the bank capital gross flow model. OG-1, OG-2, OG-3, and OG-4 are combined together to specify the other-sector capital gross flow model. Finally, FG-1, FG-2, FG-3, and FG-4 are combined together to specify the FDI gross flow model.

Let us begin with the total capital gross flow model. The four factors are combined together into one model as below:

TOTG = a + b1(ABINTD) + b2(ABRISKD) + b3(GNYPC) + b4(ABCAB) + b5(EXCHCONT) + b6(TREATY) + b7(CD) + b8(TELECOMM) +u   TG5

In model TG5, there are multi-collinearity problems even if we try to avoid them by including an interaction variable and weighted values in the hypothesis stage. The multi-collinearity problem is serious when TREATY and GNYPC are embedded together. Thus we decide to estimate two separate models.

First GNYPC is omitted. TG5 is rewritten as

TOTG = a + b1(ABINTD) + b2(ABRISKD) + b3(ABCAB) + b4(EXCHCONT) + b5(TREATY) + b6(CD) + b7(TELECOMM) + u   TG6

Then TREATY is omitted:

TOTG = a + b1(ABINTD) + b2(ABRISKD) + b3(GNYPC) + b4(ABCAB) + b5(EXCHCONT) + b6(CD) + b7(TELECOMM) + u   TG7

We initially suspected autocorrelation and heteroskedasticity problems in our models since the data is cross-sectional time series. We conducted the Durbin-Watson test for autocorrelation and the Breusch-Pagan test for heteroskedasticity. From the Durbin-Watson test, we did not find any serious autocorrelation problem.[21] One of the possible reasons is in the short period of time observation (11 years in our study). As the Durbin-Watson table provides the significance points of autocorrelation from 15 time intervals, it implicitly suggests that the autocorrelation problem can be captured when the time series exceed 15 intervals. Another reason will be in the fact that the dependent variables were deflated by millions of 1987 US dollars and major independent variables were standardized by the economy size (level of income).

From the Breusch-Pagan test, we found that the major causes of the heteroskedasticity are TREATY and GNYPC.[22] Since other exogenous variables were weighted over cross section by the level of income, they did not report heteroskedasticity.

One solution to correct heteroskedasticity is to use a fixed effects method. Since capital flows are seriously affected by time-and country-specific factors,[23] the OLS fixed effect method controls these specific effects by year and country dummy coefficients. When the OLS fixed effects model and the WLS (Weighted Least Squares) model were compared, the results were very similar, meaning that fixed effect methods worked in correcting heteroskedasticity. This will be discussed in the next chapter when the empirical findings are discussed in detail.

In addition to their methodological functions, we also are interested in the country and time dummy coefficients because the dummy coefficients tell us which country has contributed to what types of capital flows and which years have been most active in what types of capital flows. Thus we keep the fixed effect method not only for the gross flow models but also for capital inflow-outflow models.

Another solution to correct for heteroskedasticity problem is to transform the data into logarithmic form. Madalla (1988, pp. 165–81) showed that transforming the dependent variable to logarithmic form reduced heteroskedasticity. The log-linear function is also suggested theoretically since the interest rate differential or risk differential are not a linear function of capital flows. We conducted the BM (Bera and McAleer) test to judge whether the linear or log-linear model is better. The results clearly suggested the superiority of a log-linear model.[24]

Therefore log-linear fixed effect models were utilized in a cross-sectional time series pooled data set. The definition of time dummies and country dummies is reported in Appendix A–2. To avoid the perfect co-linearity condition, year 1980 is omitted as a year base dummy and Portugal is omitted as a country base dummy. The model specification for the total capital gross flow model now is complete. Model TG6 is rewritten as follows:

TGT model: total gross flow model with TREATY variable

TOTG = a + b1(ABINTD) + b2(ABRISKD) + b3(ABCAB) +
b4(EXCHCONT) + b5(TREATY) + b6(CD) + b7(TELECOMM) +
b8...b17(YEAR) + b18...b102(COUNTRY) + u TGT

Since the dependent variable is the logarithmic value, the logarithmic value of gross national income per capita provides the income elasticity of capital flow. Model TG7 is rewritten as follows:

TGW model: total gross flow model with wealth variable

TOTG = a + b1(ABINTD) + b2 (ABRISKD) + b3(GNYPC) + b4(ABCAB)
+ b5(EXCHCONT) + b6(CD) + b7(TELECOMM) + b8...b17(YEAR)
+ b18...b102(COUNTRY) + u TGW

where a = intercept, b = parameter, u = disturbance term, TOTG = total capital gross flow, ABINTD = average in absolute value of three interest rate differentials from the income group, ABRISKD = absolute value of risk differential from the income group, GNYPC = measurement of wealth by log of gross national income per capita, ABCAB = absolute value of current account balance in billions of US dollar, EXCHCONT = dummy variable for exchange control, TREATY = interaction variable between market openness and tax treaties, CD = dummy variable for certificate of deposit (measurement of financial innovation), TELECOMM = telecommunication development index, YEAR = 10 year dummies for 1981–1990, and COUNTRY = 85 country dummies.

The same logic applies to the gross flow of each financial item. When the TREATY is included, GNYPC is omitted to avoid multi-collinearity. The models are as below.

PGT model: portfolio gross flow model with TREATY variable

PORTG = a + b1(ABIGOVTD) + b2(ABRISKD)) + b3(ABCAB) + b4(EXCHCONT) + b5(TREATY) + b6(CD) + b7(TELECOMM) + b8...b17(YEAR) + b18...b102(COUNTRY) + u PGT

where PORTG = portfolio gross flow, and ABIGOVTD = absolute value of gov't bond yield rate differentials from the income group.

BGT model: bank capital gross flow model with TREATY variable

BANKG = a + b1(ABIDEPD) + b2(ABRISKD) + b3(ABCAB) + b4(EXCHCONT) + b5(TREATY) + b6(CD) + b7(TELECOMM) + b8...b17(YEAR) + b18...b102(COUNTRY) + u BGT

where BANKG = bank capital gross flow, and ABIDEPD = absolute value of bank deposit interest rate differentials from the income group.

OGT model: other-sector capital gross flow model with TREATY variable

OTHG = a + b1(ABIMKTD) + b2(ABRISKD) + b3(ABCAB) + b4(EXCHCONT) + b5(TREATY) + b6(CD) + b7(TELECOMM) + b8...b17(YEAR) + b18...b102(COUNTRY) + u OGT

where OTHG = other-sector capital gross flow, and ABIMKTD = absolute value of market interest rate differentials from the income group.

FGT model: FDI gross flow model with TREATY variable

FDIG = a + b1(ABPPPRC) + b2(ABRISKD) + b3(ABCAB) + b4(EXCHCONT) + b5(TREATY) + b6(INDSTP) + b7(TELECOMM) + b8...b17(YEAR) + b18...b102(COUNTRY) + u FGT

where FDIG = foreign direct investment gross flow, ABPPPRC = absolute value in change of purchasing power parity ratio and INDSTP = industrial sector products as percentage of GDP.

When the GNYPC is included while TREATY is omitted, the models are as below.

PGW model: portfolio gross flow model with wealth variable

PORTG = a + b1(ABIGOVTD) + b2(ABRISKD) + b3(GNYPC) + b4(ABCAB) + b5(EXCHCONT) + b6(CD) + b7(TELECOMM) + b8...b17(YEAR) + b18...b102(COUNTRY) + u PGW.

BGW model: bank capital gross flow model with wealth variable

BANKG = a + b1(ABIDEPD) + b2(ABRISKD) + b3(GNYPC) + b4(ABCAB) + b5(EXCHCONT) + b6(CD) + b7(TELECOMM) + b8...b17(YEAR) + b18...b102(COUNTRY) + u BGW.

OGW model: other-sector capital gross flow model with wealth variable

OTHG = a + b1(ABIMKTD) + b2(ABRISKD) + b3(GNYPC) + b4(ABCAB) + b5(EXCHCONT) + b6(CD) + b7(TELECOMM) + b8...b17(YEAR) + b18...b102(COUNTRY) + u OGW.

FGW model: FDI gross flow model with wealth variable

FDIG = a + b1(ABPPPRC) + b2(ABRISKD) + b3(GNYPC) + b4(ABCAB) + b5(EXCHCONT) + b6(INDSTP) + b7(TELECOMM) + b8...b17(YEAR) + b18...b102(COUNTRY) + u FGW.

Model Specification for Capital Inflows and Outflows

As discussed in chapter 2, previous studies found simultaneity of capital inflow and outflow. This is theoretically and empirically evident as international capital mobility has increased in the globalized financial markets. The major interest in the capital inflow and outflow models is to investigate causes of capital inflow and capital outflow by incorporating the flow, portfolio, monetary, and globalization factors into a single simultaneous framework. We initially estimate the inflow and outflow of five financial types in five simultaneous equation models: portfolio, bank capital, other-sector capital, FDI, and total capital. Then we estimate the inflow and outflow of four financial items in a single simultaneous equation model in order to examine the interactions among different types of capital flows. Finally, we separately study the short-term capital to investigate four types of capital flows (type 1 inflow, type 2 inflow, type 1 outflow, and type 2 outflow).

The 3SLS (three-stage least squares) technique is applied to the capital inflow-outflow simultaneous equation models. Since our two equation systems (inflow and outflow) are simultaneous, the 2SLS (two-stage least squares) estimator can provide consistent parameter estimates. However, the 2SLS technique applies to a single equation within the system of two equations. This may yield inefficient estimates. The 2SLS technique also does not account for the cross-equation correlation among the error terms. The loss of efficiency in the 2SLS can be improved by 3SLS, which accounts for the correlation between the error terms caused by unmodelled events in the 2SLS parameters and correlation between exogenous variables of the system and error terms (Madansky, 1964, p. 55).

In our models, the efficiency level for parameter estimates of major exogenous variables improved slightly. When a variable was included in both equations, the efficiency level improved even more. The efficiency level of the dummy coefficients also improved. Since the dummy variables were included in both equations, this can be attributed to the fact that the 2SLS method applies to a single equation while 3SLS method applies to both equations. Appendix B–4 reports the comparison of efficiency levels between 2SLS and 3SLS methods by t-statistic.

In applying the 3SLS technique, equations should not be under-identified. In our models, all equations are over-identified by order condition and identified by rank condition. The identification issue is discussed in Appendix A–3. Following the same logic in the gross flow models, we apply the log-linear model with the year and country dummy variables. Unlike the gross flow model, we do not have a multi-co-linearity problem in the inflow-outflow simultaneous equation models, since TREATY is included only in the inflow equation while GNYPC is included only in the outflow equation.

In-outflows by financial item We assume that inflow and outflow of a financial item are simultaneously determined within that capital flow. For example, portfolio inflow and outflow are simultaneously determined within portfolio flows. As we incorporate the four factors into one framework, the inflow equation is a combination of four inflow factors and the outflow equation combines the four outflow factors. For example, the portfolio inflow equation is the combination of PI-1 (the flow factor in portfolio inflow), PI-2 (the portfolio factor in portfolio inflow), PI-3 (the monetary factor in portfolio inflow), and PI-4 (the globalization factor in portfolio inflow). The portfolio outflow equation is a combination of PO-1 (the flow factor in portfolio outflow), PO-

2 (the portfolio factor in portfolio outflow), PO-3 (the monetary factor in portfolio outflow), and PO-4 (the globalization factor in portfolio outflow).

We begin with the total capital inflow-outflow simultaneous equation model. The total capital inflow equation and the total capital outflow equation are simultaneously estimated. This model provides a general picture of aggregate capital flows. Then we estimate each financial item's inflow and outflow equations within that capital's simultaneous equation model. This will provide more specific factors that determine the inflow and outflow of each financial item.

Total capital in-outflow model in a simultaneous system:

TOTI = a1 + b1(INTD) + b2(RISKD) + b3(CAB) + b4(TAXD) +
b5(TREATY) + b6(CD) + b7(TOTO) + b8...b17(YEAR) +
b18...b102(COUNTRY) + u1 TI

TOTO = a2 + c1(INTD) + c2(RISKDC) + c3(GNYPC) + c4(CAB) +
c5(TAXD) + c6(EXCHCONT) + c7(TELECOMM) + c8(TOTI) +
c9...c18(YEAR) + c19...c103(COUNTRY) + u2 TO

where TOTI = total capital inflow, TOTO = total capital outflow, INTD = average of three interest rate differentials from the income group, RISKD = risk differential from the income group, RISKDC = annual change in RISKD, GNYPC = measurement of wealth by log of gross national income per capita, CAB = current account balance in billions of US dollar, TAXD = average of three tax rates differential, EXCHCONT = dummy variable for exchange control, TREATY = interaction variable between market openness and tax treaties, CD = dummy variable for certificate of deposit (measurement of financial innovation), TELECOMM = telecommunication development index, YEAR = 10 year dummies for 1981–1990 and COUNTRY = 85 country dummies.

Portfolio in-outflow model in a simultaneous system:

PORTI = a1 + b1(IGOVTD) + b2(RISKD) + b3(CAB) + b4(TFDIVD) +
b5(TREATY) + b6(CD) + b7(PORTO) + b8...b17(YEAR) +
b18...b102(COUNTRY) + u1 PI

PORTO = a2 + c1(IGOVTD) + c2(RISKDC) + c3(GNYPC) + c4(CAB) +

c5(TFDIVD) + c6(EXCHCONT) + c7(TELECOMM) + c8(PORTI) +
c9...18(YEAR) + c19...c103(COUNTRY) + u2 PO

where PORTI = portfolio inflow, PORTO = portfolio outflow, and TFDIVD = dividend earning tax rate differential from the average of the income group.

Bank capital in-outflow model in a simultaneous system:

BANKI = a1 + b1(IDEPD) + b2(RISKD) + b3(CAB) + b4(TFINTD) +
b5(TREATY) + b6(CD) + b7(BANKO) + b8...b17(YEAR) +
b18...b102(COUNTRY) + u1 BI

BANKO = a2 + c1(IDEPD) + c2(RISKDC) + c3(GNYPC) + c4(CAB) +
c5(TFINTD) + c6(EXCHCONT) + c7(TELECOMM) + c8(BANKI) +
c9...18(YEAR) + c19...c103(COUNTRY) + u2 BO

where BANKI = bank capital inflow, BANKO = bank capital outflow, and TFINTD = interest earning tax rate differential from the average of the income group.

Other-sector capital in-outflow model in a simultaneous system:

OTHI = a1 + b1(IMKTD) + b2(RISKD) + b3(CAB) + b4(TFINTD) +
b5(TREATY) + b6(CD) + b7(OTHO) + b8...b17(YEAR) +
b18...b102(COUNTRY) + u1 OI

OTHO = a2 + c1(IMKTD) + c2(RISKDC) + c3(GNYPC) + c4(CAB) +
c5(TFINTD) + c6(EXCHCONT) + c7(TELECOMM) + c8(OTHI) +
c9...18(YEAR) + c19...c103(COUNTRY) + u2 OO

where OTHI = other-sector capital inflow, and OTHO = other-sector capital outflow.

Foreign direct investment in-outflow model in a simultaneous system:

FDII = a1 + b1(PPPR) + b2(RISKD) + b3(CAB) + b4(TFCORD) +
b5(TREATY) + b6(INDSTP) + b7(FDIO) + b8...b17(YEAR) +
b18...b102(COUNTRY) + u1 FI

FDIO = a2 + c1(PPPR) + c2(RISKDC) + c3(GNYPC) + c4(CAB) + c5(TFCORD) + c6(EXCHCONT) + c7(TELECOMM) + c8(FDII) + c9...18(YEAR) + c19...c103(COUNTRY) + u2 FO

where FDII = foreign direct investment inflow, FDIO = foreign direct investment outflow, PPPR = purchasing power parity ratio, TFCORD = corporate income tax rate differential from the average of the income group, and INDSTP = industrial sector product as per cent of GDP.

Four financial items' in-outflow model in a simultaneous system A single simultaneous equation model for four financial items' inflow-outflow is employed to see the interactions among four financial items' capital flows. That is, eight equations (as each financial item has inflow and outflow equations) are embedded in one system. In the previous part, we assumed that inflow and outflow of a financial item are simultaneously determined within that capital flow. In this section, we now assume that inflow and outflow of a financial item are simultaneously determined by other financial items' flows as well as its own item's flow.

Due to the difficulty in identification for this model, the model specification is slightly different from the previous models. As there are eight equations in the model, the missing variables in each equation should be at least seven to be identified by the order condition (g - 1 = 7).[25] Thus we create a RISKCP variable (annual percentage change in risk estimate), which is different from the RISKDC as discussed in the hypotheses section.

The order condition is a necessary but not a sufficient condition for identification. Thus we need to take care of the rank condition as well. When all equations are to be identified by the rank condition, each equation should not share too many variables or too few variables. In both cases, the column corresponding to the missing variables may also have missing variables. This violates the rank condition for identification. The bank and other-sector capital equations share many identical variables while INDSTP (industrial sector products as a percentage of GDP) is used only in the FDI inflow equation in the previous part. When they are combined together into one model, the combination of these equations violate the rank condition identification. Thus we replace CD with INDSTP in the bank inflow equation, which obviates the rank condition identification problem. Then each equation is identified by the rank condition and over-identified by the order condition as seen Appendix A–3.

Four financial items' in-outflow model in a simultaneous system:

PORTI = a1 + b1(IGOVTD) + b2(RISKD) + b3(CAB) + b4(TREATY) + b5(FDIVD) + b6(CD) + b7(PORTO) + b8(BANKI) + b9(BANKO) + b10(OTHI) + b11(OTHO) + b12(FDII) + b13(FDIO) + b14...b23(YEAR) + b24...b108(COUNTRY) + u1

Portfolio inflow eq.

PORTO = a2 + c1(IGOVTD) + c2(RISKCP) + c3(GNYPC) + c4(CAB) + c5(EXCHCONT) + c6(TFDIVD) + c7(TELECOMM) + c8(PORTI) + c9(BANKI) + c10(BANKO) + c11(OTHI) + c12(OTHO) + c13(FDII) + c14(FDIO) + b15...b24(YEAR) + 25...b109(COUNTRY) + u2

Portfolio outflow eq.

BANKI = a3 + d1(IDEPD) + d2(RISKD) + d3(CAB) + d4(TREATY) + d5(TFINTD) + d6(INDSTP) + d7(PORTI) + d8(PORTO) + d9(BANKO) + d10(OTHI) + d11(OTHO) + d12(FDII) + d13(FDIO) + d14...d23(YEAR) + d24...d108(COUNTRY) + u3

Bank capital inflow eq.

BANKO = a4 + e1(IDEPD) + e2(RISKDC) + e3(GNYPC) + e4(CAB) + e5(EXCHCONT) + e6(TFINTD) + e7(TELECOMM) + e8(PORTI) + e9(PORTO) + e10(BANKI) + e11(OTHI) + e12(OTHO) + e13(FDII) + e14(FDIO) + e15...e24(YEAR) + e25...e109(COUNTRY) + u4

Bank capital outflow eq.

OTHI = a5 +f 1(IMKTD) + f2(RISKD) + f3(CAB) + f4(TREATY) + f5(TFINTD) + f6(CD) + f7(PORTO) + f8(POTO) + f9(BANKI) + f10(BANKO) + f11(OTHO) + f12(FDII) + f13(FDIO) + f14...f23(YEAR) + f24...f108(COUNTRY) + u5

Other-sector capital inflow eq.

OTHO = a6 + g1(IMKTD) + g2(RISKDC) + g3(GNYPC) + g4(CAB) + g5(EXCHCONT) + g6(TFINTD) + g7(TELECOMM) + g8(PORTI) + g9(PORTO) + g10(BANKI) + g11(BANKO) + g12(OTHI) + g13(FDII) + g14(FDIO) + g15...g24(YEAR) + g25...g109(COUNTRY) + u6

Other-sector capital outflow eq.

FDII = a7 + h1(PPPR) + h2(RISKD) + h3(CAB) + h4(TREATY) + h5(TFCORD) + h6(INDSTP) + h7(PORTO + h8(POTO) + h9(BANKI) + h10(BANKO) + h11(OTHI) + h12(OTHO) + h13(FDIO) + h14...h23(YEAR) + h24...h108(COUNTRY) + u7

FDI inflow eq.

FDIO = a8 + i1(PPPR) + i2(RISKCP) + i3(GNYPC) + i4(CAB) + i5(EXCHCONT) + i6(TFCORD) + i7(TELECOMM) + i8(PORTI) + i9(PORTO) + i10(BANKI) + i11(BANKO) + i12(OTHI) + i13(OTHO) + i14(FDII) + i15...i24(YEAR) + i25...i109(COUNTRY) + u8

FDI outflow eq.

Four types of short-term capital flow model in a simultaneous system There are four types of capital flows. In the inflow category, capital can be invested in the home country by foreign investors (type 1 inflow) and capital can be withdrawn from the world by domestic residents who previously invested abroad (type 2 inflow). In the outflow category, capital can be invested abroad by domestic residents (type 1 outflow), and capital can be withdrawn by foreign investors who had previously invested in the home country (type 2 outflow). These type 1 and 2 inflows and type 1 and 2 outflows are available only with respect to short-term bank capital and short-term other-sector capital.

These two flow categories are treated together in the models due to data availability problems. The models can properly explain the interest rate differential, risk differential, and monetary factors by treating foreign investors and domestic residents as one group since the residents' capital outflow factor and the foreigners' capital withdrawal factors are similar. However, when we consider the national wealth variable, the residents' capital outflow and foreigners' capital withdrawal should be separated.

One of the advantages in this model with four types of capital flows is to reveal the information about which domestic condition promotes capital investment abroad by domestic residents and which domestic condition reduces the invested capital in other countries by foreign investors. This is a very important question because securing international financial resources can be made not only by inducing new capital but also by keeping previously-invested capital. This is a critical issue for the foreign direct investment, because the loss of foreign direct investment may generate unemployment. It is also an important issue in the portfolio market since the massive withdrawal of foreigners' portfolio investment may increase in the fluctuations in the domestic money market in general.

We construct one simultaneous equation model of four equations for each type of capital flow. We utilize the same flow factors, the portfolio factors, the monetary factors, and the globalization factors as in the previous models. However, we select a different measurement for interest rates since the concern is with short-term capital, and introduce another tax rate since it is related to domestic tax rates on domestic residents for type 1 outflows and type 2 inflows. We also attempt to estimate the untested hypotheses in the previous models by relocating the variables in different equations.

As Marwah (1985, pp. 94–5) suggested, we assume that exchange rate and price level play an important role in determining the direction of short-term capital flows. Thus, we include purchasing power parity ratio (PPPR) as a measurement of rate of return in short-term capital investment. We hypothesize that a positive PPPR discourages the type 1 and 2 inflows while it encourages type 1 and 2 outflows.

We select the tax rate on interest earnings as used in the bank and other-sector capital model. In the type 1 inflow equation and the type 2 outflow equation we use the tax rate differential between domestic tax rate on foreign investors' interest earnings and the average of the income group tax rates on foreign investors' interest earnings (TFINTD). The logic behind this choice is that type 1 inflows and type 2 outflows are determined by foreign investors' decisions when they compare their tax rates among foreign countries. However, type 1 outflows and type 2 inflows are determined by domestic residents who compare their tax rates between domestic investment and foreign investments (TDINTD). TFINTD is derived from the average of the same income group since risk and financial market development are similar in the same income group countries. However, TDINTD is derived from the average of the world since the option to invest by domestic residents is not limited to a certain income group. We hypothesize that a positive value in TFINTD reduces type 1 inflow and increases type 2 outflow. We also hypothesize that a positive value in TDINTD increases type 1 outflows and discourage type 2 inflows.

Risk differential (RISKD) is embedded in type 1 inflow and type 1 outflow to see the effects on the initial capital inflow and outflow. Then change in risk differential (RISKDC) is utilized in type 2 inflow and type 2 outflow to estimate how a country's creditworthiness changes affect capital withdrawals. We hypothesize that RISKD will positively influence type 1 inflows but negatively affect type 1 outflows. We also hypothesize that RISKDC will positively influence type 2 inflows and negatively affect type 2 outflows.

Telecommunication development level (TELECOMM) has been tested only in the outflow equations and financial instrument innovation (CD) has been tested only in the inflow equations in the previous models. Now we attempt to see the effects of TELECOMM on capital inflows. TELECOMM will be critically important to type 2 inflows since investors may withdraw their previously-invested capital to the home country more efficiently by monitoring foreign market conditions through better telecommunication networks. We include CD in type 1 outflows to see the effect of developed financial markets on the initial capital outflows as well as in type 1 inflows to see the effect of financial instrument innovation on the initial capital inflows. This process also will relax the identification problem in the rank condition. Treaty and exchange control policy variables are utilized to estimate the previously untested factors and obviate the rank condition identification problems.

With the above hypotheses, we construct the following model specification. We define type 1 inflow as STKI1 (short-term capital inflow type 1), type 2 inflow as STKI2 (short-term capital inflow type 2), type 1 outflow as STKO1 (short-term capital outflow type 1), and type 2 outflow as STKO2 (short-term capital outflow type 2). Each equation is identified by the rank condition and over-identified by the order condition (see Appendix A–3).

Four types of short-term capital flow model in a simultaneous system:

STKI1 = a1 + b1(PPPR) + b2(RISKD) + b3(CAB) + b4(EXCHCONT) + b5(TFINTD) + b6(CD) + b7(TELECOMM) + b8(STKI2) + b9(STKO1) + b10(STKO2) + b11...b20(YEAR) + b21...b105(COUNTRY) + u1

Type 1 inflow eq.

STKI2 = a2 + c1(PPPR) + c2(RISKDC) + c3(CAB) + c4(TREATY) + c5(TDINTD) + c 6(TELECOMM) + c7(STKI1) + c8(STKO1) + c9(STKO2) + c10...c19(YEAR) + c20...c104(COUNTRY) + u2

Type 2 inflow eq.

STKO1 = a3 + d1(PPPR) + d2(RISKD) +d 3(GNYPC) + d4(CAB) +d5(TREATY) + d6(TDINTD) + d7(CD) + d8(STKI1) + d9(STKI2) + d10(STKO2) + d11...d20(YEAR) + d21...d105(COUNTRY) + u3

Type 1 outflow eq.

STKO2 = a4 + e1(PPPR) + e2(RISKDC) + e3(GNYPC) + e4(CAB) + e5(EXCHCONT) + e6(TFINTD) + e7(STKI1) + e8(STKI2) + e9(STKO1) + b10...b19(YEAR) + b20...b104(COUNTRY) + u4

Type 2 outflow eq.

where STKI1 = short-term capital type 1 inflow: invested in home by foreign investors, STKI2 = short-term capital type 2 inflow: withdrawn to home by domestic investors, STKO1 = short-term capital type 1 outflow: invested abroad by domestic investors, STKO1 = short-term capital type 2 outflow: withdrawn abroad by foreign investors, RISKD = risk differential from the income group, RISKDC = annual change in RISKD (risk differential), RISKCP = annual change in RISK (creditworthiness), GNYPC = measurement of wealth by log of gross national income per capita, CAB = current account balance in billions of US dollar, TFINTD = interest earning tax rate differential from the average of the income group, EXCHCONT = dummy variable for exchange control, TREATY = interaction variable between market openness and tax treaties, CD = dummy variable for certificate of deposit (measurement of financial innovation), TELECOMM = telecommunication development index, YEAR = 10 year dummies for 1981–1990, and COUNTRY = 85 country dummies.

Notes

1 See Johnson (1972), Frenkel and Johnson (1976) and Frenkel, Gylfason and Helliwell (1980).

2 It is shown here that the marginal income of foreign investment is exactly equal to expected yield differential:

$$dy_T/dI^* = \mu^* - \mu = r^* - r\ .$$

3 See Mundell (1960, 1962), Fleming (1967), Obstfeld (1986) and Frankel (1989, 1992).

4 See Frankel (1989) and Haque and Montiel (1990, 1991)

5 See Frankel (1989, p. 28, Table 5).

6 A simple mathematical proof for the equation:

$$\begin{aligned} y_T &= r(1 - C)(k - I^*) + r^*(1 - C^*)I^* \\ &= (r - rC)(k - I^*) + (r^* - r^*C^*)I^* \\ &= rk - rI^* - rCk + rCI^* + r^*I^* - r^*C^*I^* \end{aligned}$$

$$\begin{aligned} dy_T/dI^* &= -r + rC + r^* - r^*C^* \\ &= (r^* - r) - (r^*C^* - rC) \text{ or } r^*(1 - C^*) - r(1 - C) \end{aligned}$$

7 Huizinga (1991) argues that international tax competition can be socially harmful.

8 Brown (1987, pp. 389–5) discusses the capital flight from Latin America, Hong Kong and Philippines in the 1970s and 1980s.

9 Official sector capital does not necessarily mean public sector capital: public sector can access private sector capital such as public bonds and public corporate equities.

10 We refer to the four types of private capital – portfolio, bank capital, other-sector capital, and FDI – as 'financial item', and their constituents as 'components'.

11 It is more desirable if we have data for private bond yield rates and corporate equity yield

Table 6 Definition of exogenous variables

Issue	Variable	Definition
Interest rate differential	IGOVT (IGOVTD)	Government bond yield rate (difference from the income group)
	IDEP (IDEPD)	Deposit interest rate (difference from the income group)
	IMKT (IMKTD)	Market interest rate (difference from the income group)
	PPPR	Purchasing power parity ratio (base year = 1979)
	INTD	Average of all types of interest rate difference (IGOVTD, IDEPD and IMKTD)
	ABIGOVTD	Absolute value of IGOVTD
	ABIDEPD	Absolute value of IDEPD
	ABIMKTD	Absolute value of IMKTD
	ABINTD	Absolute value of INTD
Risk differential	RISK	Country credit rate measured by 100 scale (0 = worst, 100 = best)
	RISKD	RISK difference from the income group
	RISKDC	Annual change of RISKD in number
	ABRISKD	Absolute value of RISKD
	RISKCP	Annual change of RISK in %
Wealth	GNYPC	Log of gross national income per capita in 1987 US dollars
Current account balance	CAB	Current account balance in billions of 1987 US dollars
	ABCAB	Absolute value of CAB
Regulation	OWNERP	Percentage of foreign ownership allowed
	TAXTRT	Number of countries in tax treaties
	TREATY	Interaction variable between OWNERP and TAXTRT
	EXCHCONT	Dummy variable for enforcing exchange control (1) or not (0)

	Issue	Variable Definition
Tax rate	TFDIV (TFDIVD)	Tax rate on foreign investors' dividend earning (difference from the income group)
	TFCOR (TFCOR)	Tax rate on foreign investors' corporate income (difference from the income group)
	TFINT (TFINTD)	Tax rate on foreign investors' interest earning (difference from the income group)
	TDINT (TDINTD)	Difference between tax rate on domestic residents' interest earning and average of world's TFINT
Financial and tele-communication innovation	CD	Dummy variable for providing certificate of deposit in the market (1) or not (0)
	CIRCUIT	Number of international circuit ends terminating at switching exchanges in 1000
	CSDN	Dummy variable for providing circuit-switched digital network (1) or not (0)
	PSDN	Dummy variable for providing packet-switched digital network (1) or not (0)
	ISDN	Dummy bariable for providing integrated service digital network (1) or not (0)
	TELECOMM	Measurement of telecommunication innovation calculated by CIRCUIT* (CSDN + PSDN + ISDN)
Other * (1)	INDSTP	Industrial sector products as % of gross domestic product

Note (1) Only for foreign direct investment

Table 7 Data source and calculation method for exogenous variables

Variable	Raw data	Data source*	Calculation method
IGOVT (IGOVTD) IDEP (IDEPD) IMKT (IMKTD)	Nominal government bond yield rate Nominal interest at bank deposit rate Nominal interest at money market rate Inflation Rate (from Consumer Price Index)	IMF1	(ex)IGOVT = nominal government bond yield rate – inflation rate (ex)IGOVTDi = IGOVTi-average of IGOVT in country i's income group
PPPR	Price index (GDP deflator) Real effective exchange rate		PPPR = (Ei/Pi)*Pus where Ei = country i's exchange rate to US$ Pi = price of country i, Pus = price of US
RISKD RISKDC RISKCP	RISK: Country credit ratings (0–100)	Institutional investor	RISDKD = RISKi - average of country i's income group RISKDC = RISKDt - RISKDt - 1 RISKCP = (RISKt - RISKt - 1)/RISKt - 1* 100, where t = present year
GNYPC CAB	Gross national income and population Current account balance in billions	WB1 IMF2	GNYPC = GNY/population
OWNERP TAXTRT TREATY	Percentage of foreign ownership allowed Number of countries in tax treaties TREATY = OWNERP*TAXTRT	Price Waterhouse UN	
EXCHCONT	Exchange control	Price Waterhouse	If exchange control is enforced then 1; if removed then 0
TFDIV (TFDIVD) TFINT (TFINTD) TFCOR (TFCORD) TDINTD	Tax rate on foreigners' dividend earning Tax rate on foreigners' interest earning Tax rate on foreigners' corporate Income Tax rate on residents' interest earning		(ex) TFDIVDi = TFDIVDi - average of TFDIV in country i's income group TDINTDi = TDINTi - average of TFINT in the world
CD	Certificate of deposit	IFC, IMF2, OECD1, WB2	If CD is in money market then 1; if not then 0

	Variable	Raw data	Data source* Calculation method
CIRCUIT	Number of international circuit ends (1,000)	ITU	
CSDN	Circuit-switched digital network	OECD2	If CSDN is installed then 1; if not then 0
PSDN	Packet-switched digital network	Longman	If PSDN is installed then 1; if not then 0
ISDN	Integrated service digital network		If ISDN is installed then 1; if not then 0
TELECOMM			TELECOMM = CIRCUIT*(CSDN + PSDN + ISDN)
INDSTP	Industrial sector products and GDP at factor cost	WB1	INDSTP = industrial sector products/GDP* 100

Notes

Data source:

1 IMF1: *International Financial Statistics Yearbook* (International Monetary Fund), 1993.
2 IMF2: *Balance of Payments Statistics Yearbook* (International Monetary Fund), 1980–1993.
3 WB1: *World Tables* (World Bank), 1993.
4 WB2: *World Debt Tables* (World Bank), 1992–1993.
5 OECD1: *Financial Market Trends* (Organization for Economic Cooperation and Development), 1992.
6 OECD2: *Telecommunication Network-Based Services: Policy Implications* (Organization for Economic Cooperation and Development), 1989.
7 IFC: *Emerging Stock Markets Factbook* (International Finance Corporation), 1989–1992.
8 ITU: *Yearbook of Common Carrier Telecommunication Statistics* (International Telecommunication Union), 1980–1992.
9 UN: *World Investment Directory 1992* (United Nations), 1993.
10 *Institutional Investor*, September Issues, 1979–1992.
11 *Price Waterhouse: Doing Business in Foreign Countries* (Price Waterhouse Publisher), 1981–1993.
12 *Longman: International Directory of Telecommunications* (Longman Publisher), 1984, 1986.

rates; however, they are not available for most countries in the sample of this study.

12 In the FDI gross flow model, the absolute value of change in PPPR is projected since PPPR is not a differential value between countries but a ratio from year 1979 for all countries.

13 The World Bank data is not available to public, *Euromoney* places too much emphasis on loan volume and maturity in the Euromarkets, and International Research Group's *International Country Risk Guide* does not use a consistent measurement method during the time period of this study.

14 Gross national income is derived as the sum of GNP and the terms of trade adjustment, defined by the World Bank's *World Tables.*

15 IMF's Balance of *Payments Statistics Yearbook* defines of 32 items.

16 Finnerty (1988, pp. 14–39) surveyed more than 200 financial innovations in 1988.

17 CD is broadly described as a negotiable instrument certifying that a sum of money has been deposited with a bank issuing it and that, on the stated maturity date, the deposit will be repaid with interest rate by the issuing bank. It was initially developed in 1961 in the US, and developed its shape with unrelated interest rate in the early 1970s and negotiable rate in the late 1970s. CDs in the international financial markets became more popular in the 1980s as banks became more actively involved in securities brokerage and trust services.

18 Maximum byte rate varies by country, ranging from 1.2 kbyte per second in Turkey to 72 kbyte per second in France (OECD, 1990).

19 (Ex.1) If a country began to provide CSDN in 1980 and PSDN in 1985 and ISDN in 1988, then its telecommunication development levels are 1 in 1980–1984, 2 in 1985–1987, and 3 in 1988–1990.

20 (Ex.2) If the size of data transaction network of the country in Ex.1 was 100 for the whole period, the index of the country's telecommunication development are 100 in 1980–1984, 200 in 1985–1987 and 300 in 1988–1990.

21 We conducted the Durbin-Watson tests for each of 86 countries. Since we have 11 observations in each country's model, the degrees of freedom are limited. Thus we specified the model by three independent variables in each equation, which provides seven degrees of freedom. The models are DV = f(X1, X2, X3), where DV = dependent variable, and Xs = combination of three independent variables. We repeated all possible combinations of independent variables with each dependent variable, and found no serious autocorrelation problem. The result is presented in Appendix B–1.

22 See Appendix B–2 for the procedure and result of the Breusch-Pagan test.

23 See the introductory discussions in Chapter 1, including Figures 2 and 3.

24 See Appendix B–3 for the procedure and results of the BM test.

25 See Appendix A–3 for detailed explanations of identification.

4 Empirical Findings

As elaborated in the previous chapters, this study has two specific purposes. The first is to seek out the causes of globalization of international financial markets using gross capital flow models. The second is to investigate the effects of globalized financial markets on international capital flows using simultaneous capital inflow-outflow models. In this chapter, we summarize the empirical findings from the econometric models, along with the descriptive statistics.

Our models are restricted to 86 countries due to data limitations. Descriptive analyses thus refer to 86 countries in this chapter. However, the descriptive statistics for all 121 countries are reported in Appendix C. The 35 omitted countries contributed only about 1.26 per cent of the global capital flows.[1] Thus, the effect of omitting them is minimal in both the econometric and descriptive analyses.

Causes of Globalization of International Financial Markets

We measure the degree of globalization of international financial markets by gross capital transactions. The gross capital flows during the period of this study (1980–1990) tripled; see Table 8. This rapid growth of global capital transactions has been contributed mostly by the high income countries; their percentage share of global capital flows is 90 per cent. The most rapidly increasing type of capital flow during this period is portfolio investment (590 per cent increase between 1980–1989).

When we consider the portfolio gross flow for the high income countries only, the growth rate is even higher (730 per cent between 1980–1989). Thus when we consider the time and country effects on the global capital flows, it is not surprising to find that the gross capital flow gap between the high income countries and the rest of the world is increasing. The high income countries' shares of total capital transactions increased from 83 per cent in 1980 to 93 per cent in 1990. This means that non-high income[2] countries' share of global capital transactions decreased from 17 per cent to 7 per cent.

Table 8 Gross capital flows by level of income in 86 countries

Level of income	Year	Actual amount (millions of 1987 US dollars)				
		Portfolio	Bank	Others	FDI	Total
	1980	42	1,565	4,576	1,416	7,599
	1981	48	1,388	5,494	1,607	8,537
	1982	299	1,543	7,678	1,549	11,069
Low	1983	367	1,026	7,429	1,543	10,364
income	1984	450	1,942	8,880	1,444	12,716
countries	1985	1,105	1,988	14,867	2,396	20,356
(19)	1986	508	2,187	11,433	2,090	16,217
	1987	1,373	2,763	11,864	2,407	18,408
	1988	821	3,123	11,026	2,544	17,514
	1989	382	3,131	12,074	4,109	19,696
	1990	352	3,889	15,560	2,696	22,496
	Sum	**5,746**	**24,546**	**110,882**	**23,801**	**164,974**
	1980	587	5,577	31,477	3,861	41,502
	1981	2,259	6,164	42,650	4,729	55,803
	1982	3,729	6,304	34,326	4,183	48,542
Lower-	1983	2,942	7,208	31,177	3,707	45,034
middle	1984	3,053	12,366	35,084	3,629	54,132
income	1985	4,214	9,475	33,522	4,134	51,345
countries	1986	1,573	8,402	31,153	3,274	44,403
(27)	1987	3,215	7,799	30,517	4,406	45,938
	1988	5,615	7,899	33,436	6,058	53,007
	1989	10,296	6,335	39,222	7,650	63,503
	1990	4,782	8,585	45,657	9,607	68,631
	Sum	**42,265**	**86,115**	**388,222**	**55,239**	**571,841**
	1980	20,085	21,106	46,969	9,889	98,054
	1981	28,001	32,472	53,351	13,983	127,808
	1982	14,294	22,936	56,266	18,201	111,696
Upper-	1983	15,580	24,917	41,272	8,204	89,973
middle	1984	17,772	21,068	44,918	10,615	94,372
income	1985	12,441	24,243	56,113	5,429	98,226
countries	1986	6,498	25,544	50,521	6,482	89,045
(17)	1987	11,389	27,657	52,150	8,943	100,140
	1988	10,470	27,482	42,549	9,855	90,356
	1989	4,095	24,788	39,863	9,776	78,522
	1990	30,581	30,971	36,840	10,965	109,356
	Sum	**171,210**	**283,185**	**520,812**	**112,341**	**1,087,548**

Level of income	Year	Actual amount (millions of 1987 US dollars)				
		Portfolio	Bank	Others	FDI	Total
High income countries (23)	1980	84,326	449,132	134,044	71,656	739,157
	1981	113,263	505,910	170,792	96,059	886,025
	1982	130,842	403,579	170,038	81,173	785,631
	1983	136,963	323,221	164,497	81,699	706,381
	1984	190,773	386,430	212,115	126,455	915,773
	1985	326,599	507,262	215,926	114,699	1,164,486
	1986	460,844	953,491	318,205	172,947	1,905,487
	1987	440,240	1,188,450	371,404	252,914	2,253,008
	1988	518,282	990,328	454,299	308,115	2,271,024
	1989	614,456	1,073,756	578,035	372,203	2,638,450
	1990	433,203	1,019,754	763,296	395,502	2,611,755
	Sum	**3,449,791**	**7,801,312**	**3,552,652**	**2,073,421**	**16,877,176**
All countries (86)	1980	105,044	477,380	217,066	86,822	886,312
	1981	143,572	545,935	272,288	116,378	1,078,173
	1982	149,164	434,361	268,308	105,105	956,938
	1983	155,852	356,372	244,375	95,153	851,753
	1984	212,048	421,806	300,997	142,143	1,076,993
	1985	344,359	542,968	320,428	126,658	1,334,414
	1986	469,423	989,624	411,312	184,793	2,055,153
	1987	456,217	1,226,669	465,936	268,671	2,417,494
	1988	535,187	1,028,832	541,310	326,571	2,431,901
	1989	629,229	1,108,010	669,194	393,739	2,800,171
	1990	468,917	1,063,199	861,354	418,769	2,812,239
	Sum	**3,669,012**	**8,195,158**	**4,572,567**	**2,264,802**	**18,701,540**

Level of income	Year	Share of world total (%)				
		Portfolio	Bank	Others	FDI	Total
Low income countries (19)	1980	0.04	0.33	2.11	1.63	0.86
	1981	0.03	0.25	2.02	1.38	0.79
	1982	0.20	0.36	2.86	1.47	1.16
	1983	0.24	0.29	3.04	1.62	1.22
	1984	0.21	0.46	2.95	1.02	1.18
	1985	0.32	0.37	4.64	1.89	1.53
	1986	0.11	0.22	2.78	1.13	0.79
	1987	0.30	0.23	2.55	0.90	0.76
	1988	0.15	0.30	2.04	0.78	0.72
	1989	0.06	0.28	1.80	1.04	0.70
	1990	0.08	0.37	1.81	0.64	0.80
	Sum	**0.16**	**0.30**	**2.42**	**1.05**	**0.88**

Level of income	Year	Share of world total (%) Portfolio	Bank	Others	FDI	Total
	1980	0.56	1.17	14.50	4.45	4.68
	1981	1.57	1.13	15.66	4.06	5.18
	1982	2.50	1.45	12.79	3.98	5.07
Lower-	1983	1.89	2.02	12.76	3.90	5.29
middle	1984	1.44	2.93	11.66	2.55	5.03
income	1985	1.22	1.75	10.46	3.26	3.85
countries	1986	0.34	0.85	7.57	1.77	2.16
(27)	1987	0.70	0.64	6.55	1.64	1.90
	1988	1.05	0.77	6.18	1.85	2.18
	1989	1.64	0.57	5.86	1.94	2.27
	1990	1.02	0.81	5.30	2.29	2.44
	Sum	**1.15**	**1.05**	**8.49**	**2.44**	**3.06**
	1980	19.13	4.42	21.64	11.39	11.06
	1981	19.50	5.95	19.59	12.02	11.85
	1982	9.58	5.28	20.97	17.32	11.67
Upper-	1983	9.00	6.99	16.89	8.62	10.56
middle	1984	8.38	4.99	14.92	7.47	8.76
income	1985	3.61	4.46	17.51	4.29	7.36
countries	1986	1.38	2.58	12.28	3.51	4.33
(17)	1987	2.50	2.25	11.19	3.33	4.14
	1988	1.96	2.67	7.86	3.02	3.72
	1989	0.65	2.24	5.96	2.48	2.80
	1990	6.52	2.91	4.28	2.62	3.89
	Sum	**4.67**	**3.46**	**11.39**	**4.96**	**5.82**
	1980	80.28	94.08	61.75	82.53	83.40
	1981	78.89	92.67	62.72	82.54	82.18
	1982	87.72	92.91	63.37	77.23	82.10
High	1983	87.88	90.70	67.31	85.86	82.93
income	1984	89.97	91.61	70.47	88.96	85.03
countries	1985	94.84	93.42	67.39	90.56	87.27
(23)	1986	98.17	96.35	77.36	93.59	92.72
	1987	96.50	96.88	79.71	94.14	93.20
	1988	96.84	96.26	83.93	94.35	93.38
	1989	97.65	96.91	86.38	94.53	94.22
	1990	92.38	95.91	88.62	94.44	92.87
	Sum	**94.03**	**95.19**	**77.69**	**91.55**	**90.24**

Level of income	Year	Share of world total (%)				
		Portfolio	Bank	Others	FDI	Total
	1980	100.00	100.00	100.00	100.00	100.00
	1981	100.00	100.00	100.00	100.00	100.00
	1982	100.00	100.00	100.00	100.00	100.00
All countries (86)	1983	100.00	100.00	100.00	100.00	100.00
	1984	100.00	100.00	100.00	100.00	100.00
	1985	100.00	100.00	100.00	100.00	100.00
	1986	100.00	100.00	100.00	100.00	100.00
	1987	100.00	100.00	100.00	100.00	100.00
	1988	100.00	100.00	100.00	100.00	100.00
	1989	100.00	100.00	100.00	100.00	100.00
	1990	100.00	100.00	100.00	100.00	100.00
	Sum	**100.00**	**100.00**	**100.00**	**100.00**	**100.00**

Level of income	Year	Proportion of total gross flows (%)				
		Portfolio	Bank	Others	FDI	Total
	1980	0.55	20.60	60.22	18.63	100.00
	1981	0.57	16.26	64.36	18.82	100.00
	1982	2.70	13.94	69.36	13.00	100.00
Low income countries (19)	1983	3.54	9.90	71.68	14.89	100.00
	1984	3.54	15.27	69.83	11.36	100.00
	1985	5.43	9.77	73.03	11.77	100.00
	1986	3.13	13.48	70.50	12.89	100.00
	1987	7.46	15.01	64.45	13.08	100.00
	1988	4.69	17.83	62.96	14.52	100.00
	1989	1.94	15.90	61.30	20.86	100.00
	1990	1.56	17.29	69.17	11.98	100.00
	Sum	**3.48**	**14.88**	**67.21**	**14.43**	**100.00**
	1980	1.41	13.44	75.84	9.30	100.00
	1981	4.05	11.05	76.43	8.48	100.00
	1982	7.68	12.99	70.71	8.62	100.00
Lower-middle income countries (27)	1983	6.53	16.01	69.23	8.23	100.00
	1984	5.64	22.84	64.81	6.70	100.00
	1985	8.21	18.45	65.29	8.05	100.00
	1986	3.54	18.92	70.16	7.37	100.00
	1987	6.00	16.98	66.43	9.59	100.00
	1988	10.59	14.90	63.08	11.43	100.00
	1989	16.21	9.98	61.76	12.05	100.00
	1990	6.97	12.51	66.53	13.00	100.00
	Sum	**7.39**	**15.06**	**67.89**	**9.66**	**100.00**

Level of income	Year	Proportion of total gross flows (%)				
		Portfolio	**Bank**	**Others**	**FDI**	**Total**
	1980	20.49	21.52	47.90	10.09	100.00
	1981	21.91	25.41	41.74	10.94	100.00
	1982	12.80	20.53	50.37	16.29	100.00
Upper-	1983	17.32	27.69	45.87	9.12	100.00
middle	1984	18.83	22.32	47.60	11.25	100.00
income	1985	12.67	24.68	57.13	5.53	100.00
countries	1986	7.30	28.69	56.74	7.28	100.00
(17)	1987	11.37	27.62	52.08	8.93	100.00
	1988	11.59	30.42	47.09	10.91	100.00
	1989	5.22	31.57	50.77	12.45	100.00
	1990	27.96	28.32	33.69	10.03	100.00
	Sum	**15.74**	**26.04**	**47.89**	**10.33**	**100.00**
	1980	11.41	60.76	18.13	9.69	100.00
	1981	12.78	57.0:	19.28	10.84	100.00
	1982	16.65	51.37	21.64	10.33	100.00
High	1983	19.39	45.76	23.29	11.57	100.00
income	1984	20.83	42.20	23.16	13.81	100.00
countries	1985	28.05	43.56	18.54	9.85	100.00
(23)	1986	24.19	50.04	16.70	9.08	100.00
	1987	19.54	52.75	16.48	11.23	100.00
	1988	22.82	43.61	20.00	13.57	100.00
	1989	23.29	40.70	21.91	14.11	100.00
	1990	16.59	39.05	29.23	15.14	100.00
	Sum	**20.44**	**46.22**	**21.05**	**12.29**	**100.00**
	1980	11.85	53.86	24.49	9.80	100.00
	1981	13.32	50.64	25.25	10.79	100.00
	1982	15.59	45.39	28.04	10.98	100.00
All	1983	18.30	41.84	28.69	11.17	100.00
countries	1984	19.69	39.17	27.95	13.20	100.00
(86)	1985	25.81	40.69	24.01	9.49	100.00
	1986	22.84	48.15	20.01	8.99	100.00
	1987	18.87	50.74	19.27	11.11	100.00
	1988	22.01	42.31	22.26	13.43	100.00
	1989	22.47	39.57	23.90	14.06	100.00
	1990	16.67	37.81	30.63	14.89	100.00
	Sum	**19.62**	**43.82**	**24.45**	**12.11**	**100.00**

Source: Balance of Payments Statistics Yearbook (IMF).

Subdividing by financial item, level of income and year, we examine differences in external capital formation by each group. In the low income and lower middle income countries, the proportion of portfolio gross flow is minimal. Instead their major external financial resources are other-sector capital,[3] bank capital and FDI. In the upper middle income countries, bank capital is the most important external financial resource. However, unlike the previous two groups, portfolio investment is a more important external financial resource than FDI and other-sector capital. In the high income countries, bank capital has the largest proportion, but its proportion decreased from 61 per cent in 1980 to 39 per cent in 1990, while the proportion of portfolio and other-sector capital increased. When all countries are counted, the proportion of bank capital decreased from 54 per cent to 31 per cent during this period. On the other hand, portfolio investment and other-sector capital in proportion have increased rapidly.

Three important questions are raised by these descriptive statistics: (1) What are the causes of this rapid growth of global capital flows? (2) Why have the high income countries' global capital transactions increased more than the rest of the world? and (3) Why have particular types of capital increased in both proportional and absolute terms? As flow theorists suggest, is this due to the increase of rate of return in international investment? Or as portfolio theorists suggest, is it due to the increase of information relating to risk allocation and wealth for foreign investment? Or as monetary theorists suggest, is it due to increases in the current account imbalance and the deregulation of monetary policy? Or as this study hypothesizes, is it due to the globalization factors such as improved international tax treaty relations, financial innovation, and telecommunication development? All of the above questions will be answered in the gross flow models.

Gross Flows of Total Capital

We begin with the total capital gross flows, which are the aggregate of portfolio, bank capital, other-sector capital, and foreign direct investment. Then, each financial item's gross flow is investigated in a separate model. All models are log-linear, with the dependent variables in the logarithmic form of millions of 1987 US dollars. Due to multi-co-linearity problems, the income and treaty variables are not included together in the same model. Instead, we compute two different models, one with the treaty variable and the other with the income variable. The total gross flow model is estimated by the OLS fixed effects method as well as the WLS method to compare efficiency levels.

Table 9 overleaf presents the result of the total capital gross flow models. When the income variable is not considered in model A, we find that the major contributors to the gross capital flow are telecommunication technology (TELECOMM: number of data circuit ends weighted by telecommunication network technology innovation), financial instrument innovation (CD), and tax treaties (TREATY: interaction between financial market openness and number of countries in tax treaties) as the standardized estimates[4] in Model A suggest.

The next most important variables are current account balances (ABCAB: absolute value of current account balance)[5] and risk differentials (ABRISKD: absolute value of risk differential between home and the average of the same income countries). The interest rate differentials (ABINTD: absolute value of average in three interest rate differentials)[6] and exchange control policy (EXCHCONT) are not statistically significant.

When the income variable is included while the treaty variable is excluded in model B, the most important variable is income (log of gross national income per capita) as we expected. The order of importance for the other variables is the same as in model A, and the significance levels are all the same as in model A.

Interest rate differentials have negative signs and are not significant in both models. As flow theorists have found, interest rate differentials are decreasing among the high income countries. As a result, high interest rate differentials will be negatively associated with gross capital flows.

Another interesting finding in the total gross flow model is that exchange control policy is not statistically significant. It does, however, show a negative sign, as we expected, meaning that exchange control policy disturbs the capital flows. The fact that the exchange control policy is not statistically significant is, however, because of the aggregated dependent variable. Exchange control can be effective in some financial items such as bank capital or miscellaneous capital transactions (which is categorized as other-capital in this study) but ineffective over institutional capital transactions such as portfolio or foreign direct investment. These differences will be captured when we estimate gross capital flows by financial item below.

The WLS method is utilized to compare the parameters with the fixed effects models. WLS model A is weighted by the treaty variable while WLS model B is weighted by the income variable since heteroskedasticity was found in the treaty and income variables when the Breusch-Pagan test was used (see Appendix B–2). Compared with OLS model A, the increase in efficiency level with WLS model A is minimal. The results are very similar when we compare OLS model B and WLS model B. The improved efficiency provided by the WLS method is not high enough to shift the significance level of the OLS fixed effects parameters. This suggests that our OLS fixed effects models are not distorted by the heteroskedasticity problem.

Gross Flows by Financial Item

Since we have found that the OLS fixed effects method controls the heteroskedasticity problem, we will utilize it rather than WLS estimation hereafter. As in the total capital gross flow model, we estimate the treaty and income variables in separate models. Table 10 presents the results of the gross flow models for portfolio, bank capital, other-sector capital, and FDI. The parameters in both models, whether the income variable is omitted (model A) or the treaty variable is omitted (model B), are consistent.

As discussed in the model specification, the measurement for rate of return differs by financial item. Surprisingly none of the flow factors is statistically significant: absolute value of government bond yield rate differential (ABIGOVTD) in the portfolio gross flow model, absolute value of bank deposit interest rate differential (ABIDEPD) in the bank capital gross flow model, absolute value of market interest rate differential (ABIMKTD) in other capital gross flow model, and absolute value of purchasing power parity ratio change (ABPPPRC) in FDI gross flow model.

When we compare the standardized estimates within the model, they reveal more important information, however. In the portfolio gross flow model, telecommunication development is the most important factor; it is critical in portfolio investment to collect information and respond in a timely fashion. The next most important variable is the financial instrument innovation variable which provides various investment options as well as reducing investment costs. Also important is the treaty variable which safeguards investment, reduces regulation costs, and lowers national financial boundaries. Thus, significant variables in portfolio gross flows are transaction cost-related variables.

On the other hand, the exchange control policy variable shows an unexpected positive sign even though it is not significant. This is expected by the fact that portfolio products have been developed recently to avoid regulatory barriers (Yumoto et al., 1988). Another reason can be found in the fact that many countries that do control foreign exchange have been actively involved in public bond transactions. As portfolio investment is not designed to balance the current account, the negative sign of the current account

Table 9 Gross flows of total capital with OLS and WLS fixed effects estimations

(Model A: with treaty variable)

Model	OLS fixed effects method				WLS fixed effects method			
Dep. var.	TOTG (log of total capital gross flow)				TOTG (log of total capital gross flow)			
F-value	209.631				216.295			
R-square	0.9621				0.9632			
Adj. R-Sq	0.9575				0.9587			
Obs	946				946			
Ind. var.	**Par est**	**SE**	**(t-stat)**	**Std est**	**Par est**	**SE**	**(t-stat)**	**Std est**
INTERCEPT	7.73400	0.22026	(35.113) ***	0.0000	7.74445	0.21974	(35.243) ***	0.0000
ABINTD	-0.01555	0.08531	(-.182)	-0.0016	-0.01236	0.08316	(-.149)	-0.0013
ABRISKD	0.00969	0.00432	(2.242) **	0.0362	0.00978	0.00433	(2.256) **	0.0362
ABCAB	0.06082	0.01817	(3.348) ***	0.0469	0.06032	0.01804	(3.343) ***	0.0463
EXCHCONT	-0.02657	0.07813	(-.340)	-0.0050	-0.03447	0.07754	(-.445)	-0.0065
TREATY	8.0989E-05	3.708E-05	(2.184) **	0.0532	7.8498E-05	3.591E-05	(2.186) **	0.0530
CD	0.50130	0.09460	(5.299) ***	0.0688	0.49556	0.09191	(5.392) ***	0.0693
TELECOMM	0.07794	0.02097	(3.716) ***	0.0694	0.07940	0.02078	(3.822) ***	0.0715

(Model B: with income variable)

Model	OLS fixed effect method				WLS fixed effects method			
Dep. var.	TOTG (log of total capital gross flow)				TOTG (log of total capital gross flow)			
F-value	212.861				216.802			
R-square	0.9621				0.9633			
Adj. R-sq	0.9581				0.9588			
Obs.	946				946			
Ind. var.	**Par est**	**SE**	**(t-stat)**	**Std est**	**Par est**	**SE**	**(t-stat)**	**Std est**
INTERCEPT	4.21066	0.88950	(4.734) ***	0.0000	4.31324	0.87273	(4.942) ***	0.0000
ABINTD	-0.01647	0.08446	(-.195)	-0.0017	-0.01790	0.08229	(-.218)	-0.0019
ABRISKD	0.00823	0.00431	(1.910) *	0.0307	0.00830	0.00429	(1.935) *	0.0310
GNYPC	0.45051	0.10820	(4.164) ***	0.2945	0.45043	0.10604	(4.248) ***	0.2856
ABCAB	0.06138	0.01797	(3.415) ***	0.0473	0.06082	0.01782	(3.413) ***	0.0470
EXCHCONT	-0.11040	0.07136	(-1.54)	-0.0207	-0.11453	0.07128	(-1.587)	-0.0223
CD	0.51965	0.08985	(5.784) ***	0.0691	0.51406	0.08762	(5.867) ***	0.0694
TELECOMM	0.06406	0.02111	(3.034) ***	0.0710	0.06608	0.02080	(3.177) ***	0.0726

Notes

1 *** = significant at 1 % level; ** = significant at 5 % level; * = significant at 10 % level.
2 See Appendix D–1 for country and year dummy coefficients.
3 See Table 6 for variable definitions.
4 Par est = Parameter estimate
SE: Standard Error
t-stat: t statistics
Std est: Standardized estimate.

Table 10 Gross flows of four financial items with OLS fixed effects estimation

(Model A: with treaty variable)

Capital type	Portfolio				Bank capital			
Dep. var.	PORTG (log of portfolio gross flow)				BANKG (log of bank K gross flow)			
F-value	115.230				116.235			
R-square	0.9331				0.9336			
Adj. R-sq	0.9250				0.9256			
Obs.	946				946			
Ind. var.	Par est	(t-stat)		Std est	Par est	(t-stat)		Std est
INTERCEPT	4.371569	(12.695)	***	0.0000	6.721237	(20.807)	***	0.0000
ABIGOVTD	0.000107	(.025)		0.0004				
ABIDEPD					0.155531	(1.528)		0.0182
ABIMKTD								
ABPPPRC								
ABRISKD	0.001176	(.172)		0.0037	-0.002906	-(.459)		-0.0098
ABCAB	-0.017232	(-.606)		-0.0111	0.044827	(1.68)	*	0.0312
EXCHCONT	0.197633	(1.593)		0.0309	-0.229414	(-2.003)	**	-0.0388
TREATY	0.000098	(1.673)	*	0.0539	0.000001	(.016)		0.0005
CD	0.477679	(3.183)	***	0.0549	0.604752	(4.363)	***	0.0749
INDSTP								
TELECOMM	0.277108	(8.357)	***	0.2065	0.076765	(2.492)	**	0.0617

Capital type	Other-sector capital				FDI			
Dep. var.	OTHG (log of other K gross flow)				FDIG (log of FDI gross flow)			
F-value	96.834				72.113			
R-square	0.9214				0.9447			
Adj. R-sq	0.9118				0.9316			
Obs.	946				946			
Ind. var.	Par est	(t-stat)		Std est	Par est	(t-stat)		Std est
INTERCEPT	7.646267	(25.884)	***	0.0000	3.233743	(7.199)	***	0.0000
ABIGOVTD								
ABIDEPD								
ABIMKTD					-0.061366	(-.496)		-0.0064
ABPPPRC					-0.001595	(-.958)		-0.0131
ABRISKD	0.012207	(2.104)	**	0.0488	0.028839	(4.045)	***	0.1190
ABCAB	0.034905	(1.44)		0.0289	0.067249	(2.147)	**	0.0532
EXCHCONT	-0.264444	(-2.521)	**	-0.0531	0.140515	(1.055)		0.0281
TREATY	0.000004	(.087)		0.0030	0.000195	(3.263)	***	0.1315
CD	0.552565	(4.339)	***	0.0813				
INDSTP	0.029681	(4.722)	***	0.1746				
TELECOMM	0.089027	(3.172)	***	0.0850	0.134460	(3.9)	***	0.1202

(Model B: with income variable)

Capital type	Portfolio				Bank capital			
Dep. var.	PORTG (log of portfolio gross flow)				BANKG (log of bank K gross flow)			
F-value	115.892				116.776			
R-sqaure	0.9334				0.9339			
Adj. R-Sq	0.9254				0.9259			
Obs.	946				946			
Ind. var.	**Par est**	**(t-stat)**		**Std est**	**Par est**	**(t-stat)**		**Std est**
INTERCEPT	0.722786	(.510)		0.0000	4.289341	(3.276)	***	0.0000
ABIGOVTD	0.000839	(.198)		0.0028				
ABIDEPD					0.161621	(1.598)		0.0190
ABIMKTD								
ABPPPC								
ABRISKD	-0.000333	(-.049)		-0.001	-0.003993	(-.629)		-0.0134
GNYPC	0.467707	(2.707)	***	0.256	0.304995	(1.914)	*	0.1800
ABCAB	-0.015752	(-.558)		-0.0102	0.042607	(1.605)		0.0297
EXCHCONT	0.098036	(.861)		0.0154	-0.239663	(-2.281)	**	-0.0405
CD	0.508182	(3.55)	***	0.0584	0.572250	(4.326)	***	0.0709
INDSTP								
TELECOMM	0.262737	(7.827)	***	0.1957	0.066809	(2.143)	**	0.0537

Capital type	Other-sector Capital				FDI			
Dep. var.	OTHG (log of other K gross flow)				FDIG (log of FDI gross flow)			
F-value	98.026				71.125			
R-square	0.9222				0.9439			
Adj. R-Sq	0.9128				0.9307			
Obs.	946				946			
Ind. var.	**Par est**	**(t-stat)**		**Std est**	**Par est**	**(t-stat)**		**Std est**
INTERCEPT	4.052774	(3.387)	***	0.0000	0.744372	(.575)		0.0000
ABIGOVTD								
ABIDEPD								
ABIMKTD	-0.044545	(-.363)		-0.0046				
ABPPPC					-0.001138	-(.682)		-0.0093
ABRISKD	0.010609	(1.832)	*	0.0424	0.027629	(3.818)	***	0.1140
GNYPC	0.450192	(3.093)	***	0.3156	0.351090	(2.195)	**	0.2533
ABCAB	0.031464	(1.31)		0.0260	0.070810	(2.248)	**	0.0560
EXCHCONT	-0.277642	(-2.89)	***	-0.0557	-0.051492	(-.429)		-0.0103
CD	0.503550	(4.149)	***	0.0741				
INDSTP					0.027311	(4.237)	***	0.1607
TELECOMM	0.074132	(2.618)	***	0.0708	0.125141	(3.569)	***	0.1119

Notes

1 *** = significant at 1 % level; ** = significant at 5 % level; * = significant at 10 % level.
2 See Appendix D–2 for country and year dummy coefficients.

imbalance is not surprising. The risk differential and interest rate differential have expected positive signs, but they are not significant at the 10 per cent level.

In the bank capital gross flow model, financial instrument innovation is the most important variable – CDs were initially designed to promote stable bank capital resources. The next most important variable is telecommunication development. Unlike portfolio investment, bank capital transactions are affected significantly by exchange control policy. This implies that diversified financial instruments that avoid exchange control are not yet available for bank capital. The bank capital gross flow model reveals that the current account imbalance is balanced by bank capital borrowing or lending as the parameter shows a significantly positive sign.

With respect to other-sector capital gross flows, the telecommunication and financial instrument innovation variables are the most important variables, as with the previous two financial items. The exchange control policy and the risk differential variables are the next most important. In this other-sector capital category, all other types of capital excluding portfolio, bank capital, and FDI are included. The major source of other-sector capital is trade related credits, non-bank institutions' borrowing, and non-portfolio sector investment institutions' capital transactions. These sources are all dependent on the country's financial market structure. Thus we can infer that the significant effects of telecommunication development and financial instrument innovation are due to the investment institutions' capital transactions, while effectiveness of the exchange control policy is due to the non-bank institutions' borrowing or lending.

The financial instrument innovation variable is not included in the FDI gross flow model. Instead, industrial sector product as a percentage of GDP (INDSTP) is used as a counterpart, and it is statistically significant in the model. This is an important result because it tells us that FDI gross flows are different from non-FDI gross flows.[7] Countries with a higher proportion of industrial sector product are the countries with a lower proportion of service sector product. Since countries with higher proportion of service sector product also have advanced financial markets, the significant parameter for the industrial sector product variable implies that the developing countries have a greater chance of providing FDI compared to other financial items.

The next most important variable is the treaty variable. Since FDI is relatively a long-term investment, the safeguarding of investment via international treaties will be important. The telecommunication development variable is not as important as in the previous three models. It is the third most important variable in the FDI gross flow model, which is followed by the current account balance variable.

When income is included in model B, it becomes the most important variable throughout all four models, with the order of importance for the preexisting variables in model A remaining unchanged. This implies that the global capital flows of all financial items are influenced principally by the national wealth. As the country dummy coefficients in Appendix D–2 indicate, the high income countries are the major sources of gross capital flows of all financial items.

Major Findings Concerning Globalization of International Financial Markets

We thus conclude that interest rate differentials have not contributed to global capital transactions in any of the financial items, contrary to the flow factor hypothesis. Among the portfolio factors, national wealth is the primary source of investment capacity for all financial items, and risk differential is one of the key factors with respect to other-sector capital and FDI gross flows, and thus to the aggregated total capital gross flows. With respect to the monetary factors, the current account balance variable is significant in the bank capital and FDI gross flow models, and thus in the total capital flow model. Even though exchange control policy is effective in the bank and other-sector capital gross flow models, it is not quite significant in the total capital gross flow model. Thus we conclude that the monetary factor is not the most important factor in overall capital transactions, as the monetarists have argued.

If we consider flow, portfolio and monetary factors in separate models, none of these models can adequately explain why the globalization of international financial markets has accelerated in recent years. The fact that global capital transactions tripled during the period cannot be explained by the fact that the interest rate or risk differentials became greater over time. The fact that high income countries' share of global capital transactions was more than 90 per cent cannot be adequately explained by the fact that high income countries' national wealth and current account imbalances became greater over time. The fact that portfolio, other-sector capital, and FDI have increased their proportion as a percentage of global financial resources cannot be explained by the fact that these financial products became more profitable than bank capital investment.

Rather, in our econometric models, we show that the globalization of international financial markets has been promoted by such factors as market openness with favoured international tax treaties, financial instrument innovations and telecommunication network development. These three variables are statistically significant in all models and ranked as the most important variables in most of the models. We thus conclude that whereas each financial item has its own set of influences and serves its own function in markets, such as allocating risk and balancing the current account imbalances, portfolio and monetary factors are promoted by the globalization factors that lower national financial boundaries (market openness and treaty), provide various financial options with less investment costs (financial instrument innovation), and deliver improved information with less transaction costs (telecommunication network development).

Since these globalization factors have been developed primarily in and by the high income countries, gross capital flows are dominated by the high income countries. The higher numbers for high income countries' dummy coefficients in Appendix D–1 capture these effects. Since different types of capital have been developed or used by different countries, the country dummy coefficients in each financial item's gross flow model (Appendix D–2) capture the country's specific effect on each financial item.

The globalization factors have been rapidly developed in recent years. This pattern is captured by year dummy coefficients in Appendices D–1 and D–2. The year dummy coefficients after 1984 are significant in the total capital gross flow model. Portfolio investment is the most rapidly increasing type of capital, and the portfolio gross flow model is the one in which all globalization factor variables are significant. This implies that the portfolio market has been the greatest beneficiary of globalization. In the portfolio gross flow model, the recent years' dummy coefficients are significantly different from the earlier years' dummy coefficients, as shown in Appendix D–2.

Globalization affects the amount of gross capital flows as well as the type of external financial resources available to different income groups. In globalized financial markets, the direction and amount of capital inflow and outflow thus will also be influenced by the globalization factors. The consequences for capital inflow and outflow will be investigated in the next section.

Consequences of Globalization for Capital Flows

We have found that such factors as financial market openness and international tax treaties, financial instrument innovations and telecommunication development are the major causes of the globalization of international financial markets. The gross flow model cannot show which globalization factor has contributed to what types of capital flows (inflow or outflow), however. In this section, we will investigate impacts of the globalization factors on capital inflows and outflows.

Flow factors (e.g., interest rate differentials) did not contribute to global capital transactions for any financial item, and both portfolio factors (e.g., risk differential) and monetary factors (e.g., current account balance) had relatively small effects. Since we have used the absolute values of these variables in the gross flow model, we did not confront any confounding effects that the variables might pose. If they were not significant, it means that the differentials, either negative or positive, did not contribute significantly to global capital transactions. However, if either a negative differential or a positive differential contributed only to a one way flow, this differential effect would not have been captured in the gross flow analysis. It is thus necessary to analyze whether flow, portfolio, or monetary factors influence directional flows (inflows or outflows).

Figures 6 and 7 illustrate capital inflows and outflows by financial item and level of income, respectively. These figures, which depict financial market structure, reveal that there are distinctive patterns by income group. The low income and lower middle income countries are heavily dependent on other-sector capital and FDI for their capital inflows. The upper middle income countries' dependency on other-sector capital is far lower than the previous two groups, and bank capital becomes the second most important capital for their external finance. The major source of capital inflows to the high income countries is bank capital, and other-sector capital and portfolio are the next most important external financial resources. The sources of capital outflow are also very similar to these inflow patterns by income level.

Under these different financial market structures, the impact of the globalization factors on capital inflow and outflow should vary across country categories. The globalization process emerged first in the high income countries and is specifically effective in portfolio markets. As a result, the portfolio markets have grown more rapidly than any other capital market.

There are two effects of the globalization on capital in-outflows. The first is that countries with more globalization institutions and technologies (international treaties, financial instrument innovations, and telecommunication development) will have greater in-outflows across all financial items. The second is that there will be a shift effect from other capital to portfolio investment or more globalization-effective (or globalization-

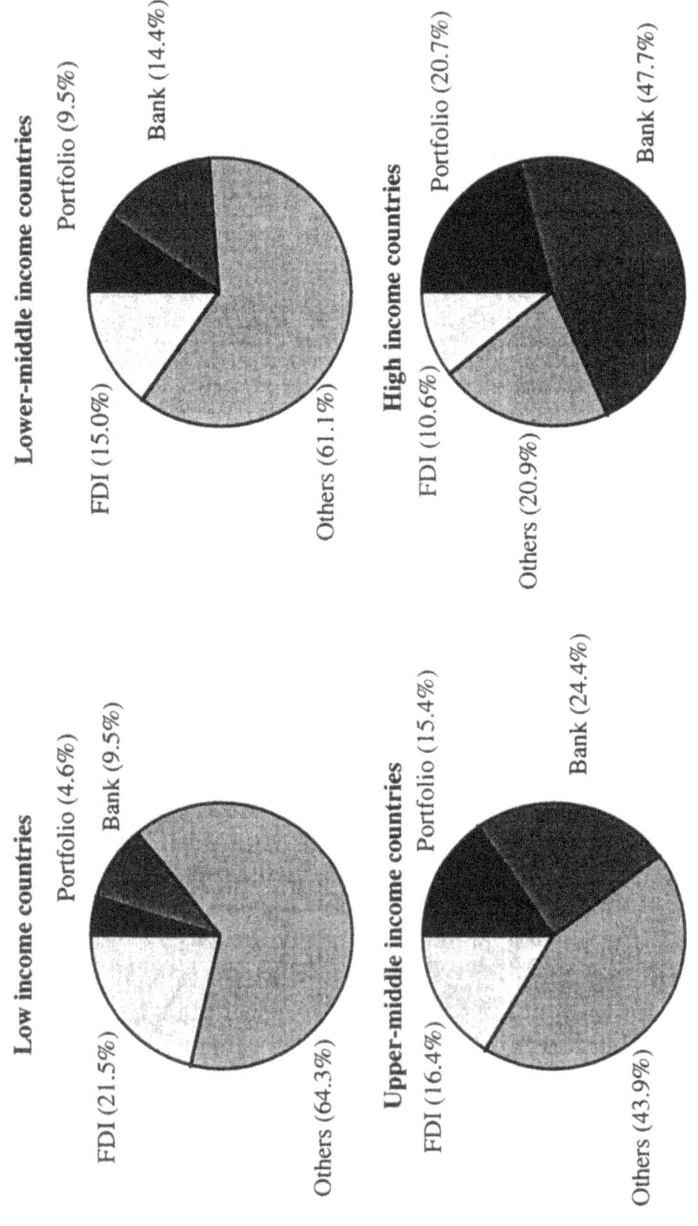

Figure 6 Source of capital inflows by level of income in 1980–1990
Source: Balance of Payments Statistics Yearbook (IMF).

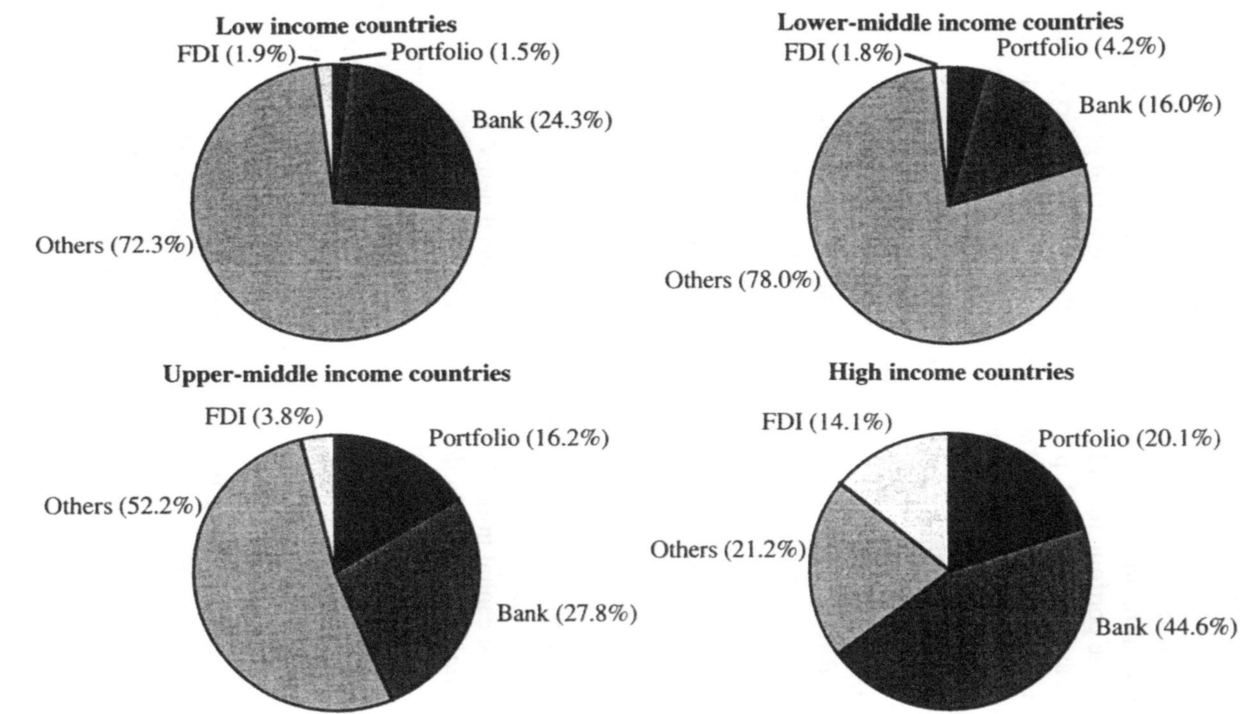

Figure 7 Source of capital outflows by level of income in 1980–1990
Source: Balance of Payments Statistics Yearbook (IMF).

sensitive) capital. The growth of portfolio investment can be a result of the movement of new capital into portfolio markets as well as the shift of old capital from other capital markets. Portfolio theorists have analyzed flow effects and stock effects on portfolio growth. The flow effect refers to an equilibrium portfolio flow into foreign assets from total portfolio growth due to increasing wealth, while the stock effect is a shift in the equilibrium distribution of the portfolio toward foreign assets due to changes in interest rates. Branson and Willet (1972, p. 295) argue that the flow effect is small relative to the stock effect, and most studies thus have ignored flow effects on portfolio growth. However, globalization factors, by reducing transaction costs, could augment these flow and stock effects.

In summary, globalization factors can change the traditional direction of international capital flows in two ways: (1) via the effects of globalization factors in general financial items; and (2) via the effect of capital shift from general financial items to globalization-effective capital. In combination these two factors will increase capital inflow to countries with more globalization facilities and produce rapid growth of their advanced portfolio markets. On the other hand, capital inflow to countries with fewer globalization facilities and less developed portfolio markets will shrink. Tables 11 and 12 present the evidence that support these conclusions. The descriptive statistics will be discussed in the next section.

To explore the relationships three different simultaneous equation systems are examined. Firstly we assume that each financial item's inflow and outflow are determined in isolation from other financial items. Five models are used to investigate total capital in-outflows and four financial items' in-outflows in section *Capital Inflow and Outflow by Financial Item.*

Then, we assume that all financial items' in-outflows are determined not only within the financial item but also by other financial items. The interactions of all financial items' in-outflows are estimated in one model with eight flow equations in section *In-Outflows of Four Financial Items in One System.* Lastly, four types of short-term capital flows are modelled in section *Four Types of Short-Term Capital Flows.*

Each model is a log-linear function using the fixed effects method, as discussed earlier. The primary concern is to investigate the effects of the globalization factors on each capital flow. The second purpose is to examine whether flow theory, portfolio theory, and the monetary approach to balance of payments provide any insights when sector-specific directional flows are investigated.

Table 11 Capital inflows by level of income in 86 countries

Level of income	Year	Actual amount (millions of 1987 US dollars)				
		Portfolio	Bank	Others	FDI	Total
Low income countries	1980	42	627	2,363	802	3,833
	1981	48	833	3,517	1,588	5,986
	1982	299	1,030	5,471	1,519	8,319
	1983	367	559	5,592	1,523	8,041
	1984	437	1,149	5,678	1,418	8,681
	1985	1,061	1,067	6,382	2,350	10,859
	1986	507	1,193	6,701	1,933	10,334
	1987	1,285	757	7,484	2,352	11,878
	1988	726	1,102	6,074	2,472	10,375
	1989	16	927	8,122	4,025	13,091
	1990	92	791	10,367	2,660	13,909
	Sum	**4,878**	**10,035**	**67,750**	**22,644**	**105,307**
Lower-middle income countries (27)	1980	429	4,052	18,479	3,440	26,399
	1981	2,138	5,073	23,897	4,464	35,571
	1982	3,661	3,963	18,427	3,794	29,845
	1983	2,779	4,146	15,496	3,329	25,750
	1984	2,692	6,373	18,485	3,288	30,839
	1985	3,438	4,566	17,531	3,916	29,450
	1986	819	3,206	17,741	3,151	24,917
	1987	2,314	3,918	15,809	3,441	25,483
	1988	3,413	3,924	16,858	5,720	29,915
	1989	8,582	3,996	19,381	7,294	39,252
	1990	2,252	6,211	26,930	9,334	44,727
	Sum	**32,517**	**49,428**	**209,033**	**51,171**	**342,149**
Upper-middle income countries (17)	1980	613	12,991	26,716	4,835	45,154
	1981	1,358	21,468	34,990	12,028	69,843
	1982	1,176	13,346	31,488	16,881	62,891
	1983	14,581	11,431	17,092	7,206	50,309
	1984	16,468	10,165	14,182	9,723	50,537
	1985	10,826	9,512	21,490	4,337	46,165
	1986	4,377	8,347	19,161	4,904	36,789
	1987	7,136	10,758	24,196	6,739	48,829
	1988	8,152	10,546	17,420	8,926	45,045
	1989	1,557	12,548	18,803	8,127	41,036
	1990	20,488	16,539	22,165	8,865	68,056
	Sum	**86,733**	**137,650**	**247,703**	**92,569**	**564,655**

Level of income	Year	Actual amount (millions of 1987 US dollars)				
		Portfolio	Bank	Others	FDI	Total
High income countries (23)	1980	49,418	229,252	69,800	32,329	380,799
	1981	64,101	249,293	84,498	43,980	441,872
	1982	66,526	179,957	89,246	41,096	376,825
	1983	64,007	172,180	78,666	43,577	358,431
	1984	95,580	217,428	105,764	57,559	476,330
	1985	182,779	276,739	104,804	47,705	612,027
	1986	231,773	518,372	133,465	72,827	956,436
	1987	237,024	659,173	204,371	112,635	1,213,203
	1988	264,247	548,151	225,592	137,169	1,175,159
	1989	336,105	568,014	307,695	166,475	1,378,289
	1990	219,486	554,609	426,823	172,158	1,373,077
	Sum	**1,811,045**	**4,173,167**	**1,830,724**	**927,510**	**8,742,446**
All countries (86)	1980	50,501	246,921	117,357	41,406	456,185
	1981	67,645	276,667	146,902	62,059	553,273
	1982	71,663	198,296	144,632	63,289	477,880
	1983	81,734	188,315	116,846	55,636	442,531
	1984	115,177	235,115	144,109	71,988	566,388
	1985	198,103	291,884	150,206	58,307	698,501
	1986	237,476	531,118	177,068	82,815	1,028,477
	1987	247,759	674,606	251,860	125,167	1,299,392
	1988	276,538	563,724	265,944	154,288	1,260,494
	1989	346,259	585,485	354,001	185,922	1,471,667
	1990	242,318	578,149	486,284	193,017	1,499,769
	Sum	**1,935,173**	**4,370,280**	**2,355,210**	**1,093,894**	**9,754,557**

Level of income	Year	Share of world total (%)				
		Portfolio	Bank	Others	FDI	Total
Low income countries (19)	1980	0.08	0.25	2.01	1.94	0.84
	1981	0.07	0.30	2.39	2.56	1.08
	1982	0.42	0.52	3.78	2.40	1.74
	1983	0.45	0.30	4.79	2.74	1.82
	1984	0.38	0.49	3.94	1.97	1.53
	1985	0.54	0.37	4.25	4.03	1.55
	1986	0.21	0.22	3.78	2.33	1.00
	1987	0.52	0.11	2.97	1.88	0.91
	1988	0.26	0.20	2.28	1.60	0.82
	1989	0.00	0.16	2.29	2.17	0.89
	1990	0.04	0.14	2.13	1.38	0.93
	Sum	**0.25**	**0.23**	**2.88**	**2.07**	**1.08**

Level of income	Year	Share of world total (%) Portfolio	Bank	Others	FDI	Total
Lower-middle income countries (27)	1980	0.85	1.64	15.75	8.31	5.79
	1981	3.16	1.83	16.27	7.19	6.43
	1982	5.11	1.00	12.74	5.99	6.25
	1983	3.40	2.20	13.26	5.98	5.82
	1984	2.34	2.71	12.83	4.57	5.44
	1985	1.74	1.56	11.67	6.72	4.22
	1986	0.34	0.60	10.02	3.80	2.42
	1987	0.93	0.58	6.28	2.75	1.96
	1988	1.23	0.70	6.34	3.71	2.37
	1989	2.48	0.68	5.47	3.92	2.67
	1990	0.93	1.07	5.54	4.84	2.98
	Sum	**1.68**	**1.13**	**8.88**	**4.68**	**3.51**
Upper-middle income countries (17)	1980	1.21	5.26	22.76	11.68	9.90
	1981	2.01	7.76	23.82	19.38	12.62
	1982	1.64	6.73	21.77	26.67	13.16
	1983	17.84	6.07	14.63	12.95	11.37
	1984	14.30	4.32	9.84	13.51	8.92
	1985	5.46	3.26	14.31	7.44	6.61
	1986	1.84	1.57	10.82	5.92	3.58
	1987	2.88	1.59	9.61	5.38	3.76
	1988	2.95	1.87	6.55	5.79	3.57
	1989	0.45	2.14	5.31	4.37	2.79
	1990	8.46	2.86	4.56	4.59	4.54
	Sum	**4.48**	**3.15**	**10.52**	**8.46**	**5.79**
High income countries (23)	1980	97.85	92.84	59.48	78.08	83.47
	1981	94.76	90.11	57.52	70.87	79.87
	1982	92.83	90.75	61.71	64.93	78.85
	1983	78.31	91.43	67.32	78.33	80.00
	1984	82.99	92.48	73.39	79.96	84.10
	1985	92.26	94.81	69.77	81.82	87.62
	1986	97.60	97.60	75.37	87.94	92.00
	1987	95.67	97.71	81.14	89.99	93.37
	1988	95.56	97.24	84.83	88.91	93.23
	1989	97.07	97.02	86.92	89.54	93.65
	1990	90.58	95.93	87.77	89.19	91.55
	Sum	**93.59**	**95.49**	**77.73**	**84.79**	**89.62**

Level of income	Year	Share of world total (%)				
		Portfolio	Bank	Others	FDI	Total
All countries (86)	1980	100.00	100.00	100.00	100.00	100.00
	1981	100.00	100.00	100.00	100.00	100.00
	1982	100.00	100.00	100.00	100.00	100.00
	1983	100.00	100.00	100.00	100.00	100.00
	1984	100.00	100.00	100.00	100.00	100.00
	1985	100.00	100.00	100.00	100.00	100.00
	1986	100.00	100.00	100.00	100.00	100.00
	1987	100.00	100.00	100.00	100.00	100.00
	1988	100.00	100.00	100.00	100.00	100.00
	1989	100.00	100.00	100.00	100.00	100.00
	1990	100.00	100.00	100.00	100.00	100.00
	Sum	**100.00**	**100.00**	**100.00**	**100.00**	**100.00**

Level of income	Year	Proportion of total inflows (%)				
		Portfolio	Bank	Others	FDI	Total
Low income countries (19)	1980	1.08	16.36	61.63	20.92	100.00
	1981	0.80	13.92	58.75	26.53	100.00
	1982	3.60	12.38	65.76	18.26	100.00
	1983	4.56	6.95	69.54	18.94	100.00
	1984	5.03	13.23	65.41	16.33	100.00
	1985	9.77	9.83	58.77	21.64	100.00
	1986	4.90	11.55	64.84	18.71	100.00
	1987	10.82	6.37	63.01	19.81	100.00
	1988	6.00	10.62	58.55	23.83	100.00
	1989	0.12	7.08	62.05	30.75	100.00
	1990	0.66	5.68	74.53	19.13	100.00
	Sum	**4.63**	**9.53**	**64.34**	**21.50**	**100.00**
Lower-middle income countries (27)	1980	1.62	15.35	69.00	13.03	100.00
	1981	6.01	14.26	67.18	12.55	100.00
	1982	12.27	13.28	61.74	12.71	100.00
	1983	10.79	16.10	60.18	12.93	100.00
	1984	8.73	20.67	59.94	10.66	100.00
	1985	11.67	15.50	59.53	13.30	100.00
	1986	3.29	12.87	71.20	12.64	100.00
	1987	9.08	15.38	62.04	13.50	100.00
	1988	11.41	13.12	56.35	19.12	100.00
	1989	21.86	10.18	49.37	18.58	100.00
	1990	5.04	13.89	60.21	20.87	100.00
	Sum	**9.50**	**14.45**	**61.09**	**14.96**	**100.00**

Level of income	Year	Proportion of total inflows (%)				
		Portfolio	**Bank**	**Others**	**FDI**	**Total**
Upper-middle income countries (17)	1980	1.36	28.77	59.17	10.71	100.00
	1981	1.94	30.74	50.0:	17.22	100.00
	1982	1.87	21.22	50.07	26.84	100.00
	1983	28.98	22.72	33.97	14.32	100.00
	1984	32.58	20.11	28.06	19.24	100.00
	1985	23.45	20.60	46.55	9.40	100.00
	1986	11.90	22.69	52.08	13.33	100.00
	1987	14.61	22.03	49.55	13.80	100.00
	1988	18.0:	23.41	38.67	19.82	100.00
	1989	3.79	30.58	45.82	19.81	100.00
	1990	30.10	24.30	32.57	13.03	100.00
	Sum	**15.36**	**24.38**	**43.87**	**16.39**	**100.00**
High income countries (23)	1980	12.98	60.20	18.33	8.49	100.00
	1981	14.51	56.42	19.12	9.95	100.00
	1982	17.65	47.76	23.68	10.91	100.00
	1983	17.86	48.04	21.95	12.16	100.00
	1984	20.07	45.65	22.20	12.08	100.00
	1985	29.86	45.22	17.12	7.79	100.00
	1986	24.23	54.20	13.95	7.61	100.00
	1987	19.54	54.33	16.85	9.28	100.00
	1988	22.49	46.64	19.20	11.67	100.00
	1989	24.39	41.21	22.32	12.08	100.00
	1990	15.98	40.39	31.09	12.54	100.00
	Sum	**20.72**	**47.73**	**20.94**	**10.61**	**100.00**
All countries (86)	1980	11.07	54.13	25.73	9.08	100.00
	1981	12.23	50.01	26.55	11.22	100.00
	1982	14.00	41.49	30.27	13.24	100.00
	1983	18.47	42.55	26.40	12.57	100.00
	1984	20.34	41.51	25.44	12.71	100.00
	1985	28.36	41.79	21.50	8.35	100.00
	1986	23.09	51.64	17.22	8.05	100.00
	1987	19.07	51.92	19.38	9.63	100.00
	1988	21.94	44.72	21.0:	12.24	100.00
	1989	23.53	39.78	24.05	12.63	100.00
	1990	16.16	38.55	32.42	12.87	100.00
	Sum	**19.84**	**44.80**	**24.14**	**11.21**	**100.00**

Source: Balance of Payments Statistics Yearbook (IMF).

Table 12 Capital outflows by level of income in 86 countries

Level of income	Year	Actual amount (millions of 1987 US dollars)				
		Portfolio	**Bank**	**Others**	**FDI**	**Total**
Low income countries (19)	1980	0	938	2,214	614	3,766
	1981	0	555	1,978	18	2,551
	1982	0	512	2,207	30	2,750
	1983	0	466	1,837	20	2,323
	1984	13	794	3,202	27	4,035
	1985	44	921	8,485	46	9,497
	1986	1	993	4,732	156	5,883
	1987	88	2,007	4,380	55	6,530
	1988	95	2,021	4,952	71	7,139
	1989	366	2,204	3,951	84	6,605
	1990	260	3,098	5,193	35	8,587
	Sum	**868**	**14,510**	**43,132**	**1,157**	**59,667**
Lower-middle income countries (27)	1980	158	1,526	12,998	422	15,103
	1981	121	1,091	18,753	266	20,231
	1982	67	2,341	15,899	389	18,696
	1983	163	3,062	15,681	378	19,284
	1984	361	5,992	16,599	341	23,293
	1985	776	4,909	15,991	218	21,895
	1986	754	5,196	13,412	124	19,486
	1987	901	3,881	14,708	965	20,456
	1988	2,202	3,975	16,578	338	23,092
	1989	1,714	2,340	19,842	356	24,251
	1990	2,530	2,374	18,728	272	23,904
	Sum	**9,748**	**36,687**	**179,189**	**4,068**	**229,692**
Upper-middle income countries (17)	1980	19,477	8,115	20,254	5,054	52,900
	1981	26,643	11,004	18,361	1,956	57,965
	1982	13,117	9,590	24,778	1,320	48,805
	1983	999	13,487	24,180	998	39,664
	1984	1,304	10,903	30,736	892	43,835
	1985	1,616	14,731	34,623	1,092	52,062
	1986	2,121	17,198	31,360	1,577	52,256
	1987	4,253	16,900	27,954	2,205	51,311
	1988	2,317	16,936	25,128	929	45,310
	1989	2,538	12,240	21,060	1,649	37,486
	1990	10,092	14,432	14,675	2,100	41,300
	Sum	**84,478**	**145,535**	**273,109**	**19,772**	**522,894**

Level of income	Year	Actual amount (millions of 1987 US dollars)				
		Portfolio	Bank	Others	FDI	Total
High income countries (23)	1980	34,908	219,880	64,244	39,327	358,359
	1981	49,162	256,618	86,294	52,079	444,153
	1982	64,316	223,622	80,792	40,077	408,806
	1983	72,956	151,041	85,831	38,122	347,951
	1984	95,193	169,002	106,351	68,895	439,442
	1985	143,820	230,522	111,122	66,995	552,459
	1986	229,071	435,120	184,740	100,120	949,051
	1987	203,216	529,276	167,034	140,279	1,039,805
	1988	254,035	442,177	228,707	170,946	1,095,865
	1989	278,351	505,743	270,340	205,728	1,260,161
	1990	213,717	465,145	336,473	223,343	1,238,678
	Sum	**1,638,746**	**3,628,145**	**1,721,928**	**1,145,911**	**8,134,730**
All countries (86)	1980	54,542	230,459	99,709	45,417	430,127
	1981	75,927	269,268	125,386	54,319	524,900
	1982	77,501	236,065	123,676	41,816	479,058
	1983	74,118	168,057	127,529	39,518	409,222
	1984	96,871	186,691	156,888	70,155	510,605
	1985	146,256	251,084	170,221	68,351	635,913
	1986	231,947	458,507	234,245	101,978	1,026,676
	1987	208,458	552,064	214,076	143,504	1,118,101
	1988	258,650	465,108	275,366	172,283	1,171,407
	1989	282,970	522,526	315,193	207,816	1,328,504
	1990	226,599	485,050	375,070	225,752	1,312,46
	Sum	**1,733,840**	**3,824,878**	**2,217,358**	**1,170,908**	**8,946,983**

Level of income	Year	Share of world total (%)				
		Portfolio	Bank	Others	FDI	Total
Low income countries (19)	1980	0.00	0.41	2.22	1.35	0.88
	1981	0.00	0.21	1.58	0.03	0.49
	1982	0.00	0.22	1.78	0.07	0.57
	1983	0.00	0.28	1.44	0.05	0.57
	1984	0.01	0.43	2.04	0.04	0.79
	1985	0.03	0.37	4.98	0.07	1.49
	1986	0.00	0.22	2.02	0.15	0.57
	1987	0.04	0.36	2.05	0.04	0.58
	1988	0.04	0.43	1.80	0.04	0.61
	1989	0.13	0.42	1.25	0.04	0.50
	1990	0.11	0.64	1.38	0.02	0.65
	Sum	**0.05**	**0.38**	**1.95**	**0.10**	**0.67**

Level of income	**Year**	**Share of world total (%)**				
		Portfolio	**Bank**	**Others**	**FDI**	**Total**
	1980	0.29	0.66	13.04	0.93	3.51
	1981	0.16	0.41	14.96	0.49	3.85
	1982	0.09	0.99	12.86	0.93	3.90
Lower-	1983	0.22	1.82	12.30	0.96	4.71
middle	1984	0.37	3.21	10.58	0.49	4.56
income	1985	0.53	1.96	9.39	0.32	3.44
countries	1986	0.33	1.13	5.73	0.12	1.90
(27)	1987	0.43	0.70	6.87	0.67	1.83
	1988	0.85	0.85	6.02	0.20	1.97
	1989	0.61	0.45	6.30	0.17	1.83
	1990	1.12	0.49	4.99	0.12	1.82
	Sum	**0.56**	**0.96**	**8.08**	**0.35**	**2.57**
	1980	35.71	3.52	20.31	11.13	12.30
	1981	35.09	4.09	14.64	3.60	11.04
	1982	16.93	4.06	20.03	3.16	10.19
Upper-	1983	1.35	8.03	18.96	2.52	9.69
middle	1984	1.35	5.84	19.59	1.27	8.58
income	1985	1.10	5.87	20.34	1.60	8.19
countries	1986	0.91	3.75	13.39	1.55	5.09
(17)	1987	2.04	3.06	13.06	1.54	4.59
	1988	0.90	3.64	9.13	0.54	3.87
	1989	0.90	2.34	6.68	0.79	2.82
	1990	4.45	2.98	3.91	0.93	3.15
	Sum	**4.87**	**3.80**	**12.32**	**1.69**	**5.84**
	1980	64.00	95.41	64.43	86.59	83.31
	1981	64.75	95.30	68.82	95.88	84.62
	1982	82.99	94.73	65.33	95.84	85.34
High	1983	98.43	89.88	67.30	96.47	85.03
income	1984	98.27	90.52	67.79	98.21	86.06
countries	1985	98.33	91.81	65.28	98.02	86.88
(23)	1986	98.76	94.90	78.87	98.18	92.44
	1987	97.49	95.87	78.03	97.75	92.00
	1988	98.22	95.07	83.06	99.22	93.55
	1989	98.37	96.79	85.77	98.00	94.86
	1990	94.32	95.90	89.71	98.93	94.38
	Sum	**94.52**	**94.86**	**77.66**	**97.87**	**90.92**

Level of income	Year	Share of world total (%)				
		Portfolio	Bank	Others	FDI	Total
	1980	100.00	100.00	100.00	100.00	100.00
	1981	100.00	100.00	100.00	100.00	100.00
	1982	100.00	100.00	100.00	100.00	100.00
All	1983	100.00	100.00	100.00	100.00	100.00
countries	1984	100.00	100.00	100.00	100.00	100.00
(86)	1985	100.00	100.00	100.00	100.00	100.00
	1986	100.00	100.00	100.00	100.00	100.00
	1987	100.00	100.00	100.00	100.00	100.00
	1988	100.00	100.00	100.00	100.00	100.00
	1989	100.00	100.00	100.00	100.00	100.00
	1990	100.00	100.00	100.00	100.00	100.00
	Sum	**100.00**	**100.00**	**100.00**	**100.00**	**100.00**

Level of income	Year	Proportion of total outflows (%)				
		Portfolio	Bank	Others	FDI	Total
	1980	0.00	24.91	58.79	16.30	100.00
	1981	0.01	21.75	77.52	0.72	100.00
	1982	0.01	18.63	80.27	1.09	100.00
Low	1983	0.00	20.08	79.07	0.85	100.00
income	1984	0.32	19.67	79.35	0.66	100.00
countries	1985	0.47	9.70	89.34	0.49	100.00
(19)	1986	0.02	16.89	80.44	2.66	100.00
	1987	1.35	30.73	67.08	0.84	100.00
	1988	1.33	28.31	69.36	0.00	100.00
	1989	5.55	33.36	59.82	1.27	100.00
	1990	3.03	36.08	60.48	0.41	100.00
	Sum	**1.45**	**24.32**	**72.29**	**1.94**	**100.00**
	1980	1.04	10.10	86.06	2.79	100.00
	1981	0.60	5.39	92.69	1.31	100.00
	1982	0.36	12.52	85.04	2.08	100.00
Lower-	1983	0.85	15.88	81.32	1.96	100.00
middle	1984	1.55	25.73	71.26	1.46	100.00
income	1985	3.54	22.42	73.04	0.00	100.00
countries	1986	3.87	26.66	68.83	0.63	100.00
(27)	1987	4.41	18.97	71.90	4.72	100.00
	1988	9.54	17.21	71.79	1.46	100.00
	1989	7.07	9.65	81.82	1.47	100.00
	1990	10.58	9.93	78.34	1.14	100.00
	Sum	**4.24**	**15.97**	**78.01**	**1.77**	**100.00**

Level of income	Year	Proportion of total outflows (%)				
		Portfolio	Bank	Others	FDI	Total
Upper-middle income countries (17)	1980	36.82	15.34	38.29	9.55	100.00
	1981	45.96	18.98	31.68	3.37	100.00
	1982	26.88	19.65	50.77	2.70	100.00
	1983	2.52	34.00	60.96	2.52	100.00
	1984	2.97	24.87	70.12	2.03	100.00
	1985	3.10	28.30	66.50	2.1	100.00
	1986	4.06	32.91	60.01	3.02	100.00
	1987	8.29	32.94	54.48	4.30	100.00
	1988	5.11	37.38	55.46	2.05	100.00
	1989	6.77	32.65	56.18	4.40	100.00
	1990	24.44	34.94	35.53	5.09	100.00
	Sum	**16.16**	**27.83**	**52.23**	**3.78**	**100.00**
High income countries (23)	1980	9.74	61.36	17.93	10.97	100.00
	1981	11.07	57.78	19.43	11.73	100.00
	1982	15.73	54.70	19.76	9.80	100.00
	1983	20.97	43.41	24.67	10.96	100.00
	1984	21.66	38.46	24.20	15.68	100.00
	1985	26.03	41.73	20.11	12.13	100.00
	1986	24.14	45.85	19.47	10.55	100.00
	1987	19.54	50.90	16.06	13.49	100.00
	1988	23.18	40.35	20.87	15.60	100.00
	1989	22.09	40.13	21.45	16.33	100.00
	1990	17.25	37.55	27.16	18.03	100.00
	Sum	**20.15**	**44.60**	**21.17**	**14.09**	**100.00**
All countries (86)	1980	12.68	53.58	23.18	10.56	100.00
	1981	14.47	51.30	23.89	10.35	100.00
	1982	16.18	49.28	25.82	8.73	100.00
	1983	18.11	41.07	31.16	9.66	100.00
	1984	18.97	36.56	30.73	13.74	100.00
	1985	22.00	39.48	26.77	10.75	100.00
	1986	22.59	44.66	22.82	9.93	100.00
	1987	18.64	49.38	19.15	12.83	100.00
	1988	22.08	39.71	23.51	14.71	100.00
	1989	21.30	39.33	23.73	15.64	100.00
	1990	17.27	36.96	28.58	17.20	100.00
	Sum	**19.38**	**42.75**	**24.78**	**13.09**	**100.00**

Source: Balance of Payments Statistics Yearbook (IMF).

Capital Inflow and Outflow by Financial Item

In-Outflows of Total Capital The proportion of world total capital inflow and outflow of the low, lower middle, and upper middle income countries was about 10 per cent in the period studied (see Tables 11 and 12). Figure 8 captures the different patterns of total capital inflow and outflow for these groups of countries, and for the high income group, which accounted for a dominant 90 per cent of the total. Note that different scales are used in each income group's graph in Figure 8. If we use the same scale, the patterns of the low and lower middle income countries cannot be seen since their capital flows are too small, compared to the high income countries.

Total capital inflows to the low income countries increased by only a small amount during the period when total capital outflow increased more than twofold. Total capital inflows to the lower middle and upper middle income countries actually decreased during the mid and late 1980s while their outflows were relatively stable. On the other hand, both inflows and outflows of total capital in the high income countries increased rapidly after 1985.

We investigate what led to these shifts, utilizing flow, portfolio, monetary and globalization factors in a simultaneous equation model. The results are in Table 13 .

The flow factor (defined by average value of three interest rate differentials: government bond yield rate; bank deposit interest rate; and market interest rate) is not significant in either the inflow or outflow equation, though the sign for inflow is positive and the sign for outflow is negative as expected. On the other hand, portfolio factors are significant in both the inflow and outflow equations. A positive risk differential (RISKD) induces total capital inflow while a negative change in risk differential (RISKDC) induces capital outflow.

The national wealth variable is statistically significant in the total capital outflow equation. National wealth is measured by the log value of gross national income per capita, and thus, the coefficient measures the income elasticity of international capital outflow.[8] The current account balance (CAB) condition is critical in determining the both inflow and outflow of total capital.[9] However, exchange control policy (EXCHCONT) is not significant enough to control capital outflow effectively. The tax rate differential (TAXD: average of three tax rate differentials such as tax on dividend earning, interest earning, and corporate income) is not significant in either equation.

All of the globalization factors are statistically significant in both equations. The international tax treaty (TREATY) and financial instrument innovation

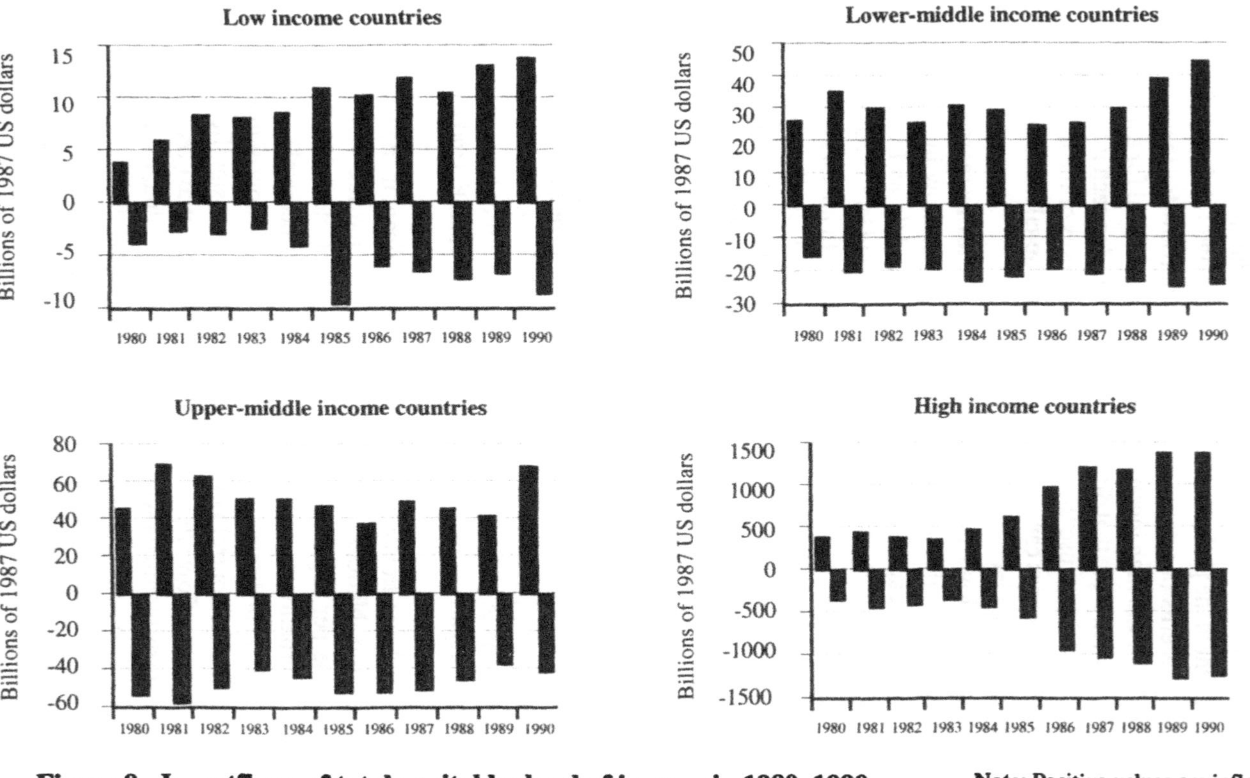

Figure 8 In-outflows of total capital by level of income in 1980–1990
Source: Balance of Payments Statistics (IMF).

Note: Positive values are inflows and negative values are outflows

Table 13 In-outflows of total capital with 3SLS simultaneous estimation

Equation	Total capital inflow				Total capital outflow			
	DV:TOTI (log of total K inflow)				DV: TOTO (log of total K outflow)			
Ind. var.	Par est	SE	(t-stat)		Par st	SE	(t-stat)	
INTERCEPT	6.564184	0.282180	(23.262)	***	2.850162	0.716313	(3.979)	***
INTD	0.000309	0.001621	(.191)		-0.000986	0.001560	(-.632)	
RISKD	0.017147	0.002876	(5.963)	***				
RISKDC					-0.027838	0.005147	(-5.408)	***
GNYPC					0.471966	0.090998	(5.187)	***
CAB	-0.005267	0.001591	(-3.311)	***	0.011592	0.001530	(7.575)	***
EXCHCONT					-0.082167	0.059095	(-1.39)	
TAXD	0.003099	0.003413	(.908)		0.008270	0.003274	(2.526)	**
TREATY	0.000109	0.000030	(3.673)	***				
CD	0.489737	0.080949	(6.05)	***				
TELECOMM					0.112782	0.025314	(4.455)	***
TOTI					0.105145	0.036512	(2.88)	***
TOTO	0.150757	0.036113	(4.175)	***				
System weighted R-sq: 0.9520		N = 946			Degree of freedom = 1685			

Notes

1 *** = significant at 1% level; ** = significant at 5% level.
2 See Appendix D–3 for country and year dummy coefficients.

(CD) variables positively influence total capital inflow[10] while telecommunication network development (TELECOMM) accelerates total capital outflow.[11]

The system variables (TOTI and TOTO) are statistically significant with positive signs.[12] This implies a high level of speculation in global financial markets, meaning that countries with more capital inflows provide more capital outflows.

Appendix D–3 reports the country and year dummy coefficients. It shows that most of the high income countries and a small number of upper middle income countries are the major contributors to total capital inflows and outflows. The year coefficients become significant after 1987 in the inflow equation and after 1984 in the outflow equation.

In the total capital in-outflow simultaneous equation model, we thus find that, once again, flow theory does not explain much about total capital in-outflows. Global capital in-outflows are explained by combination of the portfolio theory, the monetary approach to the balance of payments, and the globalization factors.

In-outflows of portfolio capital Tables 11 and 12 reveal that 94 per cent of global portfolio inflow and outflow is contributed by the high income countries. When we look at the portfolio inflow and outflow by income group in Figure 9, we find considerable year-to-year fluctuation in the developing countries, but a rapid and steady increase in the high income countries. Portfolio outflows from the low and lower middle income countries appeared only in the late 1980s, but for the upper middle income countries were large in the early 1980s. The upper middle income countries' large capital outflows in 1980–1982 were due in large part to the second oil shock; most OPEC countries are included in this group of upper middle income countries. After the oil money circulation period, the pattern of capital outflow from the upper middle income countries is similar to other developing country groups. However, the high income countries' portfolio inflows and outflows show a rapid increase over time until 1989. In 1990, both inflow and outflow of portfolio in the high income countries decreased to the 1988 level.

Portfolio capital is the most unstable financial resource for the developing countries, compared to other financial items that will be discussed in the next three parts. On the other hand, it is the most rapidly increasing capital type in the high income countries. What are the forces that shape this pattern? The answer can be found in Table 14 on p. 138.

Let us begin with the outflow equation first, as investment starts with outflow. Government bond yield differential (IGOVT) and change in risk differential (RISKDC) show unexpected positive signs although they are not significant. National wealth (GNYPC) and current account balance (CAB) are statistically significant with positive signs.

The unexpected signs of IGOVT and RISKDC in the outflow equation can be a result of the fact that the low and lower middle income countries' negligible portfolio outflows until the mid 1980s and the OPEC members' massive portfolio outflows in the early 1980s were not due to risk estimation but rather to a wealth effect. As the coefficient of GNYPC tells us, a one per cent increase in gross national income per capita yields an 0.41 per cent increase in portfolio outflow: portfolio outflow is a result of the portfolio allocation process by wealthy countries.

The current account balance is statistically significant in the portfolio outflow equation,[13] which is another version of the financial capability of portfolio outflow via trade surplus and foreign credit surplus. The significance of the telecommunication development variables is a correlative indicator of capacity for portfolio outflow. However, the exchange control (EXCHCONT) and tax rate variables (differentials between the home country's tax rate on

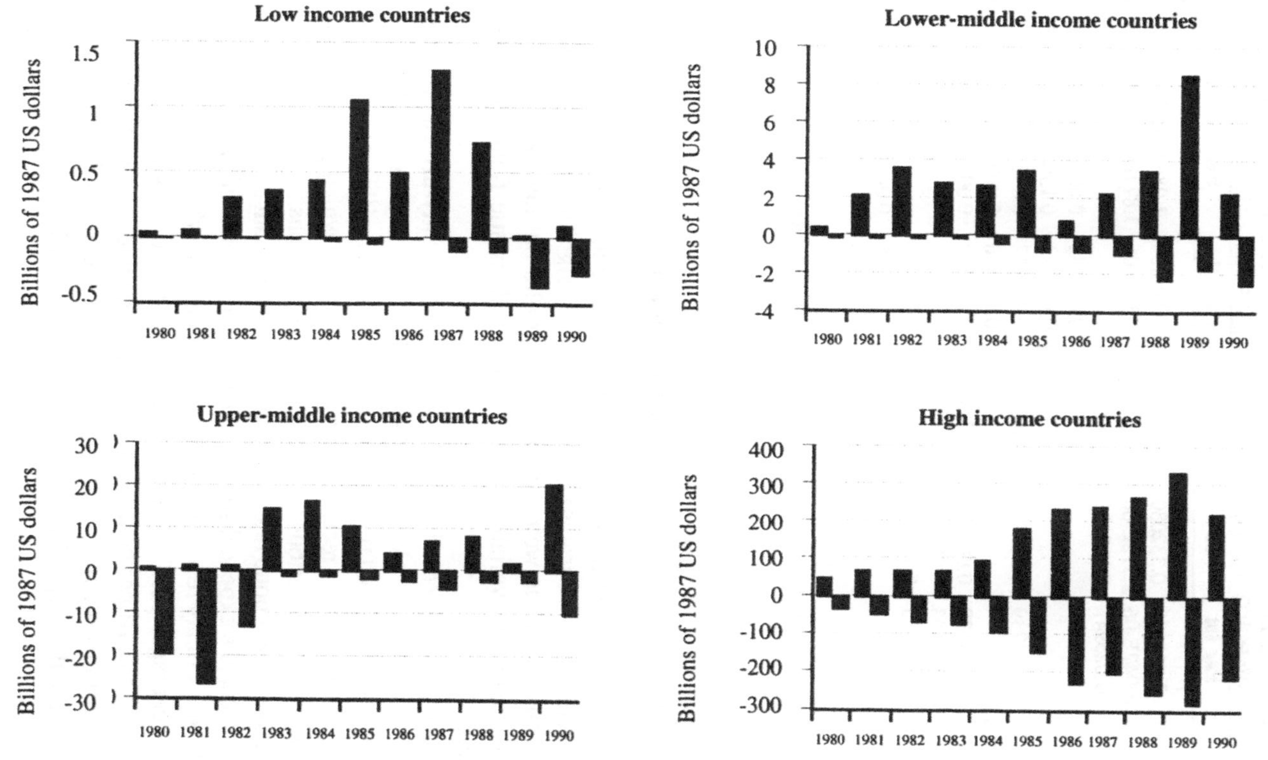

Figure 9 In-outflows of portfolio by level of income in 1980–1990
Source: Balance of Payments Statistics (IMF).

Table 14 In-outflows of portfolio with 3SLS simultaneous estimation

Equation	Portfolio inflow				Portfolio outflow			
	DV: PORTI (log of portfolio inflow)				DV: PORTO (log of portfolio outflow)			
Ind. var.	Par est	SE	(t-stat)		Par est	SE	(t-stat)	
INTERCEPT	3.528040	0.332080	(10.624)	***	-1.116860	1.088333	(-1.026)	
IGOVTD	4.042E-06	2.572E-06	(1.572)		1.098E-06	1.874E-06	(.586)	
RISKD	0.025947	0.005589	(4.643)	***				
RISKDC					0.007393	0.007689	(.962)	
GNYPC					0.407813	0.138073	(2.954)	***
CAB	-0.004739	0.003203	(-1.48)		0.014352	0.002250	(6.379)	***
EXCHCONT					0.107326	0.090172	(1.19)	
TFDIVD	-0.009127	0.005957	(-1.532)		0.006710	0.004398	(1.526)	
TREATY	0.008593	0.005956	(1.443)					
CD	0.747593	0.163847	(4.563)	***				
TELECOMM					0.209795	0.044886	(4.674)	***
PORTI					0.138388	0.050506	(2.74)	***
PORTO	0.228736	0.054841	(4.171)	***				
System weighted R-sq: 0.9204		N = 946			Degree of freedom = 1685			

Notes

1 *** = significant at 1% level.
2 See Appendix D–4 for country and year dummy coefficients.

foreigner dividends earning and the average of same income group's tax rate on foreigner dividends earning) are not statistically significant in the portfolio outflow equation. Thus we conclude that portfolio outflows are driven by investment capacity variables, rather than by domestic financial market conditions.

The question is then where these investment capacity-driven portfolios were invested. As the risk differential (RISKD) variable and the financial instrument innovation (CD) variables are statistically significant in the inflow equation,[14] the portfolio receiving countries are those which provide higher creditworthiness and various financial instrument options.

The government bond rate differential, current account balance and treaty variables show the expected signs. Higher government bond rates and more countries in tax treaty relations induce portfolio inflow while current account surplus discourages portfolio inflow. However, these three variables are not significant at the 10 per cent level. We thus conclude that in the portfolio inflow equation a country's creditworthiness and financial instrument availability are the major forces that drive portfolio inflow.

We infer that portfolio capital is exported from the countries with investment capabilities to the countries with higher creditworthiness and more financial options. Most developing countries are disadvantaged in this respect. This is why the high income countries contributed more than 94 per cent to the global portfolio inflow and outflow.

Two system variables (PORTI and PORTO) are positively significant in each equation, meaning that countries with greater portfolio inflow also export more portfolio capital, and vice versa. The effect of portfolio outflow on portfolio inflow is greater than the opposite case. If a country increases portfolio outflow by one per cent, the country induces foreign portfolios by 0.23 per cent. On the other hand, if a country increases portfolio inflow by 1 per cent, the increase in portfolio exports is 0.14 per cent.

Appendix D–4 presents the country and year dummy coefficients. The positive country dummy coefficients in the inflow equation are found mostly in the high income countries and a few Latin American 'emerging portfolio market' countries such as Argentina and Mexico, while the positive country coefficients in the outflow equations are found in the those portfolio inflow countries plus oil exporting countries and newly industrialized countries. The year dummy coefficients become significant after 1985 in both inflow and outflow equations.

In-outflows of bank capital Unlike portfolio outflows, Figure 10 shows that the proportion of bank capital outflows to inflows in the developing countries is relatively large and stable during the entire time period. One possible reason for the large proportion of bank capital outflows in the developing countries is the repayment of bank loans received. As indicated in Table 5, the repayment of bank loans received is treated as bank capital outflow while the repayment of loans extended is treated as bank capital inflow.

Compared to portfolio inflows, bank capital inflows in the developing countries fluctuated less. Also, on average, the actual amount of bank capital inflows to the developing countries did not increase over time. On the other hand, both inflows and outflows of bank capital in the high income countries were relatively stable until 1984 but increased rapidly in 1985. After 1985 they became relatively stable again. Because of this pattern, bank capital is the financial type that increased least during the period of this study.

The bank capital inflow-outflow simultaneous equation model reported in Table 15 explores why bank capital and portfolio capital flows are different. In the outflow equation of bank capital, most of the financial and monetary variables are significant. A positive interest rate differential in home country

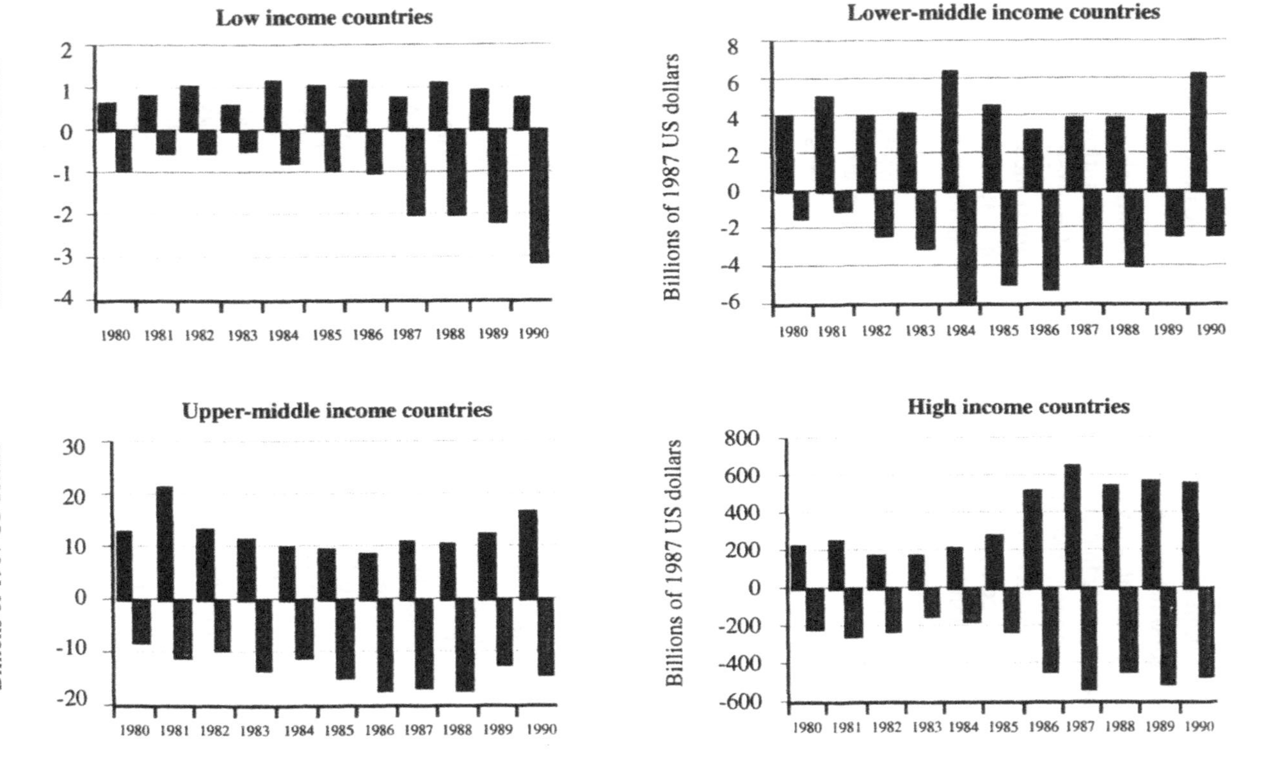

Figure 10 In-outflows of bank capital by level of income in 1980–1990
Source: Balance of Payments Statistics Yearbook (IMF).

Table 15 In-outflows of bank capital with 3SLS simultaneous estimation

Equation	Bank capital inflow				Bank capital outflow			
	DV: BANKI (log of bank K inflow)				DV: BANKI (log of bank K outflow)			
Ind. var.	**Par est**	**SE**	**(t-stat)**		**Par est**	**SE**	**(t-stat)**	
INTERCEPT	4.637126	0.412737	(11.235)	***	4.261308	1.398773	(3.046)	***
IDEPD	0.000850	0.003129	(.272)		-0.00953:	0.002922	(-3.265)	***
RISKD	0.025426	0.005647	(4.503)	***				
RISKDC					-0.038516	0.010135	(-3.8)	***
GNYPC					0.206686	0.175566	(1.177)	
CAB	-0.002080	0.003087	(-.674)		0.010602	0.002939	(3.607)	***
EXCHCONT					-0.338624	0.119127	(-2.843)	***
TFINTD	-0.003552	0.006087	(-.584)		-0.004154	0.005727	(-.725)	
TREATY	0.000001	0.000064	(.021)					
CD	0.664663	0.162776	(4.083)	***				
TELECOMM					0.125034	0.048752	(2.565)	**
BANKI					0.090831	0.058170	(1.561)	
BANKO	0.243979	0.066111	(3.69)	***				
System weighted R-sq: 0.9061		N = 946			Degree of freedom = 1685			

Notes

1 *** = significant at 1% level; ** = significant at 5% level.
2 See Appendix D–5 for country and year dummy coefficients.

discourages bank capital outflows: the coefficient of IDEPD (bank deposit interest rate differential) shows a negative sign. A positive creditworthiness differential in the home country also discourages bank capital outflows. Exchange control policy is effective in controlling bank capital outflows.[15] The current account surplus condition encourages bank capital outflows.[16]

The wealth variable in the outflow equation is not statistically significant even though it shows the expected positive sign. Remember that national wealth was a major factor in the portfolio outflow equation. Also remember that the interest rate differential and change in risk differential variables were not significant in the same equation. These different significance levels in the portfolio and bank capital outflow equations provide insights into the different patterns evident in the descriptive statistics of Figures 9 and 10. The results from the econometric analyses imply that domestic financial market conditions are more influential with respect to bank capital outflows than with respect to portfolio outflows. The results also suggest that national wealth is less influential for bank capital outflows than for portfolio outflows.

Comparing Figures 9 and 10, for example, the upper middle income countries in the early 1980s showed significant portfolio outflows due to the effects of OPEC members' wealth increases, while their bank capital outflows did not show this oil money circulation effect.

Telecommunication development is statistically significant but tax rate differential (TFINTD: differential between home country's tax rate on foreigner's interest earning and the average of the same income groups' tax rate on foreigner's interest earning) is not significant in the bank capital outflow equation. These two variables show the same effects as in the portfolio outflow equation. However, the bank capital inflow system variable (BANKI) in the bank capital outflow equation is not significant although it shows the expected positive sign. This implies that the countries with greater bank capital outflows also induce greater bank capital inflows; however, the effect of bank capital inflow on bank capital outflow is smaller than the effect of portfolio capital inflow on portfolio capital outflow.

The question then becomes where this domestic financial market condition-driven bank capital is invested. In the bank capital inflow equation, the risk differential and financial instrument innovation variables are statistically significant, similar to the results of the portfolio inflow equation. The countries with higher creditworthiness and provide CDs in their banking industry induce greater bank capital inflows.[17] The system variable, bank capital outflow, is statistically significant, meaning that the countries with greater capital outflows also display greater bank capital inflows.[18] This is similar to the portfolio inflow equation.

In general, the forces that determine inflows of bank and portfolio capital are the same. That is why bank capital inflows to the developing countries did not increase over time, like portfolio capital inflows. On the other hand, variables that are insignificant in determining portfolio capital outflows become significant in bank capital outflows. This is why bank capital outflows from the developing countries were relatively large compared to portfolio outflows.

In sum, bank capital outflows are driven by domestic financial market conditions. Bank capital outflows are transferred as bank capital inflows to countries with higher creditworthiness and various financial options. The country and year dummy coefficients are reported in Appendix D–5. The coefficients of the high income countries and year dummies after 1984 show positive signs in both the inflow and outflow equations.

In-outflows of other-sector capital The developing countries' inflow and outflow shares of other-sector capital from the pool of world total other-sector capital inflow and outflow was 22 per cent during the period studied (see Tables 11 and 12). Other-sector capital, thus, is the primary external financial resource for the developing countries (see Figures 6 and 7). As shown in Figure 11, the actual amount of other-sector capital outflow from the developing countries was relatively stable, but the actual amount of other-sector capital inflow to the developing countries decreased over time. This pattern is similar to bank capital inflows and outflows in the developing countries. In the high income countries, on the other hand, both inflows and outflows of other-sector capital increased over time. The pattern of other-sector capital flows differs from their bank capital flows. There is no downhill trend in the mid 1980s or a peak in 1987, as was found for bank capital flows. The pattern of other-sector capital flows is similar to portfolio flows in the high income countries.

We thus find that in-outflows of other sector-capital in the developing countries are similar to their bank capital in-outflows, while those in the high income countries are similar to the high income countries' portfolio in-outflows. Why is this the case? The other-sector capital in-outflow simultaneous equation model investigates the forces that shape this pattern.

In the other-sector capital outflow equation in Table 16, change in risk differential, national wealth, current account balance, and telecommunication development are statistically significant. However, interest rate differential (IMKTD: money market interest rate differential), exchange control and tax rate differential (TFINTD: same as in the bank capital in-outflow model) are not statistically significant.

As introduced in the gross flow model of other-sector capital, trade related credits, non-bank institutions' borrowing and lending, and non-portfolio sector investment institutions' capital transactions are treated as other-sector capital. The similarity between outflows of other-sector capital and bank capital is the significance level of change in risk differential, which is not found in the portfolio outflow equation. This can be attributed to the non-bank financial institutions' capital lending.

The similarities between outflows of other-sector and portfolio capital are found in an unexpected positive sign of interest rate differential, insignificant exchange control policy, and significant national wealth.[19] This can be attributed to non-portfolio sector investment institutions' capital investment. In the bank capital outflow equation, interest rate differential is positively significant, exchange control policy is negatively significant while national wealth is not significant.

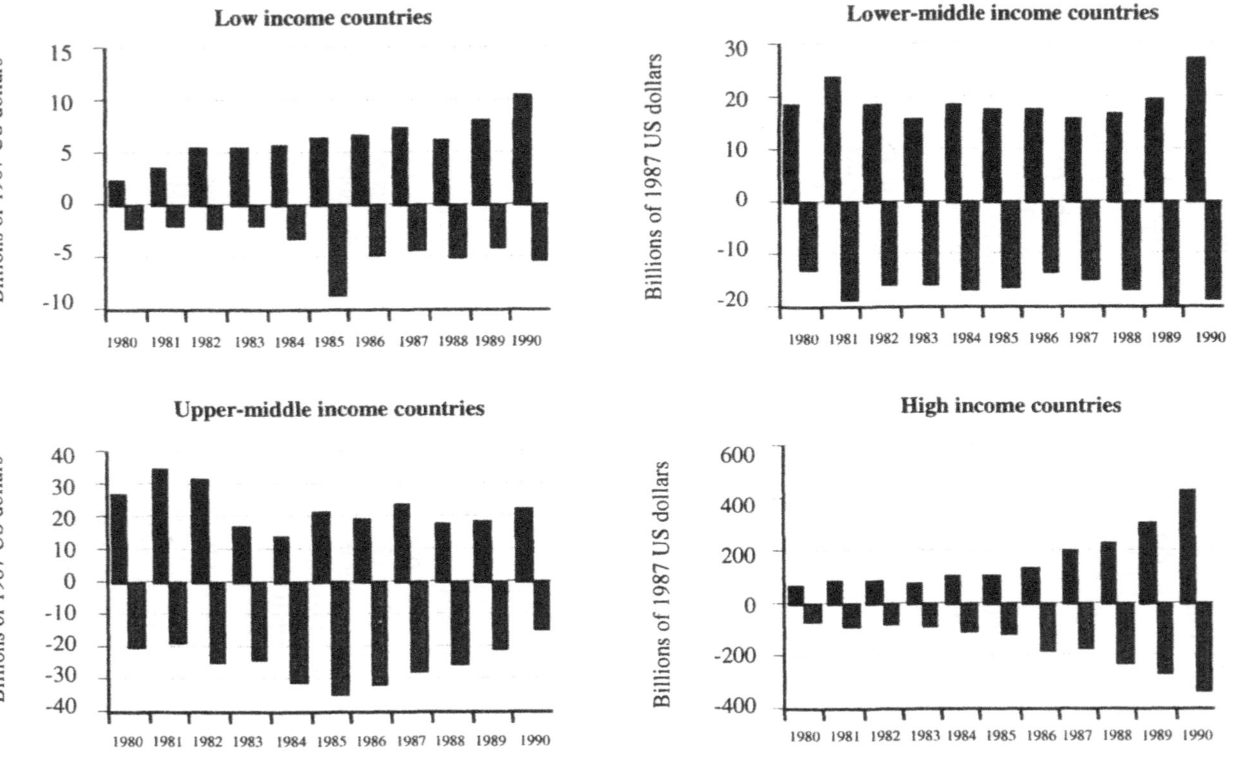

Figure 11 In-outflows of other-sector capital by level of income in 1980–1990 **Note:** Positive values are inflows and negative values are outflows

Source: Balance of Payments Statistics (IMF).

Table 16 In-outflows of other-sector capital with 3SLS simultaneous estimation

Equation	Other sector capital inflow				Other sector capital outflow			
	DV: OTHI (log of other K inflow)				DV: OTHO (log of other K outflow)			
Ind. var.	**Par est**	**SE**	**(t-stat)**		**Par est**	**SE**	**(t-stat)**	
INTERCEPT	6.423551	0.357329	17.977	***	1.954013	1.184244	1.650	*
IMKTD	0.001834	0.002748	0.667		0.001274	0.002594	0.491	
RISKD	0.023462	0.004872	4.816	***				
RISKDC					-0.037939	0.008670	-4.376	***
GNYPC					0.629885	0.149169	4.223	***
CAB	-0.007916	0.002690	-2.943	***	0.007855	0.002600	3.022	***
EXCHCONT					-0.083659	0.100472	-0.833	
TFINTD	-0.001647	0.005311	-0.310		0.003072	0.004947	0.621	
TREATY	0.000088	0.000049	1.769	*				
CD	0.571621	0.134031	4.265	***				
TELECOMM					0.124005	0.039795	3.116	***
OTHI					-0.016788	0.047294	-0.355	
OTHO	0.082744	0.046594	1.776	*				
System weighted R-sq: 0.8818		N = 946			Degree of freedom = 1685			

Notes

1 *** = significant at 1 % level; * = significant at 10% level.

2 See Appendeix D–6 for country and year dummy coefficients.

The current account balance[20] and telecommunication development variables are all significant in the three financial items' outflows but tax rate is not significant in any equation. In the other-sector capital inflow equation, the risk differential and financial instrument innovation variables[21] are significant, but the tax rate differential variable is not. The significance level of these variables is similar to the level in inflows both the portfolio and bank capital equations. Current account balance[22] and international tax treaty relations become statistically significant only in the other-sector capital inflow equation. This can be attributed to trade-related credit inflows since these variables are not significant in either the portfolio or the bank capital inflow equation.

We thus find that some of the variables in the inflow equation of other-sector capital have the same significance level in the inflow equations for portfolio and bank capital, while other variables are found to be significant only in the other-sector capital inflow equation since other-sector capital is composed of several miscellaneous types of capital.

The system variable in the outflow equation of other-sector capital, OTHI, is negative though it is not significant. It is not a surprising result if we consider the components of other-sector capital. In the portfolio and bank capital in-outflow simultaneous equation models, we include in-outflow system variables for the same financial item. For example, the portfolio inflow system variable is not included in the bank capital outflow equation. If we did so, then the portfolio inflow system variable would have a negative sign, meaning that the effect of portfolio inflow on bank capital outflow is negatively associated.

The fact that other-sector capital includes several miscellaneous financial items is similar to the case when the portfolio inflow system variable is included in the bank capital outflow equation. We did not consider the in-outflow equations of miscellaneous capital in our simultaneous equation model. Thus the negative sign of OTHI should be interpreted to mean that non-bank financial institutions' capital inflow may be negatively related with non-portfolio sector investment institutions capital outflow and/or with trade related credit outflow and so on.

We speculate that non-bank financial institutions' capital inflows may not be associated with non-portfolio sector investment institutions' capital outflow or that non-portfolio sector institutions' capital inflow may not be associated with non-bank financial institutions' capital outflows. The logic is that the forces that determine bank capital outflow and portfolio outflow are different, as we have found in the previous models. This will be revealed in section *In-Outflows of Four Financial Items in One System*, when all financial items' in-outflow equations are included in one system so that interactions among different financial items may be examined.[23]

On the other hand, the system variable in the other-sector capital inflow equation, OTHO, is positive and significant. The correct interpretation is that one or combinations in three components' inflows are positively related with one or combinations in three components' outflows. However, we do not know which components are related to which components. We speculate that non-bank financial institutions' capital outflow may be positively related with non-portfolio sector investment institutions capital inflow or vice versa. The logic is that the forces that determine portfolio inflow and bank capital inflow are the same as we found in the previous models.[24]

If financial items are not homogenous, a simultaneous equation model may not be an adequate method since there will be no simultaneity. In the other-sector capital in-outflow model, three financial components are not homogenous. In addition, there are many more categories of miscellaneous components, based on the financial market structure of each country. Thus parameter estimates in the other-sector capital in-outflow model may be inefficient if the unidentified equation does not account for the cross-equation correlation among the error terms. This problem can be found in several of the country dummy coefficients reported in Appendix D–6. If a country has a different inflow and outflow financial components, inflow and outflow cannot be simultaneously determined. For example, the major source of other-sector capital inflow might be non-bank financial institutions' capital borrowing whereas the major source of other-sector capital outflow might be non-portfolio sector investment in a country. This problem will be solved in section *Four Types of Short-term Capital Flows*, when all financial items' in-outflow equations are included in one simultaneous system.

In-outflows of FDI Foreign direct investment has been an important external financial source for developing countries, as Figures 6 and 7 indicated. FDI inflows to the low and lower middle income countries have increased over time while those to the upper middle income countries have fluctuated, as shown in Figure 12. FDI outflows from the low income countries have been minimal. FDI outflows from the lower middle and upper middle income countries have been relatively stable over time with an exception of 1980 in the upper middle income countries, which was attributed to multinational enterprises' withdrawal from FDI.

On the other hand, FDI inflows and outflows in the high income countries were relatively stable until 1985 but have increased rapidly since then. As indicated in Tables 11 and 12, the high income countries' proportion of FDI inflows and outflows to world total FDI inflows and outflows increased from 83 per cent in 1980 to 92 per cent in 1990 and 83 per cent in 1980 to 93 per cent in 1990.

Table 17 presents the results of the FDI in-outflow simultaneous equation model. In the outflow equation, the purchasing power parity ratio (PPPR) is negative and significant. Purchasing power parity ratio is purchasing power of the dollar in a country in comparison to that of the US, all expressed as a ratio to the relative purchasing power in 1979. Thus, the negative purchasing power parity ratio means that the county's present purchasing power of the dollar become stronger compared to 1979 (see Appendix A–1 for detailed explanations). This tells us that a one unit increase in PPPR (relatively less strong purchasing power of the dollar) decreases FDI outflows by 1.3 million dollars (decomposed log value of 0.269 is 1.31). In other words, if value of the currency decreases, FDI outflow decreases (or if value of the currency becomes strong, FDI outflow increases).

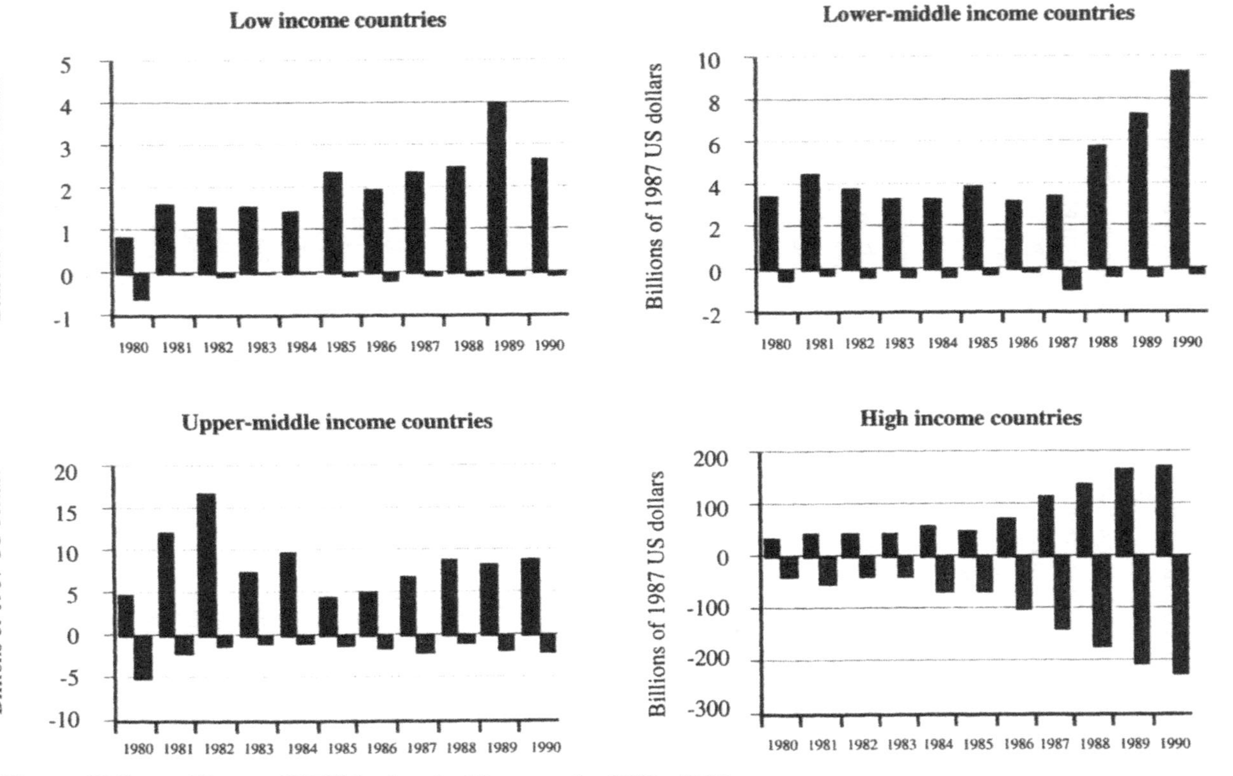

Figure 12 In-outflows of FDI by level of income in 1980–1990
Source: Balance of Payments Statistics (IMF).

Table 17 In-outflows of FDI with 3SLS simultaneous estimation

Equation	FDI inflow				FDI outflow			
	DV: FDII (log of FDI inflow)				DV: FDIO (log of FDI outflow)			
Ind. var.	Par est	SE	(t-stat)		Par est	SE	(t-stat)	
INTERCEPT	3.442720	0.381621	(9.021)	***	-2.745033	1.188192	(-2.310)	**
PPPR	-0.348012	0.123028	(-2.829)	***	-0.269283	0.135031	(-1.994)	**
RISKD	0.014863	0.004216	(3.525)	***				
RISKDC					-0.000091	0.008168	(-.011)	
GNYPC					0.633876	0.144542	(4.385)	***
CAB	-0.003614	0.002320	(-1.557)		0.009705	0.002525	(3.844)	***
EXCHCONT					-0.184722	0.098520	(-1.875)	*
TFCORD	0.005956	0.004186	(1.423)		-0.004763	0.004264	(-1.117)	
TREATY	0.000126	0.000044	(2.854)	***				
INDSTP	0.022101	0.004856	(4.551)	***				
TELECOMM					0.000455	0.042149	(.011)	
FDII					0.386862	0.060460	(6.399)	***
FDIO	0.362312	0.054563	(6.640)	***				
System weighted R-sq: 0.9303		N = 946			Degree of freedom = 1685			

Notes

1 *** = significant at 1% level; ** = significant at 5% level; * = significant at 10% level.
2 See Appendix D–7 for country and year dummy coefficients.

The exchange control variable is negative and significant.[25] This is a different result from the FDI gross flow model in which the exchange control variable was not significant. One possible explanation is that the less significant effect of exchange control on FDI gross flow is attributed to the less significant effect of exchange control on FDI inflow only. Exchange control policy was enforced by a small number of the high income countries in the early 1980s and by a large number of the developing countries during the entire period of the study. Since FDI is a major source of the developing countries' external finance, the developing countries received FDI inflow regardless of their exchange control policy. On the other hand, since the developing countries provide little FDI outflow, the significant level of the exchange control variable in the outflow equation is captured.

As expected, national wealth[26] and current account balance[27] are positive and significant in the FDI outflow equation. However, change in risk differential, tax rate (TFCORD: differential between home country's tax rate on foreigner's corporate income and the average of the same income group's tax rate on foreigner's corporate income) and telecommunication development are not significant at the 10 per cent level.

In the FDI inflow equation, the purchasing power parity ratio is negative and significant as in the inflow equation. It tells us that a relatively strong currency value compared to the currency value in 1979 increases FDI inflow. One of the reasons for the same sign in both equations is that PPPR is not a differential value between home and foreign countries. FDI decreases in both directions when purchasing power of the dollar decreases compared the purchasing power of the dollar in 1979. In other words, when a country has a higher purchasing power of the dollar (negative in PPPR), both inflow and outflow of FDI increases. The other reason for the similar sign may be the calculation method. Investment earnings are outflow of FDI from the FDI recipient countries' point of view. The actual outflow of FDI thus includes the outflow of earnings that have been contributed by the higher purchasing power parity in the outflow equation.

A positive country creditworthiness differential significantly induces FDI inflow, as it does other financial items' inflows. International tax treaty relations are also positive and significant to FDI inflow, an indicator of the safeguarding of FDI investment. Countries with a higher proportion of industrial sector product induce greater FDI inflows, compared to countries with a higher proportion in service sector or agricultural sector. However, current account imbalance and tax rate differential are not statistically significant in the FDI inflow equation.

The system variables (FDII and FDIO) are positively related to each other, meaning that countries with greater FDI outflow induce greater FDI inflow and vice-versa. In Appendix D–7, positive coefficients of country dummy variables are found not only in several high income countries but also in developing countries in both the inflow and outflow equations. The year dummy coefficients become significant after 1987 in both the inflow and outflow equations.

One important note in the FDI in-outflow model is that telecommunication development in the outflow equation is not significant and financial instrument innovation is irrelevant in the inflow equation. These two globalization factors are not as important as in the previous three models. The only globalization factor significant is the treaty variable in the FDI in-outflow model due to the characteristics of FDI. We thus conclude that FDI outflow is determined in its own function by purchasing power parity, national wealth, and exchange control policy, while FDI inflow is influenced by country creditworthiness, international tax treaties, and hosting countries' industrial structure.

Major findings concerning in-outflows by financial item We find that such globalization factors as international tax treaty relations, telecommunication development and financial instrument innovation are important in determining capital in-outflows. International tax treaty relations effectively induce FDI and other sector capital inflows, financial instrument innovation attracts all financial items' inflows except FDI, and telecommunication development promotes all types of capital outflows except FDI.

The current account balance condition is more sensitive in outflows than inflows: current account surplus is significant in all financial items' outflow, but current account deficit is significant only in other-sector capital inflow. Country creditworthiness is the common denominator that influences inflows of all financial items. We thus conclude that the monetary approach to the balance of payments effectively explains the capital outflow phenomenon, while portfolio theory fits the capital inflow phenomenon.

We also find that each financial item has its unique function in determining inflow and outflow of capital. In the outflow functions, portfolio capital and FDI are more sensitive to investment capacities, while bank capital is more sensitive to domestic financial market conditions such as interest rates and risk estimates. Other-sector capital outflow, on the other hand, is determined by a mixture of the forces that drive portfolio and bank capital outflows due to its miscellaneous financial components. We thus conclude that portfolio capital and FDI flows are better explained by portfolio theory, while bank capital movement is better explained by flow theory.

In the inflow functions, most financial items are influenced by the same forces that induce capital inflows. All types of capital inflows are affected by country creditworthiness and financial instrument innovation (industrial structure in FDI inflow). In addition to these forces, international tax treaty relations are associated with FDI and other-sector capital inflows. We thus conclude that globalization factors and country creditworthiness are the major forces that drive capital inflows of most financial items.

We also find that capital inflow and outflow are positively related within a capital type. That is, capital importing countries have a greater chance to export capital compared to less capital importing countries, and capital exporting countries have a greater chance to import capital compared to less capital exporting countries. This suggests that capital speculation within the same type of financial markets is evident as a result of globalization. In summary, capital outflows of most financial items are driven by investment capacity variables with better telecommunication facilities. These capital outflows are transferred as capital inflows to the countries where higher creditworthiness with more financial instrument options are provided. These inflow and outflow processes are accelerated in advanced financial markets that are equipped with globalization institutions and technologies. Because globalization of international financial markets has proceeded farther in the most-developed parts of the world, the developing countries have less chance to access external financial resources, while the high income countries have greatly increased their external financial resources.

In-Outflows of Four Financial Items in One System

In the previous section we estimated the forces that drive inflow and outflow within each financial item. In doing so, we ignored the shift effect across the financial items. In globalized financial markets, we hypothesize that the shift effect will be greater than before, however. If there are significant amounts of capital shifted across financial items, the in-outflow simultaneous equation model for any particular type of capital may be inefficient. In this section we estimate eight equations, one for each financial item's inflow and outflow, in one simultaneous system. This model will provide us with the ability: (1) to see the interactions among capital flows in globalized financial markets; and (2) to relax the simultaneous equation bias that may have existed when we considered in-outflows only within each financial item.

For convenience, we define each financial item's in-outflow models as 'partial flow models,' and the comprehensive in-outflow model as the 'general flow model' hereafter. We begin by comparing the partial flow models and the general flow model. Then we illustrate the interactions among capital flows with system variables in the general flow model. Lastly we will discuss the major findings from the general flow model.

Comparison of partial flow model and general flow model Most exogenous variables are assigned in the same equation in the general flow model as they were in the partial flow models but with the following exceptions. We select the industrial sector product (INDSTP) in the bank inflow equation, and we replace change in risk differential (RISKDC) with annual change in risk estimates (RISKCP) in the portfolio outflow and FDI outflow equations in order to obviate the rank condition identity problem, as was discussed in the model specification. We thus are able to compare most of the parameter estimates in the general flow model with partial flow models.

In Table 18, we find that the variables that are significant in the partial flow models remain significant in the general flow model. However, some of the insignificant variables in the partial flow models become significant. This suggests that the general flow model provides more efficient parameter estimates than the partial flow model.

In the portfolio inflow equation, risk differential and financial instrument innovation are statistically significant, as in the partial flow model. Unlike the partial flow model, the tax rate differential becomes significant and negative, however. That is, a higher tax rate on foreigner's dividends earning disturbs portfolio inflows.

In the portfolio outflow equation, national wealth, current account balance, and telecommunication development are significant, as in the partial flow model. However, government bond yield rate differential and annual change in risk estimates become negative, which is more reasonable, though they are not significant.[28]

In the bank capital inflow equation, risk differential is the same as in the partial flow model. Industrial sector product is positive but not significant. This is an important result since it reveals that bank capital is not significantly transferred to the countries with a higher proportion of industrial sector product. Other variables remain insignificant with the same sign as in the partial flow model. With respect to bank capital outflows, interest rate differential, annual change in risk estimate, current account balance and exchange control are significant, as in the partial flow model. The insignificant variables in the partial flow model such as national wealth and tax rate differential also remain insignificant in the general flow model. However, the bank capital inflow system variable that was insignificant in the partial flow model becomes significant in the general flow model.

In the other-sector capital inflow equation, risk differential, current account balance, international tax treaty relations, and financial instrument innovation are significant as in the partial flow model. The insignificant variables in the partial flow model such as interest rate differential and tax rate differential also remain insignificant in the general model. In the other-sector capital outflow equation, change in risk differential, national wealth, current account balance, and telecommunication development are significant, as in the partial flow model. However, interest rate differential becomes negative, which is more reasonable, but not significant.[29] Tax rate differential is positive but not significant, as in the partial flow model. As noted in the partial flow model, the system variable (other-sector capital outflow) becomes positive and significant when all financial items' in-outflows are included in one system.

In the FDI inflow equation, purchasing power parity, risk differential, international tax treaty relations and industrial sector production are all

Table 18 In-outflows of four financial items in one system with 3SLS simultaneous estimation

K type equation	Portfolio						Bank capital					
	Inflow (PORTI)			Outflow (PORTO)			Inflow (BANKI)			Outflow (BANKO)		
Ind. var.	Par est	(t-stat)		Par est	(t-stat)		Par est	(t-etat)		Par est	(t-etat)	
INTERCEPT	2.1114	(4.457)	***	0.454	(.425)		3.3347	(6.512)	***	3.7446	(2.667)	***
IGOVTD	3.3E-06	(1.292)		-0.0015	(-.619)							
IDEPD				0.0005	(.171)		-0.0105	(-3.544)	***			
IMKTD												
PPPR												
RISKD	0.019	(3.07)	***	0.0166	(2.737)	***						
RISKCP				-3.3E-05	(-.016)							
RISKDC							-0.0356	(-3.378)	***			
GNYPC				0.3169	(2.24)	**				0.2335	(1.32)	
CAB	-0.0039	(-1.147)		0.0082	(3.236)	**	0.0016	(.45)		0.0122	(3.789)	
EXCHCONT				0.1221	(1.366)					-0.2523	-(2.146)	**
TFDIVD	-0.0138	(-2.276)	**	0.0026	(.604)							
TFINTD							-0.0046	(-.724)		-0.006	(-1.042)	
TFCORD												
TREATY	7.3E-05	(1.228)					8.2E-05	(1.412)				
CD	0.4277	(2.504)	**									
INDSTP							0.0014	(.22)				
TELECOMM				0.1461	(3.668)	***				0.1594	(2.963)	***
PORTI				0.1699	(3.81)	***	0.1315	(1.808)	*	0.0185	(.276)	
PORTO	0.273	(4.246)	***				0.1844	(2.347)	**	0.2494	(3.32)	
BANKI	0.0891	(1.032)		0.0909	(1.438)					0.2561	(4.397)	***
BANKO	0.0634	(.806)		0.0563	(.965)		0.1475	(2.639)	***			

K type	Portfolio				Bank capital			
equation	Inflow (PORTI)		Outflow (PORTO)		Inflow (BANKI)		Outflow (BANKO)	
Ind. var.	**Par est**	**(t-stat)**	**Par est**	**(t-stat)**	**Par est**	**(t-etat)**	**Par est**	**(t-etat)**
OTHI	-0.0259	(-.281)	-0.4719	(-8.011) ***	0.5722	(6.928) ***	-0.1117	(-1.353)
OTHO	0.0285	(.314)	0.3155	(4.966) ***	-0.4673	(-5.514) ***	0.0199	(.238)
FDII	0.2103	(2.603) ***	-0.0024	(-.04)	0.038	(.461)	0.1024	(1.306)
FDIO	0.0742	(.802)	0.2268	(3.36) ***	0.2257	(2.498) **	0.0774	(.891)

K type	Other-sector capital				FDI			
equation	Inflow (OTHI)		Outflow (OTHO)		Inflow (FDII)		Outflow (FDIO)	
Ind. var.	**Par est**	**(t-stat)**	**Par est**	**(t-stat)**	**Par est**	**(t-stat)**	**Par est**	**(t-stat**
INTERCEPT	5.4539	(13.82) ***	1.649	(1.416)	3.738	(9.435) ***	-2.9591	(-2.764) ***
IGOVTD								
IDEPD								
IMKTD	0.0008	(.312)	-0.0007	(-.301)				
PPPR					-0.1812	(-3.235) ***	-0.1365	(-2.474) **
RISKD	0.019	(3.797) ***			0.0146	(3.263) ***		
RISKCP							-0.004	(-1.991) **
RISKDC			-0.0278	(-3.297) ***				
GNYPC			0.5111	(3.512) ***			0.7138	(5.439) ***
CAB	-0.0059	(-2.048) **	0.0074	(2.75) ***	-0.0033	-(-1.308)	0.0089	(3.622) ***
EXCHCONT			-0.1219	(-1.25)			-0.1977	(-2.243) **
TFDIVD								
TFINTD	-0.0023	(-.456)	0.0062	(1.235)				
TFCORD					0.0064	(1.205)	-0.001	(-1.289)
TREATY	8.1E-05	(1.684) *			0.0001	(3.217) ***		
CD	0.5616	(4.2) ***						
INDSTP					0.0238	(4.897) ***		
TELECOMM			0.0813	(1.829) *			0.0099	(.25)

K type equation	Other-sector capital				FDI			
	Inflow (OTHI)		Outflow (OTHO)		Inflow (FDII)		Outflow (FDIO)	
Ind. var.	Par est	(t-stat)	Par est	(t-stat)	Par est	(t-stat)	Par est	(t-stat
PORTI	0.1256	(2.075) **	-0.092	(-1.633)	0.306	(5.96) ***	0.0165	(.331)
PORTO	-0.3693	(-6.113) ***	0.1829	(2.966) ***	-0.1664	(-2.865) ***	0.1244	(2.23) **
BANKI	0.2675	(3.909) ***	-0.1921	(-2.884) ***	0.2244	(3.515) ***	0.101	(1.623)
BANKO	-0.1155	(-1.767) *	0.0953	(1.567)	0.1467	(2.55) **	0.0289	(.516)
OTHI			0.2171	(4.509) ***	-0.0684	(-1.008)	0.2756	(4.375) ***
OTHO	0.2267	(4.534) ***			0.027	(.415)	0.2912	(4.645) ***
FDII	0.2305	(3.278) ***	0.0559	(.856)			0.269	(5.459) ***
FDIO	0.3167	(4.135) ***	-0.073	(-1.015)	0.263	(4.728) ***		

System weighted R-sq: 0.9008 N = 946 Degree of freedom = 6692

Notes

1 *** = significant at 1% level; ** = significant at 10% level.

2 See Appendix D–8 for country and year dummy coefficients.

significant, as in the partial flow model. Current account balance and tax rate differential are not significant again as in the partial flow model. In the FDI outflow equation, purchasing power parity, annual change in risk estimate, national wealth, current account balance, and exchange control policy are significant, as in the partial flow model. Telecommunication and tax rate differential remain insignificant.

These results revealed that the major variables that played important roles in the partial flow models (globalization factors, risk differential, national wealth, current account balance, etc.) are unchanged. However, the interest rate differential variables that had unexpected positive signs in the portfolio and other-sector capital outflow equations in the partial flow models now have negative signs although they are not significant. The insignificant system variables such as bank capital inflow and other-sector capital inflow become significant. When all types capital flows are included in one simultaneous equation system, we thus conclude, the shift effects are captured and more efficient estimates are provided. As the ongoing process of globalization of international financial markets promotes more capital shift across financial items, the in-outflow analysis within each financial item will provide less efficient estimates. It is necessary to perform a comprehensive flow model if one is to estimate global capital flows.

Interactions of capital flows We must now analyze the interactions among the eight different types capital flows. We will discuss the significant parameters only in the system variables, which are summarized in Figure 13. In the portfolio inflow equation, the portfolio outflow variables is positive and significant. The positive relationship between portfolio in-outflows is the same as in the partial flow model. We call the positive relationship between inflow and outflow within each financial item 'synchronized intra-item movement,' which implies that inflow of a financial item (e.g., portfolio inflow) encourages outflow of the same financial item (e.g., portfolio outflow).

In addition, the FDI inflow variable is positive and significant, meaning that greater FDI inflows also induce greater portfolio inflow. That is, there are common factors in inflows of portfolio and FDI. We call the positive relationships between inflows of different financial items 'synchronized inflow movement', which implies that one type of inflow (e.g., FDI inflow) encourages the other type of inflow (e.g., portfolio inflow).

In the portfolio outflow equation, portfolio inflow, other-sector capital outflow and FDI outflow are positive and significant. The significant influence of portfolio inflow on portfolio outflow is the same as in the partial flow model, which is the synchronized intra-item movement. In addition, portfolio outflow is positively affected by other sector outflow and FDI outflow, meaning that countries with greater other-sector capital outflows and/or FDI outflows export more portfolio capital. That is, there are common factors in outflows of portfolio, other-sector, and FDI. We call the positive relationship between outflows of different financial items 'synchronized outflow movement', which implies that one type of outflow (e.g., FDI outflow) encourages the other type of outflow (e.g., portfolio outflow). Thus there are three types of synchronized movements such as synchronized intra-item movement, synchronized inflow movement, and synchronized outflow movement. We call these all together 'synchronized movement'.

On the other hand, portfolio outflow is negatively affected by other-sector inflows, meaning that countries with greater other-sector capital inflows induce less portfolio outflow. There are two ways to interpret the negative relationship between other-sector inflow and portfolio outflow. First, the fact that countries have greater other-sector capital inflows may be evidence of more profitable domestic financial markets compared to foreign financial markets. Thus portfolio investment abroad may be discouraged under conditions of more profitable domestic financial markets, which also encourages other-sector capital inflows. A second interpretation is that countries with more other-sector inflows are not capable of investing portfolio capital abroad: other-sector capital inflows are a major financial resource for the developing countries and portfolio outflow is driven by the investment capacity variables. We call the negative relationship between different directional flows of different type of financial items 'counteractive movement', which implies that one type of inflow (e.g., other-sector inflow) discourages the other type of outflow (e.g., portfolio outflow) or vice versa.

Bank capital inflow is positively related to bank capital outflow (synchronized intra-item movement), as in the partial flow model. In addition, bank capital inflow is positively related to both inflows and outflows of portfolio capital. The synchronized movement between bank capital inflow and portfolio inflow are expected. This tells us that countries with greater portfolio inflows also induce bank capital inflows. However, the synchronized movement between portfolio outflow and bank capital inflow is an unexpected one: one might expect the counteractive movements. The result shows that countries with greater portfolio outflows also induce bank capital inflows. This is a very important result, however. As found in the descriptive statistics, high income countries are the major contributors to portfolio inflows and outflows as well as to bank capital inflows and outflows, so the positive relationship between them is captured. The synchronized movement between portfolio outflow and bank capital inflow implies an agglomeration effect of international capital flows.

In the portfolio in-outflow equations, portfolio in-outflows and bank capital in-outflows are positive but not significant. However, in the bank capital in-outflow equations, these relationships show a higher significance level. This suggests that the effects of portfolio in-outflows on bank capital in-outflow is greater than the effects of bank capital in-outflow on portfolio in-outflows. That is, portfolio flows have greater influence on bank capital flows than the opposite case.

On the other hand, other-sector capital outflow is negatively related to bank capital inflows (counteractive movement), meaning that countries with greater other-sector capital outflows reduce bank capital inflows. Since other-sector capital is composed of several miscellaneous financial components, countries with more inflows of miscellaneous financial components have lower bank capital inflows. This can be interpreted as a type 2 outflow of other-sector capital: if domestic financial markets are profitable, other-sector capital withdrawal from the home country to other countries will be discouraged (negative other-sector capital outflow) and bank capital inflows will be encouraged. We temporarily postpone this discussion until we investigate four types of short-term capital flows in section *Four Types of Short-Term Capital Flows*.

Bank capital outflow is positively related to bank capital inflow (synchronized intra-item movement) and portfolio outflow (synchronized outflow movements), meaning that countries with more portfolio outflows and/or bank capital outflows provide more bank capital outflows. These relationships are similar to the relationship found in the bank capital inflow, portfolio inflow and portfolio outflow equations.

Other-sector capital inflow is positively related to portfolio and bank capital inflows. That is, there are the synchronized inflow movements between other-sector capital inflow and portfolio inflow and between other-sector capital inflow and bank capital inflow. This is a predicted pattern from the previous four equations. It reveals that the forces that induce other-sector capital inflow are the same forces that induce inflows of portfolio and bank capital.

On the other hand, other sector inflow is negatively related to portfolio outflow and bank capital outflow. That is, there are the counteractive movements between portfolio outflow and other-sector inflow and between bank capital outflow and other-sector capital inflow. The fact that other-sector capital inflow is negatively related to portfolio and bank capital outflows is explained by the developing countries' inflow resources, as was found in the portfolio inflow and bank capital inflow equations. This confirms that other-sector capital is the developing countries' principal external financial resource. The developing countries have little portfolio and bank capital outflow, however.

Other sector capital outflow is positively and significantly related to other-sector capital inflow (synchronized intra-item movement). This is a different result from the partial flow model.[30] When the other-sector capital outflow equation is simultaneously determined by the other-sector capital inflow equation, the model cannot capture the simultaneous relationship between financial components in the other-sector capital category. The financial components in the other-sector capital category are non-bank institutions' capital, non-portfolio sector investment institutions' capital, trade related credits and so on. In the general flow model, outflows of the different miscellaneous financial components are simultaneously determined by the four different inflow equations and three different outflows equations. Thus, outflow of non-bank financial institutions' capital is simultaneously determined by bank capital inflow and bank capital outflow, and outflow of non-portfolio sector investment institutions' capital is simultaneously determined by portfolio inflow and portfolio outflow, and so on. Under this condition, other-sector capital outflow becomes positively related to other sector capital inflow. Since the unit of analysis in this study is the country, the result suggests that one country has one dominant other-sector financial component. That is, a country's other-sector capital should be dominated by one component in order to be simultaneously determined by one of the three financial items. Otherwise, the relationship cannot be estimated. In addition, in the other-sector capital outflow equation, portfolio outflow is positively related (synchronized outflow movement) and bank capital inflow is negatively related (counteractive movement).

FDI inflow is positively related to FDI outflow as in the partial flow model (synchronized intra-item movement). In addition, FDI inflow is positively related to bank capital inflow (synchronized inflow movement), as we found the synchronized inflow movement between portfolio inflow and FDI inflow in the portfolio inflow equation. However, FDI inflow is negatively related to portfolio outflow (counteractive movement). This counteractive movement was found in the portfolio outflow equation: portfolio outflow is negatively associated with FDI inflow. This confirms that FDI inflow is one of the most important external financial resources of the developing countries. In turn, the developing countries have little portfolio capital outflow.

FDI outflow is positively related to FDI inflow as in the partial flow model (synchronized intra-item movement). FDI outflow is also positively related to portfolio outflow and other-sector capital outflow. That is, there are synchronized outflow movements between portfolio capital and FDI and between other-sector capital and FDI. However, other-sector capital inflow is negatively related to FDI outflow (counteractive movement). This confirms that the countries that have capability to invest FDI abroad are the high income countries, the most active contributors to globalization. In these countries, all types of capital flows traffic are heavy. Thus, all interactions in the FDI outflow equation are positive. In fact, although not significant, other variables are all positive in the FDI outflow equation.

Major findings concerning interactions among capital flows We thus far have estimated global capital flow interactions in one system, which requires eight equations of four financial items within a simultaneous system. We do not claim that this is a general equilibrium model since we have not included official sector capital flows and omitted capital transactions, which are often treated as capital flight. However, our model presents an inclusive analysis for all private sector capital flows, which thus allows us to understand the impacts of globalization on capital flows.

The result is summarized in Figure 13. The upper level boxes are inflows and the lower level boxes are outflows. The solid arrows represent positive relationship, while the empty arrows represent negative relationship. The solid arrows between the upper level boxes represent the synchronized inflow movements. The solid arrows between the lower level boxes represent the synchronized outflow movements. The solid arrows between an upper level box and a lower level box within each financial item represent the synchronized intra-item movement. The empty arrows represent the counteractive movement.

Three important findings emerge from this analysis: an improvement in the efficiency of global capital resource allocation, an agglomeration effect, and the pre-eminence of portfolio flows in influencing other types of capital flows.

The inflow and outflow synchronized movements are shown in the same directional capital flows of different financial items. That is, countries with more capital inflows of one financial item promote more capital inflows of other types of financial item, and countries with more capital outflows of one financial item promote more capital outflows of other types of financial item. This implies that the global capital moves to more profitable places and moves

Note: statistically significant relationships are reported

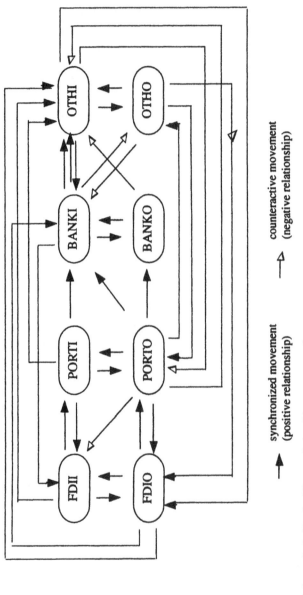

Figure 13 Interactions of global capital flows

out from less profitable places facilitated by globalization institutions and technologies. This suggests that the efficiency of global capital resource allocation is improved as a result of globalization of international financial markets.

Countries with one financial item's inflow induce more other types of capital inflows by the synchronized inflow movement. In addition, the synchronized intra-item movements also provide more capital inflow to the countries. That is, countries with more capital inflows of one financial item promote more capital outflow of the financial item, and vice versa. On the other hand, countries with less capital inflows induce less capital inflows of other types of capital. This is evidence of an agglomeration effect. When we consider the counteractive movements, this agglomeration effect is even greater. In Figure 13, bank capital and other-sector capital show the counteractive movements. For example, countries with more bank capital inflow do not induce other-sector capital outflow and countries with more other-sector capital outflows do not induce bank capital inflow. Recall that other-sector capital is a major source of the developing countries' external financial resources. On the other hand, there is no counteractive movement between bank capital and portfolio capital flows which are mostly carried by the high income countries. Thus the international capital agglomeration phenomenon is found among the high income countries.

In Appendix D–8, where the country and year dummy coefficients are reported, each country dummy coefficient shows a different sign in different flow equations. One thing in common is that major globalization actors such as the USA, Japan, and the UK show positive and significant coefficients in the most of eight equations. This pattern are also found such European countries as France and Germany. This means that countries that induce inflows of most financial items also provide outflows of most financial items. This suggests that countries with more globalization institutions and technologies have greater access to all types of capital flows. The country dummy coefficients of many high income countries also are positive in portfolio and bank capital flows. We thus conclude that there is an agglomeration effect in international capital flows as a result of globalization of international financial markets.

The third major finding is that portfolio market conditions are the most influential factors in determining other financial items' capital flows. That is, the forces that drive portfolio inflow or outflow also induce all other types of capital inflows or outflows. The portfolio inflow variables in the three inflow equations[31] in Table 18 are positive and significant. This suggests that countries with more portfolio inflows are more likely to induce all types of capital inflows. We do not see any other variable that is similarly positively and significantly related to all other types of capital inflows. The portfolio outflow variables in the three outflow equations also are positive and significant. This also suggests that countries with more portfolio outflows are more likely to provide all other types of capital outflows. No other variables are similarly positively and significantly related to all other types capital outflows. Figure 13 provides a clear picture of this idea.

One of the reasons for the significant effect of portfolio flows on other financial items' flows is that the performance of portfolio markets is a barometer of general domestic financial market conditions. Portfolio markets have been the greatest beneficiaries of globalization facilities and technologies, and portfolio capital mobility is the highest among financial items.

The other reason is that countries with advanced portfolio markets also display the same level in other financial markets. The forces that drive portfolio flows are similar to the forces that drive other financial items' flows under the parallel development of portfolio and other financial markets. We thus conclude that an improvement of the efficiency in the global capital allocation, an agglomeration effect in international capital flows and the pre-eminence of portfolio markets in influencing other financial markets' performance have emerged as a result of globalization.

Four Types of Short-term Capital Flows

Due to the data availability problem in the previous models, we did not differentiate domestic and foreign investors, treating them as a homogenous group. The endogenous variable in the inflow equation, capital inflow, was the actual amount of capital transferred to a country from the rest of the world as the sum of capital invested in the home country by foreign investors (type 1 inflow) and capital withdrawal to the home country by domestic investors (type 2 inflow). The endogenous variable in the outflow equation, capital outflow was the actual amount of capital moved from the country to the rest of the world as the sum of capital invested abroad by domestic investors (type 1 outflow) and capital withdrawal by foreign investors (type 2 outflow).

In this section, we investigate the forces that influence the four different types of flows in short-term capital in a simultaneous equation model. From these analyses, we will see which domestic condition promotes the capital investment abroad by domestic investors and which domestic condition leads to withdrawal of invested capital to other countries by foreign investors. This is an important issue because securing international financial resources means not only inducing new capital but also keeping previously-invested capital.

In integrated international financial markets, the forces that drive type 1 and 2 inflows will be similar to each other since the investment decisions made by domestic and foreign investors will be homogenous under one financial market system. However, the forces that drive type 1 and 2 outflows can be different due to the level of wealth. Type 1 outflow is more likely to be influenced by domestic investors' capabilities and type 2 outflow more by domestic financial market conditions. For example, if domestic financial markets are not profitable, there will be synchronized movement of type 1 and 2 outflows. However, if a country has no capability to invest abroad, there will be little type 1 outflow. If domestic financial markets are profitable, there will be little type 2 outflow, but there can still be type 1 outflow due to the capital allocation process by the domestic investors in the wealthy countries. This is why the interpretation of the outflow equations was difficult, especially in the financial items that developing countries were actively involved. A large proportion of capital outflows from the developing countries are not capital investment by the developing countries (type 1 outflow), but capital withdrawal by the high income countries (type 2 outflow).

Short-term capital should include short-term portfolio capital, short-term FDI capital, short-term bank capital, and short-term other-sector capital. However, data for the four types of capital flows are available only for short-term bank capital and short-term other-sector capital. In our analyses, type 1 inflows of short-term bank capital and short-term other-sector capital are defined as STKI1, type 2 inflows of the two financial items are defined as STKI2, type 1 outflows of the two financial items are defined as STKO1, and type 2 outflows of the two financial items are defined as STKO2. For convenience, short-term capital in this study means short-term bank capital and short-term other-sector capital only.

Descriptive Statistics

Out of global total capital flows in 1980–1990, short-term capital transactions accounted for 40.17 per cent, as shown in the right column of Table 19. The proportion of short-term capital flows to total capital flows has decreased in all income groups, especially in the high income countr-ies. The reason for this decrease is that portfolio investment has increased its proportion. Actual amounts of type 1 inflow and type 1 outflow increased by 190 per cent and

Table 19 Four types of short-term capital flows by level of income in 86 countries

Level of income	Year	Actual amount (millions of 1987 US dollars) (1)			
		STKI1 (a)	STKI2 (b)	STKO1 (c)	STKO2 (d)
Low income countries (19)	1980	1,196	152	1,008	677
	1981	950	826	342	646
	1982	2,337	814	492	421
	1983	2,224	427	481	154
	1984	2,220	595	1,207	401
	1985	2,204	237	5,551	586
	1986	2,543	666	1,628	1,305
	1987	3,526	195	2,745	1,121
	1988	1,113	1,099	1,712	2,036
	1989	2,419	781	1,835	1,046
	1990	1,911	438	3,685	1,493
	Sum	**22,643**	**6,230**	**20,685**	**9,886**
Lower-middle income countries (27)	1980	6,651	750	1,567	5,585
	1981	5,485	373	3,570	7,043
	1982	4,096	1,229	3,375	5,165
	1983	4,099	1,080	2,353	4,733
	1984	5,863	2,783	3,907	4,418
	1985	4,250	2,685	1,408	6,084
	1986	4,321	1,640	1,527	3,571
	1987	6,284	362	2,556	2,734
	1988	6,293	1,200	4,045	2,823
	1989	7,681	448	2,205	6,069
	1990	14,064	1,957	2,342	4,207
	Sum	**69,088**	**14,507**	**28,856**	**52,431**
Upper-middle income countries (17)	1980	14,714	73	14,515	1,930
	1981	18,749	183	12,371	975
	1982	6,909	4,823	9,799	5,364
	1983	6,705	1,913	5,812	11,197
	1984	4,515	1,212	11,747	4,611
	1985	3,321	8,745	9,551	5,062
	1986	6,290	7,236	10,071	3,369
	1987	7,854	13,379	10,861	2,484
	1988	6,641	5,772	11,591	3,158
	1989	7,972	9,147	7,591	4,314
	1990	16,217	2,550	11,335	2,329
	Sum	**99,885**	**55,032**	**115,243**	**44,792**

Level of income	Year	Actual amount (millions of 1987 US dollars) (1)			
		STKI1 (a)	STKI2 (b)	STKO1 (c)	STKO2 (d)
High income countries (23)	1980	222,022	1,467	195,137	4,916
	1981	236,531	1,738	223,418	14,505
	1982	151,935	15,821	156,405	23,701
	1983	141,949	18,743	105,233	14,061
	1984	197,365	9,597	131,376	7,372
	1985	226,540	11,019	186,381	9,880
	1986	458,402	9,878	404,618	28,927
	1987	608,079	23,685	466,666	7,499
	1988	441,540	27,292	370,433	23,504
	1989	481,035	33,054	445,836	16,170
	1990	426,154	34,713	339,994	18,531
	Sum	**3,591,550**	**187,006**	**3,025,496**	**169,067**
All countries (86)	1980	244,583	2,441	212,227	13,108
	1981	261,716	3,119	239,701	23,169
	1982	165,277	22,687	170,071	34,651
	1983	154,978	22,163	113,879	30,145
	1984	209,962	14,188	148,237	16,803
	1985	236,314	22,686	202,891	21,613
	1986	471,556	19,420	417,844	37,171
	1987	625,743	37,620	482,829	13,837
	1988	455,587	35,363	387,780	31,521
	1989	499,106	43,430	457,467	27,599
	1990	458,346	39,658	357,355	26,558
	Sum	**3,783,167**	**262,775**	**3,190,280**	**276,177**

Level of income	Year	Share of world total (%) (2)				Proportion of total flows (%) (3)		
		STKI1	STKI2	STKO1	STKO2	Inflow(a)	Outflow(b)	Gross(c)
Low income countries (19)	1980	0.49	6.22	0.47	5.16	35.16	44.73	39.91
	1981	0.36	26.48	0.14	2.79	29.67	38.75	32.38
	1982	1.41	3.59	0.29	1.21	37.88	33.19	36.72
	1983	1.44	1.93	0.42	0.51	32.97	27.36	31.71
	1984	1.06	4.20	0.81	2.39	32.43	39.85	34.78
	1985	0.93	1.05	2.74	2.71	22.48	64.62	42.14
	1986	0.54	3.43	0.39	3.51	31.05	49.86	37.87
	1987	0.56	0.52	0.57	8.10	31.32	59.21	41.21
	1988	0.24	3.11	0.44	6.46	21.32	52.50	34.03
	1989	0.48	1.80	0.40	3.79	24.45	43.61	30.87
	1990	0.42	1.11	1.03	5.62	16.89	60.29	33.46
	Sum	**0.60**	**2.37**	**0.65**	**3.58**	**27.42**	**51.24**	**36.03**

Level of income	Year	Share of world total (%) (2)				Proportion of total flows (%) (3)		
		STKI1	STKI2	STKO1	STKO2	Inflow(a)	Outflow(b)	Gross(c)
Lower-middle income countries (27)	1980	2.72	30.72	0.74	42.61	28.03	47.36	35.07
	1981	2.0:	11.95	1.49	30.40	16.47	52.46	29.52
	1982	2.48	5.42	1.98	14.91	17.84	45.68	28.56
	1983	2.65	4.87	2.07	15.70	20.11	36.75	27.24
	1984	2.79	19.62	2.64	26.29	28.04	35.74	31.35
	1985	1.80	11.83	0.69	28.15	23.55	34.22	28.0:
	1986	0.92	8.45	0.37	9.61	23.93	26.16	24.91
	1987	1.00	0.96	0.53	19.76	26.08	25.86	25.98
	1988	1.38	3.39	1.04	8.95	25.05	29.74	27.09
	1989	1.54	1.03	0.48	21.99	20.71	34.12	25.83
	1990	3.07	4.94	0.66	15.84	35.82	27.39	32.89
	Sum	**1.83**	**5.52**	**0.90**	**18.98**	**24.43**	**35.39**	**28.83**
Upper-middle income countries (17)	1980	6.02	2.98	6.84	14.72	32.75	31.09	31.85
	1981	7.16	5.86	5.16	4.21	27.11	23.03	25.26
	1982	4.18	21.26	5.76	15.48	18.65	31.07	24.08
	1983	4.33	8.63	5.10	37.14	17.13	42.88	28.48
	1984	2.15	8.54	7.92	27.45	11.33	37.32	23.40
	1985	1.41	38.55	4.71	23.42	26.14	28.07	27.16
	1986	1.33	37.26	2.41	9.06	36.77	25.72	30.28
	1987	1.26	35.56	2.25	17.95	43.49	26.01	34.53
	1988	1.46	16.32	2.99	10.02	27.56	32.55	30.06
	1989	1.60	21.06	1.66	15.63	41.72	31.76	36.96
	1990	3.54	6.43	3.17	8.77	27.57	33.08	29.65
	Sum	**2.64**	**20.94**	**3.61**	**16.22**	**27.44**	**30.61**	**28.96**
High income countries (23)	1980	90.78	60.08	91.95	37.50	58.69	55.82	57.30
	1981	90.38	55.72	93.21	62.60	53.92	53.57	53.74
	1982	91.93	69.74	91.96	68.40	44.52	44.06	44.28
	1983	91.59	84.57	92.41	46.64	44.83	34.28	39.64
	1984	94.00	67.64	88.63	43.88	43.45	31.57	37.75
	1985	95.86	48.57	91.86	45.72	38.82	35.52	37.25
	1986	97.21	50.86	96.83	77.82	48.96	45.68	47.33
	1987	97.18	62.96	96.65	54.20	52.07	45.60	49.09
	1988	96.92	77.18	95.53	74.57	39.90	35.95	37.99
	1989	96.38	76.11	97.46	58.59	37.30	36.66	36.00
	1990	92.98	87.53	95.14	69.77	33.56	28.94	31.37
	Sum	**94.94**	**71.17**	**94.83**	**61.22**	**43.22**	**39.27**	**41.32**
All countries (86)	1980	100.00	100.00	100.00	100.00	54.15	52.39	53.29
	1981	100.00	100.00	100.00	100.00	47.87	50.08	48.94
	1982	100.00	100.00	100.00	100.00	39.33	42.73	41.04
	1983	100.00	100.00	100.00	100.00	40.03	35.19	37.71
	1984	100.00	100.00	100.00	100.00	39.58	32.32	36.14
	1985	100.00	100.00	100.00	100.00	37.08	35.30	36.23
	1986	100.00	100.00	100.00	100.00	47.74	44.32	46.03
	1987	100.00	100.00	100.00	100.00	51.05	44.42	47.98

Level of income	Year	Share of world total (%) (2)				Proportion of total flows (%) (3)		
		STKI1	STKI2	STKO1	STKO2	Inflow(a)	Outflow(b)	Gross(c)
	1988	100.00	100.00	100.00	100.00	38.95	35.79	37.43
	1989	100.00	100.00	100.00	100.00	36.87	36.51	36.70
	1990	100.00	100.00	100.00	100.00	33.21	29.25	31.36
	Sum	**100.00**	**100.00**	**100.00**	**100.00**	**41.48**	**38.74**	**40.17**

Source: Balance of Payments Statistics Yearbook (IMF).

Notes

1 Short-term bank capital and short-term other-sector capital are included.
(a) Short-term capital type 1 inflow: short-term capital invested from world to home by foreign investors.
(b) Short-term capital type 2 inflow: short-term capital withdrawn from world to home by domestic investors.
(c) Short-term capital type 1 outflow: short-term capital invested from home to world by domestic investors.
(d) Short-term capital type 2 outflow: short-term capital withdrawn from home to world by foreign investors.

2 Share of world total short-term capital flows.

3 Proportion of short-term capital flows from total capital flows.
(a) (STKI1 + STKI2) /TOTI *100, where TOTI = total capital inflow.
(b) (STKO1 + STKO2) /TOTO *100, where TOTO = total capital outflow.
(c) (STKI1 + STKI2 + STKO1+STKO2) /TOTG *100, where TOTG = total gross capital flow.

170 per cent respectively, but actual amounts of type 2 inflow and type 2 outflow increased by 1625 per cent and 203 per cent respectively from 1980 to 1990 (see the first column of all countries in Table 19).

The rapid increase of type 2 inflow is one of the important evidences of the high level of capital mobility. It tells us that investors have greater ability to reallocate their previously invested capital than to invest new capital. Why is this the case?

The four types of short-term capital flows in each income group are plotted in Figure 14. For purpose of readability, different sales are used. The high income countries' shares of the world total type 1 inflows were 94.93 per cent and those of type 1 outflows were 94.83 per cent in 1980–1990.[32] This tells us that about 95 per cent of the world's total short-term capital was invested in the high income countries and invested by the high income countries. Why are type 1 short-term capital inflows and outflows so concentrated in the high income countries?

Figure 14 shows that the short-term capital flows fluctuate more than the capital flows we have examined thus far. Type 1 inflows to the lower middle and upper middle income countries had a u-shape during 1980–1990, while those of the low income countries displayed no distinctive pattern. Type 1 inflows to the high income countries decreased until 1985 and increased rapidly after 1986 with a peak in 1987.

On the other hand, type 1 outflows were relatively stable in the lower middle and upper middle income countries, while those of low income countries had no distinctive pattern. Type 1 outflows from the high income countries are similar to their type 1 inflows. Type 2 inflows to the low and lower middle income countries have not increased over time, but type 2 inflows to the upper middle and high income countries increased over time with fluctuating patterns. Type 2 outflows in all four income groups increased over time with fluctuating patterns.

Econometric Analyses

In the four types of short-term capital flows simultaneous equation model, we measure the rate of return by the purchasing power parity ratio (PPPR), since the concern is with short-term capital which considers the price level and exchange rate. Since we have four equations in this model, we attempt to estimate the untested hypotheses in the two equation model by allocating the variables in different equations. We include the tax rate differential between domestic tax rate on foreign investors' interest earnings and the average of countries' income group tax rates on foreign investors' interest earnings (TFINTD) in the type 1 inflow and type 2 outflow equations since these two types of flows are dependent on foreign investors' decisions. In the type 2 inflow and type 1 outflow equations, we use the differential between domestic tax rate on domestic investors' interest earnings and the world average of tax rate on foreign investors' interest earning (TDINTD) since type 2 inflow and type 1 outflow are determined by domestic investors. In each equation, the system variables excluding its own system variable are included as exogenous variables in a simultaneous system.

Let us begin with Type 1 outflow, as it is the starting point for investment. In the type 1 outflow equation in Table 20, national wealth (GNYPC), current account balance (CAB), and financial instrument innovation (CD) are all positive and significant. A 1.5 per cent increase in gross national income per capita provides an 0.51 per cent increase in the short-term capital investment abroad. A surplus of one billion dollar in current account balance increases short-term capital investment abroad by 1.01 million dollars. Countries with

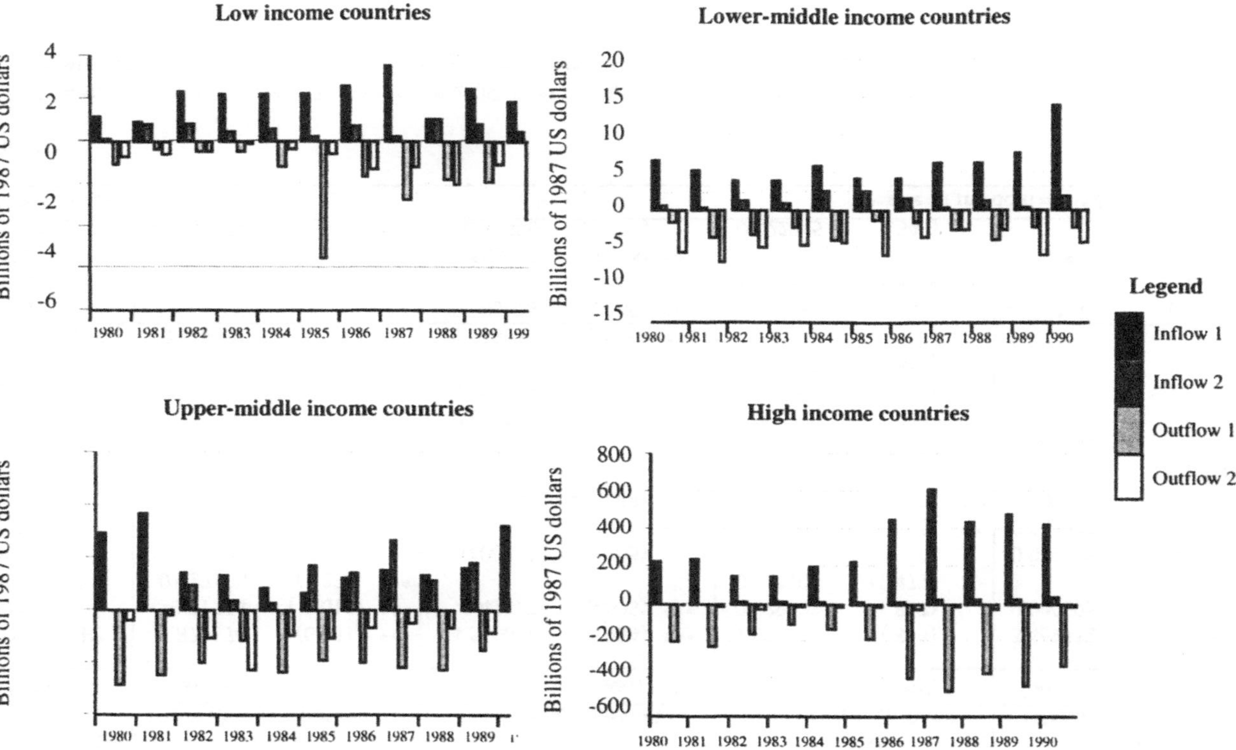

Figure 14 Four types of short-term capital flows by level of income in 1980–1990
Source: Balance of Payments Statistics (IMF)

Note: Positive values are inflows and negative values are outflows

Table 20 Four types of short-term capital flows with 3SLS simultaneous estimation

Equation	Type 1 inflow		Type 2 inflow		Type 1 outflow		Type 2 outflow	
DV	STKI1 (log of type 1 inflow)		STKI2 (log of type 2 inflow)		STKO1 (log of type 1 outflow)		STKO2 (log of type 2 outflow)	
Ind. var.	Par est	(t-stat)	Par est	(t-stat)	Par est	(t-stat)	Par est	(t-stat)
INTERCEPT	3.820176	(6.031) ***	4.566011	(6.954) ***	1.691478	(.819)	3.469412	(1.491)
PPPR	-0.31764	(-3.018) ***	-0.42317	-(3.673) ***	0.089503	(.867)	-0.090695	(-.731)
RISKD	0.027106	(3.332) ***			0.011706	(1.477)		
RISKDC			0.00333	(.205)			-0.069035	(-4.197) ***
GNYPC					0.512782	(2.06) **	0.165827	(.568)
CAB	-0.003528	(-.780)	-0.008	-(1.648) *	0.013129	(3.113) ***	0.009434	(1.839) *
EXCHCONT	-0.374721	(-2.157) **					-0.279166	(-1.420)
TFINTD	-0.01022	(-1.229)					0.002241	(.237)
TDINTD			0.011014	(1.513)	0.001792	(.274)		
TREATY			7.97E-05	(.94)	2.55E-05	(.32)		
CD	0.46625	(2.102) **			0.40759	(1.845) *		
TELECOMM	0.118301	(1.722) *	0.218942	(2.975) ***				
STKI1			0.205628	(2.239) **	0.057	(.801)	-0.220645	(-2.313) **
STKI2	0.310501	(3.436) ***			-0.188456	(-2.227) **	0.145364	(1.532)
STKO1	0.109286	(1.51)	-0.505463	(-5.805) ***			-0.206509	(-2.263) **
STKO2	-0.21434	(-3.049) ***	0.10526	(1.391)	0.022045	(.343)		
System weighted R-sq: 7028			N = 946			Degree of freedom = 3362		

Notes

1 *** = significant at 1% level; ** = significant at 5% level; * = significant at 10% level.

2 See Appendix D–9 for country and year dummy coefficients.

CDs in their financial markets have 1.5 million dollars more short-term capital investment abroad compared to countries without CDs. All of these three variables are investment capacity-related variables.

The purchasing power parity ratio is positive, meaning that weak local currency value to purchase the US dollar provides more type 1 outflow. This is an expected sign in the short-term capital outflow equation, but the variable is not significant at the 10 per cent level. Tax rate differential and international tax treaties are positive as we hypothesized, but they are not significant. The positive sign of risk differential is an important result even though it is not significant. It suggests that type 1 outflow is not driven by the negative risk differentials. Overall, type 1 outflow is influenced by capital investment capacity.

In the system variables, type 2 inflow (STKI2) is negatively and significantly related to type 1 outflow. This is the counteractive movement, implying that type 2 inflow discourages type 1 outflow: an one per cent increase in type 2 inflow reduces type 1 outflow by 0.19 per cent. This suggests that withdrawal of capital to the home country is evidence that domestic financial markets perform better than foreign financial markets. Thus, new investment abroad by domestic investors decreases.

On the other hand, type 2 outflow are positively related to type 1 outflow although it is not significant. This is the synchronized outflow movement, implying that type 2 outflow encourages type 1 inflow. Type 1 inflow is positively but insignificantly related to type 1 outflow. This is the synchronized intra-item movement, which implies that type 1 inflow and type 1 outflow positively influence each other. Even though type 2 outflow and type 1 inflow are not significant at the 10 per cent level, the positive signs of these variables reveal that there is no counteractive movement between type 1 inflow and type 1 outflow as we found in the previous section. That is, countries that export short-term capital (type 1 outflow) also import the short-term capital (type 1 inflow) at the same time. As seen in the descriptive statistics, 95 per cent of the world total type 1 short-term capital inflows are contributed by the high income countries which are well equipped with globalization institutions and technologies. That is why countries with greater type 1 outflows provide greater type 1 inflow at the same time. This is captured in the country dummy coefficients in Appendix D–9.

In the type 1 inflow equations, the purchasing power parity is negative and significant. It tells us that a one unit increase in the purchasing power parity ratio reduces type 1 short-term capital inflows by 1.37 million dollars.

Risk differential is positive and significant while exchange control is negative and significant as expected. A one unit increase in risk differential induce 1.03 million dollars of type 1 short-term inflows. We did not test the exchange control policy variable in the inflow equations of the previous models. We now confirm that exchange control effectively disturbs short-term capital inflow: countries that enforce exchange control policies attract 1.45 million dollars less than countries that do not control foreign exchange.

Globalization factors such as financial instrument innovation and telecommunication network development are all positive and significant. Countries with CDs in the financial markets induce 1.59 million dollars of type 1 short-term capital more than countries without CDs. A one unit increase in telecommunication network development induces 1.13 million dollars of type 1 short-term capital. However, tax rate differential is not significant though it is negatively related as we hypothesized.

Type 2 short-term capital inflow is positive and significant in the type 1 inflow equation, showing synchronized movement. A one per cent increase in capital withdrawal by domestic investors (type 2 inflow) induces an 0.31 per cent increase in new investment by foreign investors (type 1 inflow). It implies that withdrawal of capital to the home country is evidence that domestic financial markets perform better than foreign financial markets. Thus, new investment in the home country by foreign investors also increases.

On the other hand, type 2 outflow is negative and significant, which is the counteractive movement. It states that a 1 per cent increase in withdrawal by foreign investors (type 2 outflow) reduces new investment by foreign investors (type 1 inflow) by 0.21 per cent. This implies that short-term capital withdrawal from the home country to other countries by foreign investors is evidence that domestic financial markets perform worse than foreign financial markets. Thus new investment in the home country by foreign investors decreases.

Although type 1 outflow is not significant, the positive sign of this variable is an important finding. We showed that type 2 outflow is negative in the previous paragraph; however, type 1 outflow is positive in the same equation. In the general flow model in the previous section, we treated these type 1 outflow and type 2 outflow together, and we found that bank capital inflow is negatively related with other-sector capital outflow. Recall that we temporarily postponed the explanation on why bank capital inflow was negatively related to other-sector capital outflow in section *In-Outflows of Four Financial Items in One System*. We now show that the effects of type 1 outflow and type 2 outflow on type 1 inflow are opposite. The fact that the coefficient of type 2 outflow is higher and more significant than type 1 outflow in the type 1 inflow equation suggests that the effect of type 2 outflow is more influential on type

1 inflow. That is why we had a negative sign of the other-sector capital outflow variable in the bank capital inflow equation in that section.

We thus far have found that initial short-term capital outflows (type 1 outflow) are driven by countries with investment capacities. These type 1 outflows are transferred as initial short-term capital inflows (type 1 inflow) to countries with higher yield rates, higher creditworthiness, more financial instrument options, better telecommunication networks, and lesser exchange control. Type 1 outflow can be reallocated by domestic investors' withdrawal (type 2 inflow) and type 1 inflow can be reallocated by foreign investors' withdrawal (type 2 outflow). Let us first look at the forces that produce type 2 outflow.

In the type 2 outflow equation, change in risk differential is negative and significant while current account balance is positive and significant. When the home country's risk differential decreases by one per cent, 0.07 per cent of previously-invested capital will be withdrawn to other countries. Since a negative change in risk differential is determined by either bad domestic financial market condition or good foreign financial market conditions, change in risk differential can be relatively large in the real world.

When a country increases current account surplus by one billion dollars, the country's previously-invested short-term capital will be drawn down by one million dollars. This is attributable to the repayment of short-term capital loans. As current account conditions improves, a country has the capability to repay previously borrowed short-term capital.

In the type 2 outflow equation, purchasing power parity is negative but not significant. Since it is a short-term capital movement, local currency's purchasing power parity to buy the dollar can be still strong in countries that provide type 2 outflows, even though the effect is not significant. National wealth is positive but not significant. This variable is significant in the type 1 outflow equation. The significance level difference between the type 1 and 2 outflow equations suggests that type 1 outflows are clearly dominated by the high income countries while type 2 outflows are not. Although exchange control is negative and tax rate differential is positive as we hypothesized, they are not significant at the 10 per cent level.

The system variables, STKI1 and STKO1 in the type 2 outflow equation are all negative and significant. That is, there is a counteractive movement between type 1 inflow and type 2 outflow and between type 1 outflow and type 2 outflow. We saw this counteractive movement between type 1 inflow and type 2 outflow in the type 1 inflow equation. It appears again in the type 2 outflow equation: a one per cent increase in type 1 inflow reduces type 2 outflow by 0.22 per cent. When domestic financial markets are so attractive that type 1 inflows are induced, withdrawal by foreign investors to other countries decreases.

The counteractive movement between type 1 outflow and type 2 outflow is an unexpected result. However, type 1 outflow is mainly determined by the capital investment capacity variables and type 2 outflow by the risk differential variable. Thus, it tells us that countries with capital investment capacities are not so poorly creditworthy as to yield type 2 outflows. This is confirmed in the country dummy coefficients in Appendix D–9. Most countries with negative coefficients in the type 2 outflow equation have positive coefficients in the type 1 outflow equation. Most countries with positive coefficients in the type 2 outflow equation do have negative coefficients in the type 1 outflow equation.

The counteractive movements between type 1 inflow and type 2 outflow and between type 1 outflow and type 2 outflow reveal that the synchronized intra-item movement (positive relationships between the in-outflows equations for particular financial items) explained in the previous sections is not influenced by the relationships between type 1 inflow and type 2 outflow. Rather this synchronized intra-item movement is the result of the synchronized movements between type 1 inflow and type 1 outflow that we found in the type 1 inflow and type 1 outflow equations.

In the type 2 inflow equation, we find the forces that lead to withdrawal of previously invested capital to the home country by domestic investors. Purchasing power parity ratio and current account balance are negative and significant. When a domestic currency's purchasing power parity increases by one per cent, domestic investors withdraw 0.42 per cent of their capital to the home country. When a country has a one billion dollar of current account deficit, domestic investors withdraw one million dollars of their capital to the home country.

Telecommunication network development is positive and significant in the type 2 inflow equation. This implies that telecommunication networks provide the information to compare domestic and foreign financial markets, and thus domestic investors have greater ability to reallocate their previously-invested capital. Change in risk differential in domestic financial markets is positively related to type 2 inflow though it is not significant. Tax rate differential and international tax treaties are not significant. Thus, the major forces that induce type 2 inflow are domestic purchasing power parity and current account balance conditions.

In the type 2 inflow equation, we find synchronized movement between type 1 inflow and type 2 inflow, as seen in the type 1 inflow equation. A one per cent increase in type 1 inflow yields an 0.21 per cent increase in type 2 inflow. We also find a counteractive movement between type 1 outflow and type 2 inflow, as seen in the type 1 outflow equation. A 1 per cent increase in type 1 outflow yields an 0.51 per cent decrease in type 2 inflow. These two system variables reveal that type 2 inflow is very sensitive to domestic financial market conditions. If domestic financial markets are attractive as type 1 inflow is induced, then type 2 inflow becomes positive. If domestic financial markets are not attractive as type 1 outflow is induced, type 2 inflow becomes negative. In the different directional flows of short-term capital, all relationships are counteractive movements, implying more agglomeration effects in short-term capital flows compared to longer-term capital flows in the previous section.

Summary and Findings

We raised four questions when the descriptive statistics of short-term flows were discussed: (1) Why are 95 per cent of the type 1 inflows to the high income countries? (2) Why are 95 per cent of the type 2 inflows contributed by the high income countries? (3) Why are type 2 inflows increasingly induced by the upper-middle and high income countries? and (4) Why are type 2 outflows not concentrated in the high income countries? The answers are summarized in Figure 15, which shows the forces that shape the four types of short-term capital flows.

The factors that induce type 1 inflow are higher yield rates, higher creditworthiness, more financial instrument options, better telecommunication networks, and removal of exchange controls. Except for higher yield rate,[33] all of the above factors are characteristic of the high income countries. This is why the high income countries induce most of the type 1 inflows.

The factors that influence type 1 outflows are national wealth, current account surplus, and developed financial markets, indicated by financial instrument innovation. Thus, type 1 outflows are driven by capital investment capacity factors rather than risk-avoiding factors. That is why the high income countries provide most of the type 1 outflows.

The factors that induce type 2 inflows are rate of return, current account deficit, and telecommunication network development. Type 2 inflow is a part of previously-invested capital (type 1 outflow), which is mostly contributed by the high income countries. However, the reason why type 2 inflows are increasingly induced by the upper middle income and high income countries in recent years can be found in telecommunication development.

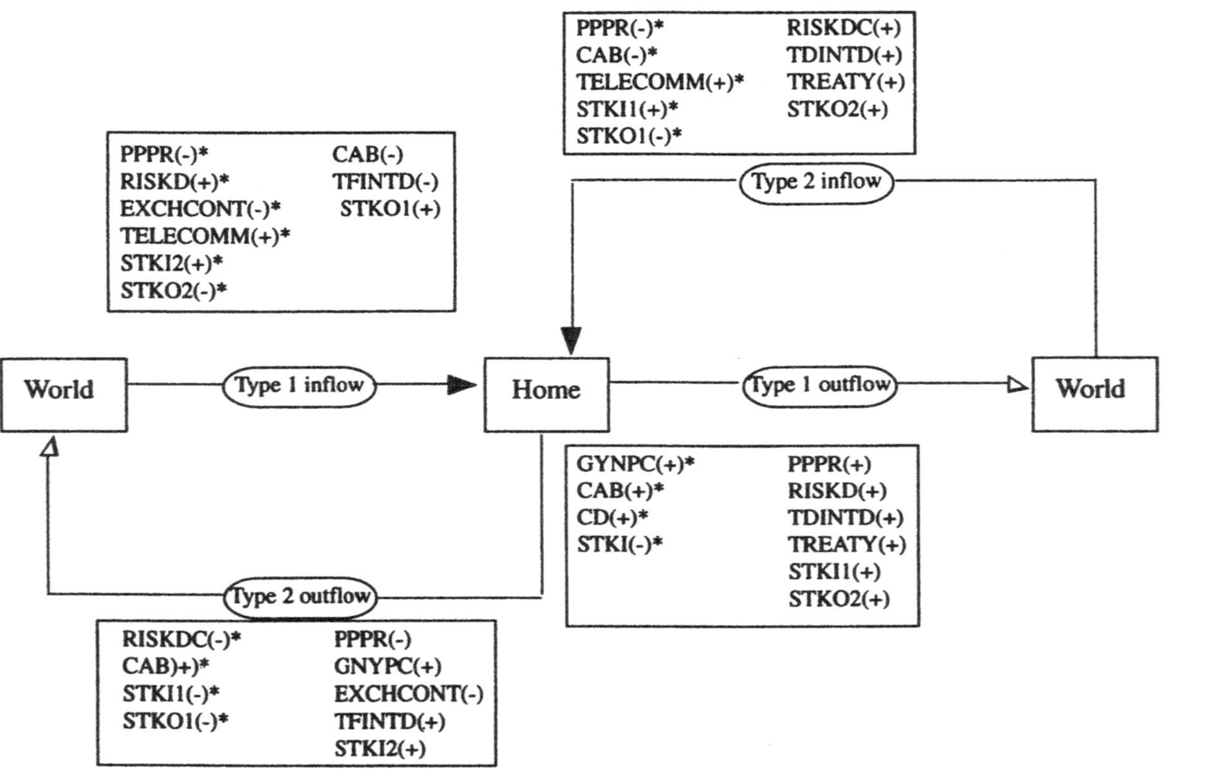

Figure 15 Determinants of four types of short-term capital flows

Note: variables in the left column with * are statistically significant

Telecommunication network development in the upper middle and high income countries in recent years extends the ability to reallocate previously-invested capital with less transportation and information collection costs.

The factors that yield type 2 outflows are the change in risk differentials and current account balance surplus. That is, type 2 outflows are driven by risk avoiding factors as well as by repayment capacity factors. These factors apply to all income groups, not just to the high income countries. That is why type 2 outflows are not concentrated in the high income countries, as was seen for the type 1 and 2 inflows and type 1 outflow.

These analyses also provide empirical evidence in support of the three major theories, information about interactions among four types of flows, and insights into the impacts of globalization on capital flows.

Rate of return, which is measured by purchasing power parity, is significant in both type 1 and type 2 inflows. However, it is not significant for type 1 and type 2 outflows. We thus confirm that flow theory explains inflow factors rather than outflow factors.

Current account balance is significant in the type 2 inflow, the type 1 outflow, and the 2 outflow equations. Exchange control policy is effective in controlling short-term capital type 1 inflow. We thus confirm that the monetary approach to the balance of payments helps explain both short-term capital inflows and outflows.

Risk differential is critical in both type 1 inflow and type 2 outflow, but is not significant in type 1 outflow and type 2 inflow. National wealth is significant in type 1 outflow but it is not significant in type 2 outflow. Thus, portfolio theory fits overall short-term capital inflows and outflows.

With respect to flow, portfolio and monetary factors, we thus conclude that type 1 inflows are explained by all of three factors, type 1 outflow by portfolio and monetary factors, type 2 inflow by flow and monetary factors, and type 2 outflow by portfolio and monetary factors. These results suggest that short-term capital flows are jointly determined by rate of return, wealth, and the current and current account condition, thus confirming that the portfolio balance model performs best in explaining short-term capital flows.

The next important finding is that there are both synchronized and counteractive movements among the four type of capital flows. Type 1 inflow and type 2 inflow are synchronized. That is, if a country induces type 2 inflows, then it also induces more type 1 inflows and vice versa. Type 2 inflow and type 1 outflow are counteractive. That is, if a country induces more type 1 outflows, it reduces type 2 inflows and vice versa. From the synchronized movement between type 1 inflow and type 2 inflow and the counteractive movement between type 1 outflow and type 2 inflow, we conclude that the common denominator, type 1 inflow, is a good measure of domestic financial market conditions.

Type 2 outflow and type 1 inflow are counteractive as well. That is, if a country induces type 1 inflows, it reduces type 2 outflow and vice versa. However, we do not find any synchronized movement between type 1 outflow and type 2 outflow; rather their relationship is counteractive. This counteractive movement is explained by the fact that type 1 outflow is determined by the capital investment capacity variables while type 2 outflow is influenced by the risk-avoiding factors. Thus, countries with capital investment capacities are not so uncreditworthy as to yield type 2 outflows. This is confirmed by the country dummy coefficients in Appendix D–9.

Type 1 inflow and type 1 outflow are synchronized. That is, if a country induces type 1 inflows, it increases type 1 outflows and vice versa. Since the concern is the relationship between inflow and outflow, we might expect a counteractive movement. However, this result is consistent with the previous models, and is also confirmed by the country dummy coefficients in Appendix D–9.

The most important forces that contribute to these interactions are globalization institutions and technologies. Telecommunication network development provides more information with less costs, which extends the ability to reallocate previously-invested capital. That is why there are the synchronized movements between same-directional flows and counteractive movements between different-directional flows. Capital moves in the same direction in globalized financial markets. This implies that the efficiency of global short-term capital allocation has been improved by globalization.

In the general picture of four types of short-term capital flows in Figure 15, type 1 outflows are provided by investment-capable countries in order to be transferred as type 1 inflow to the countries that provide higher rates of return, more financial options, and less-regulated environments. Type 1 inflows are converted into type 2 outflows if recipient countries' creditworthiness decreases and type 1 outflows are converted into type 2 inflows if the home country increases its own rate of return. The conversion process is facilitated by improvements in information flows between the home country and invested countries. This implies that an agglomeration effect in global short-term capital has been accelerated by globalization institutions and technologies.

In the upper level boxes of Figure 15, type 1 and type 2 inflows are induced by similar factors, all of which favour the high income countries. These factors produce cumulative effects of short-term capital inflows on the high income countries in the presence of globalized financial markets. In the lower level boxes, type 1 outflows are driven by investment capacity and type 2 outflows by risk avoiding factor. Since the developing countries are less able to attract type 1 inflows, and type 1 inflows are easily converted to type 2 outflows as a result of globalized financial markets, the developing countries are doubly disadvantage in any attempt to keep external financial resources. We conclude that globalization of financial markets improves the efficiency of short-term capital allocation, and accelerates the agglomeration in short-term capital flows. Globalization of financial markets, thus, has resulted and will result in wider external financial resource gaps between the capital-rich countries and capital-poor countries for the foreseeable future.

Notes

1 In the 11 year period, the global capital transactions were approximately $18.940 trillion (1987 US dollar base) for 121 countries. Among them the 35 missing countries' capital transactions were $ 238.210 billion. Thus the proportion of missing countries' international capital transaction was 1.26 per cent. Additional numbers are provided in Appendix C–1.

2 The term non-high income country is also interchangeably used with developing country in this study.

3 As defined in the model specification, other-capital is a miscellaneous capital category including the international capital transactions of non-bank financial institutions, non-portfolio sector investment institutions, trade related credits and so on.

4 To determine the order of importance, we calculated the standard estimate by dividing partial regression coefficients by the ratio of the sample standard deviation of the independent variable to the sample standard deviation of independent variable.

5 In fact this is current account imbalance. For convenience, we follow the term (current account balance) as it was used by previous studies.

6 As specified in the previous chapter, it is the average of absolute value in ABIGOVTD (government bond yield rate differential), ABIDEPD (bank deposit rate interest rate differential), and ABIMKTD (market interest rate differential).

7 We have some research notes regarding the selection of exogenous variables. When CD was estimated in the FDI gross flow model, it was positive but not significant. When INDSTP was estimated in non-FDI gross flow models, all parameters were statistically significant with negative signs. The service sector products as a percentage of GDP were also used in the non-FDI capital gross flows as an experiment. The parameters of service sector product in all three models were positively significant. But we decided not to use this variable since it is seriously correlated with the income, telecommunication development, and treaty variables. We also attempted to measure the financial sector activities by financial sector employment as a percentage of total employment, and number of companies listed in the domestic financial markets. These variable also have the similar problem with multi-collinearity since any measurement of financial development is almost perfectly correlated with the national wealth.

8 A 1 per cent change in gross national income per capita yields a 0.47 per cent increases in international capital outflows when other things are held constant. Hereafter, in interpretation of regression coefficients, we do not repeat the assumption that all other values for the remaining explanatory variables are held constant.
9 Since CAB is defined as billions of dollars, one billion dollars of current account deficit induce approximately one million dollars of capital inflow (decomposed log value of 0.005267 = 1.0052 since the dependent variables are log of million dollars) and the one billion dollars of current account balance surplus also induce approximately one million (1.011) dollars of capital outflow.
10 Countries that have CDs in their financial markets have capital inflows that average 1.63 million dollars more than for countries without CDs.
11 Since TREATY is defined by interactions between market openness and international tax treaties, and TELECOMM is measured by the telecommunication network innovation level and size of circuit ends, we do not attempt to interpret their coefficients.
12 Since both are log values, a 1 per cent change in total capital outflow yields an 0.151 per cent change in total capital inflow, while a 1 per cent change in total capital inflow yields an 0.105 per cent change in capital outflow.
13 A one billion dollar surplus in current account balance yields 1.05 million dollar portfolio outflows.
14 Countries that have CDs in their financial markets receives 2.1 million dollar more portfolio when compared with country without CDs.
15 Countries with exchange control policy provide 1.4 million dollar less bank capital outflow when compared to countries without exchange control policy.
16 A one billion dollar surplus in current account balance create 1.01 million dollars for bank capital outflow.
17 Countries with CDs induce 1.94 million dollars more bank capital inflows when compared to countries without CDs.
18 A one per cent increase in bank capital outflow yields a 0.24 per cent increase in bank capital inflow.
19 When gross national income per capita increases by 1 per cent, other-sector capital outflow increases by 0.63 per cent.
20 When a country has one billion dollars of current account balance surplus, the country provides approximately one million dollars of other-sector capital outflow.
21 If a country provides CDs in its domestic financial markets, the country induces 1.78 million dollars more other-sector capital inflows compared to the countries without CDs.
22 If a country has one billion dollars of current account surplus, the country decreases approximately one million dollars of other-sector capital inflows.
23 When all financial items' in-outflows are included in one simultaneous model, the bank capital outflow equation in Table 18 reveals that portfolio inflow is negatively related with bank capital outflow. Thus our speculation that non-portfolio sector investment institutions' capital inflow may be negatively associated with non-bank financial institutions' capital outflow is found to be adequate.
24 When all financial items' in-outflows are included in one simultaneous model, the portfolio inflow equation in Table 18 reveals that bank capital outflow is positively related with portfolio inflow. In the bank capital inflow equation, portfolio outflow is also positively related to bank capital inflow. Thus both speculations are found to be correct.
25 If a country enforces exchange control, the country provides 1.2 million dollar less FDI outflow when compared to countries without exchange control.

26 A 1 per cent increase in gross national income per capita yields 0.63 per cent increase in FDI outflow.
27 A one billion dollar surplus in current account balance provides one million dollar increase in FDI outflow.
28 Note that IGOVTD and RISKDC are positive and not significant in the partial flow model.
29 Note that IMKTD is positive and not significant in the partial flow model.
30 Note that other-sector capital outflow is negatively but not significantly related with other sector capital inflow in the partial flow model.
31 Inflow equations of bank capital, other-sector capital, and FDI: Of course portfolio inflow variable itself is an endogenous variable in the portfolio inflow equation.
32 See 'sum' of high income countries in the second column of Table 19.
33 As purchasing power parity ratio is weighted based on each country's 1979 purchasing power parity, it is not a differential value between countries.

5 Overview

The principal purposes of this study were to investigate the causes of globalization of international financial markets and the consequences of globalization for international capital flows. By incorporating flow, portfolio, monetary and globalization factors into a single framework, the factors that accelerate globalization and the impacts of globalization on inflows and outflows of all types of private sector capital, including portfolio investment, bank capital, foreign direct investment, and other private sector capital have been clarified.

The major causes of globalization are market openness/international tax treaty relations, financial instrument innovation, and telecommunication network development. The determinants of each type of capital flow are different, and as a result of globalization, a pattern of both synchronized flows among same-directional capital movements and counteractive flows among opposite-directional movements has emerged. These synchronized and counteractive movements are evidence of the efficiency of international capital resource allocation and agglomeration of international capital in countries with globalization institutions and technologies. Thus, capital flows to and from developed countries increased rapidly, while capital flows to and from most developing countries maintained low and fluctuating levels. As a result, the external financial resource gap between developed and developing countries widened.

These major findings need to be discussed in conjunction with an evaluation of received theory, as do available policy options for countries needing external financial resources. Table 21 summarizes the principal findings with respect to the key variables suggested by flow, portfolio, and monetary theory and by analysts of globalization in the context of gross capital flows in four types of capital markets.

Whereas each financial item has its own set of influences and serves its own function in markets, such as allocating risk and balancing current account imbalances, it is evident that portfolio and monetary factors are reinforced by such globalization factors as market openness/international tax treaties, financial instrument innovation, and telecommunication network development.

No support is found for flow theory hypotheses.

Portfolio markets are the greatest beneficiaries of the globalization factors. The banking industry and other private sector financial institutions are not influenced by market openness/international tax treaties, but are primarily affected by financial instrument innovation and telecommunication network development. However, multinationals' global investment activities are effectively accelerated by market openness/international tax treaties along with telecommunication network development. Thus, overall, globalization of financial markets, is accelerated by the following globalization institutions and technologies: market openness and international tax treaties that lower national financial boundaries; financial instrument innovation that provides new financial options with lower investment costs; and telecommunication network development that delivers improved information, also with lower transaction costs.

Interest rate differentials did not contribute to global capital transactions in any of the financial items, contrary to the flow factor hypothesis. Among the portfolio factors, national wealth is the primary source of investment capacity for all financial items, and risk differential is one of the key factors with respect to other-sector capital and FDI gross flows and thus to the aggregate capital gross flows. With respect to monetary factors, a current account imbalance is one of the motives for transferring bank capital and FDI, thus affecting gross flows of aggregate total capital. Even though exchange control policy is effective in bank and other-sector capital transactions, it is not effective in overall capital transactions.

During the period 1980–1990 global capital transactions tripled. The high income countries contributed more than 90 per cent to global capital transactions, with portfolio investment flows being the items that increased most rapidly. These shifts cannot be explained by separate models incorporating only flow, portfolio and monetary theory hypotheses, but when such hypotheses are complemented by inclusion of the globalization factors, it becomes clear that it is the globalization institutions and technologies that have been developed by the high income countries in recent years that have facilitated this global capital mobility, especially in portfolio markets.

What are the consequences of this globalization for specific types of capital flows in specific capital markets? The factors that drive capital inflows are summarized in Table 22 and those that influence capital outflows in Table 23.

With respect to capital inflows, strong purchasing power parity induces FDI and short-term capital movements, but high interest rates do not attract inflows of portfolio investment, bank capital and other-sector capital, and

Table 21 Causes of globalization by financial market

Theories (factor)	Key propositions	Portfolio markets	Banking industries	Other secors	FDI (multinationals)	Overall Markets
Flow	Interest rate differential	weak	weak	no	no	no
Portfolio	Risk differential	weak	no	effective	effective	effective
Monetary	National wealth	effective	effective	effective	effective	effective
	Current account imbalance	no	effective	weak	effective	effective
	Removal of exchange control	no	effective	effective	no	weak
(Globalization)	Market openness and tax treaties	effective	weak	weak	effective	effective
	Financial instrument innovation	effective	effective	effective	n/a	effective
	Telecommunication development	effective	effective	effective	effective	effective

Table 22 Capital inflow factors by financial item

Theories (factor)	Key propositions	Portfolio capital	Bank capital	Other capital	FDI capital	Short-term capital		Total capital
						Type 1	Type 2	
Flow	High interest rate (strong PPP)	weak	weak	weak	(effective)	(effective)	(effective)	weak
Portfolio	Low risk	effective	effective	effective	effective	effective	weak	effective
Monetary	Current account deficit	weak	weak	effective	effective	weak	effective	effective
	Removal of exchange control	n/a	n/a	n/a	n/a	effective	n/a	n/a
	Low tax rate	effective	weak	weak	no	weak	weak	weak
(Globalization)	Market openness and tax treaties	weak	effective	effective	effective	n/a	weak	effective
	Financial instrument innovation	effective	effective	effective	n/a	effective	n/a	effective
	Telecommunication development	n/a	n/a	n/a	n/a	effective	effective	n/a

Notes

1 Effective = statistically significant with supportive sign.

2 Weak = statistically insignificant with supportive sign.

3 No = statistically insignificant with non-supportive sign.

4 N/a = not available or not tested.

thus overall capital. Thus, capital inflows are not explained well by flow theory. Rather, all types of capital inflows are effectively explained by portfolio theory. Low risk is an essential factor in all types of capital inflows, except type 2 short-term capital (capital withdrawal by domestic investors to the home country). Monetary theory explains a large part of capital inflows. Current account deficits demand foreign capital via other-sector capital and short-term capital, and thus overall capital. We did not test the effect of exchange control on capital inflows of the major financial items, but it is effective in inducing short-term capital inflows. Low tax rates do not attract foreign capital, except portfolio investment.

Globalization factors effectively enhance most types of capital inflows. Market openness and international tax treaties induce bank capital, other-sector capital and FDI and thus overall capital inflows. Financial instrument innovation is effective in inducing all types of foreign capital imports. Telecommunication network development was not tested for its effect on major financial items' inflows but it is effective in inducing short-term capital inflows. The results strongly support that globalization factors are the key forces that drive capital inflow for most financial items.

What are the implication for countries needing external financial resources? Since controlling interest rates or current account deficits are not practicable approaches to attract foreign capital, strategies to lower transaction costs should be considered. Transaction costs can be reduced by telecommunication network development, financial instrument innovation, lowering tax rates, and negotiating favoured treaty relations. An improved telecommunication technology lowers both information collection and transportation costs since telecommunication networks provide up-to-data information of financial markets as well as massive, instantaneous fund transfer. Financial instrument innovation lowers investment costs, offers various options to investors, and improves allocation of risk. Lowered tax rates and favoured treaty relations reduce regulation-related costs by easing tax burdens and safeguarding investment.

Each country may need different types of capital, based on its domestic financial market structure or industrial demands. The results indicate that countries needing portfolio investment should focus on tax rate policies and financial instruments. Countries needing bank capital should concentrate on international tax treaties and financial instruments. Countries needing FDI should permit more foreign ownership and provide security to foreign investors via international tax treaties. Countries needing short-term capital should remove exchange controls, and develop new financial instruments and work to advance their telecommunication networks.

Most of all, managing country risk is a key factor, because foreign investors now have greater ability to reallocate their capital in response to change in country risk as financial markets have globalized. Then the question is how to manage country risk. Country risk consists of two separate risks – political risk and economic risk. Political risk involves the will to honour one's obligations, whereas economic risk (often called 'transfer risk') depends on the capability to honour one's debts. They can be mutually influential. A country cannot adequately adjust all of its political and economic risk factors at one time. However, the developing countries should consider the following political and economic risk factors since these factors are of major concern in calculating country risk: political risk factors include the constitutional environment, quality of government, foreign policy, social conflict, bureaucratic corruption, and war or warlike conflicts; economic risk include inflation, currency parity policy, economic policies, use of foreign funds, tax policies, management of foreign debt, trade barriers, economic growth, labour relations, and membership in some larger economic grouping (Krayenbuehl, 1985).

The forces that drive capital outflows are similar to the capital inflow factors. As shown in Table 23, low interest rate is only effective in bank capital outflows. Overall capital outflows are not influenced by low interest rate. Thus, flow theory does not explain any capital outflow item except bank capital.

On the other hand, portfolio theory is effective in explaining most of the capital outflows. High risk is a key contributor to capital outflows of bank capital, other-sector capital and short-term capital, while national wealth is a major source of capital investment capacity for all financial items. Likewise, monetary theory explains a part of capital inflows: current account surplus is an important source of capital outflows for all financial items. However, exchange control policy does not effectively control capital outflows, except for bank capital and FDI. Neither do high tax rates induce capital outflows. But when we combine all tax rates in a measure of the level of a county's tax policy, it serves as a capital outflow factor for overall capital.

Market openness/international tax treaties and financial instrument innovation were not tested in the outflow equations of the major financial items. They do not influence short-term capital outflows but financial instrument innovations do. Telecommunication network development is the key contributor to capital outflows for all financial items but FDI.

Three different policy objectives may be addressed in light of these conclusions. The first is the desire to secure previously invested capital. The

Table 23 Capital outflow factors by financial item

Theories (factor)	Key propositions	Portfolio capital	Bank capital	Other capital	FDI capital	Short-term capital		Total capital
						Type 1	Type 2	
Flow	Low interest rate (weak PPP)	weak	effective	weak	(no)	(weak)	(no)	weak
Portfolio	High risk	weak	effective	effective	effective	no	effective	effective
	High national income	effective	weak	effective	effective	effective	weak	effective
Monetary	Current account surplus	effective	effective	effective	effective	effective	effective	effective
	Removal of exchange control	no	effective	weak	effective	n/a	weak	weak
	High tax rate	weak	no	weak	no	weak	weak	effective
(Globalization)	Market openness and tax treaties	n/a	n/a	n/a	n/a	weak	n/a	n/a
	Financial instrument innovation	n/a	n/a	n/a	n/a	effective	n/a	n/a
	Telecommunication development	effective	effective	effective	effective	n/a	n/a	effective

Notes

1 Effective = statistically significant with supportive sign.
2 Weak = statistically insignificant with supportive sign.
3 No = statistically insignificant with non-supportive sign.
4 N/a = not available or not tested.

second is the attempt to discourage domestic investors' capital flight. The third is to promote the efficiency of domestic capital resource allocation.

Short-term capital outflows by domestic investors are mostly influenced by investment capacity-driven factors such as national wealth and current account surplus. However, short-term capital withdrawal by foreign investors is very sensitive to domestic financial market conditions, especially to risk avoiding factors. Previously-invested capital can be secured by country risk management. High country risk inhibits new capital investment and repels previously-invested capital.

Data availability limited analysis of the extent to which outflows in portfolio, bank capital, other-sector capital, and FDI are driven by domestic or foreign investors. We do know that portfolio outflow is not a result of high risk, however, implying a portfolio allocation process. On the other hand, outflows of bank capital, other sector capital and FDI can be a result of domestic investors' responses to domestic risk levels. To discourage domestic capital outflow in the globalized financial markets is difficult. The only policy options appear to be country risk management and the provision of a favourable domestic investment environment.

The efficiency of domestic capital resource allocation can be increased by investing surplus domestic capital in places where more profits are available. Telecommunication network development helps lower information collection costs and lowers transportation cost, and hence can improve profitability. Likewise, favourable international treaties can help safeguard investment.

In globalized financial markets, the direction of capital inflows and outflows is both influenced and shaped by the new globalization factors. How do interactions among different types of capital flows change as a result of financial markets globalization? Table 24 summarizes the principal findings.

There are many examples of synchronized flow movements. Large directional movements of one type of capital are accompanied by large movements of others. This synchronization produces positive feedback that widens the capital resource gap between the developed and developing countries as globalization enhances international capital mobility. An agglomeration effect among countries best endowed with globalization institutions and technologies emerges.

There are also counteractive flow movements when a particular financial item's inflows (e.g., other-sector capital inflow) discourage other financial item's outflows (e.g., portfolio outflow) or vice versa. These counteractive movements are particularly evident among short-term capital flow interactions. This is evidence that efficiency of short-term capital resource allocation is

Table 24 Synchronized and counteractive movements by capital type

A *All types of capital flow interactions*

Endogenous		Inflows				Outflows			
Exogenous		Portfolio	Bank K	Other K	FDI	Portfolio	Bank K	Other K	FDI
Inflows	Portfolio	n/a	+	+	+	+*			
	Bank K		n/a	+	+		+*	-	
	Other K		+	n/a		-		+*	+
	FDI	+		+	n/a				+*
Outflows	Portfolio	+*	+	-	-	n/a	+	+	+
	Bank K		+*	-	+		n/a		
	Other K		-	+*		+		n/a	+
	FDI		+	+	+*	+			n/a

B *Short-term capital flow interactions*

Endogenous		Short-term K inflows		Short-term K outflows	
Exogenous		Type 1	Type 2	Type 1	Type 2
Short-term K Inflows	Type 1	n/a	+		-
	Type 2	+	n/a	-	
Short-term K Outflows	Type 1		-	n/a	-
	Type 2	-			n/a

Notes

Statistically significant relationships are reported.

1 (+) synchronized movement.
2 (-) counteractive movement.
3 (*) intra-item movement.
4 (n/a) not available.

much higher than for other types of capital as a result of these counteractions.

In summary, then, the globalization of international financial markets improves the efficiency of international capital resource allocations, accelerates agglomeration of international capital in countries with globalization institutions and technologies and widens the gap between the capital-rich developed countries and capital-poor developing countries.

In addressing such issues as the effect of domestic monetary policies on actual capital inflows, the effect of domestic monetary management on capital outflows, and the efficiency of resource allocation, there appears to be a very limited role for monetary policies, restricted to specific financial items such as lower tax rates on portfolio investment, and removal of exchange controls on short-term capital inflows. Rather, more effective means of creating a better investment environment appear to include the provision of new financial instruments, development of advanced telecommunication networks, and improved country risk management. With respect to the effect of domestic monetary management on capital outflows, the policy options are very limited in globalized financial markets. The efficiency of domestic capital resource allocation can likewise be improved by telecommunication network development and favourable international treaties.

But there is a downside: globalized financial markets promote global efficiency of capital allocation, but undermine global equity of access to international capital. The ongoing process of globalization may widen global inequity in the short-run and not be desirable for the world as a whole. However, to the extent that less developed countries, perhaps with the assistance of international development organizations, are successful in attracting foreign capital through the strategies suggested above, the twin goals of increased global efficiency and equity may be realized.

Appendix A
Variable Creation and Identification

A–1 Calculation method for purchasing power parity ratio

The purchasing power parity ratio (PPPR) is calculated to compare each country's purchasing power of the US dollar, which is expressed as a ratio to the relative purchasing power in 1979. Four countries are selected to show how the PPPR is calculated and what the PPPR means as shown on the next page.

Panel 1 of the table on the next page shows the exchange rates with the US dollar for selected countries in 1979-1990.

Panel 2 shows a general price index, measured by the deflator for gross domestic product.

Panel 3 computes purchasing power parity (PPP). It is calculated by

PPP = Ei*(Pus/Pi) = (Ei/Pi)*Pus

where Ei = exchange rate of country i's local currency to US dollar,
Pus = price level of the US
Pi = price level of country i measured by the deflator for gross domestic product

Purchasing power parity connects a country's exchange rate with US dollar to the ratio of that country's price level to the US price level.

For example, Japan's exchange rate in 1990 was 144.79 as shown in Panel 1. It means that 144.79 1990 Japanese yen bought one 1990 US dollar. Since the price levels of Japan and the US affect the real terms of purchasing power, we multiply the exchange rate by the ratio of Japan's price level to the US price level. Thus Japan's purchasing power of one dollar is 144.7920* (164.90/123.29) = 193.67 yens in 1990.

Panel 4 computes purchasing power parity ratio (PPPR), expressed as a ratio to the relative purchasing power in 1979 to standardize the purchasing power parity.

PPPR tells us that the purchasing power of the dollar in country i in comparison to that of the US from the 1979 level. If the PPPR falls, it means that goods become relatively more expensive in country i than in the US.

For example, the value 0.88 for Japan's PPPR in 1990 means that in 1990 the dollar bought only 88 per cent as much in Japan as in the US, relative to the situation in 1979. Thus goods in Japan became more expensive than in the US. On the other hand, the value 1.04 for Germany's PPPR in 1990 means that in 1990 the dollar bought 4 per cent more goods in Germany relative to the US in comparison to the relative purchasing power in 1979. Thus goods in Germany became cheaper than in the US.

Since the PPP of the US for the dollar is always 1, the PPP of the US for the pound is calculated by multiplying the US exchange rate with the UK pound by the ratio of the US price level to the UK price level in our models.

Panel 1 Exchange rates (domestic currency per US dollar)

Year	Canada (dollar)	Germany (mark)	Japan (yen)	UK (pound)	USA (dollar)
1979	1.1714	1.8329	219.1400	0.4722	1.0000
1980	1.1692	1.8177	226.7410	0.4303	1.0000
1981	1.1989	2.2600	220.5360	0.4976	1.0000
1982	1.2337	2.4266	249.0770	0.5724	1.0000
1983	1.2324	2.5533	237.5120	0.6597	1.0000
1984	1.2951	2.8459	237.5220	0.7518	1.0000
1985	1.3655	2.9440	238.5360	0.7792	1.0000
1986	1.3895	2.1715	168.5200	0.6822	1.0000
1987	1.3260	1.7974	144.6370	0.6119	1.0000
1988	1.2307	1.7562	128.1520	0.5622	1.0000
1989	1.1840	1.8800	137.9640	0.6112	1.0000
1990	1.1668	1.6157	144.7920	0.5632	1.0000

Panel 2 Price levels (GDP deflator, 1979 = 100)

Year	Canada	Germany	Japan	UK	USA
1979	100.0000	100.0000	100.0000	100.0000	100.0000
1980	110.5602	104.8956	104.6739	118.2720	109.3010
1981	122.4433	109.1907	108.5319	130.8475	119.5957
1982	133.1127	113.9661	110.3610	140.9956	127.3926
1983	139.5542	117.9555	111.9319	148.3173	131.9200
1984	143.9593	120.4531	114.5106	155.0516	136.7227
1985	147.7678	123.0809	116.2774	163.9766	140.4153
1986	151.2321	127.1951	118.2906	169.6149	143.3789
1987	158.3678	129.7087	118.3270	178.0297	147.6746
1988	165.9687	131.7606	118.7528	190.0234	152.5653
1989	173.7227	135.1739	120.9773	203.1192	158.3991
1990	178.8700	139.7540	123.2867	216.9313	164.9059

Panel 3 Purchasing power parity

Year	Canada	Germany	Japan	UK	USA
1979	1.1714	1.8329	219.1400	0.4722	1.0000
1980	1.1559	1.8940	236.7640	0.3977	1.0000
1981	1.1710	2.4754	243.0176	0.4548	1.0000
1982	1.1807	2.7125	287.5161	0.5172	1.0000
1983	1.1650	2.8555	279.9252	0.5868	1.0000
1984	1.2300	3.2303	283.5950	0.6629	1.0000
1985	1.2975	3.3586	288.0532	0.6673	1.0000
1986	1.3173	2.4478	204.2615	0.5767	1.0000
1987	1.2365	2.0463	180.5100	0.5076	1.0000
1988	1.1313	2.0335	164.6408	0.4514	1.0000
1989	1.0796	2.2031	180.6403	0.4766	1.0000
1990	1.0757	1.9065	193.6710	0.4281	1.0000

Panel 4 Purchasing power parity ratios (1979 = 1)

Year	Canada	Germany	Japan	UK	USA
1979	1.0000	1.0000	1.0000	1.0000	1.0000
1980	0.9868	1.0333	1.0804	0.8422	1.0000
1981	0.9997	1.3505	1.1090	0.9633	1.0000
1982	1.0079	1.4799	1.3120	1.0954	1.0000
1983	0.9945	1.5579	1.2774	1.2427	1.0000
1984	1.0500	1.7624	1.2941	1.4040	1.0000
1985	1.1077	1.8324	1.3145	1.4132	1.0000
1986	1.1246	1.3355	0.9321	1.2213	1.0000
1987	1.0555	1.1165	0.8237	1.0750	1.0000
1988	0.9658	1.1095	0.7513	0.9559	1.0000
1989	0.9216	1.2020	0.8243	1.0094	1.0000
1990	0.9183	1.0402	0.8838	0.9067	1.0000

A–2 Cross-section and time dummy variables

Cross-section dummies

If country = Algeria then ALGERIA =1 otherwise ALGERIA =0
If country = Argentina then ARGENTIN =1 otherwise ARGENTIN =0
If country = Australia then AUSTRALI =1 otherwise AUSTRALI =0
If country = Austria then AUSTRIA =1 otherwise AUSTRIA =0
If country = Bahrain then BAHRAIN =1 otherwise BAHRAIN =0
If country = Bangladesh then BANGLADE =1 otherwise BANGLADE =0
If country = Barbados then BARBADOS =1 otherwise BARBADOS =0
If country = Belgium and Luxembourg then BELGIUML =1 otherwise BELGIUML =0

Cross-section dummies

If country =	Bolivia	then	BOLIVIA	=1 otherwise	BOLIVIA	=0
If country =	Brazil	then	BRAZIL	=1 otherwise	BRAZIL	=0
If country =	Canada	then	CANADA	=1 otherwise	CANADA	=0
If country =	Chile	then	CHILE	=1 otherwise	CHILE	=0
If country =	Colombia	then	COLOMBIA	=1 otherwise	COLOMBIA	=0
If country =	Congo	then	CONGO	=1 otherwise	CONGO	=0
If country =	Costa Rica	then	COSTARIC	=1 otherwise	COSTARIC	=0
If country =	Cote d' Ivoire	then	COTEIVOR	=1 otherwise	COTEIVOR	=0
If country =	Cyprus	then	CYPRUS	=1 otherwise	CYPRUS	=0
If country =	Denmark	then	DENMARK	=1 otherwise	DENMARK	=0
If country =	Dominican Rep.	then	DOMINIRP	=1 otherwise	DOMINIRP	=0
If country =	Ecuador	then	ECUADOR	=1 otherwise	ECUADOR	=0
If country =	Egypt	then	EGYPT	=1 otherwise	EGYPT	=0
If country =	El Salvador	then	ELSALVAD	=1 otherwise	ELSALVAD	=0
If country =	Ethiopia	then	ETHIOPIA	=1 otherwise	ETHIOPIA	=0
If country =	Finland	then	FINLAND	=1 otherwise	FINLAND	=0
If country =	France	then	FRANCE	=1 otherwise	FRANCE	=0
If country =	Gabon	then	GABON	=1 otherwise	GABON	=0
If country =	West Germany	then	GERMANY	=1 otherwise	GERMANY	=0
If country =	Greece	then	GREECE	=1 otherwise	GREECE	=0
If country =	Guatemala	then	GUATEMAL	=1 otherwise	GUATEMAL	=0
If country =	Haiti	then	HAITI	=1 otherwise	HAITI	=0
If country =	Honduras	then	HONDURAS	=1 otherwise	HONDURAS	=0
If country =	Iceland	then	ICELAND	=1 otherwise	ICELAND	=0
If country =	India	then	INDIA	=1 otherwise	INDIA	=0
If country =	Indonesia	then	INDONESI	=1 otherwise	INDONESI	=0
If country =	Ireland	then	IRELAND	=1 otherwise	IRELAND	=0
If country =	Israel	then	ISRAEL	=1 otherwise	ISRAEL	=0
If country =	Italy	then	ITALY	=1 otherwise	ITALY	=0
If country =	Jamaica	then	JAMAICA	=1 otherwise	JAMAICA	=0
If country =	Japan	then	JAPAN	=1 otherwise	JAPAN	=0
If country =	Kenya	then	KENYA	=1 otherwise	KENYA	=0
If country =	South Korea	then	KOREA	=1 otherwise	KOREA	=0
If country =	Libya	then	LIBYA	=1 otherwise	LIBYA	=0
If country =	Madagascar	then	MADAGASC	=1 otherwise	MADAGASC	=0
If country =	Malaysia	then	MALAYSIA	=1 otherwise	MALAYSIA	=0
If country =	Mauritius	then	MAURITIU	=1 otherwise	MAURITIU	=0
If country =	Mexico	then	MEXICO	=1 otherwise	MEXICO	=0
If country =	Morocco	then	MOROCCO	=1 otherwise	MOROCCO	=0
If country =	Mozambique	then	MOZAMBIQ	=1 otherwise	MOZAMBIQ	=0
If country =	Nepal	then	NEPAL	=1 otherwise	NEPAL	=0
If country =	Netherlands	then	NETHERLA	=1 otherwise	NETHERLA	=0
If country =	New Zealnd	then	NEWZEALA	=1 otherwise	NEWZEALA	=0
If country =	Nigeria	then	NIGERIA	=1 otherwise	NIGERIA	=0
If country =	Norway	then	NORWAY	=1 otherwise	NORWAY	=0
If country =	Oman	then	OMAN	=1 otherwise	OMAN	=0
If country =	Pakistan	then	PAKISTAN	=1 otherwise	PAKISTAN	=0

Cross-section dummies

If country =	Papua New Guinea	then PAPUANEW	=1 otherwise	PAPUANEW	=0
If country =	Paraguay	then PARAGUAY	=1 otherwise	PARAGUAY	=0
If country =	Peru	then PERU	=1 otherwise	PERU	=0
If country =	Philippines	then PHILIPPI	=1 otherwise	PHILIPPI	=0
If country =	Portugal	then PORTUGAL	=1 otherwise	PORTUGAL	=0
If country =	Saudi Arabia	then SAUDIARA	=1 otherwise	SAUDIARA	=0
If country =	Senegal	then SENEGAL	=1 otherwise	SENEGAL	=0
If country =	Seychelles	then SEYCHELL	=1 otherwise	SEYCHELL	=0
If country =	Sierra Leone	then SIERRALE	=1 otherwise	SIERRALE	=0
If country =	Singapore	then SINGAPOR	=1 otherwise	SINGAPOR	=0
If country =	South Africa	then SOUTHAFR	=1 otherwise	SOUTHAFR	=0
If country =	Spain	then SPAIN	=1 otherwise	SPAIN	=0
If country =	Sri Lanka	then SRILANKA	=1 otherwise	SRILANKA	=0
If country =	Sudan	then SUDAN	=1 otherwise	SUDAN	=0
If country =	Swaziland	then SWAZILAN	=1 otherwise	SWAZILAN	=0
If country =	Sweden	then SWEDEN	=1 otherwise	SWEDEN	=0
If country =	Switzerland	then SWITZERL	=1 otherwise	SWITZERL	=0
If country =	Syria	then SYRIA	=1 otherwise	SYRIA	=0
If country =	Tanazania	then TANZANIA	=1 otherwise	TANZANIA	=0
If country =	Thailand	then THAILAND	=1 otherwise	THAILAND	=0
If country =	Trinidad and Tobago	then TRINIDAD	=1 otherwise	TRINIDAD	=0
If country =	Tunisia	then TUNISIA	=1 otherwise	TUNISIA	=0
If country =	Turkey	then TURKEY	=1 otherwise	TURKEY	=0
If country =	United Kingdom	then UK	=1 otherwise	UK	=0
If country =	The United States	then USA	=1 otherwise	USA	=0
If country =	Uruguay	then URUGUAY	=1 otherwise	URUGUAY	=0
If country =	Venezuela	then VENEZUEL	=1 otherwise	VENEZUEL	=0
If country =	Yugoslavia	then YUGOSLAV	=1 otherwise	YUGOSLAV	=0
If country =	Zaire	then ZAIRE	=1 otherwise	ZAIRE	=0
If country =	Zambia	then ZAMBIA	=1 otherwise	ZAMBIA	=0
If country =	Zimbabwe	then ZIMBABWE	=1 otherwise	ZIMBABWE	=0

Time dummies

If year =	1980	then YR1980	=1 otherwise	YR1980	=0
If year =	1981	then YR1981	=1 otherwise	YR1981	=0
If year =	1982	then YR1982	=1 otherwise	YR1982	=0
If year =	1983	then YR1983	=1 otherwise	YR1983	=0
If year =	1984	then YR1984	=1 otherwise	YR1984	=0
If year =	1985	then YR1985	=1 otherwise	YR1985	=0
If year =	1986	then YR1986	=1 otherwise	YR1986	=0
If year =	1987	then YR1987	=1 otherwise	YR1987	=0
If year =	1988	then YR1988	=1 otherwise	YR1988	=0
If year =	1989	then YR1989	=1 otherwise	YR1989	=0
If year =	1990	then YR1990	=1 otherwise	YR1990	=0

A–3 Identification for simultaneous equation models

Identification for Two Equations of Each Financial Item's In-Outflow Model

Since there are two equations in each financial item's in-out flow simultaneous equation model (3.4.2:A), we consider identification by order condition. The model is under-identified when g - 1 < k, exactly identified when g-1 = k, and over-identified when g - 1 < k, where g = number of equation in the model, and k = number of missing variables.

Model	Equation	INTD	RISKD	RISKDC	GNYPC	TREATY	EXCHCONT	TAXD	CD	TELECOMM
Total capital	TOTI	X	X	0	0	X	0	X	X	0
	TOTO	X	0	X	X	0	X	X	0	X
Portfolio	PORTI	X^1	X	0	0	X	0	X^5	X	0
	PORTO	X	0	X	X	0	X	X	0	X
Bank capital	BANKI	X^2	X	0	0	X	0	X^6	X	0
	BANKO	X	0	X	X	0	X	X	0	X
Other capital	OTHI	X^3	X	0	0	X	0	X^6	X	0
	OTHO	X	0	X	X	0	X	X	0	X
FDI	FDII	X^4	X	0	0	X	0	X^7	X^8	0
	FDIO	X	0	X	X	0	X	X	0	X

Notes

1 = IGOVTD 2 = IDEPD 3 = IMKTD 4 = PPPR 5 = tfdivd
6 =TFINTD 7 = TFCORD 8 = INDSTP

The above table shows that all equations are over-identified; g - 1 = 1 < k = 4 in the inflow equations, g - 1 = 1 < k =3 in the outflow equations. The missing variables are represented by 0, and the included variables by X. Since the both endogenous variables are included as the exogenous variables in the counterpart equations, and dummy variables are included in both equations, we do not report them. If we do, they will be all marked as X.

Identification for Eight Equations of Four Financial Items' In-Outflow Model

The following table represents the four financial items' in-outflow model (3.4.2: B). Since each financial item has two equations (inflow and outflow), there are eight equations for four financial items in one simultaneous equation system. The system, year, and country dummy variables are not reported here, since they are all marked by X.

Equation	I1	I2	I3	I4	R1	R2	R3	GNY	CAB	TR	EXCH	T1	T2	T3	IND	CD	TEL
PORTI	X	0	0	0	X	0	0	0	X	X	0	X	0	0	0	X	0
PORTO	X	0	0	0	0	0	X	X	X	0	X	X	0	0	0	0	X
BANKI	0	X	0	0	X	0	0	0	X	X	0	0	X	0	X	0	0
BANKO	0	X	0	0	0	X	0	X	X	0	X	0	X	0	0	0	X
OTHI	0	0	X	0	X	0	0	0	X	X	0	0	X	0	0	X	0
OTHO	0	0	X	0	0	X	0	X	X	0	X	0	X	0	0	0	X
FDII	0	0	0	X	X	0	0	0	X	X	0	0	0	X	X	0	0
FDIO	0	0	0	X	0	0	X	X	X	0	X	0	0	X	0	0	X

Notes

I1 = IGOVTD I2 = IDEPD I3 = IMKRD I4 = PPPR R1 = RISKD
R2 = RISKDC R3 = RISKCP GNY = GNYPC TR = TREATY EXCH = EXCHCONT
T1 = TFDIVD T2 = TFINTD T3 = TFCORD IND = INDSTP TEL = TELECOMM

The rule for identification of any equation is as follows (Maddala, 1988, pp. 301–2): 1) delete the particular row; 2) pickup the column corresponding to the elements that have zeros in that row; 3) if from this array of column we can find (g - 1 = 7) rows and (g - 7 < k) column that are not zeros, then the equation is identified. otherwise, not.

Applying the rule, the following are the results:

PORTI equation

0 0 0 0 X X X 0 0 0 X
X 0 0 0 0 0 0 X 0 X 0
X 0 0 X 0 X X X 0 0 X
0 X 0 0 0 0 0 X 0 0 0
0 X 0 X 0 X X X 0 0 X
0 0 X 0 0 0 0 0 X X 0
0 0 X 0 X X X 0 X 0 X

PORTO equation

0 0 0 X 0 X 0 0 0 X
X 0 0 X 0 X X 0 X 0
X 0 0 0 X 0 X 0 0 0
0 X 0 X 0 X X 0 0 X
0 X 0 0 X 0 X 0 0 0
0 0 X X 0 X 0 X X 0
0 0 X 0 0 0 X X 0 0

PORTI has 11 non-zero columns and seven non-zero rows: it is over-identified by the order condition and identified by rank condition. PORTO has 10 non-zero columns and seven non-zero rows: it is over-identified by the order condition and identified by the rank condition.

BANKI equation

X 0 0 0 0 0 0 X 0 X 0
X 0 0 0 X X X X 0 0 X
0 0 0 X 0 X X 0 0 0 X
0 X 0 0 0 0 0 0 0 X 0
0 X 0 X 0 X X 0 0 0 X
0 0 X 0 0 0 0 0 X 0 0
0 0 X 0 X X X 0 X 0 X

BANKO equation

X 0 0 X 0 X X 0 0 X
X 0 0 0 X 0 X 0 0 0
0 0 0 X 0 X 0 0 X 0
0 X 0 X 0 X 0 0 0 X
0 X 0 0 0 0 0 0 0 0
0 0 X X 0 X 0 X X 0
0 0 X 0 X 0 0 X 0 0

BANKI has 11 non-zero columns and seven non-zero rows: it is over-identified by the order condition and identified by rank condition. BANKO has 10 non-zero columns and seven non-zero rows: it is over-identified by the order condition and identified by the rank condition.

OTHI equation

X 0 0 0 0 0 0 X 0 0 0
X 0 0 0 X X X X 0 0 X
0 X 0 0 0 0 0 0 0 X 0
0 X 0 X 0 X X 0 0 0 X
0 0 0 X 0 X X 0 0 0 X
0 0 X 0 0 0 0 0 X X 0
0 0 X 0 X X X 0 X 0 X

OTHO equation

X 0 0 X 0 X X 0 0 X
X 0 0 0 X 0 X 0 0 0
0 X 0 X 0 X 0 0 X 0
0 X 0 0 0 0 0 0 0 X
0 0 0 X 0 X 0 0 0 0
0 0 X X 0 X 0 X X 0
0 0 X 0 X 0 0 X 0 0

OTHI has 11 non-zero columns and seven non-zero rows: it is over-identified by the order condition and identified by rank condition. OTHO has 10 non-zero columns and seven non-zero rows: it is over-identified by the order condition and identified by the rank condition.

FDII equation

X 0 0 0 0 0 0 X 0 X 0
X 0 0 0 X X X X 0 0 X
0 X 0 0 0 0 0 0 X 0 0
0 X 0 X 0 X X 0 X 0 X
0 0 X 0 0 0 X 0 X X 0
0 0 X X 0 X 0 0 X 0 X
0 0 0 0 X X X 0 0 0 X

FDIO equation

X 0 0 X 0 X X 0 0 X
X 0 0 0 0 0 X 0 0 0
0 X 0 X 0 X 0 X X 0
0 X 0 0 X 0 0 X 0 0
0 0 X X 0 X 0 X 0 X
0 0 X 0 X 0 0 X 0 0
0 0 0 X 0 X 0 0 X 0

FDII has 11 non-zero columns and seven non-zero rows: it is over-identified by the order condition and identified by rank condition. FDIO has 10 non-zero columns and seven non-zero rows: it is over-identified by the order condition and identified by the rank condition.

Identification for Four Equations of Four Types of Short-term Capital Flow Model

The same process is applied to verify the identification for the four types of short-term capital flow model (3.4.2.:C).

Equation	PPPR	RISKD	RISKDC	GNYPC	CAB	EXCHCONT	TREATY	TFINTD	TDINTD	CD	TELECO
STKI1	X	X	0	0	X	X	0	X	0	X	X
STKI2	X	0	X	0	X	0	X	0	X	0	X
STKO1	X	X	0	X	X	0	X	0	X	X	0
STKO2	X	0	X	X	X	X	0	X	0	0	0

Note: TELECO = TELECOMM

As shown below, there are four non-zero columns andthree non- zero rows in equations STKI 1 and STKO1, and five non-zero columns and three non-zero rows in equations STKI2 and STKO2. Thus, all equations are over-identified by order condition and identified by rank condition.

STKI1

X	0	X	X
0	X	X	X
X	X	0	0

STKI2

X	0	X	X	X
X	X	0	0	X
0	X	X	X	0

STKO1

0	X	X	X
X	0	0	X
X	X	X	0

STKO2

X	0	0	X	X
0	X	X	0	X
X	X	X	X	0

Appendix B
Statistical Tests

B–1 Detection of autocorrelation by the Durbin-Watson test

The Durbin-Watson test was used to detect autocorrelation in our models. Since the data set is a cross-sectional time series pooled data, we separated the data set by country (86 models) to detect autocorrelation. Number of observation in each model is 11 since each country has 11 years (1980-1990) of observation.

The small number of observation limits the use of exogenous variables due to the degree of freedom. Thus, we repeated all possible combinations by using three exogenous variables with different endogenous variables. We report the most problematic combinations in the table.

We calculated the DW statsitic from the following models.

TOTG = a + b1(abintd) + b2(abcab) + b3(TELECOMM) + u
PORTG = a + b1(abintd) + b2(abcab) + b3(TELECOMM) + u
BANKG = a + b1(abintd) + b2(abcab) + b3(TELECOMM) + u
OTHG = a + b1(abintd) + b2(abcab) + b3(TELECOMM) + u
FDIG = a + b1(abintd) + b2(abcab) + b3(TELECOMM) + u

The Durbin-Watson ststistic provides the following information when k = 3 and n = 15.

$3.18<DW<4$	negative autocorrelation
$0<DW<0.82$	positive autocorrelation
$2.25<DW<3.18$ or $0.82<1.75$	indeterminate
$1.75<DW<2.25$	no autocorrelation

The models (named after its country name) with more than 3.18 or less than 0.82 in DW statistic are marked by asterisks in the table. Note that this resut is based on n = 15. Since n=11 in our models, it may be over-estimated. Even in the over-estimated result, the problematic countries are less than 7 per cent of the the total, when BANKG is estimated.

With other exogenous variables, less than 2 per cent were detected to be serially correlated. Thus we conclude that the autocorrelation problem is not serious in our pooled models.

DV / Model by country	Durbin-Watson statistic				
	TOTG	PORTG	BANKG	OTHG	FDIG
Algeria	1.752	1.817	2.958	1.594	2.718
Argentina	1.687	1.533	2.011	0.798*	1.595
Australia	1.906	2.614	2.535	2.582	2.327
Austria	2.59	2.486	1.883	2.124	0.974
Bahrain	1.992	2.166	2.341	2.731	1.815
Bangladesh	1.315	1.614	2.015	1.846	2.082
Barbados	2.080	1.901	3.267*	2.444	2.836
Belgium and Luxembourg	1.660	2.403	2.328	2.482	2.003
Bolivia	2.571	2.759	2.501	3.364*	1.835
Brazil	1.277	1.797	1.237	2.499	1.823
Canada	2.438	1.485	2.46:	2.290	2.800
Chile	2.708	1.442	1.540	1.949	2.125
Colombia	2.626	3.018	1.608	1.206	2.303
Congo	2.903	2.415	3.061	3.333*	2.089
Costa Rica	2.495	2.566	2.282	2.640	2.913
Cote d' Ivoire	1.612	2.306	1.882	2.580	1.59
Cyprus	2.075	2.566	2.087	1.160	1.486
Denmark	2.657	2.901	3.369*	2.743	1.659
Dominican Republic	1.038	1.786	0.973	1.845	2.197
Ecuador	2.130	1.987	2.777	2.201	1.232
Egypt	1.924	2.240	2.299	3.006	0.946
El Salvador	1.241	2.911	1.653	2.305	1.898
Ethiopia	2.087	2.224	2.673	2.476	1.986
Finland	2.972	1.365	2.317	1.383	1.948
France	1.992	2.035	2.212	2.377	1.697
Gabon	2.423	2.015	3.471*	2.914	2.108
Germany, West	2.728	2.780	1.280	2.159	1.433
Greece	1.612	2.015	2.486	2.054	1.495
Guatemala	2.142	1.954	1.710	2.864	1.204
Haiti	2.669	2.124	3.007	2.200	1.758
Honduras	1.664	2.130	2.220	2.265	1.727
Iceland	1.717	2.703	1.754	2.011	2.050
India	2.285	2.014	2.597	1.700	2.061
Indonesia	2.596	1.812	2.651	1.835	1.908
Ireland	2.762	2.738	1.484	3.048	3.143
Israel	2.610	2.432	3.030	2.867	1.621
Italy	1.695	2.461	2.232	1.930	2.934
Jamaica	2.227	2.324	2.306	2.765	2.697
Japan	2.124	1.849	2.114	2.172	1.535
Kenya	2.861	2.124	2.501	2.233	1.939
Korea, South	2.775	1.813	2.924	2.055	2.088
Libya	2.919	1.294	2.878	2.466	1.481
Madagascar	1.168	2.144	1.168	2.124	2.354
Malaysia	0.976	2.274	1.988	2.208	2.003
Mauritius	2.002	1.194	2.454	1.199	1.472
Mexico	2.502	3.416*	2.586	1.828	1.587

DV / Model by country	Durbin-Watson statistic				
	TOTG	**PORTG**	**BANKG**	**OTHG**	**FDIG**
Morocco	1.841	2.011	2.043	2.369	2.569
Mozambique	2.451	2.147	2.155	1.982	2.512
Nepal	3.264*	1.187	2.725	2.817	1.47
Netherlands	1.696	1.745	2.332	2.111	2.153
New Zealnd	1.823	1.174	2.753	2.244	2.535
Nigeria	2.217	2.567	2.239	2.391	1.509
Norway	2.467	1.321	1.790	2.480	3.269*
Oman	2.086	2.210	2.023	2.658	1.936
Pakistan	2.148	2.523	1.572	2.770	2.166
Papua New Guinea	1.029	2.733	2.371	1.717	2.58:
Paraguay	2.200	2.086	1.886	2.538	2.843
Peru	2.633	1.928	3.448*	2.330	2.202
Philippines	2.493	2.535	2.324	2.005	2.485
Portugal	1.978	1.585	2.421	2.347	2.459
Saudi Arabia	2.048	2.063	2.222	2.611	1.793
Senegal	1.337	1.971	2.371	2.258	2.772
Seychelles	2.358	1.208	1.768	2.462	1.521
Sierra Leone	2.466	1.898	2.535	2.425	2.031
Singapore	2.438	2.457	2.838	2.851	1.815
South Africa	2.163	1.207	2.745	2.325	2.524
Spain	1.675	1.824	2.137	3.095	1.837
Sri Lanka	2.583	2.054	2.474	2.719	1.665
Sudan	1.571	2.114	2.794	2.305	2.199
Swaziland	2.115	1.757	2.120	1.349	2.250
Sweden	1.576	2.644	1.823	1.591	1.511
Switzerland	2.015	1.717	2.259	2.273	1.756
Syria	2.143	2.110	2.062	2.249	3.046
Tanazania	1.409	1.742	1.953	2.496	1.871
Thailand	1.653	2.464	2.729	1.909	1.727
Trinidad and Tobago	2.433	2.148	3.194*	2.151	2.200
Tunisia	1.736	2.291	2.017	1.660	1.934
Turkey	2.202	2.315	2.603	1.687	1.243
United Kingdom	1.910	1.684	2.204	2.395	2.480
United States	1.934	2.103	1.922	2.006	1.516
Uruguay	1.936	2.236	2.741	2.717	2.676
Venezuela	1.496	1.710	2,334	1.677	1.061
Yugoslavia	1.907	2.015	2.605	2.384	2.053
Zaire	2.629	2.258	3.223*	1.893	1.999
Zambia	2.094	1.905	2.622	1.861	2.338
Zimbabwe	1.980	2.048	1.987	2.457	2.094

B-2 Detection of heteroskedasticity by the Breusch-Pagan test

The Breusch-Pagan test was used to detect heteroskedasticity. Each model has the similar result that the heteroskedasticity problem is caused by TREATY add GNYPC. We demonstrate here an example in the total gross flow model with GNYPC.

TOTG = a + b1(ABINTD) + b2(ABRISKD) + b3(GNYPC) + b4(ABCAB) + b5(EXCHCONT) + b6(CD) + b7(TELECOMM) + e   original model

We initially estimated the residuals from the original model to test the Breusch-Pagan's hypothesis: $\alpha 1 = \alpha 2 = \alpha 3 = \alpha 4 = \alpha 5 = \alpha 6 = \alpha 7 = 0$ in the auxiliary model as shown below.

$\sigma^2 = f\{\alpha 0 + \alpha 1(\text{ABINTD}) + \alpha 2(\text{ABRISKD}) + \alpha 3(\text{GNYPC}) + \alpha 4(\text{ABCAB}) + \alpha 5(\text{EXCHCONT}) + \alpha 6(\text{CD}) + \alpha 7(\text{TELECOMM}) + u\}$ auxiliary regression

where $\sigma^2 = \dfrac{\Sigma e^2}{N}$

from the original model.

From the auxiliary regression, we estimated the following parameters.

Variable	Par. Est	St. Error	t-Stat	Prob>ITI
INTERCEPT	0.415909	0.09788660	4.249	0.0001
ABINTD	0.028482	0.05243136	0.543	0.5871
ABCAB	0.009698	0.00833719	1.163	0.2451
ABRISKD	-0.001681	0.00143136	-1.174	0.2406
GNYPC	-0.034212	0.01089616	-3.140	0.0017
EXCHCONT	-0.002992	0.03614479	-0.083	0.9340
CD	0.029393	0.05420033	0.542	0.5877
TELECOMM	-0.003659	0.01008507	-0.363	0.7168

We found that GNYPC is significantly different from 0 at the 1 per cent level, meaning that GNYPC is not independent from the error terms. We estimated the regression sum of squares (RSS), and σ^2 from the auxiliary regression to check the Breusch-Pagan test statistic:

$$\lambda = \frac{RSS}{2\sigma^4} \sim \chi^2.$$

From the auxiliary regression, RSS = 2.3793, and $\sigma^2 = 0.20219$. Thus λ = 29.0997, which is significant at 0.1 per cent level in χ^2-distribution.

Based on the Breusch-Pagan test, we found heteroskedasticity in this model. However, as discussed in chapter 4, the OLS fixed effects models provided the consistent parameter and the WLS models weighted by GNYPC increased only a small amount of efficiency. The difference between the OLS fixed effects models and WLS models was not significant. Thus we conclude that the heteroskedasticity problem does not seriously affect the parameter estimates in our models.

B–3 Model selection procedure of log-linear function by the BM test

The BM-test involves three steps to test whether a model is better specified by a log-linear or linear function. Model A is a log-linear model and Model B is a linear model for total capital gross flow.

Model A: log(TOTG) = a + b1(ABINTD) + b2*(ABRISKD) + b3(GNYPC) + b4(ABCAB) + b5(EXCHCONT) + b6(CD) + b7(TELECOMM) + b8 ... b92(COUNTRY) + b93 ... b102(YEAR) + u1

Model B: TOTG = a + b1(ABINTD) + b2(ABRISKD) + b3(GNYPC) + b4(ABCAB) + b5(EXCHCONT) + b6(CD) + b7(TELECOMM) + b8 ... b92(COUNTRY) + b93 ... b102(YEAR) + u2

1 Obtain the predicted values from A and B. Put ^Y1 and ^Y2 for predicted values of A and B.
2 Then compute the artificial regressions for the predicted values:

Model A': ^Y= a + b1(ABINTD) + b2*(ABRISKD) + b3(GNYPC) + b4(ABCAB) + b5(EXCHCONT) + b6(CD) + b7(TELECOMM) + b8 ... b92(COUNTRY) + b93 ... b102(YEAR) + v1

Model B': ^Y2 = a + b1(ABINTD) + b2(ABRISKD) + b3(GNYPC) + b4(ABCAB) + b5(EXCHCONT) + b6(CD) + b7(TELECOMM) + b8 ... b92(COUNTRY) + b93 ... b102(YEAR) + v2

3 Keep the estimated residuals from A' and B': put ^v1 from A' and ^v2 from B'. Then compute another artificial regression for the original dependent variable by the the estimated residual.

Model A":log (TOTG) = a + b1(^v1) + b2(ABINTD) + b3*(ABRISKD) + b4(GNYPC) + b5(ABCAB) + b6(EXCHCONT) + b7(CD) + b8(TELECOMM) + b9 … b93(COUNTRY) + b94… b103(YEAR) + e1
Model B": TOTG = a + b1(^v2) + b2(ABINTD) + b3(ABRISKD) + b4(GNYPC) + b5(ABCAB) + b6(EXCHCONT) + b7(CD) + b8(TELECOMM) + b9 … b93(COUNTRY) + b94 … b103(YEAR) + e2

We use the t-test to test the hypotheses b1=0 in A" and B".

If b1=0 is accepted, the model is correctly specified; if b1 = 0 is not accepted, the model is not properly specified.

The regression reults of models A" and B" show that the log-linear model (A") is clearly a better selection.

As shown below, we reject the hypothesis b1 = 0 at the 0.1 per cent significant level in the linear model (B"), while we accept b1 = 0 in the log-linear model (A") as the t-statistic of ^v1 is not statistically significant at all.

BM Model	Log-linear model (Model A")				Linear model (Model B")			
Variable	Par est	St. error	t-stat	Prob>[T]	Par est	St. error	t-stat	Prob>[T]
INTERCEPT	-4.929603	24.21045766	-0.204	0.8387	2973463	723818.60423	4.108	0.0001
^v1	-6.0012E+12	1.15553E+13	-0.519	0.6037				
^v2					-4.432387E+14	1.06649E+14	-4.156	0.0001
ABINTD	0.948747	1.82325393	0.52	0.6029	-251049	53722.029198	-4.673	0.0001
ABRISKD	-0.006332	0.0320043	-0.198	0.8432	4737.737787	1141.566419	4.15	0.0001
GNYPC	-0.00014	0.00038769	-0.36	0.7189	336.715611	79.20531775	4.251	0.0001
ABCAB	1.455777	2.691640971	0.541	0.5888	-262372	64273.55425	-4.082	0.0001
EXCHCONT	0.150223	0.460990301	0.326	0.7446	-195066	42530.67569	-4.586	0.0001
CD	0.124797	0.725629141	0.172	0.8635	-113589	32084.075021	-3.54	0.0004
TELECOMM	-0.01164	0.15040548	-0.077	0.9383	-105677	25893.995493	-4.081	0.0001
ALGERIA	4.03458	7.02416811	0.574	0.5659	-1901139	459519.49006	-4.137	0.0001
ARGENTIN	1.189064	1.236346	0.962	0.3364	-1284047	309352.57497	-4.151	0.0001
AUSTRALI	2.932391	2.67986493	1.094	0.2742	-3504695	846987.36605	-4.138	0.0001
AUSTRIA	6.250393	12.15223757	0.514	0.6071	-5777791	1366156.7279	-4.229	0.0001
BAHRAIN	3.691341	11.33739691	0.326	0.7448	-3626131	866015.06398	-4.187	0.0001
BANGLADE	-0.191601	5.08757127	-0.038	0.97	-917800	226415.7139	-4.054	0.0001
BARBADOS	4.52972	15.17801339	0.298	0.7654	-3567481	854339.66878	-4.176:	0.0001
BELGIUML	5.447034	7.9261315	0.687	0.4921	-4615784	1104983.0267	-4.177	0.0001
BOLIVIA	1.425769	7.77481411	0.183	0.8545	-1339045	328602.97251	-4.075	0.0001
BRAZIL	1.896941	0.97746681	1.941	0.0526	-815432	203332.50061	-4.01	0.0001
CANADA	3.776015	6.07846199	0.621	0.5346	-4507808	1065078.2795	-4.232	0.0001
CHILE	1.689829	2.76830305	0.61	0.5417	-1005468	246695.61785	-4.076	0.0001
COLOMBIA	2.07599	4.69873282	0.442	0.6587	-1086137	265060.36943	-4.098	0.0001

BM Model	Log-linear model (Model A")				Linear model (Model B")			
Variable	Par est	St. error	t-stat	Prob>|T|	Par est	St. error	t-stat	Prob>|T|
INTERCEPT	-4.929603	24.21045766	-0.204	0.8387	2973463	723818.60423	4.108	0.0001
^v1	-6.0012E+12	1.15553E+13	-0.519	0.6037				
^v2					-4.432387E+14	1.06649E+14	-4.156	0.0001
CONGO	1.991688	7.41666066	0.269	0.7883	-1477039	359128.35237	-4.113	0.0001
COSTARIC	1.671318	7.08724171	0.236	0.8136	-1476543	359688.86807	-4.105	0.0001
COTEIVOR	0.905757	4.50280335	0.201	0.8406	-1090076	266464.91286	-4.091	0.0001
CYPRUS	3.737743	12.49326862	0.299	0.7649	-3128408	749853.65304	-4.172	0.0001
DENMARK	4.078643	8.62904192	0.473	0.6366	-6409576	1512162.281	-4.239	0.0001
DOMINIRP	0.602447	6.64834256	0.091	0.9278	-1250531	305701.86989	-4.091	0.0001
ECUADOR	1.656442	5.79903757	0.286	0.7752	-1371302	331907.40273	-4.132	0.0001
EGYPT	1.067621	2.38933833	0.447	0.6551	-802349	197403.27327	-4.065	0.0001
ELSALVAD	2.416505	10.68140921	0.226	0.8211	-1726213	420930.39861	-4.101	0.0001
ETHIOPIA	0.999449	7.75560155	0.129	0.8975	-1170499	288186.25773	-4.062	0.0001
FINLAND	4.837284	9.6257341	0.503	0.6154	-5913271	1398572.024	-4.228	0.0001
FRANCE	5.482072	7.5747504	0.724	0.4694	-5007094	1199406.6703	-4.175	0.0001
GABON	2.479689	8.43392006	0.294	0.7688	-2696096	644258.15251	-4.185	0.0001
GERMANY	2.543822	1.63193698	1.559	0.1194	-3780342	915342.23431	-4.13	0.0001
GREECE	0.931057	2.92318822	0.319	0.7502	-1947629	464831.27098	-4.19	0.0001
GUATEMAL	1.598655	7.05192021	0.227	0.8207	-1323962	323823.68411	-4.089	0.0001
HAITI	1.388363	10.23893995	0.136	0.8922	-1439561	353567.07483	-4.072	0.0001
HONDURAS	1.337833	7.22126347	0.185	0.8531	-1330477	325210.0649	-4.091	0.0001
ICELAND	4.856801	16.46314708	0.2945	0.7681	-7688678	1821309.8048	-4.222	0.0001
INDIA	-1.278958	0.34184364	-3.741	0.0002	-400418	98914.082078	-4.048	0.0001
INDONESI	0.17792	1.69509592	0.105	0.9164	-528022	130459.52307	-4.047	0.0001
IRELAND	2.73136	6.46846245	0.422	0.6729	-3095744	733273.76123	-4.222	0.0001
ISRAEL	2.939628	7.11642661	0.413	0.6797	-3294532	782419.83982	-4.211	0.0001
ITALY	3.969478	4.76994548	0.832	0.4055	-3874432	926493.41284	-4.182	0.0001
JAMAICA	1.587012	8.07123576	0.197	0.8442	-1507348	366666.14157	-4.111	0.0001
JAPAN	3.052619	2.73847026	1.115	0.2653	-5190043	1284509.9619	-4.04	0.0001
KENYA	1.118822	6.83787631	0.164	0.8701	-1153676	283630.57953	-4.068	0.0001
KOREA	0.71656	1.31283976	0.546	0.5853	-921300	220612.84122	-4.176	0.0001
LIBYA	1.015034	4.25690478	0.238	0.8116	-2846324	677882.08031	-4.199	0.0001
MADAGASC	-0.561079	6.87206097	-0.082	0.9349	-1103172	272641.13991	-4.046	0.0001
MALAYSIA	2.075147	4.71498261	0.44	0.66	-1306534	313210.34376	-4.171	0.0001
MAURITIU	2.081174	10.72563704	0.194	0.8462	-1840610	448232.8738	-4.106	0.0001
MEXICO	1.180509	0.51281795	2.302	0.0216	-700331	174870.20933	-4.005	0.0001
MOROCCO	0.86939	4.18225662	0.208	0.8354	-996723	244378.40135	-4.079	0.0001
MOZAMBIQ	-2.585494	6.11034857	-0.423	0.6723	-1067286	260688.88662	-4.094	0.0001
NEPAL	0.602245	9.13701696	0.066	0.9475	-1285355	316868.19962	-4.056	0.0001
NETHERLA	3.969442	5.12267706	0.775	0.4386	-4998945	1188794.031	-4.205	0.0001
NEWZEALA	1.695733	6.62197231	0.256	0.798	-3649632	861840.49638	-4.235	0.0001
NIGERIA	0.897353	2.69242026	0.333	0.739	-738451	183290.72772	-4.029	0.0001
NORWAY	4.628091	9.42741286	0.491	0.6236	-6800925	1603016.2618	-4.243	0.0001
OMAN	0.995318	6.99815532	0.142	0.8869	-2434104	583127.96682	-4.174	0.0001
PAKISTAN	0.401778	3.7559204	0.107	0.9148	-825583	203697.60733	-4.053	0.0001
PAPUANEW	1.43037	6.67606568	0.214	0.8304	-1260213	307953.26954	-4.092	0.0001
PARAGUAY	1.866881	8.04368164	0.232	0.8165	-2172805	520617.60152	-4.174	0.0001
PERU	0.612822	4.4255643	0.138	0.8899	-1080742	265455.00965	-4.071	0.0001
PHILIPPI	1.339008	3.09289788	0.433	0.6652	-778477	192250.968	-4.049	0.0001
SAUDIARA	0.722368	0.24043417	3.004	0.0027	-2351865	555892.20228	-4.231	0.0001
SENEGAL	0.81712	6.77981323	0.121	0.9041	-1224786	299937.35172	-4.083	0.0001

BM Model	Log-linear model (Model A")				Linear model (Model B")			
Variable	Par est	St. error	t-stat	Prob>lTl	Par est	St. error	t-stat	Prob>lTl
INTERCEPT	-4.929603	24.21045766	-0.204	0.8387	2973463	723818.60423	4.108	0.0001
^v1	-6.0012E+12	1.15553E+13	-0.519	0.6037				
^v2					-4.432387E+14	1.06649E+14	-4.156	0.0001
SEYCHELL	2.898005	15.1244589	0.192	0.8481	-2918315	704265.93655	-4.144	0.0001
SIERRALE	2.546105	11.6115202	0.219	0.8265	-1582325	389695.27365	-4.06	0.0001
SINGAPOR	3.983698	8.15451602	0.489	0.6253	-2906378	687471.10708	-4.228	0.0001
SOUTHAFR	1.101604	3.07344583	0.358	0.7201	-1072107	258322.31012	-4.15	0.0001
SPAIN	2.225372	2.88854304	0.77	0.4413	-2294894	545428.5334	-4.208	0.0001
SRILANKA	1.573466	6.56679465	0.24	0.8107	-1119878	275647.53744	-4.063	0.0001
SUDAN	-1.012161	4.67416747	-0.217	0.8286	-1050104	257415.65447	-4.079	0.0001
SWAZILAN	2.114093	11.1914	0.189	0.8502	-1575643	387031.00042	-4.071	0.0001
SWEDEN	5.689877	10.20813644	0.557	0.5774	-6345514	1500198.074	-4.23	0.0001
SWITZERL	5.44815	10.44583814	0.522	0.6021	-8857682	2091605.8644	-4.235	0.0001
SYRIA	0.57171	4.90525228	0.117	0.9072	-1174101	287533.13542	-4.083	0.0001
TANZANIA	-1.411248	5.50047991	-0.257	0.7976	-948278	235140.68791	-4.033	0.0001
THAILAND	1.430207	2.68862501	0.532	0.5949	-807379	198186.75961	-4.074	0.0001
TRINIDAD	2.104153	7.78929556	0.27	0.7871	-2380069	571494.56444	-4.165	0.0001
TUNISIA	2.013666	6.34362272	0.317	0.751	-1365735	332455.41639	-4.108	0.0001
TURKEY	0.86232	2.38497289	0.362	0.7178	-889828	217952.57131	-4.083	0.0001
UK	4.248091	4.23018184	1.004	0.3156	-3139919	775911.18463	-4.047	0.0001
USA	2.005528	0.63389963	3.164	0.0016	-4591869	1130277.1024	-4.063	0.0001
URUGUAY	3.282074	9.45152315	0.347	0.7285	-2047158	493862.58913	-4.145	0.0001
VENEZUEL	0.322745	0.69870713	0.462	0.6443	-1254924	299568.69215	-4.189	0.0001
YUGOSLAV	2.332316	3.72557566	0.626	0.5315	-1514805	366011.57722	-4.139	0.0001
ZAIRE	-1.227586	4.91094734	-0.25	0.8027	-918864	228096.43941	-4.028	0.0001
ZAMBIA	1.355847	6.18751538	0.219	0.8266	-1055197	259549.65555	-4.065	0.0001
ZIMBABWE	1.844827	8.89325623	0.207	0.8357	-1434695	351799.44112	-4.078	0.0001
YR1981	0.240043	0.25667601	0.935	0.35	-122780	29871.522647	-4.11	0.0001
YR1982	0.512476	0.82180964	0.624	0.5331	-133265	31832.805799	-4.186	0.0001
YR1983	1.119812	2.12744104	0.526	0.5988	-269449	64368.325002	-4.186	0.0001
YR1984	1.712786	2.97540957	0.576	0.565	-371661	88940.22317	-4.179	0.0001
YR1985	1.967566	3.3524988	0.587	0.5574	-500733	119684.77514	-4.184	0.0001
YR1986	1.813945	3.05321799	0.594	0.5526	-387006	94477.631226	-4.096	0.0001
YR1987	1.727975	2.7617054	0.626	0.5317	-369440	90933.119843	-4.063	0.0001
YR1988	1.796815	2.92042768	0.615	0.5386	-366119	89389.059417	-4.096	0.0001
YR1989	1.840249	3.03148908	0.607	0.544	-361063	88604.294094	-4.075	0.0001
YR1990	1.511384	2.26022648	0.669	0.5039	-277513	67909.316834	-4.087	0.0001

B–4 Comparison of efficiency level between 2SLS and 3SLS by T-statistic

Note: T-statistics from total capital in-out flow model and portfolio in-outflow model are presented.

Model and method / Var.	Total capital In-outflow model: Total K inflow 2SLS	Total K inflow 3SLS	Total K outflow 2SLS	Total K outflow 3SLS	Model and method / Var.	Portfolio in-outflow model: Portfolio inflow 2SLS	Portfolio inflow 3SLS	Portfolio outflow 2SLS	Portfolio outflow 3SLS
INTERCEPT	22.831	23.262	3.731	3.979	INTERCEPT	10.276	10.624	-0.996	-1.026
INTD	0.182	0.191	-0.622	-0.632	IGOVTD	1.479	1.572	0.468	0.586
RISKD	5.452	5.963			RISKD	4.462	4.643		
RISKDC			-5.228	-5.408	RISKDC			0.862	0.962
GNYPC			4.939	5.187	GNYPC			2.819	2.954
CAB	-3.228	-3.311	7.454	7.575	CAB	-1.46	-1.48	6.299	6.379
TREATY	3.465	3.673			TREATY	1.524	1.443		
EXCHCONT			-1.225	-1.39	EXCHCONT		1.201	1.19	
TAXD	0.872	0.908	2.359	2.526	TFDIVD	-1.497	-1.532	1.449	1.526
CD	5.895	6.05			CD	4.558	4.563		
TELECOMM			4.326	4.455	TELECOMM			4.663	4.674
TOTI			2.563	2.88	PORTI			2.691	2.74
TOTO	4.114	4.175			PORTO	4.129	4.171		
ALGERIA	0.624	0.536	4.164	4.191	ALGERIA	-7.734	-7.839	-2.388	-2.431
ARGENTIN	2.712	2.773	4.836	4.994	ARGENTIN	3.618	3.632	9.187	9.189
AUSTRALI	7.093	7.693	5.541	5.92	AUSTRALI	4.54	4.828	5.494	5.613
AUSTRIA	-0.308	0.163	-1.136	-0.92	AUSTRIA	3.265	3.578	6.395	6.488
BAHRAIN	-11.424	-11.475	-9.165	-9.28	BAHRAIN	-5.621	-5.679	-2.763	-2.864
BANGLADE	-10.977	-11.041	-1.378	-1.514	BANGLADE	-4.824	-4.952	1.699	1.698
BARBADOS	-11.579	-11.551	-11.131	-11.374	BARBADOS	-5.132	-5.188	-1.177	-1.375
BELGIUML	6.017	6.856	6.942	7.251	BELGIUML	1.929	2.313	11.182	11.324
BOLIVIA	-8.888	-8.886	-4.566	-4.812	BOLIVIA	-4.34	-4.417	0.65	0.578
BRAZIL	6.225	6.41	9.778	9.888	BRAZIL	-0.656	-0.623	6.642	6.667
CANADA	4.363	5.063	1.716	2.071	CANADA	4.106	4.591	8.124	8.409
CHILE	0.553	0.568	1.767	1.763	CHILE	-0.504	-0.591	1.793	1.753
COLOMBIA	-2.145	-2.224	-0.478	-0.484	COLOMBIA	-6.175	-6.245	-1.959	-1.927
CONGO	-6.427	-6.436	-3.736	-3.97	CONGO	-4.577	-4.672	-0.114	-0.231
COSTARIC	-8.150	-8.1178	-7.203	-7.344	COSTARIC	-4.899	-4.933	-0.433	-0.476
COTEIVOR	-6.166	-6.208	-4.095	-4.245	COTEIVOR	-5.759	-5.884	0.713	0.639
CYPRUS	-5.223	-5.064	-11.637	-11.954	CYPRUS	-2.274	-2.244	-2.865	-2.989
DENMARK	0.980	1.373	-2.056	-1.933	DENMARK	0.788	1.067	3.726	3.773
DOMINIRP	-9.516	-9.552	-6.225	-6.473	DOMINIRP	-4.731	-4.842	0.607	0.521
ECUADOR	-6.899	-6.891	-3.638	-3.703	ECUADOR	-6.129	-6.231	-0.164	-0.248
EGYPT	-1.544	-1.571	2.217	2.17	EGYPT	-4.942	-5.074	0.284	0.239
ELSALVAD	-8.447	-8.48	-7.422	-7.74	ELSALVAD	-3.218	-3.305	-0.172	-0.256
ETHIOPIA	-9.246	-9.3	-1.194	-1.335	ETHIOPIA	-4.354	-4.455	1.707	1.727
FINLAND	3.056	3.317	-1.709	-1.62	FINLAND	5.352	5.569	4.522	4.606
FRANCE	5.460	6.168	5.854	6.254	FRANCE	4.511	4.912	8.155	8.352
GABON	-6.416	-6.424	-7.161	-7.406	GABON	-5.042	-5.122	-2.297	-2.487
GERMANY	6.111	6.706	6.239	6.664	GERMANY	3.279	3.691	9.208	9.454
GREECE	-1.219	-1.243	-6.228	-6.336	GREECE	-6.093	-6.151	-4.521	-4.587

Model and method / Var.	Total capital In-outflow model				Model and method / Var.	Portfolio in-outflow model			
	Total K inflow		Total K outflow			Portfolio inflow		Portfolio outflow	
	2SLS	3SLS	2SLS	3SLS		2SLS	3SLS	2SLS	3SLS
GUATEMAL	-5.868	-5.89	-4.947	-5.188	GUATEMAL	-1.849	-1.954	3.422	3.326
HAITI	-11.714	-11.743	-3.339	-3.527	HAITI	-4.577	-4.668	1.506	1.511
HONDURAS	-8.658	-8.688	-5.597	-5.813	HONDURAS	-4.99	-5.087	-0.033	-0.104
ICELAND	-8.703	-8.528	-10.100	-10.468	ICELAND	-4.143	-4.153	-2.887	-3.105
INDIA	-5.742	-5.741	-0.578	-0.549	INDIA	-7.956	-8.076	0.552	0.59
INDONESI	-4.652	-4.646	1.251	1.328	INDONESI	-4.478	-4.559	3.42	3.49
IRELAND	0.015	0.209	-4.745	-4.739	IRELAND	3.74	3.837	5.666	5.621
ISRAEL	2.104	2.48	-2.748	-2.803	ISRAEL	4.582	4.791	4.785	4.853
ITALY	7.354	7.906	5.654	6.015	ITALY	1.795	2.143	7.04	7.164
JAMAICA	-9.634	-9.598	-7.505	-7.726	JAMAICA	-4.324	-4.391	-0.681	-0.773
JAPAN	9.303	9.918	8.839	9.292	JAPAN	5.303	5.72	10.551	10.837
KENYA	-10.966	-11.051	-3.966	-4.095	KENYA	-6.507	-6.645	0.602	0.598
KOREA	0.008	0.009	0.853	0.929	KOREA	-1.027	-1.063	0.34	0.439
LIBYA	-2.667	-2.632	-4.409	-4.646	LIBYA	-1.378	-1.448	6.188	6.014
MADAGASC	-12.778	-12.87	-3.548	-3.717	MADAGASC	-5.44	-5.596	1.669	1.639
MALAYSIA	-3.729	-3.77	-1.591	-1.412	MALAYSIA	-0.066	-0.001	4.387	4.531
MAURITIU	-12.695	-12.738	-9.821	-10.046	MAURITIU	-5.377	-5.49	-0.465	-0.589
MEXICO	7.326	7.421	9.837	9.882	MEXICO	3.529	3.504	12.263	12.27
MOROCCO	-6.385	-6.362	-2.352	-2.481	MOROCCO	-6.017	-6.101	0.07	0.018
MOZAMBIQ	-13.290	-13.267	-2.757	-2.904	MOZAMBIQ	-4.4	-4.5	1.914	1.916
NEPAL	-13.742	-13.872	-2.075	-2.198	NEPAL	-5.509	-5.677	1.825	1.847
NETHERLA	6.084	6.558	5.783	6.032	NETHERLA	3.965	4.277	9.186	9.281
NEWZEALA	-4.512	-4.234	-9.226	-9.264	NEWZEALA	-6.247	-6.159	-5.603	-5.662
NIGERIA	-2.437	-2.559	1.999	1.947	NIGERIA	-0.4	-0.567	4.555	4.561
NORWAY	0.318	0.885	0.261	0.463	NORWAY	1.671	2.016	6.256	6.344
OMAN	-10.334	-10.401	-9.707	-9.862	OMAN	-6.364	-6.483	-2.4	-2.55
PAKISTAN	-5.592	-5.68	-1.696	-1.813	PAKISTAN	-2.376	-2.517	1.72	1.715
PAPUANEW	-9.500	-9.613	-5.844	-5.985	PAPUANEW	-6.68	-6.824	-0.348	-0.389
PARAGUAY	-9.725	-9.785	-6.809	-6.913	PARAGUAY	-6.534	-6.644	-0.363	-0.462
PERU	-7.427	-7.429	-5.368	-5.527	PERU	-4.713	-4.794	-1.522	-1.574
PHILIPPI	-1.701	-1.657	1.286	1.268	PHILIPPI	-3.897	-3.928	-0.669	-0.629
SAUDIARA	5.214	5.174	3.225	3.365	SAUDIARA	4.635	4.761	11.714	11.799
SENEGAL	-8.869	-8.919	-4.195	-4.423	SENEGAL	-4.484	-4.616	1.06	0.97
SEYCHELL	-10.518	-10.472	-13.114	-13.476	SEYCHELL	-3.296	-3.328	-1.904	-2.078
SIERRALE	-11.233	-11.255	-2.672	-2.807	SIERRALE	-4.329	-4.431	1.699	1.696
SINGAPOR	-1.162	-0.573	-2.788	-2.649	SINGAPOR	-3.714	-3.559	2.33	2.29
SOUTHAFR	-3.740	-3.626	-1.307	-1.27	SOUTHAFR	-1.836	-1.729	5.493	5.571
SPAIN	6.187	6.551	1.008	1.155	SPAIN	1.997	2.214	1.9	2.018
SRILANKA	-8.323	-8.399	-2.056	-2.188:	SRILANKA	-5.752	-5.898	0.992	0.96
SUDAN	-11.057	-11.091	-5.808	-6.071	SUDAN	-4.279	-4.372	0.515	0.438
SWAZILAN	-12.251	-12.32	-5.105	-5.327	SWAZILAN	-4.627	-4.752	1.202	1.166
SWEDEN	3.131	3.648	1.657	1.885	SWEDEN	1.775	2.092	4.755	4.836
SWITZERL	2.374	2.762	2.054	2.309	SWITZERL	2.509	2.891	9.165	9.326
SYRIA	-7.298	-7.272	-5.642	-5.835	SYRIA	-5.333	-5.412	-0.237	-0.331
TANZANIA	-11.329	-11.392	-3.176	-3.358	TANZANIA	-4.587	-4.685	1.439	1.451
THAILAND	0.336	0.225	2.588	2.649	THAILAND	0.702	0.606	4.698	4.748
TRINIDAD	-8.949	-8.95	-8.968	-9.115	TRINIDAD	-6.147	-6.218	-3.001	-3.129
TUNISIA	-6.997	-7.062	-4.289	-4.331	TUNISIA	-4.628	-4.725	-0.34	-0.361
TURKEY	0.373	0.352	1.179	1.103	TURKEY	-1.44	-1.556	2.4	2.301
UK	9.365	10.133	9.392	9.848	UK	5.431	5.851	11.678	11.924

Model and method / Var.	Total capital In-outflow model: Total K inflow 2SLS	Total K inflow 3SLS	Total K outflow 2SLS	Total K outflow 3SLS	Model and method / Var.	Portfolio in-outflow model: Portfolio inflow 2SLS	Portfolio inflow 3SLS	Portfolio outflow 2SLS	Portfolio outflow 3SLS
USA	7.622	8.246	9.188	9.608	USA	4.452	4.924	11.116	11.387
URUGUAY	-4.711	-4.72	-4.910	-5.121	URUGUAY	-1.558	-1.666	1.03	0.834
VENEZUEL	-0.472	-0.438	1.608	1.682	VENEZUEL	-4.864	-4.869	-0.991	-1.037
YUGOSLAV	3.526	3.655	3.996	3.894	YUGOSLAV	-5.353	-5.386	-2.494	-2.627
ZAIRE	-10.116	-10.161	-4.383	-4.596	ZAIRE	-4.307	-4.403	1.205	1.198
ZAMBIA	-6.248	-6.244	-0.929	-1.07	ZAMBIA	-4.852	-4.935	1.268	1.259
ZIMBABWE	-11.125	-11.156	-5.349	-5.537	ZIMBABWE	-3.005	-3.093	4.794	4.758
YR1981	2.740	2.717	1.195	1.208	YR1981	0.332	0.321	0.448	0.461
YR1982	1.582	1.573	0.564	0.633	YR1982	0.348	0.355	0.551	0.612
YR1983	-0.347	-0.315	0.100	0.18	YR1983	0.958	0.997	0.989	1.059
YR1984	0.885	0.984	1.811	1.937	YR1984	1.964	2.054	1.135	1.216
YR1985	0.904	1.074	2.454	2.601	YR1985	3.341	3.473	2.321	2.424
YR1986	0.807	1.028	2.719	2.925	YR1986	2.699	2.858	2.788	2.916
YR1987	2.194	2.461	3.329	3.56	YR1987	2.961	3.137	2.753	2.896
YR1988	1.146	1.557	3.497	3.79	YR1988	3.314	3.532	3.637	3.811
YR1989	1.811	2.286	2.776	3.099	YR1989	2.627	2.89	3.237	3.432
YR1990	3.109	3.603	2.970	3.301	YR1990	1.914	2.203	3.178	3.4

Appendix C
Descriptive Statistics for 121 Countries

C–1 Total capital flows by country (1980–1990) (unit: billions of 1987 US dollars)

K Type / Country	Portfolio Inflow	Portfolio Outflow	Portfolio Gross	Portfolio Net	Bank capital Inflow	Bank capital Outflow	Bank capital Gross	Bank capital Net	Other-sector capital Inflow	Other-sector capital Outflow	Other-sector capital Gross	Other-sector capital Net	FDI Inflow	FDI Outflow	FDI Gross	FDI Net	Total capital Inflow	Total capital Outflow	Total capital Gross	Total capital Net
Algeria	0.00	0.00	0.01	0.00	1.43	0.47	1.90	0.97	38.64	38.14	76.78	0.51	0.33	0.17	0.50	0.16	40.41	38.78	79.19	1.63
Antigua *	0.00	0.00	0.00	0.00	0.11	0.01	0.11	0.10	0.01	0.00	0.01	0.01	0.32	0.00	0.32	0.32	0.44	0.01	0.45	0.44
Argentina	10.67	6.08	16.75	4.58	4.01	2.85	6.86	1.16	28.57	45.77	74.34	-17.20	8.13	0.56	8.69	7.57	51.39	55.26	106.65	-3.88
Australia	29.52	10.02	39.54	19.50	163.23	144.12	307.36	19.11	455.10	414.00	869.11	41.10	44.14	28.88	73.02	15.26	691.00	597.03	1289.03	94.97
Austria	22.04	10.39	32.43	11.66	35.67	36.82	72.49	-1.15	9.66	9.95	19.61	-0.29	4.38	4.11	8.49	0.27	71.76	61.26	133.02	10.49
Bahamas *	0.00	0.01	0.01	-0.01	0.20	0.05	0.25	0.15	0.46	0.33	0.79	0.13	0.13	0.1	0.23	0.03	0.79	0.48	1.27	0.31
Bahrain	0.29	0.08	0.37	0.21	1.28	2.98	4.26	-1.70	0.72	0.78	1.50	-0.07	0.64	0.41	1.05	0.24	2.93	4.25	7.18	-1.31
Bangladesh	0.00	0.01	0.01	-0.00	0.57	1.07	1.63	-0.50	0.38	0.21	0.58	0.17	0.01	0.00	0.01	0.01	0.96	1.28	2.24	-0.32
Barbados	0.02	0.03	0.05	-0.00	0.10	0.02	0.12	0.07	0.62	0.68	1.30	-0.06	0.09	0.02	0.11	0.06	0.82	0.75	1.58	0.07
Belgium-Lux.	33.26	72.47	105.73	-39.20	387.26	376.58	763.85	10.68	26.86	22.37	49.23	4.49	29.27	22.49	51.77	6.78	476.66	493.91	970.57	-17.26
Benin *	0.00	0.00	0.00	0.00	0.08	0.10	0.18	-0.01	0.67	0.34	1.01	0.33	0.00	0.00	0.00	0.00	0.76	0.44	1.19	0.32
Bolivia	0.00	0.00	0.00	-0.00	0.20	0.35	0.55	-0.15	0.93	1.10	2.04	-0.17	0.33	0.11	0.44	0.22	1.45	1.57	3.02	-0.11
Botswana *	0.00	0.00	0.00	0.00	0.11	0.14	0.25	-0.04	0.80	0.52	1.32	0.28	0.89	0.30	1.19	0.59	1.79	0.97	2.76	0.83
Brazil	1.71	2.95	4.67	-1.24	29.80	40.15	69.95	-10.34	49.76	73.50	123.27	-23.74	18.37	3.43	21.80	14.95	99.66	120.03	219.69	-20.37
Burkina Faso *	0.00	0.00	0.00	0.00	0.05	0.08	0.13	-0.03	0.18	0.11	0.29	0.08	0.01	0.01	0.01	0.00	0.24	0.19	0.44	0.05
Canada	185.60	94.12	279.71	91.48	57.97	42.72	100.69	15.26	43.38	20.75	64.12	22.63	24.08	53.58	77.66	-29.51	311.02	211.16	522.18	99.86
C. African R. *	0.00	0.00	0.00	0.00	0.02	0.03	0.05	-0.01	0.10	0.16	0.26	-0.06	0.02	0.00	0.02	0.02	0.14	0.19	0.33	-0.04
Chad *	0.00	0.00	0.00	0.00	0.02	0.05	0.08	-0.03	0.11	0.24	0.36	-0.13	0.12	0.03	0.16	0.09	0.26	0.33	0.59	-0.07
Chile	3.76	0.01	3.77	3.74	13.28	10.00	24.28	2.29	18.16	12.02	30.17	6.14	2.13	0.07	2.19	2.06	37.32	23.09	60.41	14.23
Colombia	0.25	0.02	0.26	0.23	1.38	2.45	3.83	-1.07	14.78	10.55	25.33	4.23	4.99	0.44	5.44	4.55	21.40	13.46	34.85	7.94
Comoros *	0.00	0.00	0.00	-0.00	0.01	0.01	0.02	0.00	0.02	0.02	0.05	-0.00	0.01	0.00	0.01	0.01	0.05	0.03	0.08	0.01
Congo	0.00	0.00	0.00	0.00	0.07	0.08	0.14	-0.01	3.47	3.21	6.68	0.26	0.27	0.00	0.27	0.27	3.81	3.29	7.10	0.52
Costa Rica	0.10	0.07	0.17	0.03	0.25	0.22	0.47	0.03	2.20	2.14	4.35	0.06	0.87	0.07	0.94	0.79	3.42	2.50	5.93	0.92
Cote d'Ivoire	0.00	0.03	0.03	-0.02	4.05	0.78	4.83	3.26	2.58	1.00	4.58	0.58	0.55	0.00	0.55	0.55	7.18	2.81	9.99	4.37
Cyprus	0.09	0.03	0.12	0.05	1.12	0.54	1.65	0.58	1.25	0.74	1.99	0.51	0.73	0.00	0.73	0.73	3.18	1.31	4.49	1.87
Denmark	11.82	7.50	19.32	4.32	33.16	32.58	65.74	0.59	21.50	0.57	22.08	20.93	3.33	6.18	9.51	-2.85	69.82	46.83	116.65	22.99
Dominica *	0.00	0.00	0.00	0.00	0.03	0.04	0.08	-0.01	0.05	0.00	0.05	0.05	0.04	0.00	0.04	0.04	0.12	0.04	0.17	0.08
Dominican R.	0.00	0.00	0.00	0.00	0.34	0.32	0.66	0.02	0.45	0.40	0.86	0.05	0.77	0.00	0.77	0.77	1.56	0.72	2.29	0.84
Ecuador	0.00	0.00	0.00	0.00	0.20	0.24	0.43	-0.04	5.87	5.25	11.12	0.63	0.70	0.01	0.72	0.69	6.77	5.49	12.27	1.28
Egypt	0.05	0.00	0.05	0.05	2.96	6.54	9.50	-3.58	8.09	7.68	15.77	0.41	9.65	0.12	9.77	9.52	20.74	14.34	35.08	6.40
El Salvador	0.00	0.00	0.00	-0.00	0.19	0.27	0.46	-0.08	0.29	0.39	0.68	-0.10	0.75	0.10	0.85	0.65	1.23	0.76	1.99	0.47
Ethiopia	0.00	0.00	0.00	0.00	0.04	0.03	0.07	0.01	1.18	0.79	1.96	0.39	0.00	0.00	0.00	0.00	1.21	0.82	2.03	0.39
Fiji *	0.00	0.00	0.00	0.00	0.24	0.25	0.49	-0.01	0.29	0.36	0.65	-0.07	0.46	0.07	0.53	0.39	0.00	0.68	1.67	0.32
Finland	30.01	11.58	41.58	18.43	25.18	9.59	34.77	15.60	24.80	20.47	45.27	4.32	2.92	12.37	15.30	-9.45	82.91	54.01	136.92	28.89
France	124.77	36.86	161.63	87.91	294.03	259.04	553.07	34.99	121.94	129.61	251.55	-7.67	52.66	94.98	147.64	-42.32	593.40	520.50	1113.90	72.91

K Type / Country	Portfolio				Bank capital				Other-sector capital				Foreign direct investment (FDI)				Total capital			
	Inflow	Outflow	Gross	Net	Inflow	Outflow	Gross	Net	Inflow	Outflow	Gross	Net	Inflow	Outflow	Gross	Net	Inflow	Outflow	Gross	Net
Gabon	0.00	0.00	0.00	0.00	0.22	0.29	0.51	-0.06	2.92	3.01	5.93	-0.10	1.07	0.46	1.53	0.61	4.21	3.76	7.97	0.45
Gambia *	0.00	0.00	0.00	0.00	0.04	0.04	0.08	-0.00	0.01	0.01	0.01	0.00	0.02	0.00	0.02	0.02	0.06	0.04	0.11	0.02
Germany W.	114.71	145.55	260.26	-30.84	369.26	458.97	828.23	-89.71	122.73	208.11	330.85	-85.38	34.24	107.24	141.48	-72.99	640.94	919.87	1560.81	-278.93
Ghana *	0.00	0.00	0.00	0.00	0.17	0.16	0.34	0.01	0.42	0.64	1.06	-0.23	0.10	0.01	0.10	0.09	0.68	0.81	1.50	-0.13
Greece	0.00	0.00	0.00	0.00	3.63	0.74	4.36	2.89	14.48	7.29	21.77	7.19	6.49	0.00	6.49	6.49	24.59	8.03	32.62	16.56
Greneda *	0.00	0.00	0.00	0.00	0.03	0.03	0.07	0.00	0.00	0.00	0.00	0.00	0.05	0.00	0.05	0.05	0.09	0.03	0.12	0.05
Guatemala	0.47	0.51	0.98	-0.03	0.16	0.10	0.27	0.06	2.05	0.98	3.04	1.07	1.08	0.00	1.08	1.08	3.77	1.59	5.36	2.18
Haiti	0.00	0.00	0.00	0.00	0.05	0.08	0.13	-0.03	0.31	0.10	0.41	0.20	0.08	0.00	0.08	0.08	0.44	0.18	0.62	0.25
Honduras	0.00	0.00	0.01	-0.00	0.08	0.16	0.24	-0.07	1.72	1.22	2.94	0.49	0.30	0.01	0.31	0.29	2.10	1.39	3.49	0.71
Hungary *	0.00	0.00	0.00	0.00	0.01	1.08	1.09	-1.06	0.77	0.48	1.24	0.29	0.00	0.00	0.00	0.00	0.78	1.55	2.34	-0.77
Iceland	0.00	0.00	0.00	0.00	0.80	0.54	1.35	0.26	1.07	0.86	1.93	0.21	0.17	0.10	0.26	0.07	2.04	1.50	3.54	0.54
India	0.00	0.00	0.00	0.00	1.18	1.37	2.55	-0.19	17.76	4.01	21.78	13.75	0.00	0.00	0.00	0.00	18.94	5.38	24.33	13.56
Indonesia	1.02	0.48	1.49	0.54	0.00	0.00	0.00	0.00	17.54	10.83	28.37	6.71	4.15	0.00	4.15	4.15	22.71	11.31	34.02	11.40
Ireland	9.51	3.08	12.59	6.43	14.59	10.06	24.65	4.53	0.00	6.48	6.48	-6.48	1.46	0.04	1.50	1.41	25.56	19.66	45.21	5.90
Israel	9.96	3.36	13.32	6.61	6.37	5.28	11.64	1.09	11.29	11.00	23.29	-0.70	1.35	0.80	2.15	0.56	28.98	21.42	50.40	7.55
Italy	37.57	44.19	81.76	-6.62	135.03	85.00	221.03	49.03	290.45	246.19	536.64	44.27	24.96	28.54	53.51	-3.58	488.02	404.92	892.93	83.10
Jamaica	0.00	0.00	0.00	0.00	0.11	0.14	0.24	-0.03	1.26	0.85	2.11	0.41	0.49	0.30	0.79	0.20	1.86	1.28	3.14	0.57
Japan	300.77	649.12	949.89	-348.35	895.14	740.31	1635.45	154.82	245.03	220.91	465.94	24.12	5.66	181.45	187.11	-175.79	1446.60	1791.80	3238.39	-345.20
Jordan *	0.00	0.00	0.00	0.00	1.26	0.13	1.40	1.13	0.01	0.05	0.07	-0.04	0.28	0.04	0.32	0.24	1.56	0.22	1.78	1.34
Kenya	0.00	0.00	0.00	0.00	0.09	0.08	0.17	0.01	1.75	0.87	2.62	0.88	0.48	0.07	0.55	0.41	2.32	1.03	3.35	1.30
Korea S.	2.88	0.78	3.66	2.11	13.37	11.74	25.11	1.63	20.30	17.62	37.92	2.68	3.83	1.85	5.68	1.99	40.39	31.98	72.37	8.41
Kuwait *	1.44	3.05	4.49	-1.61	4.65	6.91	11.56	-2.27	5.76	6.46	12.22	-0.70	0.13	1.94	2.07	-1.80	11.98	18.36	30.34	-6.38
Lao PDR *	0.00	0.00	0.00	0.00	0.00	0.00	0.00	0.00	0.08	0.00	0.08	0.08	0.00	0.00	0.00	0.00	0.08	0.00	0.08	0.08
Lesotho *	0.00	0.00	0.00	0.00	0.08	0.13	0.21	-0.05	0.00	0.00	0.00	-0.00	0.08	0.00	0.08	0.08	0.16	0.13	0.29	0.03
Libya	0.11	4.46	4.57	-4.35	1.58	0.51	2.09	1.06	8.83	3.27	12.10	5.56	1.01	3.41	4.42	-2.39	11.53	11.65	23.18	-0.13
Madagascar	0.00	0.00	0.00	0.00	0.21	0.26	0.47	-0.05	0.00	0.00	0.00	0.00	0.03	0.00	0.03	0.03	0.24	0.26	0.50	-0.02
Malaysia	8.42	1.70	10.12	6.73	4.44	4.74	9.18	-0.30	8.31	8.27	16.58	0.04	11.41	0.00	11.41	11.41	32.58	14.71	47.29	17.88
Mali *	0.00	0.00	0.00	0.00	0.08	0.06	0.14	0.02	0.02	0.01	0.03	0.02	0.05	0.02	0.07	0.04	0.16	0.08	0.24	0.08
Malta *	0.05	0.18	0.23	-0.14	0.32	0.58	0.89	-0.26	0.20	0.14	0.34	0.06	0.33	0.01	0.34	0.32	0.89	0.91	1.80	-0.02
Mauritania *	0.00	0.00	0.00	0.00	0.14	0.08	0.22	0.06	0.72	0.35	1.07	0.37	0.09	0.00	0.09	0.09	0.95	0.43	1.38	0.52
Mauritius	0.00	0.00	0.00	-0.00	0.03	0.14	0.17	-0.11	0.62	0.29	0.91	0.33	0.14	0.00	0.14	0.13	0.78	0.44	1.22	0.35
Mexico	7.08	12.03	19.12	-4.95	46.10	22.67	68.78	23.43	42.12	76.36	118.48	-34.25	19.94	0.68	20.62	19.25	115.24	111.75	226.99	3.48
Morocco	0.00	0.00	0.00	0.00	0.24	0.56	0.81	-0.32	5.55	3.69	9.24	1.85	0.77	0.00	0.77	0.76	6.56	4.26	10.82	2.30
Mozambique	0.00	0.00	0.00	0.00	0.00	0.00	0.00	-0.00	0.00	0.00	0.00	0.00	0.02	0.00	0.02	0.02	0.02	0.00	0.03	0.02
Nepal	0.00	0.00	0.00	0.00	0.04	0.03	0.07	0.02	0.32	0.15	0.47	0.17	0.00	0.00	0.00	0.00	0.36	0.18	0.54	0.18
Netherlands	39.91	32.40	72.31	7.50	200.27	200.63	400.91	-0.36	34.80	35.80	70.61	-1.00	37.35	64.48	101.82	-27.13	312.33	333.32	645.65	-20.99
New Zealand	0.18	0.00	0.18	0.18	1.43	1.03	2.46	0.40	9.48	2.61	12.09	6.86	6.65	5.73	12.38	0.92	17.74	9.37	27.11	8.37
Nicaragua *	0.00	0.00	0.00	0.00	0.17	0.04	0.21	0.13	0.11	0.39	0.50	-0.27	0.01	0.00	0.01	0.01	0.29	0.43	0.72	-0.13

K Type / Country	Portfolio				Bank capital				Other-sector capital				Foreign direct investment (FDI)				Total capital			
	Inflow	Outflow	Gross	Net	Inflow	Outflow	Gross	Net	Inflow	Outflow	Gross	Net	Inflow	Outflow	Gross	Net	Inflow	Outflow	Gross	Net
Niger *	0.00	0.00	0.00	0.00	0.18	0.14	0.31	0.04	0.31	0.37	0.67	-0.06	0.09	0.02	0.11	0.07	0.57	0.52	1.09	0.05
Nigeria	3.25	0.38	3.63	2.86	0.53	1.25	1.78	-0.72	7.30	11.15	18.45	-3.85	5.38	0.59	5.97	4.79	16.46	13.37	29.83	3.09
Norway	25.22	10.96	36.18	14.26	23.99	19.06	43.05	4.93	39.93	40.35	80.28	-0.42	6.04	10.67	16.71	-4.63	95.17	81.04	176.21	14.13
Oman	0.00	0.00	0.00	0.00	0.51	1.01	1.52	-0.51	0.26	0.44	0.70	-0.18	1.33	0.00	1.33	1.33	2.09	1.45	3.54	0.65
Pakistan	0.56	0.00	0.56	0.56	2.20	1.41	3.61	0.79	2.87	1.00	3.87	1.86	1.28	0.07	1.35	1.20	6.90	2.49	9.38	4.41
Panama *	1.21	1.39	2.60	-0.17	38.48	39.18	77.66	-0.70	25.08	25.24	50.32	-0.16	0.78	0.51	1.29	0.27	65.55	66.31	131.87	-0.76
Papua N-G	0.00	0.00	0.00	-0.00	0.13	0.02	0.15	0.11	2.62	1.75	4.37	0.87	1.39	0.05	1.44	1.33	4.13	1.82	5.96	2.31
Paraguay	0.00	0.00	0.00	0.00	0.34	0.33	0.68	0.01	2.42	1.32	3.74	1.10	0.20	0.00	0.20	0.20	2.97	1.66	4.62	1.31
Peru	0.00	0.00	0.00	0.00	0.11	0.09	0.21	0.02	4.16	3.41	7.58	0.75	0.48	0.19	0.67	0.29	4.75	3.70	8.45	1.06
Philippines	0.36	0.05	0.41	0.31	2.80	1.88	4.69	0.92	11.56	11.70	23.25	-0.14	3.34	0.57	3.91	2.77	18.06	14.19	32.25	3.87
Portugal	4.95	0.01	4.95	4.94	6.63	8.29	14.92	-1.66	18.88	15.86	34.74	3.01	6.21	0.34	6.55	5.88	36.67	24.51	61.17	12.16
Romania *	0.00	0.00	0.00	0.00	20.72	31.01	51.73	-10.29	0.00	0.00	0.00	0.00	0.00	0.00	0.00	0.00	20.72	31.01	51.73	-10.29
Rwanda *	0.00	0.00	0.00	0.00	0.02	0.02	0.04	0.00	0.18	0.13	0.30	0.05	0.17	0.00	0.17	0.17	0.37	0.15	0.52	0.22
St. Lucia *	0.00	0.00	0.00	0.00	0.03	0.06	0.09	-0.02	0.03	0.00	0.04	0.03	0.23	0.00	0.23	0.23	0.30	0.06	0.36	0.24
St. Vincent *	0.00	0.00	0.00	0.00	0.02	0.05	0.08	-0.03	0.03	0.00	0.03	0.03	0.04	0.00	0.04	0.04	0.09	0.05	0.14	0.04
Sao T and P *	0.00	0.00	0.00	0.00	0.00	0.00	0.00	0.00	0.08	0.03	0.11	0.05	0.00	0.00	0.00	0.00	0.08	0.03	0.11	0.05
Saudi Arabia	50.03	59.18	109.20	-9.15	7.83	35.40	43.23	-27.57	37.45	7.56	45.02	29.89	27.78	4.31	32.09	23.47	123.09	106.45	229.54	16.64
Senegal	0.01	0.01	0.02	0.01	0.38	0.38	0.76	0.01	0.86	0.61	1.47	0.25	0.21	0.20	0.41	0.01	1.47	1.19	2.67	0.28
Seychelles	0.00	0.00	0.00	0.00	0.01	0.01	0.02	0.00	0.00	0.00	0.00	0.00	0.15	0.06	0.22	0.09	0.17	0.07	0.24	0.10
Sierra Leone	0.00	0.00	0.00	0.00	0.03	0.07	0.10	-0.04	0.32	0.17	0.50	0.15	0.22	0.28	0.49	-0.06	0.57	0.52	1.09	0.05
Singapore	1.63	1.78	3.41	-0.15	20.73	21.61	42.34	-0.88	7.24	8.34	15.57	-1.10	22.79	0.00	22.79	22.79	52.39	31.73	84.12	20.66
Solomon Isl. *	0.00	0.00	0.00	0.00	0.02	0.01	0.03	0.00	0.07	0.02	0.08	0.05	0.04	0.01	0.04	0.03	0.12	0.03	0.15	0.09
South Africa	2.53	2.82	5.35	-0.29	4.42	0.84	5.26	3.58	8.52	11.39	19.91	-2.87	2.15	3.24	5.39	-1.09	17.63	18.29	35.92	-0.67
Spain	21.91	2.01	23.92	19.90	24.97	7.45	32.42	17.52	62.40	46.40	108.79	15.00	45.11	8.08	53.19	37.04	154.39	63.93	218.32	90.45
Sri Lanka	0.00	0.00	0.00	0.00	0.47	0.43	0.90	0.03	2.92	2.31	5.23	0.61	0.43	0.01	0.44	0.42	3.82	2.75	6.57	1.07
Sudan	0.00	0.00	0.00	0.00	0.53	1.09	1.62	-0.57	0.00	0.03	0.03	-0.03	0.01	0.00	0.02	0.01	0.54	1.12	1.66	-0.58
Suriname *	0.00	0.00	0.00	-0.00	0.08	0.02	0.01	0.06	0.19	0.09	0.28	0.09	0.10	0.44	0.54	-0.35	0.36	0.56	0.92	-0.19
Swaziland	0.02	0.00	0.02	0.02	0.05	0.08	0.12	-0.03	0.10	0.22	0.32	-0.12	0.35	0.06	0.40	0.30	0.52	0.36	0.87	0.16
Sweden	22.19	14.77	36.96	7.43	103.36	47.29	150.65	56.07	67.46	43.47	110.94	23.99	7.48	43.54	51.03	-36.06	200.50	149.07	349.58	51.43
Switzerland	41.72	95.80	137.52	-54.08	78.46	64.48	142.94	13.98	8.38	46.78	55.16	-38.40	26.22	36.72	62.95	-10.50	154.79	243.78	398.57	-88.99
Syria	0.00	0.00	0.00	0.00	1.77	0.67	2.44	1.10	3.06	1.97	5.02	1.09	0.00	0.00	0.00	0.00	4.83	2.64	7.46	2.19
Tanzania	0.00	0.00	0.00	0.00	0.05	0.07	0.11	-0.02	0.53	0.16	0.69	0.37	0.00	0.00	0.00	0.00	0.58	0.23	0.81	0.35
Thailand	4.40	0.82	5.22	3.58	3.50	1.54	5.03	1.96	30.96	13.09	44.05	17.88	7.49	0.98	8.47	6.51	46.35	16.42	62.78	29.93
Togo *	0.01	0.00	0.01	0.00	0.21	0.17	0.37	0.04	0.41	0.13	0.54	0.28	0.12	0.04	0.15	0.09	0.74	0.33	1.08	0.41
Tonga *	0.00	0.00	0.00	0.00	0.01	0.00	0.01	0.01	0.00	0.00	0.00	0.00	0.01	0.00	0.01	0.01	0.02	0.00	0.03	0.02
Trinidad & T.	0.00	0.00	0.00	0.00	0.14	0.21	0.36	-0.07	2.04	2.46	4.50	-0.42	1.72	0.48	2.20	1.23	3.90	3.16	7.06	0.74
Tunisia	0.31	0.01	0.32	0.30	1.14	0.71	1.85	0.42	4.96	3.43	8.40	1.53	1.58	0.04	1.62	1.54	7.99	4.19	12.19	3.80
Turkey	3.54	0.00	3.54	3.54	8.54	6.09	14.63	2.46	13.93	6.39	20.32	7.54	2.36	0.01	2.36	2.35	28.37	12.49	40.86	15.88

K Type / Country	Portfolio				Bank capital				Other-sector capital				Foreign direct investment (FDI)				Total capital			
	Inflow	Outflow	Gross	Net	Inflow	Outflow	Gross	Net	Inflow	Outflow	Gross	Net	Inflow	Outflow	Gross	Net	Inflow	Outflow	Gross	Net
Uganda *	0.00	0.00	0.00	0.00	0.08	0.11	0.19	-0.03	0.21	0.15	0.36	0.06	0.00	0.00	0.00	0.00	0.29	0.26	0.55	0.03
UK	155.30	202.91	358.21	-47.61	718.71	586.10	1304.81	132.61	94.29	82.42	176.71	11.86	116.23	183.64	299.87	-67.42	1084.52	1055.07	2139.59	29.45
USA	593.35	189.86	783.20	403.49	582.42	477.35	1059.78	105.07	131.70	102.74	234.44	28.95	430.29	252.28	682.56	178.01	1737.75	1022.23	2759.98	715.52
Uruguay	0.38	0.06	0.44	0.32	2.78	2.28	5.06	0.49	1.70	1.50	3.20	0.20	0.42	0.03	0.45	0.39	5.28	3.87	9.16	1.41
Venezuela	16.75	2.08	18.82	14.67	3.28	3.25	6.53	0.03	12.03	28.29	40.32	-16.26	1.36	1.06	2.41	0.30	33.42	34.68	68.10	-1.26
W. Samoa *	0.00	0.00	0.00	0.00	0.00	0.00	0.00	0.00	0.01	0.02	0.03	-0.01	0.00	0.00	0.00	0.00	0.01	0.02	0.03	-0.01
Yugoslavia	0.00	0.00	0.00	0.00	15.97	15.13	31.10	0.84	27.09	23.08	50.17	4.00	0.00	0.00	0.00	0.00	43.05	38.21	81.26	4.84
Zaire	0.00	0.00	0.00	0.00	0.74	0.07	0.81	0.67	0.12	0.00	0.12	0.12	0.04	0.00	0.04	0.04	0.91	0.07	0.98	0.84
Zambia	0.00	0.00	0.00	0.00	0.28	0.50	0.78	-0.22	4.65	2.44	7.10	2.21	0.56	0.00	0.56	0.56	5.49	2.95	8.43	2.54
Zimbabwe	0.20	0.43	0.63	-0.23	0.28	0.20	0.48	0.09	0.65	0.24	0.89	0.41	0.07	0.15	0.21	-0.08	1.19	1.01	2.21	0.18
86 Countries (1)	1935.17	1733.84	3669.01	201.33	4370.28	3824.88	8195.16	545.40	2355.21	2217.36	4572.57	137.85	1093.89	1170.91	2264.80	-77.01	9754.56	8946.98	18701.54	807.57
35 Countries (2)	2.71	4.64	7.35	-1.93	67.68	80.76	148.44	-13.07	37.38	36.78	74.16	0.60	4.73	3.53	8.27	1.20	112.51	125.70	238.21	-13.19
121 Countries (3)	1937.88	1738.48	3676.36	199.41	4437.97	3905.63	8343.60	532.33	2392.59	2254.13	4646.73	138.46	1098.63	1174.44	2273.07	-75.81	9867.07	9072.69	18939.75	794.38

Source: Balance of Payments Statistics Yearbook (IMF).

Notes

* Countries not included in the model due to the availability of exogenous variables.
(1) Sum of countries included in the model.
(2) Sum of countries not included in the model.
(3) Sum of all countries.

C-2 Gross capital flows by level of income in 121 countries

Level of income	Year	Actual amount (millions of 1987 US dollars) Portfolio	Bank	Others	FDI	Total	Share of world total (%) Portfolio	Bank	Others	FDI	Total	Proportion of total gross flows (%) Portfolio	Bank	Others	FDI	Total
	1980	44	1804	4808	1542	8199	0.04	0.37	2.15	1.76	0.90	0.54	22.01	58.65	18.81	100.00
	1981	51	1542	6326	1724	9643	0.04	0.27	2.26	1.47	0.87	0.53	15.99	65.61	17.88	100.00
	1982	300	1768	8353	1663	12084	0.20	0.39	3.04	1.57	1.23	2.48	14.63	69.12	13.76	100.00
Low	1983	367	1286	8102	1606	11360	0.23	0.35	3.19	1.67	1.30	3.23	11.32	71.32	14.13	100.00
income	1984	450	2255	9397	1522	13623	0.21	0.52	3.04	1.07	1.24	3.31	16.55	68.98	11.17	100.00
countries	1985	1108	2188	15392	2519	21207	0.32	0.40	4.73	1.98	1.57	5.22	10.32	72.58	11.88	100.00
(36)	1986	512	2364	12018	2174	17068	0.11	0.24	2.88	1.17	0.82	2.00	13.85	70.41	12.74	100.00
	1987	1374	2985	12413	2481	19254	0.30	0.24	2.64	0.92	0.79	7.14	15.50	64.47	12.89	100.00
	1988	823	3286	11472	2634	18215	0.15	0.31	2.07	0.80	0.74	4.52	18.04	62.98	14.46	100.00
	1989	382	3320	12732	4232	20665	0.06	0.30	1.89	1.07	0.73	1.85	16.06	61.61	20.48	100.00
	1990	352	4120	16147	2756	23375	0.08	0.39	1.86	0.66	0.83	1.51	17.62	69.08	11.79	100.00
	Sum	**5762**	**26918**	**117160**	**24852**	**174692**	**0.16**	**0.32**	**2.52**	**1.09**	**0.92**	**3.30**	**15.41**	**67.07**	**14.23**	**100.00**
	1980	1333	18066	35878	4344	59620	1.26	3.67	16.06	4.95	6.55	2.24	30.30	60.18	7.29	100.00
	1981	2451	24026	47331	5181	78989	1.70	4.25	16.94	4.42	7.14	3.10	30.42	59.92	6.56	100.00
	1982	4241	19632	39042	4759	67674	2.83	4.37	14.21	4.49	6.91	6.27	29.01	57.69	7.03	100.00
Lower-	1983	3115	20930	39179	4093	67317	1.99	5.65	15.41	4.27	7.68	4.63	31.09	58.20	6.08	100.00
middle	1984	3162	22476	41159	3803	70599	1.49	5.19	13.31	2.67	6.43	4.48	31.84	58.30	5.39	100.00
income	1985	4449	14734	37558	4413	61155	1.29	2.68	11.53	3.47	4.54	7.28	24.09	61.41	7.22	100.00
countries	1986	1706	16912	34160	3564	56341	0.36	1.69	8.19	1.92	2.72	3.03	30.02	60.63	6.32	100.00
(39)	1987	3347	28153	32649	4708	68857	0.73	2.26	6.95	1.75	2.82	4.86	40.89	47.42	6.84	100.00
	1988	5900	31276	44550	6247	87973	1.10	2.97	8.03	1.91	3.56	6.71	35.55	50.64	7.10	100.00
	1989	10352	9886	41471	7876	69585	1.64	0.89	6.16	1.99	2.47	14.88	14.21	59.60	11.32	100.00
	1990	4807	12093	48245	9967	75112	1.02	1.13	5.57	2.38	2.66	6.40	16.10	64.23	13.27	100.00
	Sum	**44864**	**218183**	**441222**	**58953**	**763222**	**1.22**	**2.61**	**9.50**	**2.59**	**4.03**	**5.88**	**28.59**	**57.81**	**7.72**	**100.00**
	1980	20106	21124	46988	9940	98157	18.95	4.29	21.04	11.32	10.79	20.48	21.52	47.87	10.13	100.00
Upper	1981	28005	32518	53375	14071	127969	19.46	5.75	19.10	12.01	11.57	21.88	25.41	41.71	10.00	100.00
middle	1982	14301	22968	56304	18257	111830	9.54	5.12	20.49	17.23	11.42	12.79	20.54	50.35	16.33	100.00
income-	1983	15602	24994	41337	8280	90213	9.99	6.74	16.26	8.63	10.29	17.29	27.71	45.82	9.18	100.00
mountries	1984	17773	21232	45201	10691	94897	8.37	4.90	14.62	7.50	8.65	18.73	22.37	47.63	11.27	100.00
(21)	1985	12476	24319	56158	5480	98433	3.62	4.42	17.24	4.31	7.30	12.67	24.71	57.05	5.57	100.00

Level of income	Year	Actual amount (millions of 1987 US dollars) Portfolio	Bank	Others	FDI	Total	Share of world total (%) Portfolio	Bank	Others	FDI	Total	Proportion of total gross flows (%) Portfolio	Bank	Others	FDI	Total
Upper	1986	6544	25640	51174	6558	89916	1.39	2.57	12.27	3.53	4.34	7.28	28.52	56.91	7.29	100.00
middle	1987	11397	27819	52339	9065	100619	2.50	2.23	11.14	3.37	4.12	11.33	27.65	52.02	9.01	100.00
income-	1988	10507	27738	42728	10046	91018	1.96	2.63	7.70	3.07	3.68	11.54	30.48	46.94	11.04	100.00
mountries	1989	4149	25533	39996	10037	79716	0.66	2.29	5.95	2.54	2.84	5.20	32.03	50.17	12.59	100.00
(cont'd)	1990	30582	31498	37087	11120	110287	6.51	2.95	4.28	2.65	3.91	27.73	28.56	33.63	10.08	100.00
	Sum	**171441**	**285384**	**522686**	**113545**	**1093056**	**4.66**	**3.42**	**11.25**	**4.00**	**5.77**	**15.68**	**26.11**	**47.82**	**10.39**	**100.00**
	1980	84591	451472	135694	71984	743741	79.75	91.68	60.75	81.98	81.76	11.37	60.70	18.24	9.68	100.00
	1981	113403	507503	172360	96223	889490	78.80	89.73	61.69	82.10	80.42	12.75	57.06	19.38	10.82	100.00
	1982	131021	404464	171135	81285	787905	87.43	90.11	62.27	76.71	80.44	16.63	51.33	21.72	10.32	100.00
High	1983	137172	323484	165574	81940	708170	87.79	87.26	65.14	85.43	80.74	19.37	45.68	23.38	11.57	100.00
income	1984	191014	387250	213366	126563	918194	89.93	89.39	69.02	88.77	83.68	20.80	42.18	23.24	13.78	100.00
mountries	1985	327060	508957	216623	114805	1167446	94.77	92.50	66.50	90.24	86.59	28.02	43.60	18.56	9.83	100.00
(25)	1986	461386	954216	319655	173226	1908484	98.14	95.50	76.65	93.37	92.12	24.18	49.00	16.75	9.08	100.00
	1987	440459	1188857	372360	253050	2254726	96.47	95.28	79.27	93.96	92.28	19.53	52.73	16.51	11.22	100.00
	1988	519204	991238	455841	308414	2274697	96.79	94.09	82.19	94.22	92.02	22.83	43.58	20.04	13.56	100.00
	1989	614872	1075646	578515	372704	2641737	97.64	96.52	85.00	94.39	93.96	23.28	40.72	21.90	14.11	100.00
	1990	434110	1020026	764534	395525	2614195	92.39	95.53	88.28	94.31	92.60	16.61	39.02	29.25	15.13	100.00
	Sum	**3454292**	**7813115**	**3565658**	**2075719**	**16908784**	**93.96**	**93.64**	**76.73**	**91.32**	**89.28**	**20.43**	**46.21**	**21.09**	**12.28**	**100.00**
	1980	106073	492466	223369	87810	909717	100.00	100.00	100.00	100.00	100.00	11.66	54.13	24.55	9.65	100.00
	1981	143910	565590	279392	117198	1106090	100.00	100.00	100.00	100.00	100.00	13.01	51.13	25.26	10.60	100.00
	1982	149863	448833	274834	105963	979493	100.00	100.00	100.00	100.00	100.00	15.30	45.82	28.06	10.82	100.00
All	1983	156256	370693	254191	95920	877060	100.00	100.00	100.00	100.00	100.00	17.82	42.27	28.98	10.94	100.00
countries	1984	212399	433213	309122	142579	1097313	100.00	100.00	100.00	100.00	100.00	19.36	39.48	28.17	12.99	100.00
(121)	1985	345093	550198	325732	127218	1348241	100.00	100.00	100.00	100.00	100.00	25.60	40.81	24.16	9.44	100.00
	1986	470148	999132	417008	185521	2071809	100.00	100.00	100.00	100.00	100.00	22.69	48.23	20.13	8.95	100.00
	1987	456576	1247815	469761	269304	2443456	100.00	100.00	100.00	100.00	100.00	18.69	51.07	19.23	11.02	100.00
	1988	536434	1053539	554591	327340	2471903	100.00	100.00	100.00	100.00	100.00	21.70	42.62	22.44	13.24	100.00
	1989	629755	1114385	672715	394848	2811703	100.00	100.00	100.00	100.00	100.00	22.40	39.63	23.93	14.04	100.00
	1990	469852	1067736	866012	419368	2822969	100.00	100.00	100.00	100.00	100.00	16.64	37.82	30.68	14.86	100.00
	Sum	**3676359**	**8343600**	**4646727**	**2273068**	**18939753**	**100.00**	**100.00**	**100.00**	**100.00**	**100.00**	**19.41**	**44.05**	**24.53**	**12.00**	**100.00**

Source: Balance of Payments Statistics (IMF).

C-3 Capital inflows by level of income in 121 countries

Level of income	Year	Actual amount (millions of 1987 US dollars) Portfolio	Bank	Others	FDI	Total	Share of world total (%) Portfolio	Bank	Others	FDI	Total	Proportion of total gross flows (%) Portfolio	Bank	Others	FDI	Total
	1980	44	811	2460	920	4235	0.09	0.32	2.04	2.20	0.90	1.04	19.14	58.09	21.73	100.00
	1981	50	910	4069	1701	6730	0.07	0.32	2.70	2.71	1.19	0.75	13.52	60.46	25.27	100.00
	1982	299	1190	6029	1622	9141	0.41	0.58	4.08	2.54	1.87	3.27	13.02	65.96	17.75	100.00
Low	1983	367	698	5952	1564	8580	0.45	0.36	4.89	2.79	1.89	4.27	8.14	69.36	18.23	100.00
income	1984	437	1224	5970	1481	9112	0.38	0.51	4.04	2.05	1.58	4.80	13.43	65.52	16.25	100.00
countries	1985	1063	1198	6678	2462	11401	0.54	0.41	4.36	4.19	1.62	9.32	10.51	58.58	21.59	100.00
(36)	1986	510	1294	7020	2004	10827	0.21	0.24	3.89	2.41	1.05	4.71	11.95	64.84	18.51	100.00
	1987	1285	872	7726	2409	12292	0.52	0.13	3.05	1.92	0.94	10.46	7.09	62.85	19.60	100.00
	1988	727	1164	6299	2547	10738	0.26	0.20	2.31	1.65	0.84	6.77	10.84	58.66	23.72	100.00
	1989	16	1006	8441	4136	13598	0.00	0.17	2.37	2.22	0.92	0.12	7.40	62.07	30.41	100.00
	1990	92	863	10685	2721	14360	0.04	0.15	2.19	1.41	0.95	0.64	6.01	74.40	18.95	100.00
	Sum	**4889**	**11231**	**71329**	**23566**	**111015**	**0.25**	**0.25**	**2.98**	**2.15**	**1.13**	**4.40**	**10.12**	**64.25**	**21.23**	**100.00**
	1980	449	11141	20915	3742	36246	0.89	4.37	17.30	8.93	7.74	1.24	30.74	57.70	10.32	100.00
	1981	2326	14369	26140	4801	47635	3.43	5.02	17.36	7.65	8.39	4.88	30.16	54.88	10.08	100.00
	1982	4042	10037	20558	4291	38927	5.60	4.89	13.90	6.71	7.95	10.38	25.78	52.81	11.02	100.00
Lower-	1983	2897	10409	19388	3601	36296	3.54	5.34	15.93	6.43	7.99	7.98	28.68	53.42	9.92	100.00
middle	1984	2778	10720	21493	3433	38424	2.41	4.47	14.56	4.75	6.68	7.23	27.90	55.94	8.93	100.00
income	1985	3459	6467	19679	4150	33754	1.75	2.19	12.86	7.07	4.79	10.25	19.16	58.30	12.29	100.00
countries	1986	920	6959	19300	3312	30490	0.39	1.30	10.70	3.99	2.94	3.02	22.82	63.30	10.86	100.00
(39)	1987	2344	13666	16666	3700	36377	0.95	1.00	6.58	2.95	2.77	6.44	37.57	45.82	10.17	100.00
	1988	3681	14170	22382	5853	46086	1.33	2.47	8.21	3.78	3.60	7.99	30.75	48.57	12.70	100.00
	1989	8582	4926	20549	7477	41533	2.48	0.84	5.78	4.01	2.81	20.66	11.86	49.48	18.00	100.00
	1990	2252	7693	28380	9609	47934	0.93	1.33	5.81	4.97	3.18	4.70	16.05	59.21	20.05	100.00
	Sum	**33729**	**110555**	**235450**	**53968**	**433702**	**1.74**	**2.49**	**9.84**	**4.91**	**4.40**	**7.78**	**25.49**	**54.29**	**12.44**	**100.00**

Level of income	Year	Actual amount (millions of 1987 US dollars) Portfolio	Bank	Others	FDI	Total	Share of world total (%) Portfolio	Bank	Others	FDI	Total	Proportion of total gross flows (%) Portfolio	Bank	Others	FDI	Total
	1980	613	13000	26725	4884	45222	1.21	5.10	22.11	11.66	9.65	1.36	28.75	59.10	10.80	100.00
	1981	1358	21495	35008	12115	69975	2.00	7.50	23.26	19.30	12.33	1.94	30.72	50.03	17.31	100.00
	1982	1176	13364	31518	16928	62986	1.63	6.51	21.31	26.47	12.87	1.87	21.22	50.04	26.88	100.00
Upper-	1983	14581	11483	17141	7281	50485	17.81	5.89	14.08	12.00	11.11	28.88	22.75	33.95	14.42	100.00
middle	1984	16468	10189	14213	9756	50628	14.26	4.25	9.63	13.51	8.81	32.53	20.13	28.07	19.27	100.00
income	1985	10826	9529	21520	4387	46263	5.46	3.23	14.06	7.47	6.56	23.40	20.60	46.52	9.48	100.00
countries	1986	4423	8379	19799	4945	37546	1.86	1.57	10.98	5.95	3.62	11.78	22.32	52.73	13.17	100.00
(21)	1987	7136	10817	24227	6787	48967	2.88	1.58	9.57	5.41	3.73	14.57	22.09	49.48	13.86	100.00
	1988	8152	10674	17590	9023	45440	2.94	1.86	6.45	5.84	3.55	17.94	23.49	38.71	19.86	100.00
	1989	1557	12624	18865	8232	41278	0.45	2.15	5.30	4.42	2.80	3.77	30.58	45.70	19.94	100.00
	1990	20488	16615	22262	8981	68347	8.44	2.86	4.55	4.64	4.54	29.98	24.31	32.57	13.14	100.00
	Sum	**86779**	**138169**	**248869**	**93320**	**567137**	**4.48**	**3.11**	**10.40**	**8.49**	**5.75**	**15.30**	**24.36**	**43.88**	**16.45**	**100.00**
	1980	49418	230225	70786	32332	382761	97.81	90.22	58.56	77.21	81.71	12.91	60.15	18.49	8.45	100.00
	1981	64114	249723	85318	44144	443299	94.50	87.16	56.68	70.34	78.10	14.46	56.33	19.25	9.96	100.00
	1982	66701	180822	89802	41102	378427	92.36	88.03	60.72	64.28	77.31	17.63	47.78	23.73	10.86	100.00
High	1983	64007	172260	79228	43577	359073	78.20	88.41	65.10	77.78	79.02	17.83	47.97	22.07	12.14	100.00
income	1984	95813	217464	105964	57560	476802	82.96	90.76	71.77	79.69	82.93	20.10	45.61	22.22	12.07	100.00
countries	1985	182828	277735	105184	47705	613453	92.26	94.17	68.72	81.26	87.03	29.80	45.27	17.15	7.78	100.00
(25)	1986	231794	518580	134269	72832	957475	97.54	96.89	74.43	87.65	92.39	24.21	54.16	14.02	7.61	100.00
	1987	237243	659181	204609	112651	1213684	95.66	96.30	80.80	89.73	92.55	19.55	54.31	16.86	9.28	100.00
	1988	264472	548385	226377	137214	1176448	95.47	95.47	83.03	88.73	92.00	22.48	46.61	19.24	11.66	100.00
	1989	336127	568752	307959	166501	1379339	97.07	96.84	86.55	89.35	93.47	24.37	41.23	22.33	12.07	100.00
	1990	219967	554881	427445	172158	1374452	90.60	95.66	87.45	88.98	91.32	16.00	40.37	31.10	12.53	100.00
	Sum	**1812485**	**4178009**	**1836943**	**927774**	**8755212**	**93.53**	**94.14**	**76.78**	**84.45**	**88.73**	**20.70**	**47.72**	**20.98**	**10.60**	**100.00**

Level of income	Year	Actual amount (millions of 1987 US dollars)					Share of world total (%)					Proportion of total gross flows (%)				
		Portfolio	Bank	Others	FDI	Total	Portfolio	Bank	Others	FDI	Total	Portfolio	Bank	Others	FDI	Total
	1980	50523	255177	120887	41877	468464	100.00	100.00	100.00	100.00	100.00	10.78	54.47	25.80	8.94	100.00
	1981	67847	286496	150535	62761	567639	100.00	100.00	100.00	100.00	100.00	11.95	50.47	26.52	11.06	100.00
	1982	72219	205413	147908	63942	489482	100.00	100.00	100.00	100.00	100.00	14.75	41.97	30.22	13.06	100.00
All	1983	81852	194851	121708	56023	454434	100.00	100.00	100.00	100.00	100.00	18.01	42.88	26.78	12.33	100.00
countries	1984	115497	239598	147641	72229	574965	100.00	100.00	100.00	100.00	100.00	20.09	41.67	25.68	12.56	100.00
(121)	1985	198176	294930	153061	58703	704870	100.00	100.00	100.00	100.00	100.00	28.12	41.84	21.71	8.33	100.00
	1986	237646	535211	180389	83092	1036339	100.00	100.00	100.00	100.00	100.00	22.93	51.64	17.41	8.02	100.00
	1987	248009	684536	253228	125548	1311320	100.00	100.00	100.00	100.00	100.00	18.91	52.20	19.31	9.57	100.00
	1988	277032	574394	272648	154637	1278711	100.00	100.00	100.00	100.00	100.00	21.66	44.92	21.32	12.09	100.00
	1989	346282	587307	355814	186345	1475748	100.00	100.00	100.00	100.00	100.00	23.46	39.80	24.11	12.63	100.00
	1990	242800	580052	488772	193469	1505093	100.00	100.00	100.00	100.00	100.00	16.13	38.54	32.47	12.85	100.00
	Sum	**1937882**	**4437965**	**2392592**	**1098627**	**9867066**	**100.00**	**100.00**	**100.00**	**100.00**	**100.00**	**19.64**	**44.98**	**24.25**	**11.13**	**100.00**

Source: Balance of Payments Statistics (IMF).

C–4 Capital outflows by level of income in 121 countries

Level of income	Year	Actual amount (millions of 1987 US dollars) Portfolio	Bank	Others	FDI	Total	Share of world total (%) Portfolio	Bank	Others	FDI	Total	Proportion of total gross flows (%) Portfolio	Bank	Others	FDI	Total
	1980	0	994	2348	622	3964	0.00	0.42	2.29	1.35	0.90	0.01	25.07	59.24	15.68	100.00
	1981	0	632	2257	23	2913	0.00	0.23	1.75	0.04	0.54	0.02	21.71	77.49	0.78	100.00
	1982	1	578	2323	41	2943	0.00	0.24	1.83	0.	0.60	0.02	19.64	78.96	1.38	100.00
Low	1983	0	588	2150	42	2780	0.00	0.33	1.62	0.10	0.66	0.00	21.15	77.35	1.50	100.00
income	1984	13	1031	3427	41	4511	0.01	0.53	2.12	0.06	0.86	0.29	22.84	75.95	0.91	100.00
countries	1985	45	990	8714	58	9806	0.03	0.39	5.05	0.08	1.52	0.46	10.09	88.86	0.59	100.00
(36)	1986	2	1070	4998	170	6241	0.00	0.23	2.11	0.17	0.60	0.04	17.15	80.08	2.73	100.00
	1987	89	2113	4687	72	6961	0.04	0.38	2.16	0.05	0.61	1.28	30.36	67.34	1.03	100.00
	1988	96	2122	5173	87	7478	0.04	0.44	1.83	0.05	0.63	1.28	28.38	69.18	1.16	100.00
	1989	366	2313	4291	96	7067	0.13	0.44	1.35	0.05	0.53	5.18	32.74	60.72	1.36	100.00
	1990	260	3256	5462	35	9014	0.11	0.67	1.45	0.02	0.68	2.89	36.13	60.60	0.39	100.00
	Sum	**873**	**15687**	**45831**	**1286**	**63677**	**0.05**	**0.40**	**2.03**	**0.11**	**0.70**	**1.37**	**24.64**	**71.97**	**2.02**	**100.00**
	1980	884	6925	14963	602	23374	1.59	2.92	14.60	1.31	5.30	3.78	29.63	64.02	2.58	100.00
	1981	125	9658	21191	380	31353	0.16	3.46	16.45	0.70	5.82	0.40	30.80	67.59	1.21	100.00
	1982	199	9595	18484	468	28746	0.26	3.94	14.56	1.11	5.87	0.69	33.38	64.30	1.63	100.00
Lower-	1983	218	10520	19791	492	31022	0.29	5.98	14.94	1.23	7.34	0.70	33.91	63.80	1.59	100.00
middle	1984	383	11756	19665	370	32175	0.40	6.07	12.18	0.53	6.16	1.19	36.54	61.12	1.15	100.00
income	1985	990	8267	17880	264	27401	0.67	3.24	10.35	0.38	4.26	3.61	30.17	65.25	0.96	100.00
countries	1986	786	9953	14860	252	25851	0.34	2.15	6.28	0.25	2.50	3.04	38.50	57.48	0.97	100.00
(39)	1987	1003	14488	15982	1008	32480	0.48	2.57	7.38	0.70	2.87	3.09	44.60	49.21	3.10	100.00
	1988	2220	17106	22168	394	41887	0.86	3.57	7.86	0.23	3.51	5.30	40.84	52.92	0.94	100.00
	1989	1771	4960	20922	399	28052	0.62	0.94	6.60	0.19	2.10	6.31	17.68	74.58	1.42	100.00
	1990	2555	4400	19865	358	27178	1.13	0.90	5.27	0.16	2.06	9.40	16.19	73.09	1.32	100.00
	Sum	**11135**	**107627**	**205772**	**4986**	**329520**	**0.64**	**2.76**	**9.13**	**0.42**	**3.63**	**3.38**	**32.66**	**62.45**	**1.51**	**100.00**

Level of income	Year	Actual amount (millions of 1987 US dollars) Portfolio	Bank	Others	FDI	Total	Share of world total (%) Portfolio	Bank	Others	FDI	Total	Proportion of total gross flows (%) Portfolio	Bank	Others	FDI	Total
	1980	19493	8124	20262	5056	52935	35.09	3.42	19.77	11.01	11.00	36.82	15.35	38.28	9.55	100.00
	1981	26647	11024	18367	1956	57994	35.03	3.95	14.25	3.59	10.77	45.95	19.01	31.67	3.37	100.00
	1982	13125	9604	24786	1329	48844	16.90	3.95	19.53	3.16	9.97	26.87	19.66	50.74	2.72	100.00
Upper-	1983	1021	13510	24196	1000	39727	1.37	7.68	18.26	2.51	9.40	2.57	34.01	60.91	2.52	100.00
middle	1984	1304	11043	30988	935	44270	1.35	5.70	19.19	1.33	8.48	2.95	24.94	69.00	2.11	100.00
income	1985	1650	14790	34638	1093	52171	1.12	5.79	20.06	1.60	8.11	3.16	28.35	66.39	2.10	100.00
countries	1986	2121	17261	31374	1613	52370	0.91	3.72	13.26	1.57	5.06	4.05	32.96	59.91	3.08	100.00
(21)	1987	4260	17002	28112	2277	51652	2.04	3.02	12.98	1.58	4.56	8.25	32.92	54.43	4.41	100.00
	1988	2354	17064	25138	1022	45578	0.91	3.56	8.92	0.59	3.82	5.17	37.44	55.15	2.24	100.00
	1989	2592	13000	21131	1805	38438	0.91	2.45	6.67	0.87	2.88	6.74	33.59	54.98	4.70	100.00
	1990	10094	14883	14825	2139	41941	4.45	3.05	3.93	0.95	3.18	24.07	35.49	35.35	5.10	100.00
	Sum	**84662**	**147215**	**273817**	**20225**	**525918**	**4.87**	**3.77**	**12.15**	**1.72**	**5.80**	**16.10**	**27.99**	**52.06**	**3.85**	**100.00**
	1980	35173	221247	64908	39652	360981	63.32	93.24	63.34	86.33	81.81	9.74	61.29	17.98	10.98	100.00
	1981	49290	257780	87042	52079	446191	64.80	92.36	67.55	95.67	82.87	11.05	57.77	19.51	11.67	100.00
	1982	64319	223642	81333	40183	409478	82.84	91.88	64.08	95.63	83.57	15.71	54.62	19.86	9.81	100.00
High	1983	73164	151223	86346	38363	349097	98.33	85.00	65.18	96.16	82.60	20.96	43.32	24.73	10.99	100.00
income	1984	95201	169786	107402	69004	441392	98.24	87.69	66.51	98.09	84.50	21.57	38.47	24.33	15.63	100.00
countries	1985	144232	231222	111439	67100	553993	98.17	90.58	64.54	97.94	86.11	26.04	41.74	20.12	12.11	100.00
(25)	1986	229592	435637	185386	100394	951009	98.75	93.90	78.35	98.01	91.84	24.14	45.81	19.49	10.56	100.00
	1987	203216	529675	167751	140399	1041042	97.43	94.03	77.47	97.66	91.95	19.52	50.88	16.11	13.49	100.00
	1988	254732	442853	229464	171200	1098249	98.20	92.43	81.39	99.13	92.04	23.19	40.32	20.89	15.59	100.00
	1989	278744	506894	270556	206203	1262397	98.33	96.17	85.38	98.90	94.49	22.08	40.15	21.43	16.33	100.00
	1990	214143	465145	337088	223367	1239743	94.31	95.38	89.36	98.88	94.07	17.27	37.52	27.19	18.02	100.00
	Sum	**1641807**	**3635106**	**1728715**	**1147944**	**8153572**	**94.44**	**93.07**	**76.69**	**97.74**	**89.87**	**20.14**	**44.58**	**21.20**	**14.08**	**100.00**

Level of income	Year	Actual amount (millions of 1987 US dollars)					Share of world total (%)					Proportion of total gross flows (%)				
		Portfolio	Bank	Others	FDI	Total	Portfolio	Bank	Others	FDI	Total	Portfolio	Bank	Others	FDI	Total
	1980	55550	237289	102482	45932	441253	100.00	100.00	100.00	100.00	100.00	12.59	53.78	23.23	10.41	100.00
	1981	76063	279094	128857	54437	538451	100.00	100.00	100.00	100.00	100.00	14.13	51.83	23.93	10.11	100.00
	1982	77644	243420	126926	42021	490011	100.00	100.00	100.00	100.00	100.00	15.85	49.68	25.90	8.58	100.00
All	1983	74404	175842	132483	39897	422626	100.00	100.00	100.00	100.00	100.00	17.61	41.61	31.35	9.44	100.00
countries	1984	96902	193615	161481	70350	522348	100.00	100.00	100.00	100.00	100.00	18.55	37.07	30.91	13.47	100.00
(121)	1985	146918	255268	172670	68514	643370	100.00	100.00	100.00	100.00	100.00	22.84	39.68	26.84	10.65	100.00
	1986	232502	463921	236619	102429	1035470	100.00	100.00	100.00	100.00	100.00	22.45	44.80	22.85	9.89	100.00
	1987	208568	563278	216533	143756	1132136	100.00	100.00	100.00	100.00	100.00	18.42	49.75	19.13	12.70	100.00
	1988	259402	479145	281942	172703	1193192	100.00	100.00	100.00	100.00	100.00	21.74	40.16	23.63	14.47	100.00
	1989	283473	527078	316901	208503	1335954	100.00	100.00	100.00	100.00	100.00	21.22	39.45	23.72	15.61	100.00
	1990	227052	487684	377240	225899	1317876	100.00	100.00	100.00	100.00	100.00	17.23	37.01	28.62	17.14	100.00
	Sum	**1738476**	**3905635**	**2254135**	**1174441**	**9072687**	**100.00**	**100.00**	**100.00**	**100.00**	**100.00**	**19.16**	**43.05**	**24.85**	**12.94**	**100.00**

Source: Balance of Payments Statistics (IMF).

C–5 Four types of short-term capital flows by level of income in 121 countries

Level of income	Year	Actual amount (millions of 1987 US dollars) (1)				Share of world total (%) (2)				Proportion of total flows (%) (3)		
		STKI1 (a)	STKI2 (b)	STKO1 (c)	STKO2 (d)	STKI1	STKI2	STKO1	STKO2	Inflow(a)	Outflow(b)	Gross(c)
Low income countries (36)	1980	1323	258	1084	763	0.53	5.39	0.50	4.62	37.33	46.59	41.81
	1981	1374	858	550	733	0.51	19.90	0.22	2.83	33.17	44.05	36.46
	1982	2554	1060	527	462	1.50	4.43	0.30	1.21	39.53	33.61	38.09
	1983	2425	456	637	324	1.55	1.55	0.55	0.83	33.57	34.59	33.82
	1984	2415	650	1318	613	1.15	3.22	0.88	2.60	33.64	42.79	36.67
	1985	2372	374	5668	684	0.99	1.51	2.77	2.81	24.09	64.78	42.90
	1986	2656	867	1700	1482	0.56	3.84	0.40	3.77	32.54	50.99	39.29
	1987	3673	292	2850	1334	0.59	0.61	0.59	5.74	32.26	60.10	42.32
	1988	1225	1147	1833	2167	0.27	2.27	0.47	4.64	22.09	53.49	34.98
	1989	2671	803	1938	1171	0.53	1.81	0.42	4.03	25.55	43.00	31.86
	1990	2045	493	3777	1671	0.44	1.21	1.05	6.04	17.67	60.44	34.17
	Sum	**24734**	**7257**	**21882**	**11404**	**0.65**	**2.32**	**0.68**	**3.42**	**28.82**	**52.27**	**37.37**
Lower-middle income countries (39)	1980	11377	2975	5100	8266	4.54	62.23	2.35	50.08	39.59	57.18	46.49
	1981	13252	1468	10970	9091	4.90	34.05	4.41	35.12	30.90	63.98	44.03
	1982	7807	2149	7446	8289	4.59	8.98	4.27	21.72	25.58	54.74	37.96
	1983	5359	8032	3648	12799	3.42	27.34	3.16	32.98	36.90	53.02	44.32
	1984	6529	8569	4641	10348	3.10	42.43	3.10	43.94	39.29	46.59	42.62
	1985	6746	3510	3024	7748	2.82	14.13	1.48	31.83	30.39	39.31	34.39
	1986	6440	3725	4248	4924	1.36	16.49	1.01	12.52	33.34	35.48	34.32
	1987	6576	9992	3498	11224	1.05	21.03	0.72	48.32	45.54	45.33	45.44
	1988	6775	16129	4622	17126	1.48	31.90	1.19	36.70	49.70	51.92	50.76
	1989	8657	1163	3436	6624	1.73	2.63	0.75	22.78	23.64	35.86	28.57
	1990	16080	2396	4615	4771	3.49	5.88	1.28	17.24	38.55	34.54	37.10
	Sum	**95597**	**60109**	**55247**	**101211**	**2.50**	**19.19**	**1.71**	**30.37**	**35.90**	**47.48**	**40.90**

Level of income	Year	Actual amount (millions of 1987 US dollars) (1) STKI1 (a)	STKI2 (b)	STKO1 (c)	STKO2 (d)	Share of world total (%) (2) STKI1	STKI2	STKO1	STKO2	Proportion of total flows (%) (3) Inflow(a)	Outflow(b)	Gross(c)
	1980	14723	81	14519	1937	5.88	1.70	6.68	11.74	32.74	31.09	31.85
	1981	18762	187	12390	976	6.94	4.34	4.99	3.77	27.08	23.05	25.25
	1982	6928	4823	9812	5371	4.07	20.16	5.63	14.07	18.66	31.08	24.09
Upper-	1983	6774	1937	5812	11217	4.33	6.60	5.03	28.90	17.26	42.87	28.53
middle	1984	4526	1225	11755	4993	2.15	6.07	7.84	21.20	11.36	37.83	23.71
income	1985	3358	8747	9559	5128	1.40	35.21	4.67	21.07	26.17	28.15	27.22
countries	1986	6938	7239	10116	3385	1.46	32.03	2.40	8.61	37.76	25.78	30.78
(21)	1987	7928	13379	10890	2679	1.27	28.16	2.25	11.53	43.51	26.27	34.66
	1988	6925	5778	11628	3178	1.52	11.43	2.99	6.81	27.96	32.48	30.22
	1989	8086	9148	7668	4948	1.61	20.65	1.67	17.02	41.75	32.82	37.44
	1990	16367	2550	11494	2710	3.55	6.25	3.19	9.79	27.68	33.87	30.03
	Sum	**101315**	**55095**	**115641**	**46523**	**2.65**	**17.59**	**3.59**	**13.96**	**27.58**	**30.83**	**29.15**
	1980	222996	1467	196500	5540	89.05	30.68	90.47	33.56	58.64	55.97	57.35
	1981	236961	1798	224580	15085	87.65	41.71	90.38	58.28	53.86	53.71	53.79
	1982	152800	15897	156425	24039	89.83	66.44	89.79	62.99	44.58	44.07	44.32
High	1983	142030	18948	105400	14472	90.70	64.51	91.26	37.29	44.83	34.34	39.66
income	1984	197401	9751	132131	7598	93.61	48.28	88.18	32.26	43.45	31.66	37.78
countries	1985	226564	12210	186381	10783	94.78	49.15	91.08	44.30	38.92	35.59	37.34
(25)	1986	458425	10768	404618	29543	96.62	47.65	96.18	75.11	49.00	45.65	47.33
	1987	608087	23850	467036	7991	97.10	50.20	96.44	34.40	52.07	45.63	49.10
	1988	441774	27507	371110	24195	96.73	54.40	95.35	51.85	39.89	35.99	38.01
	1989	481773	33184	446988	16335	96.13	74.91	97.16	56.18	37.33	36.70	37.03
	1990	426377	35342	339994	18531	92.52	86.66	94.47	66.94	33.59	28.92	31.38
	Sum	**3595188**	**190722**	**3031163**	**174112**	**94.19**	**60.90**	**94.02**	**52.25**	**43.24**	**39.31**	**41.35**

Level of income	Year	Actual amount (millions of 1987 US dollars) (1)				Share of world total (%) (2)				Proportion of total flows (%) (3)		
		STKI1 (a)	STKI2 (b)	STKO1 (c)	STKO2 (d)	STKI1	STKI2	STKO1	STKO2	Inflow(a)	Outflow(b)	Gross(c)
	1980	250419	4780	217204	16506	100.00	100.00	100.00	100.00	54.48	52.96	53.74
	1981	270348	4312	248490	25885	100.00	100.00	100.00	100.00	48.39	50.96	49.64
	1982	170090	23929	174209	38162	100.00	100.00	100.00	100.00	39.64	43.34	41.49
All	1983	156588	29373	115497	38813	100.00	100.00	100.00	100.00	40.92	36.51	38.80
countries	1984	210871	20195	149845	23552	100.00	100.00	100.00	100.00	40.19	33.20	36.86
(121)	1985	239039	24842	204631	24343	100.00	100.00	100.00	100.00	37.44	35.59	36.56
	1986	474459	22599	420682	39333	100.00	100.00	100.00	100.00	47.96	44.43	46.20
	1987	626264	47513	484274	23229	100.00	100.00	100.00	100.00	51.38	44.83	48.34
	1988	456699	50560	389192	46666	100.00	100.00	100.00	100.00	39.67	36.53	38.15
	1989	501187	44299	460030	29078	100.00	100.00	100.00	100.00	36.96	36.61	36.80
	1990	460869	40781	359880	27683	100.00	100.00	100.00	100.00	33.33	29.41	31.50
	Sum	**3816834**	**313183**	**3223933**	**333250**	**100.00**	**100.00**	**100.00**	**100.00**	**41.86**	**39.21**	**40.59**

Source: Balance of Payments Statistics (IMF).

Notes

1 Short-term bank capital and short-term other-sector capital are included.
   (a) Short-term capital type 1 inflow: short-term capital invested from world to home by foreign investors.
   (b) Short-term capital type 2 inflow: short-term capital withdrawn from world to home by domestic investors.
   (c) Short-term capital type 1 outflow: short-term capital invested from home to world by domestic investors.
   (d) Short-term capital type 2 outflow: short-term capital withdrawn from home to world by foreign investors.
2 Share of world total short-term capital flows.
3 Proportion of short-term capital flows from total capital flows.
   (a) (STKI1 + STKI2) /TOTI *100, where TOTI = total capital inflow.
   (b) (STKO1 + STKO2) /TOTO *100, where TOTO = total capital outflow.
   (c) (STKI1 + STKI2 + STKO1 + STKO2) /TOTG *100, where TOTG = total gross capital flow.

Appendix D
Models with Country and Time Dummy Coefficients

D–1 Gross flow of total capital with OLS and WLS fixed effects estimations (dummy coefficients reported)

Model	OLS fixed effects method					WLS fixed effects method				
Dep. var.	TOTG (log of total capital gross flow)					TOTG (log of total capital gross flow)				
F-Value	209.631					216.295				
R-square	0.9621					0.9632				
Adj. R-Sq	0.9575					0.9587				
Obs	946					946				
Ind. var.	Par est	SE	T-stat	Prob >|T|	Std est	Par est	SE	T-stat	Prob >|T|	Std est
INTERCEPT	7.73400	0.22026	35.113	0.0001	0.0000	7.74445	0.21974	35.243	0.0001	0.0000
ABINTD	-0.01555	0.08531	-0.182	0.8554	-0.0016	-0.01236	0.08316	-0.149	0.8818	-0.0013
ABRISKD	0.00969	0.00432	2.242	0.0252	0.0362	0.00978	0.00433	2.256	0.0244	0.0362
ABCAB	0.06082	0.01817	3.348	0.0009	0.0469	0.06032	0.01804	3.343	0.0009	0.0463
EXCHCONT	-0.02657	0.07813	-0.340	0.7339	-0.0050	-0.03447	0.07754	-0.445	0.6568	-0.0065
TREATY	8.0989E-05	3.708E-05	2 184	0 0292	0.0532	7 8498E-05	3.591E-05	2.186	0.0291	0.0530
CD	0.50130	0.09460	5.299	0.0001	0.0688	0.49556	0.09191	5.392	0.0001	0.0693
TELECOMM	0.07794	0.02097	3.716	0.0002	0.0694	0.07940	0.02078	3.822	0.0001	0.0715
ALGERIA	0.40045	0.21340	1.877	0.0609	0.0185	0.40049	0.21443	1.868	0.0621	0.0181
ARGENTIN	0.61321	0.22838	2.685	0.0074	0.0283	0.60454	0.22912	2.639	0.0085	0 0272
AUSTRALI	1.93875	0.22527	8.606	0.0001	0.0894	1.94774	0.22385	8.701	0.0001	0.0899
AUSTRIA	0.42095	0.23278	1.808	0.0709	0.0194	0.41901	0.22811	1.837	0 0666	0.0198
BAHRAIN	-1.89159	0.20832	-9.080	0.0001	-0.0872	-1.89294	0.20962	-9.030	0.0001	-0.0851
BANGLADE	-2.98162	0.20791	-14.341	0.0001	-0.1374	-2.98079	0.20905	-14.258	0.0001	-0.1342
BARBADOS	-3.18051	0.21977	-14.472	0.0001	-0.1466	-3.18502	0.21992	-14.482	0.0001	-0.1445
BELGIUML	1.72361	0.23749	7.258	0.0001	0.0794	1.73405	0.23310	7.439	0.0001	0.0818
BOLIVIA	-2.73299	0.21055	-12.981	0.0001	-0.1260	-2.73382	0.21140	-12.932	0.0001	-0.1234
BRAZIL	1.32298	0.20769	6.370	0.0001	0.0610	1.32150	0.20852	6.338	0.0001	0.0597
CANADA	1.03275	0.25123	4.111	0.0001	0.0476	1.01357	0.24733	4.098	0.0001	0.0480
CHILE	0.15362	0.20672	0.743	0.4576	0.0071	0 15429	0.20744	0.744	0.4572	0.0070
COLOMBIA	-0.45593	0.20763	-2.196	0.0284	-0.0210	-0.45644	0.20883	-2.186	0.0291	-0.0205
CONGO	-1.93449	0.20929	-9.243	0.0001	-0.0892	-1.93566	0.21041	-9.200	0.0001	-0.0872
COSTARIC	-2.07496	0.20644	-10.051	0.0001	-0.0956	-2.07546	0.20754	-10.000	0.0001	-0.0935
COTEIVOR	-1.53928	0.20866	-7.377	0.0001	-0.0710	-1.53741	0.20974	-7.330	0.0001	-0.0693
CYPRUS	-2.68552	0.24517	-10.954	0.0001	-0.1238	-2.68111	0.24453	-10.965	0.0001	-0.1228
DENMARK	0.18164	0.25361	0.716	0.4740	0.0084	0.18526	0.24696	0.750	0.4534	0.0089
DOMINIRP	-2.95014	0.20836	-14.159	0.0001	-0.1360	-2.95007	0.20964	-14.072	0.0001	-0.1326
ECUADOR	-1.46148	0.21309	-6.859	0.0001	-0.0674	-1.47132	0.21332	-6.897	0.0001	-0.0669
EGYPT	-0.34197	0.20781	-1.646	0.1002	-0.0158	-0.33867	0.20809	-1.627	0.1040	-0.0154
ELSALVAD	-3.20655	0.21662	-14.803	0.0001	-0.1478	-3.20794	0.21783	-14.727	0.0001	-0.1442
ETHIOPIA	-3.15991	0.21006	-15.043	0.0001	-0.1456	-3.16043	0.21135	-14.953	0.0001	-0.1420
FINLAND	0.62972	0.21102	2.984	0.0029	0.0290	0.62752	0.21147	2.967	0.0031	0.0285
FRANCE	1.87971	0.26577	7.073	0.0001	0.0866	1.87807	0.26092	7.198	0.0001	0.0908
GABON	-1.73046	0.21235	-8.149	0.0001	-0.0798	-1.73350	0.21347	-8.121	0.0001	-0.0780
GERMANY	1.97272	0.27428	7.192	0.0001	0.0909	1.96984	0.26728	7.370	0.0001	0.0949
GREECE	-0.49417	0.20654	-2.393	0.0169	-0.0228	-0.49288	0.20738	-2.377	0.0177	-0.0223
GUATEMAL	-2.14867	0.20887	-10.287	0.0001	-0.0990	-2.14918	0.21018	-10.225	0.0001	-0.0966
HAITI	-4.08037	0.21168	-19.276	0.0001	-0.1881	-4.08037	0.21255	-19.197	0.0001	-0.1841
HONDURAS	-2.50260	0.20852	-12.002	0.0001	-0.1153	-2.50258	0.20985	-11.926	0 0001	-0.1124
ICELAND	-2.86015	0 23262	-12.296	0.0001	-0.1318	-2.85826	0.22987	-12.434	0.0001	-0.1333
INDIA	-1.38832	0.22048	-6.297	0.0001	-0.0640	-1.37778	0.21992	-6.265	0.0001	-0.0631
INDONESI	-0.91805	0.21898	-4.192	0.0001	-0.0423	-0.91707	0.21869	-4.194	0.0001	-0.0419
IRELAND	-0.39722	0.20985	-1.893	0.0587	-0.0183	-0.39890	0.20955	-1.904	0.0573	-0.0182
ISRAEL	-0.58987	0.25297	-2.332	0.0199	-0.0272	-0.59063	0.25138	-2.350	0.0190	-0.0273
ITALY	1.78928	0.24225	7.386	0.0001	0.0825	1.79246	0.23843	7.518	0.0001	0.0845
JAMAICA	-2.72736	0.20888	-13.057	0.0001	-0.1257	-2.72663	0.20920	-13.034	0.0001	-0.1238
JAPAN	2.45268	0.24378	10.061	0.0001	0.1130	2.46584	0.24184	10.196	0.0001	0.1137
KOREA	-0.02245	0.20921	-0.107	0.9146	-0.0010	-0.02775	0.20989	-0.132	0.8948	-0.0013
LIBYA	-0.92449	0.20834	-4.438	0.0001	-0.0426	-0.92373	0.20955	-4.408	0.0001	-0.0416
MADAGASC	-4.28584	0.21141	-20.273	0.0001	-0.1975	-4.28451	0.21235	-20.177	0.0001	-0.1934

Model / Ind. var.	OLS fixed effects method					WLS fixed effects method				
	Par est	SE	T-stat	Prob >|T|	Std est	Par est	SE	T-stat	Prob >|T|	Std est
KENYA	-2.58009	0.20771	-12.422	0.0001	-0.1189	-2.57924	0.20860	-12.364	0.0001	-0.1164
MALAYSIA	-0.51850	0.23869	-2.172	0.0301	-0.0239	-0.52292	0.23790	-2.198	0.0282	-0.0240
MAURITIU	-3.55246	0.21115	-16.825	0.0001	-0.1637	-3.55233	0.21223	-16.738	0.0001	-0.1599
MEXICO	1.37013	0.20917	6.550	0.0001	0.0631	1.36938	0.21046	6.507	0.0001	0.0616
MOROCCO	-1.48740	0.21014	-7.078	0.0001	-0.0686	-1.48323	0.21012	-7.059	0.0001	-0.0676
MOZAMBIQ	-5.99585	0.21199	-28.283	0.0001	-0.2764	-5.99695	0.21172	-28.325	0.0001	-0.2752
NEPAL	-4.28320	0.21183	-20.220	0.0001	-0.1974	-4.28281	0.21308	-20.100	0.0001	-0.1926
NETHERLA	1 76700	0.23612	7.484	0.0001	0.0814	1.76896	0.23114	7.653	0.0001	0 0838
NEWZEALA	-1.37079	0.20934	-6.548	0.0001	-0.0632	-1.36996	0.20953	-6.538	0.0001	-0.0623
NIGERIA	-0.62223	0.20804	-2.991	0.0029	-0.0287	-0.62170	0.20939	-2.969	0.0031	-0.0279
NORWAY	0.47028	0.23300	2.018	0.0439	0.0217	0.47217	0.22853	2.066	0.0391	0.0223
OMAN	-2.50046	0.20797	-12.023	0.0001	-0.1153	-2.50012	0.20933	-11.944	0.0001	-0.1123
PAKISTAN	-1.68425	0.20778	-8.106	0.0001	-0.0776	-1.68227	0.20899	-8.049	0.0001	-0.0757
PAPUANEW	-2.12982	0.20798	-10.240	0.0001	-0.0982	-2.13006	0.20932	-10.176	0.0001	-0.0957
PARAGUAY	-2.24776	0.21527	-10.442	0.0001	-0.1036	-2.25313	0.21620	-10.422	0.0001	-0.1016
PERU	-1 77930	0.20660	-8.612	0.0001	-0.0820	-1.77959	0.20760	-8.572	0.0001	-0.0803
PHILIPPI	-0.44193	0.20727	-2.132	0.0333	-0.0204	-0.44147	0.20768	-2.126	0.0338	-0.0200
SAUDIARA	1 06478	0.22685	4.694	0.0001	0.0491	1.05754	0.22792	4.640	0.0001	0.0475
SENEGAL	-2.81471	0.20808	-13.527	0.0001	-0.1297	-2.81422	0.20929	-13.447	0.0001	-0.1266
SEYCHELL	-4.91099	0.23419	-20.970	0.0001	-0.2264	-4 91153	0.23468	-20.929	0.0001	-0.2222
SIERRALE	-3.60442	0.21559	-16.719	0.0001	-0.1661	-3.60851	0.21647	-16.670	0.0001	-0.1626
SINGAPOR	-0.13179	0.22174	-0.594	0.5524	-0.0061	-0.13103	0.21999	-0.596	0.5516	-0.0061
SOUTHAFR	-0.61914	0.20716	-2.989	0.0029	-0.0285	-0.62070	0.20694	-2.999	0.0028	-0.0283
SPAIN	0.89686	0.21131	4 244	0.0001	0.0413	0.89747	0.21145	4.244	0.0001	0.0409
SRILANKA	-1.97259	0.20954	-9.414	0.0001	-0.0909	-1.97067	0.21067	-9.354	0.0001	-0.0888
SUDAN	-3.53618	0.20922	-16.902	0.0001	-0.1630	-3 53647	0.21053	-16.798	0.0001	-0.1589
SWAZILAN	-3.81363	0.21271	-17.929	0.0001	-0.1758	-3.81409	0.21394	-17.828	0.0001	-0.1714
SWEDEN	0.93545	0.25720	3.637	0.0003	0.0431	0.94224	0.25018	3.766	0.0002	0.0453
SWITZERL	1.27337	0.22974	5.543	0.0001	0.0587	1.26731	0.22659	5.593	0.0001	0.0592
SYRIA	-2.10879	0.20727	-10.174	0.0001	-0.0972	-2.11652	0.20762	-10.194	0.0001	-0.0961
TANZANIA	-4.39579	0.20816	-21.118	0.0001	-0.2026	-4 39645	0.20949	-20.987	0.0001	-0.1975
THAILAND	-0 10794	0.21627	-0.499	0.6178	-0.0050	-0.10748	0.21689	-0.496	0.6203	-0.0049
TRINIDAD	-1.84497	0.20797	-8.871	0.0001	-0.0850	-1.84453	0.20903	-8.824	0 0001	-0.0832
TUNISIA	-1.37453	0.20832	-6.598	0.0001	-0.0634	-1.37352	0.20921	-6.565	0.0001	-0.0620
TURKEY	-0.49808	0.20688	-2.408	0.0163	-0.0230	-0.49456	0.20750	-2.383	0.0174	-0.0224
UK	2.35934	0.24432	9.657	0.0001	0.1087	2.35986	0.24133	9.779	0.0001	0.1101
USA	2.38150	0.27505	8.658	0.0001	0.1098	2.37554	0.27046	8.783	0 0001	0 1116
URUGUAY	-1.59262	0.21698	-7.340	0.0001	-0.0734	-1.59878	0.21802	-7.333	0.0001	-0.0719
VENEZUEL	0 02281	0.21728	0.105	0.9164	0.0011	0.01793	0.21841	0.082	0.9346	0 0008
YUGOSLAV	0.34570	0.20786	1.663	0.0967	0.0159	0.34189	0.20769	1.646	0.1001	0.0156
ZAIRE	-3.89957	0.20928	-18.633	0.0001	-0.1797	-3.90046	0.21058	-18.522	0.0001	-0.1753
ZAMBIA	-2.02663	0.20781	-9.753	0.0001	-0.0934	-2.02370	0.20845	-9.708	0.0001	-0.0916
ZIMBABWE	-2.90199	0.20953	-13.850	0.0001	-0.1338	-2.90188	0.21043	-13.790	0.0001	-0.1310
YR1981	0.10805	0.07341	1.472	0.1415	0.0134	0.10680	0.07351	1.453	0.1466	0.0130
YR1982	0.07809	0 07380	1.058	0.2903	0.0097	0 07522	0.07393	1.018	0.3092	0.0092
YR1983	0.00248	0.07458	0.033	0.9735	0.0003	0.00065	0.07470	0.009	0.9931	0.0001
YR1984	0.14499	0.07702	1.883	0.0601	0.0179	0.14211	0.07701	1.845	0.0653	0.0174
YR1985	0.21629	0.07846	2.757	0.0060	0.0267	0.21275	0.07844	2.712	0.0068	0.0260
YR1986	0.19980	0.07955	2.512	0.0122	0.0247	0.19959	0.07951	2.510	0.0123	0.0245
YR1987	0.26293	0.08036	3.272	0.0011	0.0325	0.26443	0.08030	3.293	0.0010	0.0324
YR1988	0.24755	0.08233	3.007	0.0027	0.0306	0 24727	0.08225	3.007	0.0027	0.0304
YR1989	0.23067	0.08457	2.728	0.0065	0.0285	0.23311	0.08454	2.757	0.0060	0.0286
YR1990	0.30111	0.08546	3.523	0.0004	0.0372	0.30292	0.08548	3.544	0.0004	0.0372

Notes

1 Acronyms: Par est: parameter estimate; SE: standard error; T-stat: T statistics; Prob >|T|: significant level; Std est: standardized estimate.

2 Portugal and Year 1980 omitted as base dummies.

3 See Table 9 for variable definitions.

D–2 Gross flows of four financial items with OLS fixed effect estimation (dummy coefficients reported)

Model	Portfolio gross flow			Bank capital gross flow			Other-sector capital gross flow			FDI gross flow		
Dep. var.	PORTG (log of portfolio grossflow)			BANKG (log of bank K gross flow)			OTHG (log of other K gross flow)			FDIG (log of FDI gross flow)		
F-value 115.230	116.235			96.834			72.113					
R-square	0.9331			0.9336			0.9214			0.9447		
Adj. R-sq	0.9250			0.9256			0.9118			0.9316		
Obs.	946			946			946			946		
Ind. var.	Par est	(t-stat)	Std est	Par est	(t-stat)	Std est	Par est	(t-stat)	Std est	Par est	(t-stat)	Std est
INTERCEPT	4.371569	(12.695) ***	0.0000	6.721237	(20.807) ***	0.0000	7.646267	(25.884) ***	0.0000	3.233743	(7.199) ***	0.0000
ABIGOVTD	0.000107	(.025)	0.0004									
ABIDEPD				0.155531	(1.528)	0.0183						
ABIMKTD							-0.061366	(-.496)	-0.0064			
ABPPPRC										-0.001595	(-.958)	-0.0131
ABRISKD	0.001176	(.172)	0.0037	-0.002906	(-.459)	-0.0098	0.012207	(2.104) **	0.0488	0.028839	(4.045) ***	0.1190
ABCAB	-0.017232	(-.606)	-0.0111	0.044827	(1.68) *	0.0312	0.034905	(1.44)	0.0289	0.067249	(2.147) **	0.0532
EXCHCONT	0.197633	(1.593)	0.0309	-0.229414	(-2.003) **	-0.0388	-0.264444	(-2.521) **	-0.0531	0.140515	(1.055)	0.0281
TREATY	0.000098	(1.673) *	0.0539	0.000001	(.016)	0.0005	0.000004	(.087)	0.0030	0.000195	(3.263) ***	0.1315
CD	0.477679	(3.183) ***	0.0549	0.604752	(4.363) ***	0.0749	0.552565	(4.339) ***	0.0813			
INDSTP										0.029681	(4.722) ***	0.1746
TELECOMM	0.277108	(8.357) ***	0.2065	0.076765	(2.492) **	0.0617	0.089027	(3.172) ***	0.0850	0.134460	(3.9) ***	0.1202
ALGERIA	-2.373284	(-7.019) ***	-0.0916	-1.618027	(-5.173) ***	-0.0673	0.836138	(2.917) ***	0.0413	-2.605903	(-7.419) ***	-0.1402
ARGENTIN	2.493823	(6.492) ***	0.0962	-1.376145	(-4.136) ***	-0.0573	0.498804	(1.626)	0.0247	1.104370	(2.833) ***	0.0503
AUSTRALI	1.748133	(4.925) ***	0.0674	0.975574	(2.952) ***	0.0406	2.125602	(7.058) ***	0.1050	1.934323	(4.95) ***	0.0881
AUSTRIA	2.174256	(5.893) ***	0.0839	1.287323	(3.775) ***	0.0536	-1.094825	(-3.503) ***	-0.0541	-0.077946	(-0.211)	-0.0042
BAHRAIN	-1.713110	(-5.188) ***	-0.0661	-1.169284	(-3.832) ***	-0.0487	-3.116963	(-11.139) ***	-0.1540	-1.717148	(-5.132) ***	-0.0987
BANGLADE	-2.310045	(-7.006) ***	-0.0891	-1.973796	(-6.481) ***	-0.0821	-3.919679	(-14.034) ***	-0.1937	-2.428038	(-6.075) ***	-0.0990
BARBADOS	-2.039090	(-5.866) ***	-0.0787	-3.877453	(-12.035) ***	-0.1613	-3.060930	(-10.378) ***	-0.1513	-1.405808	(-2.718) ***	-0.0406
BELGIUML	2.647407	(7.052) ***	0.1021	2.653678	(7.632) ***	0.1104	-0.488591	(-1.533)	-0.0242	1.634570	(4.419) ***	0.0879
BOLIVIA	-2.426996	(-7.181) ***	-0.0936	-2.792575	(-9.051) ***	-0.1162	-2.651353	(-9.377) ***	-0.1310	-1.824166	(-5.183) ***	-0.0909
BRAZIL	0.422248	(1.257)	0.0163	1.523691	(5.015) ***	0.0634	1.291806	(4.642) ***	0.0638	2.020040	(5.681) ***	0.0920
CANADA	2.892269	(7.375) ***	0.1116	0.789574	(2.13) **	0.0328	-0.535020	(-1.597)	-0.0264	1.664800	(3.915) ***	0.0758
CHILE	-0.376743	(-1.142)	-0.0145	0.504967	(1.667) *	0.0210	0.034653	(.125)	0.0017	-0.283559	(-.801)	-0.0129
COLOMBIA	-1.883382	(-5.717) ***	-0.0727	-1.412971	(-4.646) ***	-0.0588	-0.305246	(-1.093)	-0.0151	0.592109	(1.855) *	0.0360
CONGO	-2.409853	(-7.27) ***	-0.0930	-3.852694	(-12.571) ***	-0.1603	-1.541120	(-5.48) ***	-0.0762	-2.150004	(-6.414) ***	-0.1156
COSTARIC	-1.911040	(-5.786) ***	-0.0737	-3.160293	(-10.447) ***	-0.1315	-1.933561	(-6.975) ***	-0.0956	-0.481234	(-1.149)	-0.0170
COTEIVOR	-2.175377	(-6.573) ***	-0.0839	-1.060976	(-3.47) ***	-0.0442	-1.779765	(-6.347) ***	-0.0880	-0.996755	(-2.918) ***	-0.0536
CYPRUS	-2.348070	(-6.045) ***	-0.0906	-1.910084	(-5.316) ***	-0.0795	-2.979949	(-9.053) ***	-0.1473	-1.877208	(-4.516) ***	-0.0936
DENMARK	1.302037	(3.247) ***	0.0502	1.145549	(3.083) ***	0.0477	-0.650103	(-1.913) *	-0.0321	-0.257225	(-.64)	-0.0138

Model / Ind. var.	Portfolio gross flow			Bank capital gross flow			Other-sector capital gross flow			FDI gross flow		
	Par est	(t-stat)	Std est	Par est	(t-stat)	Std est	Par est	(t-stat)	Std est	Par est	(t-stat)	Std est
DOMINIRP	-2.411262	(-7.306) ***	-0.0930	-2.766232	(-9.06) ***	-0.1151	-4.137870	(-14.777) ***	-0.2045	-1.039945	(-3.077) ***	-0.0559
ECUADOR	-2.361401	(-6.948) ***	-0.0911	-3.151645	(-10.093) ***	-0.1311	-1.191101	(-4.162) ***	-0.0589	-1.086479	(-3.201) ***	-0.0584
EGYPT	-2.162204	(-6.554) ***	-0.0834	-0.287857	(-0.945)	-0.0120	-0.733312	(-2.627) ***	-0.0362	1.379222	(4.266) ***	0.0792
ELSALVAD	-2.407205	(-7.026) ***	-0.0929	-2.902176	(-9.15) ***	-0.1208	-3.704103	(-12.726) ***	-0.1831	-1.199854	(-2.912) ***	-0.0489
ETHIOPIA	-2.419579	(-7.273) ***	-0.0934	-4.121599	(-13.393) ***	-0.1715	-2.766998	(-9.801) ***	-0.1367	-2.644293	(-7.232) ***	-0.1422
FINLAND	2.131004	(6.363) ***	0.0822	0.705738	(2.283) **	0.0294	0.117686	(.415)	0.0058	0.452263	(1.268)	0.0206
FRANCE	2.656569	(6.328) ***	0.1025	2.807478	(7.203) ***	0.1168	1.295350	(3.636) ***	0.0640	2.066650	(4.662) ***	0.0941
GABON	-2.326814	(-6.915) ***	-0.0898	-2.976449	(-9.567) ***	-0.1239	-1.647555	(-5.776) ***	-0.0814	-0.891131	(-2.485) **	-0.0444
GERMANY	2.949440	(7.008) ***	0.1138	3.027566	(7.519) ***	0.1260	1.094185	(2.994) ***	0.0541	1.469819	(3.448) ***	0.0791
GREECE	-2.603366	(-7.943) ***	-0.1004	-1.11378	(-3.68) ***	-0.0463	-0.368355	(-1.328)	-0.0182	0.954115	(2.873) ***	0.0513
GUATEMAL	-0.973157	(-2.932) ***	-0.0376	-3.481176	(-11.371) ***	-0.1449	-2.247866	(-8.013) ***	-0.1111	-0.425899	(-1.146)	-0.0212
HAITI	-2.463302	(-7.352) ***	-0.0950	-3.705297	(-11.948) ***	-0.1542	-4.009995	(-14.111) ***	-0.1982	-1.918981	(-4.209) ***	-0.0678
HONDURAS	-2.354661	(-7.128) ***	-0.0908	-3.478491	(-11.387) ***	-0.1447	-2.220733	(-7.924) ***	-0.1098	-1.296755	(-3.64) ***	-0.0646
ICELAND	-2.600020	(-7.036) ***	-0.1003	-2.192905	(-6.437) ***	-0.0913	-2.935970	(-9.376) ***	-0.1451	-2.249441	(-5.95) ***	-0.1121
INDIA	-2.691411	(-7.691) ***	-0.1038	-1.747333	(-5.408) ***	-0.0727	-1.001921	(-3.384) ***	-0.0495	-3.843398	(-10.925) ***	-0.2208
INDONESI	-0.464812	(-1.337)	-0.0179	-4.828542	(-15.047) ***	-0.2009	-0.542273	(-1.844) *	-0.0268	-0.639188	(-1.738) *	-0.0319
IRELAND	1.630055	(4.894) ***	0.0629	0.334012	(1.086)	0.0139	-2.517008	(-8.931) ***	-0.1244	-0.110746	(-0.304)	-0.0055
ISRAEL	1.291418	(3.201) ***	0.0498	-0.254234	-0.686	-0.0106	-0.883251	(-2.6) ***	-0.0437	-3.616639	(-6.793) ***	-0.1647
ITALY	1.456243	(3.8) ***	0.0562	1.953254	(5.494) ***	0.0813	1.882552	(5.798) ***	0.0930	1.408149	(3.561) ***	0.0702
JAMAICA	-2.496703	(-7.533) ***	-0.0963	-3.474704	(-11.35) ***	-0.1446	-2.626251	(-9.361) ***	-0.1298	-1.326587	(-3.72) ***	-0.0604
JAPAN	4.316947	(11.352) ***	0.1666	3.111152	(8.75) ***	0.1295	1.020158	(3.12) ***	0.0504	2.090602	(5.471) ***	0.1125
KENYA	-2.442616	(-7.418) ***	-0.0942	-3.685806	(-12.115) ***	-0.1534	-2.321740	(-8.317) ***	-0.1147	-0.889080	(-2.585) **	-0.0511
KOREA	-0.199611	(-0.601)	-0.0077	0.491908	(1.604)	0.0205	-0.162371	(-0.578)	-0.0080	-0.642169	(-1.973) **	-0.0369
LIBYA	0.530888	(1.601)	0.0205	-1.920351	(-6.291) ***	-0.0799	-1.054012	(-3.768) ***	-0.0521	-0.571241	(-1.669)	-0.0328
MADAGASC	-2.436058	(-7.267) ***	-0.0940	-3.029744	(-9.81) ***	-0.1261	-5.410839	(-19.119) ***	-0.2674	-2.110626	(-5.821) ***	-0.1213
MALAYSIA	1.195968	(3.158) ***	0.0461	-0.457859	(-1.309)	-0.0191	-1.320179	(-4.119) ***	-0.0652	0.761638	(1.971) **	0.0438
MAURITIU	-2.425884	(-7.255) ***	-0.0936	-3.569222	(-11.534) ***	-0.1485	-3.388031	(-11.956) ***	-0.1674	-2.256728	(-6.502) ***	-0.1214
MEXICO	2.078692	(6.182) ***	0.0802	1.531335	(4.996) ***	0.0637	1.159284	(4.136) ***	0.0573	1.453761	(3.835) ***	0.0593
MOROCCO	-2.504994	(-7.513) ***	-0.0966	-2.76092	(-8.966) ***	-0.1149	-1.040148	(-3.684) ***	-0.0514	-0.949236	(-2.858) ***	-0.0511
MOZAMBIQ	-2.485447	(-7.391) ***	-0.0959	-4.648830	(-14.967) ***	-0.1934	-5.677187	(-19.943) ***	-0.2806	-2.872799	(-7.32) ***	-0.1308
NEPAL	-2.421947	(-7.221) ***	-0.0934	-4.078416	(-13.147) ***	-0.1697	-3.950240	(-13.878) ***	-0.1952	-2.150987	(-5.847) ***	-0.1236
NETHERLA	3.156414	(8.467) ***	0.1218	2.849282	(8.25) ***	0.1186	0.201222	(.635)	0.0099	2.440691	(6.546) ***	0.1313
NEWZEALA	-2.732529	(-8.226) ***	-0.1054	-2.476532	(-8.071) ***	-0.1031	-1.983643	(-7.057) ***	-0.0980	1.001316	(3.018) ***	0.0539
NIGERIA	0.030808	(.093)	0.0012	-1.872467	(-6.142) ***	-0.0779	-0.924537	(-3.309) ***	-0.0457	0.969588	(2.811) ***	0.0483
NORWAY	2.321201	(6.295) ***	0.0896	0.312576	(.915)	0.0130	0.290345	(.928)	0.0143	0.790052	(2.116) **	0.0394
OMAN	-2.397157	(-7.269) ***	-0.0925	-1.940528	(-6.369) ***	-0.0808	-3.793696	(-13.581) ***	-0.1875	-0.900565	(-2.646) ***	-0.0517
PAKISTAN	-1.099232	(-3.336) ***	-0.0424	-1.656939	(-5.441) ***	-0.0689	-1.990066	(-7.13) ***	-0.0984	-0.254352	(-.776)	-0.0155
PAPUANEW	-2.439353	(-7.402) ***	-0.0941	-3.767497	(-12.365) ***	-0.1568	-2.104684	(-7.528) ***	-0.1040	-0.271468	(-.772)	-0.0135

Model / Ind. var.	Portfolio gross flow			Bank capital gross flow			Other-sector capital gross flow			FDI gross flow		
	Par est	(t-stat)	Std est	Par est	(t-stat)	Std est	Par est	(t-stat)	Std est	Par est	(t-stat)	Std est
PARAGUAY	-2.320731	(-6.804) ***	-0.0895	-2.803649	(-8.884) ***	-0.1167	-2.112231	(-7.303) ***	-0.1044	-1.835130	(-4.988) ***	-0.0915
PERU	-2.540451	(-7.515) ***	-0.0980	-3.637023	(-12.034) ***	-0.1513	-1.377306	(-4.965) ***	-0.0681	-1.154082	(-3.269) ***	-0.0526
PHILIPPI	-1.604317	(-4.877) ***	-0.0619	-0.916833	(-3.019) ***	-0.0382	-0.241865	(-.869)	-0.011:	-0.029125	(-.086)	-0.0015
SAUDIARA	3.774001	(10.482) ***	0.1456	0.771849	(2.322) **	0.0321	-0.719636	(-2.362) **	-0.0356	0.830147	(2.13) **	0.0447
SENEGAL	-2.243532	(-6.804) ***	-0.0866	-2.574396	(-8.449) ***	-0.1071	-2.927509	(-10.474) ***	-0.1447	-0.983403	(-2.67) ***	-0.0490
SEYCHELL	-2.523903	(-6.814) ***	-0.0974	-4.235840	(-12.34) ***	-0.1763	-5.689182	(-18.089) ***	-0.2812	-1.987740	(-4.59) ***	-0.0905
SIERRALE	-2.416412	(-6.701) ***	-0.0932	-3.994541	(-12.651) ***	-0.1662	-3.895809	(-13.451) ***	-0.1925	-0.962789	(-2.5) **	-0.0470
SINGAPOR	0.601964	(1.713) *	0.0232	0.310675	(.956)	0.0129	-1.498759	(-5.038) ***	-0.0741	1.737440	(4.74) ***	0.0791
SOUTHAFR	0.509090	(1.549)	0.0196	-1.058993	(-3.488) ***	-0.0441	-0.697547	(-2.508) **	-0.0345	-0.293548	(-.821)	-0.0134
SPAIN	0.755050	(2.253) **	0.0291	0.160258	(.518)	0.0067	0.855558	(3.017) ***	0.0423	2.231458	(6.327) ***	0.1112
SRILANKA	-2.419281	(-7.284) ***	-0.0933	-2.473765	(-8.061) ***	-0.1029	-1.770143	(-6.288) ***	-0.0875	-1.079554	(-3.09) ***	-0.0538
SUDAN	-2.403521	(-7.205) ***	-0.0927	-2.0715	(-6.756) ***	-0.0862	-5.480374	(-19.507) ***	-0.2708	-2.602631	(-6.663) ***	-0.1185
SWAZILAN	-2.268450	(-6.732) ***	-0.0875	-3.874021	(-12.431) ***	-0.1612	-4.307591	(-15.06) ***	-0.2129	-1.386387	(-3.935) ***	-0.0691
SWEDEN	1.633787	(4.015) ***	0.0630	1.561896	(4.14) ***	0.0640	0.480767	(1.394)	0.0238	1.068440	(2.548) **	0.0533
SWITZERL	3.594201	(10.008) ***	0.1387	1.691783	(5.04) ***	0.0704	-0.646440	(-2.044) **	-0.0310	1.540055	(4.267) ***	0.0828
SYRIA	-2.482164	(-7.441) ***	-0.0958	-1.496463	(-4.929) ***	-0.0623	-2.352984	(-8.454) ***	-0.1163	-2.763739	(-7.753) ***	-0.1378
TANZANIA	-2.405993	(-7.23) ***	-0.0928	-4.260450	(-13.969) ***	-0.1773	-3.975804	(-14.218) ***	-0.1965	-2.468261	(-6.746) ***	-0.1418
THAILAND	0.768926	(2.24) **	0.0297	-1.085971	(-3.427) ***	-0.0452	0.085806	(.295)	0.0042	-0.018352	(-.049)	-0.0008
TRINIDAD	-2.464647	(-7.472) ***	-0.0951	-3.176241	(-10.426) ***	-0.1322	-1.806130	(-6.462) ***	-0.0893	-0.397959	(-1.098)	-0.0181
TUNISIA	-1.345802	(-4.076) ***	-0.0519	-1.950872	(-6.393) ***	-0.0812	-1.245553	(-4.451) ***	-0.0616	-0.460971	(-1.375)	-0.0248
TURKEY	-0.722625	(-2.199) **	-0.0279	-0.402669	(-1.328)	-0.0168	-0.548329	(-1.974) ***	-0.0271	-0.739886	(-2.3) **	-0.0425
UK	3.303144	(8.589) ***	0.1274	3.253846	(9.04) ***	0.1354	0.173880	(.532)	0.0086	2.744736	(6.95) ***	0.1368
USA	3.900086	(9.711) ***	0.1505	2.720489	(6.542) ***	0.1132	0.420725	(1.177)	0.0208	3.788206	(8.364) ***	0.1725
URUGUAY	-0.987353	(-2.844) ***	-0.0381	-1.012376	(-3.183) ***	-0.0421	-2.420215	(-8.306) ***	-0.1196	-2.471969	(-6.631) ***	-0.1126
VENEZUEL	-1.503170	(-4.344) ***	-0.0570	-1.086804	(-3.415) ***	-0.0452	0.025246	(.087)	0.0012	-0.400252	(-1.055)	-0.0182
YUGOSLAV	-2.618503	(-7.876) ***	-0.1010	0.724198	(2.377) **	0.0301	0.413168	(1.482)	0.0204	-3.507836	(-10.606) ***	-0.1887
ZAIRE	-2.408121	(-6.985) ***	-0.0929	-2.762312	(-9.014) ***	-0.1149	-5.038593	(-17.925) ***	-0.2490	-2.795188	(-8.434) ***	-0.1606
ZAMBIA	-2.458538	(-7.462) ***	-0.0949	-2.579250	(-8.472) ***	-0.1073	-1.770502	(-6.344) ***	-0.0875	-1.818248	(-5.479) ***	-0.0978
ZIMBABWE	-0.544194	(-1.638)	-0.0210	-3.035744	(-9.885) ***	-0.1263	-3.479304	(-12.368) ***	-0.1710	-1.977091	(-6.079) ***	-0.1136

Model / Ind. var.	Portfolio gross flow			Bank capital gross flow			Other-sector capital gross flow			FDI gross flow		
	Par est	(t-stat)	Std est	Par est	(t-stat)	Std est	Par est	(t-stat)	Std est	Par est	(t-stat)	Std est
YR1981	0.031439	(.27)	0.0033	0.036719	(.342)	0.0041	0.166281	(1.686) *	0.0220	0.320920	(2.279) **	0.0503
YR1982	0.059094	(.506)	0.0061	-0.008057	(-.075)	-0.0009	0.184343	(1.855) *	0.0244	0.229321	(1.652) *	0.0381
YR1983	0.105729	(.898)	0.0109	0.011443	(.105)	0.0013	-0.004455	(-.044)	-0.0006	0.178227	(1.233)	0.0262
YR1984	0.181885	(1.493)	0.0188	0.155639	(1.382)	0.0174	0.183137	(1.768) *	0.0243	0.183646	(1.26)	0.0289
YR1985	0.360264	(2.917) ***	0.0373	0.275613	(2.404) **	0.0308	0.186664	(1.774) *	0.0247	0.200275	(1.333)	0.0303
YR1986	0.337362	(2.687) ***	0.0349	0.230752	(1.985) **	0.0258	0.191614	(1.79) *	0.0254	0.314817	(1.834) *	0.0359
YR1987	0.348528	(2.741) ***	0.0361	0.317513	(2.701) ***	0.0354	0.224770	(2.08) **	0.0298	0.405522	(2.301) **	0.0420
YR1988	0.393122	(3.017) ***	0.0407	0.314065	(2.607) ***	0.0350	0.132789	(1.2)	0.0176	0.361397	(2.151) **	0.0417
YR1989	0.361148	(2.701) ***	0.0374	0.225903	(1.827) *	0.0252	0.080347	(.708)	0.0106	0.618181	(3.829) ***	0.0896
YR1990	0.295794	(2.186) **	0.0306	0.224015	(1.791) *	0.0250	0.205919	(1.791) *	0.0273	0.514558	(2.878) ***	0.0542

Notes

1 Portugal and Year 1980 omiited as base dummies.
2 *** = significant at 1% level; ** = significant at 5% level; * = significant at 10% level.

D–3 In-outflows of total capital with 3SLS simultaneous estimation (dummy coefficients reported)

Equation / Ind. var.	Total capital inflow				Total capital outflow			
	DV: TOTI (log of total K inflow)				DV: TOTO (log of total K outflow)			
	Par est	**SE**	**t-stat**	**Prob >|T|**	**Par est**	**SE**	**t-stat**	**Prob >|T|**
INTERCEPT	6.564184	0.282180	23.262	0.0001	2.850162	0.716313	3.979	0.0001
INTD	0.000309	0.001621	0.191	0.8488	-0.000986	0.001560	-0.632	0.5274
RISKD	0.017147	0.002876	5.963	0.0001				
RISKDC					-0.027838	0.005147	-5.408	0.0001
GNYPC					0.471966	0.090998	5.187	0.0001
CAB	-0.005267	0.001591	-3.311	0.0010	0.011592	0.001530	7.575	0.0001
EXCHCONT					-0.082167	0.059095	-1.390	0.1648
TAXD	0.003099	0.003413	0.908	0.3642	0.008270	0.003274	2.526	0.0117
TREATY	0.000109	0 000030	3.673	0.0003				
CD	0.489737	0.080949	6.050	0.0001				
TELECOMM					0.112782	0.025314	4.455	0.0001
TOTI					0.105145	0.036512	2.880	0.0041
TOTO	0.150757	0.036113	4.175	0.0001				
ALGERIA	0.096045	0.179293	0.536	0.5923	0.744647	0.177685	4.191	0.0001
ARGENTIN	0.510449	0.184103	2.773	0.0057	0.946740	0.189573	4.994	0.0001
AUSTRALI	1.688815	0.219537	7.693	0.0001	1.294223	0.218629	5.920	0.0001
AUSTRIA	0.033372	0.205249	0.163	0.8709	-0.203290	0.221080	-0.920	0.3581
BAHRAIN	-2.031886	0.177073	-11.475	0.0001	-1.762641	0.189933	-9.280	0.0001
BANGLADE	-2.112183	0.191307	-11.041	0.0001	-0.463503	0.306072	-1.514	0.1303
BARBADOS	-2.219370	0.192144	-11.551	0.0001	-2.321276	0.204089	-11.374	0.0001
BELGIUML	1.431751	0.208830	6.856	0.0001	1.569579	0.216449	7.251	0.0001
BOLIVIA	-1.755971	0.197608	-8.886	0.0001	-1.053288	0.218889	-4.812	0.0001
BRAZIL	1.202477	0.187592	6.410	0.0001	1.784091	0.180434	9.888	0.0001
CANADA	1.064296	0.210227	5.063	0.0001	0.494482	0.238749	2.071	0.0386
CHILE	0.106125	0.186879	0.568	0.5703	0.350584	0.198851	1.763	0.0783
COLOMBIA	-0.397216	0.178602	-2.224	0.0264	-0.095336	0.197025	-0.484	0.6286
CONGO	-1.241876	0.192952	-6.436	0.0001	-0.779585	0.196346	-3.970	0.0001
COSTARIC	-1.506194	0.185530	-8.118	0.0001	-1.343562	0.182940	-7.344	0.0001
COTEIVOR	-1.123462	0 180966	-6.208	0.0001	-0.859063	0.202378	-4.245	0.0001
CYPRUS	-1.176361	0.232299	-5.064	0.0001	-2.313090	0.193503	-11.954	0.0001
DENMARK	0.317155	0.230956	1.373	0.1700	-0.475700	0.246114	-1.933	0.0536
DOMINIRP	-1.834047	0.192017	-9.552	0.0001	-1.390164	0.214774	-6.473	0.0001
ECUADOR	-1.262218	0.183163	-6.891	0.0001	-0.739190	0.199614	-3 703	0.0002
EGYPT	-0.297304	0.189213	-1.571	0.1165	0.498127	0.229524	2.170	0.0303
ELSALVAD	-1.848759	0.218013	-8.480	0.0001	-1.683385	0.217499	-7.740	0.0001
ETHIOPIA	-1.851945	0.199130	-9.300	0.0001	-0.451764	0.338315	-1.335	0.1821
FINLAND	0.628345	0.189410	3.317	0.0009	-0.364411	0.224956	-1.620	0.1056
FRANCE	1.465354	0.237580	6.168	0.0001	1.419165	0.226939	6.254	0.0001
GABON	-1.206027	0.187750	-6.424	0.0001	-1.412884	0.190785	-7.406	0.0001
GERMANY	1.580109	0.235635	6.706	0.0001	1.542874	0.231519	6.664	0.0001
GREECE	-0.240478	0.193493	-1.243	0.2143	-1.195120	0.188633	-6.336	0.0001
GUATEMAL	-1 149046	0.195068	-5.890	0.0001	-1.073440	0.206910	-5.188	0.0001
HAITI	-2.303043	0.196096	-11.744	0.0001	-1.074806	0.304777	-3.527	0.0004
HONDURAS	-1.655962	0.190603	-8.688	0.0001	-1.211979	0.208486	-5.813	0.0001
ICELAND	-1.806472	0.211824	-8.528	0.0001	-2.744579	0.262185	-10.468	0.0001
INDIA	-1.088978	0.189675	-5.741	0.0001	-0.149824	0.273121	-0.549	0.5835
INDONESI	-0.865426	0.186270	-4.646	0.0001	0.334918	0.252228	1.328	0.1846
IRELAND	0.039210	0.187522	0.209	0.8344	-0.906509	0.191299	-4.739	0.0001
ISRAEL	0.584287	0.235567	2.480	0.0133	-0.538851	0.192220	-2.803	0.0052
ITALY	1.742508	0.220392	7.906	0.0001	1.345688	0.223727	6.015	0.0001
JAMAICA	-1.880761	0.195950	-9.598	0.0001	-1.552528	0.200943	-7.726	0.0001
JAPAN	2.255693	0.227423	9.918	0.0001	2.317847	0.249445	9.292	0.0001
KENYA	-2.014817	0.182319	-11.051	0.0001	-1.040465	0.254100	-4.095	0.0001
KOREA	0.001522	0.177072	0.009	0.9931	0.163035	0.175486	0.929	0.3531

Equation / Ind. var.	Total capital inflow				Total capital outflow			
	Par est	SE	t-stat	Prob >|T|	Par est	SE	t-stat	Prob >|T|
LIBYA	-0.490779	0.186491	-2.632	0.0087	-0.919063	0.197801	-4.646	0.0001
MADAGASC	-2.572099	0.199858	-12.870	0.0001	-1.045297	0.281211	-3.717	0.0002
MALAYSIA	-0.725632	0.192468	-3.770	0.0002	-0.273421	0.193702	-1.412	0.1585
MAURITIU	-2.360036	0.185269	-12.738	0.0001	-1.894443	0.188572	-10.046	0.0001
MEXICO	1.334233	0.179803	7.421	0.0001	1.770182	0.179134	9.882	0.0001
MOROCCO	-1.163509	0.182894	-6.362	0.0001	-0.525335	0.211754	-2.481	0.0133
MOZAMBIQ	-2.696901	0.203272	-13.267	0.0001	-0.986463	0.339714	-2.904	0.0038
NEPAL	-2.626888	0.189361	-13.872	0.0001	-0.782397	0.355924	-2.198	0.0282
NETHERLA	1.338927	0.204168	6.558	0.0001	1.333287	0.221036	6.032	0.0001
NEWZEALA	-0.789260	0.186418	-4.234	0.0001	-1.883204	0.203277	-9.264	0.0001
NIGERIA	-0.473108	0.184844	-2.559	0.0107	0.514784	0.264391	1.947	0.0519
NORWAY	0.185631	0.209737	0.885	0.3764	0.114091	0.246518	0.463	0.6436
OMAN	-1.978873	0.190264	-10.401	0.0001	-1.888637	0.191497	-9.862	0.0001
PAKISTAN	-1.044974	0.183986	-5.680	0.0001	-0.481486	0.265532	-1.813	0.0701
PAPUANEW	-1.734069	0.180387	-9.613	0.0001	-1.252551	0.209274	-5 985	0.0001
PARAGUAY	-1.793127	0.183261	-9.785	0.0001	-1.349785	0.195265	-6.913	0.0001
PERU	-1.408238	0.189552	-7.429	0.0001	-1.099109	0.198865	-5.527	0.0001
PHILIPPI	-0.296150	0.178764	-1.657	0.0980	0.286045	0.225657	1.268	0.2053
SAUDIARA	0.967999	0.187100	5.174	0.0001	0.645225	0.191742	3.365	0.0008
SENEGAL	-1.774273	0.198928	-8.919	0.0001	-0.994601	0.224891	-4.423	0.0001
SEYCHELL	-2.225844	0.212554	-10.472	0.0001	-2.553480	0.189483	-13.476	0.0001
SIERRALE	-2.229728	0.198114	-11.255	0.0001	-0.893186	0.318235	-2.807	0.0051
SINGAPOR	-0.108555	0.189378	-0.573	0.5666	-0.493376	0.186239	-2.649	0.0082
SOUTHAFR	-0.686076	0.189236	-3.626	0.0003	-0.243315	0.191545	-1 270	0.2043
SPAIN	1.250429	0.190869	6.551	0.0001	0.220293	0.190681	1.155	0.2483
SRILANKA	-1.539202	0.183265	-8.399	0.0001	-0.54669:	0.249827	-2.188	0.0289
SUDAN	-2.182329	0.196760	-11.091	0.0001	-1.318172	0.217114	-6.071	0.0001
SWAZILAN	-2.343027	0.190179	-12.320	0.0001	-1.343510	0.252221	-5 327	0.0001
SWEDEN	0.847408	0.232283	3.648	0.0003	0.466396	0.247480	1.885	0.0598
SWITZERL	0.559195	0.202427	2.762	0.0059	0.583679	0.252800	2.309	0.0212
SYRIA	-1.362664	0.187384	-7.272	0.0001	-1.143221	0.195938	-5.835	0.0001
TANZANIA	-2.253063	0.197780	-11.392	0.0001	-1.049449	0.312552	-3.358	0.0008
THAILAND	0.041505	0.184248	0.225	0.8218	0.552523	0.208553	2.649	0.0082
TRINIDAD	-1.606812	0.179538	-8.950	0.0001	-1.643731	0.180337	-9.115	0.0001
TUNISIA	-1.254036	0.177567	-7.062	0.0001	-0.827628	0.191104	-4.331	0.0001
TURKEY	0.065690	0.186700	0.352	0.7250	0.217552	0.197262	1.103	0.2704
UK	2.179134	0.215062	10.133	0.0001	2.242631	0.227725	9.848	0.0001
USA	2.173743	0.263613	8.246	0.0001	2.674806	0.278391	9.608	0.0001
URUGUAY	-0.914924	0.193883	-4.719	0.0001	-0.980197	0.191399	-5.121	0.0001
VENEZUEL	-0.081157	0.185369	-0.438	0.6616	0.305596	0.181648	1.682	0.0929
YUGOSLAV	0.680676	0.186229	3.655	0.0003	0.684694	0.175818	3.894	0.0001
ZAIRE	-2.032900	0.200062	-10.161	0.0001	-1.306994	0.284402	-4.596	0.0001
ZAMBIA	-1.208856	0.193631	-6.243	0.0001	-0.298761	0.279296	-1.070	0.2851
ZIMBABWE	-2.095705	0.187852	-11.156	0.0001	-1.216217	0.219647	-5.537	0.0001
YR1981	0.170942	0.062924	2.717	0.0067	0.073601	0.060903	1.208	0.2272
YR1982	0.099045	0.062975	1.573	0.1161	0.038727	0.061145	0.633	0.5267
YR1983	-0.019846	0.063097	-0.315	0.7532	0.011075	0.061563	0.180	0.8573
YR1984	0.062831	0.063852	0.984	0.3254	0.121176	0.062547	1.937	0.0530
YR1985	0.069057	0.064314	1.074	0.2832	0.164254	0.063157	2.601	0.0095
YR1986	0.067013	0.065169	1.028	0.3041	0.189370	0.064745	2.925	0.0035
YR1987	0.162216	0.065911	2.461	0.0140	0.234145	0.065775	3 560	0.0004
YR1988	0.104907	0.067377	1.557	0.1198	0.259054	0.068355	3.790	0.0002
YR1989	0.156397	0.068417	2.286	0.0225	0.218783	0.070595	3.099	0.0020
YR1990	0.247962	0.068818	3.603	0.0003	0.239470	0.072546	3.301	0.0010
System weighted R-sq: 0.9520		N = 946				Degree of freedom = 1685		

Note

Portugal and Year 1980 omitted as base dummies.

D–4 In-outflows of portfolio with 3SLS simultaneous estimation (dummy coefficients reported)

Equation / Ind. var.	Portfolio inflow DV: PORTI (log of portfolio inflow)				Portfolio outflow DV: PORTO (log of portfolio outflow)			
	Par est	SE	t-stat	Prob >|T|	Par est	SE	t-stat	Prob >|T|
INTERCEPT	3 528040	0.332080	10.624	0.0001	-1.116860	1.088333	-1.026	0.3051
IGOVTD	0 000004	0.000003	1.572	0.1164	0.000001	0.000002	0.586	0.5583
RISKD	0.025947	0.005589	4.643	0.0001				
RISKDC					0.007393	0.007689	0.962	0 3366
GNYPC					0.407813	0.138073	2.954	0.0032
CAB	-0.004739	0 003203	-1.480	0.1393	0.014352	0.002250	6.379	0.0001
EXCHCONT					0.107326	0.090172	1.190	0 2343
TFDIVD	-0.009127	0.005957	-1.532	0.1258	0 006710	0.004398	1.526	0.1275
TREATY	0 008593	0.005956	1.443	0.1495				
CD	0 747593	0.163847	4.563	0 0001				
TELECOMM					0.209795	0.044886	4.674	0.0001
PORTI					0.138388	0.050506	2.740	0.0063
PORTO	0.228736	0.054841	4.171	0.0001				
ALGERIA	-2.814728	0.359059	-7.839	0.0001	-0.642438	0.264253	-2.431	0.0153
ARGENTIN	1 341573	0.369341	3.632	0.0003	2.681870	0.291856	9.189	0.0001
AUSTRALI	1.841560	0 381415	4.828	0.0001	1.807790	0.322061	5.613	0.0001
AUSTRIA	1.469228	0 410592	3.578	0.0004	2.140403	0.329918	6.488	0.0001
BAHRAIN	-1.995203	0.351328	-5.679	0.0001	-0.808930	0.282487	-2.864	0.0043
BANGLADE	-1.842926	0.372144	-4.952	0.0001	0.788528	0.464352	1.698	0.0899
BARBADOS	-1.998809	0 385258	-5.188	0.0001	-0.416127	0.302555	-1.375	0.1694
BELGIUML	0.976724	0.422285	2.313	0.0210	3.634099	0.320907	11.324	0.0001
BOLIVIA	-1.712614	0.387714	-4.417	0.0001	0.188169	0.325556	0.578	0.5634
BRAZIL	-0.227127	0.364693	-0.623	0.5336	1.770588	0.265565	6.667	0.0001
CANADA	2.183528	0.475561	4.591	0.0001	3.027524	0.360054	8.409	0.0001
CHILE	-0.215199	0.363926	-0.591	0.5545	0.497656	0.283910	1.753	0.0800
COLOMBIA	-2.204327	0.352976	-6.245	0.0001	-0.565761	0.293592	-1.927	0.0543
CONGO	-1.780031	0.380969	-4.672	0.0001	-0.067272	0.290592	-0.231	0.8170
COSTARIC	-1.820917	0.369163	-4.933	0.0001	-0.129297	0.271578	-0.476	0.6341
COTEIVOR	-2.132178	0.362345	-5.884	0.0001	0.193580	0.302895	0.639	0.5229
CYPRUS	-1.005952	0.448276	-2.244	0.0251	-0.805551	0.269487	-2.989	0.0029
DENMARK	0.483079	0.452542	1.067	0.2861	1.332917	0.353297	3.773	0.0002
DOMINIRP	-1.842522	0.380557	-4.842	0.0001	0.167589	0.321387	0.521	0.6022
ECUADOR	-2.279214	0.365765	-6.231	0 0001	-0.073908	0.298164	-0.248	0.8043
EGYPT	-1.877642	0.370083	-5.074	0.0001	0.080121	0.334543	0.239	0.8108
ELSALVAD	-1.347636	0.407711	-3.305	0.0010	-0.079226	0.309507	-0.256	0.7980
ETHIOPIA	-1.705740	0.382879	-4.455	0.0001	0.891908	0.516483	1.727	0.0846
FINLAND	2.059748	0.369850	5.569	0.0001	1.532230	0.332687	4.606	0.0001
FRANCE	2 299696	0.468224	4.912	0.0001	2.801871	0.335478	8.352	0.0001
GABON	-1.903209	0.371579	-5.122	0.0001	-0.688992	0.277088	-2 487	0.0131
GERMANY	1.784268	0.483459	3.691	0.0002	3.278887	0 346818	9.454	0.0001
GREECE	-2.282682	0.371135	-6.151	0.0001	-1.247160	0.271888	-4.587	0.0001
GUATEMAL	-0.759816	0.388856	-1.954	0.0510	1.029268	0.309465	3.326	0.0009
HAITI	-1.773060	0.379804	-4.668	0.0001	0.699881	0.463340	1.511	0.1313
HONDURAS	-1.909539	0.375411	-5.087	0.0001	-0.032319	0.310046	-0.104	0.9170
ICELAND	-1.764283	0.424837	-4.153	0.0001	-1.201618	0.387020	-3.105	0.0020
INDIA	-3.024098	0.374441	-8.076	0.0001	0.239725	0.406085	0.58:	0.5551
INDONESI	-1.686206	0 369824	-4.559	0.0001	1.314682	0.376718	3.490	0.0005
IRELAND	1.533669	0.399699	3.837	0.0001	1.748664	0.311117	5.621	0.0001
ISRAEL	2.240240	0.467564	4.791	0.0001	1.369965	0.282298	4.853	0.0001
ITALY	0.893770	0.417090	2.143	0.0324	2.337768	0.326307	7.164	0.0001
JAMAICA	-1.697164	0.386508	-4.391	0.0001	-0 229411	0.29682:	-0.773	0 4398
JAPAN	2.728916	0.477085	5.720	0.0001	4.122334	0.380411	10.837	0.0001
KENYA	-2.409005	0.362505	-6.645	0.0001	0.229637	0.383696	0.598	0.5497
KOREA	-0.374071	0.352045	-1.063	0.2883	0.114709	0.261194	0.439	0.6606

Equation / Ind. var.	Portfolio inflow Par est	SE	t-stat	Prob >|T|	Portfolio outflow Par est	SE	t-stat	Prob >|T|
LIBYA	-0.541198	0.373783	-1.448	0.1480	1.766775	0.293786	6.014	0.0001
MADAGASC	-2.210761	0.395044	-5.596	0.0001	0.701706	0.428077	1.639	0.1015
MALAYSIA	-0.000527	0.394397	-0.001	0 9989	1.412066	0.311665	4.531	0.0001
MAURITIU	-2.019023	0 367739	-5.490	0.0001	-0.165148	0.280416	-0.589	0 5561
MEXICO	1.267862	0.361784	3.504	0.0005	3.290802	0.268194	12.270	0.0001
MOROCCO	-2.219113	0 363744	-6 101	0.0001	0.005716	0.316902	0.018	0.9856
MOZAMBIQ	-1.774141	0.394254	-4.500	0.0001	0.990714	0.51707:	1.916	0.0557
NEPAL	-2.080712	0 366543	-5.677	0.0001	1.000040	0.541462	1.847	0.0651
NETHERLA	1.769513	0.413754	4.277	0.0001	3.096764	0.333664	9.281	0.0001
NEWZEALA	-2.238568	0.363462	-6.159	0.0001	-1.689349	0.298340	-5.662	0.0001
NIGERIA	-0.205552	0.362376	-0.567	0.5707	1.807855	0.396341	4.561	0 0001
NORWAY	0.831215	0.412268	2.016	0 0441	2.263784	0.356839	6.344	0.0001
OMAN	-2.478882	0.382365	-6.483	0.0001	-0.731224	0 286721	-2 550	0.0109
PAKISTAN	-0.911737	0.362273	-2.517	0.0120	0.687431	0.400904	1.715	0.0868
PAPUANEW	-2.468776	0.361752	-6.824	0.0001	-0.121250	0.311512	-0.389	0.6972
PARAGUAY	-2.426126	0.365134	-6.644	0.0001	-0.134972	0.292060	-0.462	0.6441
PERU	-1.819983	0.379673	-4.794	0.0001	-0.466178	0.296091	-1.574	0.1158
PHILIPPI	-1.417398	0.360852	-3.928	0.0001	-0.215955	0.343278	-0.629	0.5295
SAUDIARA	1.839243	0 386342	4.761	0.0001	3.406252	0.288698	11.799	0.0001
SENEGAL	-1.822422	0.394789	-4.616	0 0001	0.328209	0 338291	0 970	0.3322
SEYCHELL	-1 389531	0.417577	-3.328	0.0009	-0 554934	0.267104	-2.078	0.0380
SIERRALE	-1.700147	0 383730	-4.431	0 0001	0.810304	0.477671	1.696	0.0902
SINGAPOR	-1.341126	0.376848	-3.559	0.0004	0.646035	0.282082	2.290	0.0223
SOUTHAFR	-0.619346	0.358133	-1.729	0.0841	1.518513	0.272592	5 571	0.0001
SPAIN	0.840380	0.379579	2.214	0.0271	0 583608	0.289243	2 018	0.0439
SRILANKA	-2.142811	0.363321	-5.898	0.0001	0.361012	0 376027	0.960	0.3373
SUDAN	-1.683103	0.384986	-4.372	0.0001	0.141378	0.322472	0.438	0.6612
SWAZILAN	-1.772157	0.372949	-4.752	0.0001	0.443328	0 380260	1.166	0.2440
SWEDEN	0.938003	0.448445	2.092	0.0368	1.675610	0.346520	4.836	0.0001
SWITZERL	1.253163	0 433475	2.891	0.0039	3.590775	0 385022	9.326	0.0001
SYRIA	-2.010003	0.371399	-5.412	0 0001	-0.096192	0.290942	-0.331	0.7410
TANZANIA	-1.774114	0 378708	-4.685	0.0001	0.686503	0.473027	1.451	0.1471
THAILAND	0.219437	0.362343	0.606	0.5449	1.48777:	0.313324	4.748	0.0001
TRINIDAD	-2.217061	0 356582	-6.218	0 0001	-0 831385	0.265723	-3.129	0.0018
TUNISIA	-1.678161	0.355131	-4.725	0.0001	-0.103005	0.285308	-0.361	0.7182
TURKEY	-0.602246	0.386940	-1.556	0.1200	0.698297	0.303454	2.301	0.0216
UK	2.505462	0.428137	5.852	0.0001	3.984868	0.334194	11.924	0.0001
USA	2.789948	0 566700	4.924	0 0001	4.793504	0.420947	11.387	0.0001
URUGUAY	-0.634175	0.380762	-1.666	0.0962	0.231019	0.276989	0.834	0.4045
VENEZUEL	-1.795081	0.368664	-4.869	0.0001	-0.282460	0.272293	-1.037	0.2999
YUGOSLAV	-2.013002	0.373781	-5.386	0.0001	-0.689088	0.262301	-2.627	0.0088
ZAIRE	-1.693288	0.384543	-4 403	0.0001	0.510582	0.426319	1.198	0.2314
ZAMBIA	-1.868245	0.378534	-4.935	0.0001	0.530697	0.421548	1.259	0.2084
ZIMBABWE	-1.129445	0.365194	-3.093	0.0020	1.561777	0.328241	4.758	0.0001
YR1981	0.040167	0.125008	0.321	0.7481	0.041708	0.090517	0.461	0.6451
YR1982	0.044489	0.125188	0.355	0.7224	0.055593	0.090896	0.612	0.5410
YR1983	0.124963	0.125338	0.997	0.3190	0.096780	0.091422	1.059	0.2901
YR1984	0.261111	0.127113	2.054	0.0403	0.113061	0.092942	1.216	0.2241
YR1985	0.445934	0.128399	3.473	0.0005	0.227662	0.093929	2.424	0.0156
YR1986	0.370980	0.129788	2.858	0.0044	0.280757	0.096280	2.916	0.0036
YR1987	0.411325	0.131111	3.137	0.0018	0 283425	0.097852	2.896	0.0039
YR1988	0.470790	0.133278	3.532	0.0004	0.386585	0.101436	3.811	0 0001
YR1989	0.395718	0.136906	2.890	0.0039	0.359706	0.104824	3.432	0.0006
YR1990	0.305550	0.138727	2.203	0.0279	0.366771	0.107874	3.400	0.0007
System weighted R-sq: 0.9204		N = 946				Degree of freedom = 1685		

Note

Portugal and Year 1980 omitted as base dummies.

D-5 In-outflows of bank capital with 3SLS simultaneous estimation (dummy coefficients reported)

Equation / Ind. var.	Bank capital inflow				Bank capital outflow			
	DV: BANKI (log of bank K inflow)				DV: BANKI (log of bank K outflow)			
	Par est	SE	t-stat	Prob >|T|	Par est	SE	t-stat	Prob >|T|
INTERCEPT	4.637126	0.412737	11.235	0.0001	4.261308	1.398773	3.046	0.0024
IDEPD	0.00084:	0.003129	0.272	0.7860	-0.00953:	0.002922	-3.265	0.0011
RISKD	0.025426	0 005647	4.503	0.0001				
RISKDC					-0.038516	0.010135	-3.800	0.0002
GNYPC					0.206686	0.175566	1.177	0.2394
CAB	-0.002080	0.003087	-0 674	0 5007	0.010602	0.002939	3.607	0.0003
EXCHCONT					-0.338624	0.119127	-2.843	0.0046
TFINTD	-0.003552	0.006087	-0.584	0.5597	-0 004154	0 005727	-0.725	0.4685
TREATY	0.000001	0.000064	0.021	0.9835				
CD	0.664663	0.162776	4.083	0.0001				
TELECOMM					0.125034	0.048752	2.565	0.0105
BANKI					0.090831	0 058170	1.561	0.1188
BANKO	0.243979	0.066111	3.690	0.0002				
ALGERIA	-1.666658	0.357627	-4.660	0.0001	-2.286789	0.341460	-6.697	0.0001
ARGENTIN	-0.870702	0 359801	-2.420	0.0157	-1.651912	0.366772	-4.504	0.0001
AUSTRALI	1 246134	0 398272	3 129	0.0018	0.085576	0.433150	0.198	0.8434
AUSTRIA	0.886416	0.419962	2.111	0.0351	0 535854	0.445659	1.202	0.2296
BAHRAIN	-1.850863	0.349732	-5 292	0 0001	-1 007059	0.365428	-2.756	0.0060
BANGLADE	-1.271116	0.378664	-3.357	0.0008	-0.856829	0.597306	-1.434	0.1518
BARBADOS	-2.444202	0.389607	-6.274	0.0001	-3.823572	0.392710	-9.736	0.0001
BELGIUML	2.387129	0 433926	5.501	0.0001	2.344116	0.445223	5.265	0.0001
BOLIVIA	-1.833178	0.391996	-4.677	0.0001	-2.193855	0 425105	-5.161	0.0001
BRAZIL	1.539041	0.369567	4.164	0.0001	1.720192	0.348615	4.934	0.0001
CANADA	0.470199	0.434462	1.082	0.2794	-0.004903	0.465597	-0.011	0.9916
CHILE	0.672294	0.358268	1.877	0.0609	0.808049	0.369081	2.189	0.0288
COLOMBIA	-1.457757	0.351693	-4.145	0.0001	-1.60192:	0.381863	-4.195	0.0001
CONGO	-2.524384	0.384172	-6.571	0.0001	-3.018328	0.380797	-7 926	0.0001
COSTARIC	-2.260153	0 372909	-6 061	0.0001	-2.831764	0.358973	-7.889	0.0001
COTEIVOR	-0.334116	0.359891	-0 928	0.3535	-1.639690	0.393482	-4.167	0.0001
CYPRUS	-0.228375	0.453946	-0.503	0.6150	-2.324709	0.354545	-6.557	0.0001
DENMARK	1.396386	0.462167	3.021	0.0026	0.213064	0.476541	0.447	0.6549
DOMINIRP	-1.914832	0.382895	-5.001	0.0001	-2 181531	0.419124	-5.205	0.0001
ECUADOR	-2.406935	0.369801	-6.509	0.0001	-2.832740	0.389822	-7.267	0.0001
EGYPT	-0.225186	0.365051	-0.617	0.5375	0.151771	0.429898	0.353	0.7241
ELSALVAD	-1.678322	0.416728	-4.027	0.0001	-2.333037	0.401548	-5.810	0.0001
ETHIOPIA	-2.517449	0.394180	-6.387	0.0001	-2.718996	0.661119	-4.113	0.0001
FINLAND	0 961998	0.375761	2.560	0 0106	-0.495257	0.429795	-1.152	0.2495
FRANCE	2 512943	0.418715	6.002	0.0001	2.378163	0.444335	5.352	0.0001
GABON	-1.993145	0.373052	-5.343	0.0001	-2.790760	0.361822	-7.713	0.0001
GERMANY	2.363531	0.489693	4.827	0.0001	2.199105	0.474589	4.634	0.0001
GREECE	-0.333229	0.370972	-0.898	0.3693	-2.125756	0.354901	-5.990	0.0001
GUATEMAL	-2.149657	0.390868	-5.500	0.0001	-2.986747	0.405437	-7.367	0.0001
HAITI	-2.478116	0.389558	-6.361	0.0001	-2.538492	0.595124	-4.265	0.0001
HONDURAS	-2.484025	0.381671	-6.508	0.0001	-2.839067	0.408528	-6.950	0.0001
ICELAND	-0.879353	0 423917	-2.074	0.0383	-2.844851	0.485126	-5.864	0.0001
INDIA	-1.890492	0.377480	-5.008	0.0001	-1.058047	0 515486	-2.053	0.0404
INDONESI	-4.222177	0.377348	-11.189	0.0001	-3.508553	0.482713	-7.268	0.0001
IRELAND	1.108958	0.382176	2 902	0.0038	-0.518861	0.366792	-1.415	0.1576
ISRAEL	0.743249	0.453283	1.640	0.1014	-0.603301	0.370142	-1.630	0.1035
ITALY	2.057760	0.429331	4.793	0.0001	1.109051	0.444011	2.498	0.0127
JAMAICA	-2 369723	0.379071	-6.251	0.0001	-2.827257	0.378086	-7.478	0.0001
JAPAN	2.386177	0.480607	4.965	0 0001	2.206528	0.512073	4.309	0.0001
KENYA	-3.023886	0.366273	-8.256	0 0001	-2.853175	0.498062	-5.729	0.0001
KOREA	0.363130	0.348971	1.041	0.2984	0.039356	0.337775	0.117	0.9073

Equation / Ind. var.	Bank capital inflow				Bank capital outflow			
	Par est	SE	t-stat	Prob >|T|	Par est	SE	t-stat	Prob >|T|
LIBYA	-0.923830	0.370253	-2.495	0.0128	-2.344104	0.375133	-6.249	0.0001
MADAGASC	-2.262287	0.397244	-5.695	0.0001	-2.147440	0.558920	-3.842	0.0001
MALAYSIA	-1.355048	0.388832	-3.485	0.0005	-0.675047	0.366258	-1.843	0.0657
MAURITIU	-2.884776	0.367084	-7.859	0.0001	-2.708549	0.365497	-7.411	0.0001
MEXICO	2.315481	0.358043	6.467	0.0001	1.187219	0.347216	3.419	0.0007
MOROCCO	-2.332964	0.373007	-6.254	0.0001	-1.953898	0.417767	-4.677	0.0001
MOZAMBIQ	-2.877646	0.398819	-7.215	0.0001	-3.097498	0.665482	-4.655	0.0001
NEPAL	-2.923022	0.374825	-7.798	0.0001	-2.760446	0.694487	-3.975	0.0001
NETHERLA	2.512832	0.413067	6.083	0.0001	2.171254	0.443352	4.897	0.0001
NEWZEALA	-1.924962	0.366858	-5.247	0.0001	-3.183614	0.381480	-8.345	0.0001
NIGERIA	-1.813894	0.365397	-4.964	0.0001	-1.183471	0.508494	-2.327	0.0202
NORWAY	0.033657	0.420826	0.080	0.9363	-0.465313	0.484595	-0.960	0.3372
OMAN	-2.240866	0.381297	-5.877	0.0001	-1.734651	0.369741	-4 692	0.0001
PAKISTAN	-0.739346	0.364075	-2.031	0.0426	-1.25947:	0.517302	-2.435	0 0151
PAPUANEW	-2.790704	0.393325	-7.095	0.0001	-3.178342	0.426824	-7.446	0.0001
PARAGUAY	-2 167387	0.366652	-5.911	0.0001	-2 477851	0.381916	-6.488	0.0001
PERU	-2.667225	0.364797	-7.312	0.0001	-3.387943	0.374596	-9.044	0.0001
PHILIPPI	-0.599890	0.354085	-1.694	0.0906	-1.463993	0.439601	-3.330	0.0009
SAUDIARA	-0.489850	0 377537	-1.297	0.1948	0.806664	0.365968	2.204	0.0278
SENEGAL	-1.572468	0.397220	-3.959	0.0001	-1.947644	0.443369	-4.393	0.0001
SEYCHELL	-2.314324	0.426188	-5.430	0 0001	-3.551970	0.357349	-9.93:	0 0001
SIERRALE	-2.615706	0.397000	-6.589	0.0001	-3.007629	0.622001	-4.835	0.0001
SINGAPOR	0.534344	0.378511	1.412	0.1584	0.231486	0.363279	0.637	0.5242
SOUTHAFR	-0 300930	0.372875	-0.807	0.4199	-2.242535	0.372295	-6.024	0.0001
SPAIN	0.752105	0.374881	2.006	0.0451	-0.881483	0 368901	-2.389	0.0171
SRILANKA	-1.750596	0.363298	-4.819	0.0001	-1.846501	0.485832	-3.801	0.0002
SUDAN	-1.288035	0 390216	-3.301	0.0010	-1.431636	0.42120:	-3.399	0.0007
SWAZILAN	-2.665884	0.377276	-7.066	0.0001	-2.947963	0.493270	-5.976	0.0001
SWEDEN	1.693299	0.468729	3 613	0.0003	0.433404	0.488376	0.887	0.3751
SWITZERL	1.038256	0.417782	2.485	0.0131	0.764229	0.502789	1.520	0.1289
SYRIA	-0.582782	0.371491	-1.569	0.1171	-1.841188	0.380885	-4.834	0 0001
TANZANIA	-2.648393	0.391100	-6.772	0.0001	-3.065187	0.611279	-5.014	0.0001
THAILAND	-1.457628	0.380699	-3.829	0.0001	-1.223017	0.410018	-2.983	0.0029
TRINIDAD	-2.730225	0.351960	-7.757	0.0001	-3.124704	0.342464	-9.124	0.0001
TUNISIA	-1.860713	0.353605	-5.262	0 0001	-1.806194	0.369749	-4.885	0.0001
TURKEY	0.080048	0.363981	0.220	0.8260	-0.207217	0.382867	-0.541	0.5885
UK	2.871157	0 542930	5.288	0.0001	2.777934	0.459039	6.052	0.0001
USA	2.453922	0.509395	4.817	0.0001	3.081341	0.539539	5 711	0.0001
URUGUAY	0.175585	0.388567	0.452	0.6515	-0.914033	0.363145	-2.517	0.0120
VENEZUEL	-0.793804	0.369556	-2.148	0.0320	-1.630069	0 355030	-4.591	0.0001
YUGOSLAV	1.492735	0.369765	4.037	0.0001	0.580001	0.337364	1.719	0.0859
ZAIRE	-1.209527	0.395990	-3.054	0.0023	-2.668094	0.554772	-4.809	0.0001
ZAMBIA	-1.816853	0.383435	-4.738	0.0001	-1.721188	0.543029	-3.170	0.0016
ZIMBABWE	-2.015780	0.366382	-5.502	0.0001	-2.567426	0.426074	-6.026	0.0001
YR1981	0.109164	0 124231	0 879	0.3798	-0.044249	0.117177	-0 378	0.7058
YR1982	-0.034220	0 124422	-0.275	0.7834	-0.054757	0.117656	-0 465	0.6418
YR1983	-0.074217	0 124664	-0.595	0.5518	-0.056582	0.118490	-0.478	0.6331
YR1984	0.032469	0.126172	0.257	0.7970	0.110082	0.120435	0.914	0.3610
YR1985	0.113072	0.127080	0.890	0.3738	0.166649	0.121553	1.371	0.1707
YR1986	0.008249	0.128413	0.064	0.9488	0.238045	0.124865	1.906	0.0569
YR1987	0.183363	0.129917	1.411	0.1585	0.243949	0.127040	1.920	0.0552
YR1988	0.093396	0.132165	0.707	0.4800	0.287417	0.132131	2.175	0.0299
YR1989	0.052888	0.134140	0.394	0.6935	0.186749	0.136722	1.366	0.1723
YR1990	0.079842	0.134347	0.594	0.5525	0.183743	0.140223	1.310	0.1904
System weighted R-sq: 0.9061		N = 946				Degree of freedom = 1685		

Note

Portugal and Year 1980 omitted as base dummies.

D–6 In-outflows of other-sector capital with 3SLS simultaneous estimation (dummy coefficients reported)

Equation	Other-sector capital inflow				Other-sector capital outflow			
	DV: OTHI (log of other K inflow)				DV: OTHO (log of other K outflow)			
Ind. var.	Par est	SE	t-stat	Prob >|T|	Par est	SE	t-stat	Prob >|T|
INTERCEPT	6.423551	0.357329	17.977	0.0001	1.954013	1.184244	1.650	0.0993
IMKTD	0.001834	0.002748	0.667	0.5048	0.001274	0.002594	0.491	0.6235
RISKD	0.023462	0.004872	4.816	0.0001				
RISKDC					-0.037939	0.008670	-4.376	0.0001
GNYPC					0.629885	0.149169	4.223	0.0001
CAB	-0.007916	0.002690	-2.943	0.0033	0.007855	0.002600	3.022	0.0026
EXCHCONT					-0.083659	0.100472	-0.833	0.4053
TFINTD	-0.001647	0.005311	-0.310	0.7566	0.003072	0.004947	0.621	0.5348
TREATY	0.000088	0.000049	1.769	0.0773				
CD	0.571621	0.134031	4.265	0.0001				
TELECOMM					0.124005	0 039795	3.116	0.0019
OTHI					-0 016788	0.047294	-0.355	0.7227
OTHO	0.082744	0.046594	1.776	0.0761				
ALGERIA	0.498941	0.311590	1.601	0.1097	1.195243	0.300813	3.973	0.0001
ARGENTIN	0 372863	0.320072	1.165	0.2444	1.119422	0.320771	3.490	0.0005
AUSTRALI	2.320787	0.358180	6.479	0.0001	1.536362	0.376595	4.080	0.0001
AUSTRIA	-1.277903	0.353871	-3.611	0.0003	-1.776403	0.374733	-4.740	0.0001
BAHRAIN	-3 363905	0.305216	-11.021	0.0001	-3.570757	0.318306	-11.218	0.0001
BANGLADE	-3.284929	0.328049	-10.014	0.0001	-2.001133	0.511382	-3.913	0.0001
BARBADOS	-2.662131	0.328974	-8.092	0.0001	-3.081655	0.337394	-9.134	0.0001
BELGIUML	-0.576805	0.365193	-1.579	0.1146	-0.827156	0.370511	-2.232	0.0258
BOLIVIA	-2.040449	0.339391	-6.012	0.0001	-1.415572	0.368681	-3.840	0.0001
BRAZIL	1.169950	0.324236	3.608	0.0003	1.745317	0.302466	5.770	0.0001
CANADA	-0.579900	0.370977	-1.563	0.1184	-1.553402	0.396790	-3.915	0.0001
CHILE	0 046470	0.313272	0.148	0.8821	0.360387	0.322257	1.118	0.2637
COLOMBIA	-0.311658	0.304976	-1.022	0.3071	0.037394	0.331476	0.113	0.9102
CONGO	-1.017155	0.331236	-3.071	0.0022	-0.695086	0.331985	-2.094	0.0366
COSTARIC	-1.671017	0 324834	-5.144	0.0001	-1.471447	0.314955	-4.672	0.0001
COTEIVOR	-1 661972	0.311701	-5 332	0.0001	-1.049912	0.342139	-3.069	0.0022
CYPRUS	-1.438503	0.392527	-3.665	0.0003	-3.139762	0.328746	-9.551	0.0001
DENMARK	-0 006731	0.398089	-0.017	0.9865	-3.175532	0.408484	-7 774	0.0001
DOMINIRP	-3.347149	0.331427	-10.099	0.0001	-2.738873	0.364316	-7.518	0.0001
ECUADOR	-1.200435	0.311753	-3.851	0.0001	-0.687332	0.336490	-2.043	0.0414
EGYPT	-0 817364	0.311159	-2 627	0.0088	0.349781	0.373197	0.937	0.3489
ELSALVAD	-2.845889	0.357529	-7.960	0.0001	-2.579382	0.354662	-7.273	0.0001
ETHIOPIA	-1.934423	0.342719	-5.644	0.0001	-0.653499	0.564790	-1.157	0.2476
FINLAND	0.154761	0.319316	0.485	0.6280	-1.043984	0.371600	-2.809	0.0051
FRANCE	1.149868	0.361576	3.180	0.0015	0.751301	0.373186	2.013	0.0444
GABON	-1.201908	0.321242	-3.741	0.0002	-1.677048	0.318015	-5 273	0.0001
GERMANY	0.895983	0 402848	2.224	0.0264	0.688664	0.386541	1.782	0.0752
GREECE	-0.116764	0.324036	-0 360	0.7187	-1.004848	0.314139	-3.199	0.0014
GUATEMAL	-1 367654	0.338310	-4.043	0.0001	-1.917162	0.353246	-5.427	0.0001
HAITI	-3.032365	0.337948	-8.973	0.0001	-2.250498	0 509655	-4.416	0.0001
HONDURAS	-1.735623	0.330366	-5.254	0.0001	-1.462852	0.355843	-4.111	0 0001
ICELAND	-2.126740	0 360687	-5.896	0.0001	-3.744356	0.432882	-8.650	0.0001
INDIA	-0.962321	0.313569	-3.069	0.0022	0.149732	0.455477	0.329	0.7424
INDONESI	-0 795108	0.316503	-2.512	0.0122	0.946316	0.424913	2.227	0.0262
IRELAND	-3 139506	0.327597	-9.583	0.0001	-2.372389	0.330601	-7.176	0 0001
ISRAEL	0.640399	0.394855	1.622	0.1052	-1.056223	0.322395	-3.276	0.0011
ITALY	2.055349	0.378569	5 429	0.0001	1.252546	0.376382	3.328	0 0009
JAMAICA	-1.968356	0.328521	-5.992	0.0001	-1.939278	0.331510	-5.850	0.0001
JAPAN	1.061545	0.387273	2.741	0.0063	0.543167	0.412828	1.316	0.1886
KENYA	-2.167751	0.315546	-6.870	0.0001	-1.210334	0.428756	-2.823	0.0049
KOREA	-0.233163	0.305224	-0.764	0.4451	0.092459	0.296085	0.312	0.7549

Equation / Ind. var.	Other-sector capital inflow				Other-sector capital outflow			
	Par est	SE	t-stat	Prob >|T|	Par est	SE	t-stat	Prob >|T|
LIBYA	-0.419858	0.320386	-1.310	0.1904	-2.024228	0.330494	-6.125	0.0001
MADAGASC	-4.576244	0.350935	-13.040	0.0001	-3.052511	0.480264	-6.356	0.0001
MALAYSIA	-1.773966	0.337926	-5.250	0.0001	-0.412695	0.325087	-1.269	0.2046
MAURITIU	-2.913970	0.318916	-9 137	0.0001	-2.869550	0.319148	-8.991	0.0001
MEXICO	0.782162	0.312131	2.506	0.0124	1.752015	0.300878	5.823	0.0001
MOROCCO	-0.841782	0.323444	-2.603	0.0094	-0.326766	0.362204	-0.902	0.3672
MOZAMBIQ	-4.396369	0.342698	-12.829	0.0001	-2.599324	0.568174	-4.575	0.0001
NEPAL	-3.613696	0.322225	-11 215	0.0001	-1.749462	0.593081	-2.950	0.0033
NETHERLA	-0.029287	0.347722	-0.084	0 9329	-0.380819	0.37360:	-1.019	0.3084
NEWZEALA	-1.250453	0.316852	-3.946	0.0001	-3.254937	0.334338	-9.735	0 0001
NIGERIA	-1.099149	0.310186	-3.544	0.0004	0.427701	0.437142	0.978	0.3282
NORWAY	0.114972	0.358163	0.321	0.7483	-0.328927	0.406599	-0.809	0 4188
OMAN	-3.980602	0.334010	-11.918	0.0001	-3 614570	0.328178	-11.014	0.0001
PAKISTAN	-1.537972	0.315027	-4.882	0.0001	-0.980750	0.444040	-2.209	0 0275
PAPUANEW	-2.019068	0.335811	-6.013	0 0001	-1.320665	0.369390	-3.575	0.0004
PARAGUAY	-1.864765	0.315540	-5.910	0.0001	-1.618284	0.332081	-4.873	0.0001
PERU	-1.125175	0.314220	-3.581	0.0004	-0.795326	0.323862	-2.456	0.0143
PHILIPPI	-0 281696	0.306921	-0.918	0.3590	0.553014	0.379411	1 458	0.1453
SAUDIARA	-0.448381	0.314654	-1.425	0.1545	-1.909910	0.319865	-5.971	0 0001
SENEGAL	-2.280019	0.345321	-6.603	0.0001	-1.936467	0 386867	-5 006	0.0001
SEYCHELL	-3.943063	0.364168	-10.828	0.0001	-4.755042	0.316560	-15.021	0.0001
SIERRALE	-2.972972	0.337372	-8.812	0.0001	-1 880423	0.527788	-3.563	0.0004
SINGAPOR	-1.482912	0.327659	-4.526	0.0001	-1.644936	0.318678	-5.162	0.0001
SOUTHAFR	-1.021327	0.328683	-3 107	0.0020	-0.523858	0.324276	-1.615	0.1066
SPAIN	1.197443	0.333147	3.594	0.0003	0.278893	0.319759	0.872	0.3833
SRILANKA	-1.575006	0.314204	-5.013	0.0001	-0.670700	0.418471	-1.603	0.1094
SUDAN	-4.199452	0.336151	-12.493	0.0001	-3.624388	0.364494	-9.944	0.0001
SWAZILAN	-3.850623	0.326790	-11.783	0.0001	-2.465691	0 424300	-5.811	0.0001
SWEDEN	0.459582	0.401284	1.145	0.2524	-0.413412	0.412107	-1.003	0.3161
SWITZERL	-1.469247	0.331092	-4.438	0.0001	-1.391347	0.431311	-3 226	0.0013
SYRIA	-1.832400	0.323427	-5.666	0.0001	-1.965941	0.331213	-5.936	0.0001
TANZANIA	-3.021477	0.338909	-8.915	0.0001	-2.014372	0.520351	-3.871	0.0001
THAILAND	0.054617	0.327647	0.167	0.8676	0.932129	0.358125	2.603	0.0094
TRINIDAD	-1.921975	0.306965	-6.261	0.0001	-1.944678	0.300797	-6.465	0.0001
TUNISIA	-1.313342	0.307254	-4.274	0.0001	-0.689036	0.322786	-2.135	0.0331
TURKEY	-0.057678	0.317353	-0.182	0.8558	-0.169689	0.332293	-0.511	0.6097
UK	-0.064618	0.459705	-0.141	0.8882	0.134319	0.372847	0.360	0.7187
USA	0 077514	0.417596	0.186	0 8528	0.493331	0.463798	1.064	0.2878
URUGUAY	-1.858752	0.328196	-5.664	0.0001	-2.050747	0.321912	-6.371	0.0001
VENEZUEL	-0 077736	0.322831	-0.241	0.8098	0.430497	0.309469	1.391	0.1646
YUGOSLAV	0.911163	0.319951	2.848	0.0045	0.552038	0 296175	1.864	0.0627
ZAIRE	-3.662289	0.340394	-10.759	0.0001	-2.948950	0.472452	-6.242	0.0001
ZAMBIA	-1.116637	0.331980	-3.364	0.0008	-0.345144	0.466089	-0.741	0.4592
ZIMBABWE	-2.973238	0.317591	-9.362	0.0001	-2.578382	0.367685	-7.012	0.0001
YR1981	0.234748	0.108271	2.168	0.0304	0.125576	0.102516	1.225	0.2209
YR1982	0.262663	0 108467	2.422	0.0157	0.128693	0.103140	1.248	0 2125
YR1983	-0.002516	0.108625	-0.023	0 9815	0.000196	0.103699	0.002	0.9985
YR1984	0.128853	0.109977	1.172	0.2417	0.197674	0.105222	1.879	0.0606
YR1985	0.099845	0.110528	0.903	0.3666	0.208849	0.106089	1.969	0.0493
YR1986	0.125618	0.111494	1.127	0.2602	0.255402	0.108712	2.349	0.0190
YR1987	0.231286	0 112644	2.053	0.0404	0.270963	0.110296	2.457	0.0142
YR1988	0.070595	0.114628	0.616	0.5382	0.240971	0.114327	2.108	0.0353
YR1989	0.106981	0.116697	0.917	0.3595	0.175232	0.118185	1.483	0.1385
YR1990	0.332508	0.117433	2.831	0.0047	0.168318	0.121538	1.385	0.1664
System weighted R-sq: 0.8818		N = 946			Degree of freedom = 1685			

Note

Portugal and Year 1980 omitted as base dummies.

D–7 In-outflows of FDI with 3SLS simultaneous estimation (dummy coefficients reported)

Equation / Ind. var.	FDI inflow				FDI outflow			
	DV: FDII (log of FDI inflow)				DV: FDIO (log of FDI outflow)			
	Par est	**SE**	**t-stat**	**Prob >|T|**	**Par est**	**SE**	**t-stat**	**Prob >|T|**
INTERCEPT	3 442720	0.381621	9.021	0 0001	-2.745033	1 188192	-2.310	0.0211
PPPR	-0.348012	0 123028	-2.829	0.0048	-0.269283	0.135031	-1.994	0.0464
RISKD	0.014863	0.004216	3.525	0.0004				
RISKDC					-0.000091	0.008168	-0.011	0.9911
GNYPC					0.633876	0.144542	4.385	0.0001
CAB	-0.003614	0 002320	-1.557	0.1197	0.009705	0.002525	3.844	0.0001
EXCHCONT					-0.184722	0.098520	-1.875	0.0611
TFCORD	0.005956	0.004186	1.423	0.1551	-0.004763	0.004264	-1.117	0.2643
TREATY	0.000126	0 000044	2.854	0.0044				
INDSTP	0.022101	0.004856	4.551	0.0001				
TELECOMM					0.000455	0.042149	0.011	0.9914
OTHI					0.386862	0.060460	6.399	0.0001
OTHO	0.362312	0.054563	6.640	0.0001				
ALGERIA	-2 931536	0.269615	-10 873	0.0001	-0.689223	0.278370	-2.476	0.0135
ARGENTIN	0.778014	0.261262	2.978	0.0030	0.402877	0.297411	1.355	0.1759
AUSTRALI	0.969467	0.302702	3.203	0.0014	1 575288	0.341935	4.607	0.0001
AUSTRIA	-1.054218	0.299232	-3.523	0.0004	-0.052384	0.351727	-0.149	0.8816
BAHRAIN	-2.671436	0.262575	-10.174	0.0001	-1.472586	0.299465	-4.917	0.0001
BANGLADE	-2.169600	0.301391	-7.199	0.0001	0.937091	0.503397	1.862	0.0630
BARBADOS	-1.873284	0.293823	-6.376	0.0001	-1.236634	0.322981	-3.829	0.0001
BELGIUML	0.734523	0.311803	2.356	0.0187	1.492511	0.347741	4 292	0.0001
BOLIVIA	-1.229839	0.293667	-4 188	0.0001	0.084673	0.360279	0.235	0.8142
BRAZIL	1.405132	0.271384	5.178	0.0001	2.040859	0.284348	7.177	0.0001
CANADA	-0.561140	0.356280	-1.575	0.1156	2.141174	0.381322	5.615	0.0001
CHILE	-0.503933	0.262791	-1.918	0.0555	-0.131712	0.300103	-0.439	0.6609
COLOMBIA	0.034757	0.260812	0.133	0.8940	0.953982	0.319461	2.986	0.0029
CONGO	-1.867571	0.286777	-6.512	0.0001	-0.500758	0.315194	-1.589	0.1125
COSTARIC	-0.629091	0.287373	-2.189	0.0289	-0.083248	0.302929	-0.275	0.7835
COTEIVOR	-0.805100	0.275987	-2.917	0.0036	0.074156	0.328888	0.225	0.8217
CYPRUS	-0.228360	0.334060	-0.684	0.4944	-1.063617	0.295872	-3.595	0.0003
DENMARK	-1.558894	0.340284	-4.581	0 0001	0.301833	0.376718	0.801	0.4232
DOMINIRP	-0.641335	0.292486	-2.193	0 0286	0.244357	0.357739	0.683	0.4948
ECUADOR	-1.156652	0.271950	-4.253	0.0001	-0.403647	0.321218	-1.257	0.2092
EGYPT	1.339198	0.274349	4.881	0.0001	2.028308	0.357383	5.675	0.0001
ELSALVAD	-0.662934	0.300131	-2 209	0.0275	0.059478	0.328452	0.181	0.8563
ETHIOPIA	-2.137597	0 308742	-6 924	0.0001	1.202354	0.555262	2.165	0.0306
FINLAND	-1 260351	0 285864	-4.409	0.0001	0.748064	0 357030	2.095	0.0364
FRANCE	0.876809	0 333983	2.625	0.0088	2.592453	0.361793	7.166	0.0001
GABON	-1.088651	0 284929	-3.821	0.0001	-0.267979	0.295810	-0.906	0.3652
GERMANY	-0 565782	0.380323	-1.488	0.1372	2.574334	0.379487	6.784	0.0001
GREECE	0.668101	0.266450	2.507	0.0123	-0.123480	0.281828	-0.438	0.6614
GUATEMAL	0 070593	0.306207	0.231	0.8177	0.336719	0.344057	0.979	0.3280
HAITI	-1.493393	0.313037	-4.771	0.0001	1 082867	0 499951	2.166	0.0306
HONDURAS	-1.225421	0.285990	-4.285	0.0001	0.073357	0.339743	0.216	0.8291
ICELAND	-2 015451	0.321392	-6.271	0.0001	-1.515161	0.424033	-3.573	0.0004
INDIA	-3.349370	0.281212	-11.911	0.0001	0.165567	0.428610	0.386	0.6994
INDONESI	-0.313140	0.275940	-1.135	0.2568	0.976029	0.405029	2.410	0.0162
IRELAND	-0.364738	0.295596	-1.234	0.2176	-1.365469	0.309894	-4.406	0.0001
ISRAEL	-1.609459	0.432006	-3.726	0.0002	-0.112118	0.314137	-0.357	0.7213
ITALY	0.344155	0.318226	1 081	0 2798	1.865118	0.349196	5.341	0.0001
JAMAICA	-1.534607	0.290621	-5.280	0 0001	0.630520	0.321332	1.962	0.0501
JAPAN	-0.675885	0.361738	-1.868	0.0620	2 609290	0.397766	6.560	0.0001
KENYA	-1 119247	0.284857	-3.929	0.0001	0.817664	0 417548	1 958	0.0505
KOREA	-1.004121	0.257329	-3.902	0.0001	0.467565	0.277379	1.686	0.0922

Equation / Ind. var.	FDI inflow				FDI outflow			
	Par est	SE	t-stat	Prob >|T|	Par est	SE	t-stat	Prob >|T|
LIBYA	-1.384334	0.293463	-4.717	0.0001	0.961134	0.310419	3.096	0.0020
MADAGASC	-2.225120	0.309220	-7.196	0.0001	0.601808	0.467211	1.288	0.1981
MALAYSIA	0.398700	0.288948	1.380	0.1680	0.224538	0.319286	0.703	0.4821
MAURITIU	-1.974561	0.275061	-7.179	0.0001	-0.558656	0.305290	-1.82:	0.0676
MEXICO	1.736321	0.273653	6.345	0.0001	0.646648	0.293577	2.203	0.0279
MOROCCO	-1.194891	0.281521	-4.244	0.0001	0.170329	0.350013	0.487	0.6266
MOZAMBIQ	-2.235213	0.322379	-6.933	0.0001	1.128348	0.563386	2.003	0.0455
NEPAL	-2.291858	0.301854	-7.593	0.0001	1.359445	0.582941	2.332	0.0199
NETHERLA	0.734082	0.315739	2.325	0.0203	2.704270	0 359409	7.524	0.0001
NEWZEALA	0.302178	0.274392	1.101	0.2711	0.836257	0.319244	2.619	0.0090
NIGERIA	0.466203	0 289189	1 612	0.1073	1.846500	0.441880	4.179	0.0001
NORWAY	-1.161952	0.311342	-3.732	0.0002	0.693842	0.381117	1.821	0.0690
OMAN	-1.327531	0.288234	-4 606	0.0001	-1.096383	0.293729	-3 733	0.0002
PAKISTAN	-0 282556	0.284708	-0.992	0.3213	1.163550	0.437717	2.658	0.0080
PAPUANEW	-0.142023	0.278839	-0.509	0.6106	0.489347	0.340611	1.437	0.1512
PARAGUAY	-1.773191	0.283926	-6.245	0.0001	-0.797017	0.316982	-2.514	0.0121
PERU	-1.561535	0.270982	-5.762	0.0001	-0.218543	0.309772	-0.705	0.4807
PHILIPPI	-0.317486	0.264578	-1.200	0.2305	1.274995	0.367003	3.474	0.0005
SAUDIARA	-0 392505	0.276032	-1.422	0.1554	0.791556	0.296347	2.671	0.0077
SENEGAL	-1.211456	0.287442	-4.215	0.0001	0.878344	0.355733	2.469	0.0137
SEYCHELL	-0.969857	0.328521	-2.952	0.0032	-0.419261	0.306162	-1.369	0.1712
SIERRALE	-1.263830	0.331824	-3.809	0.0001	1.718803	0.531683	3.233	0.0013
SINGAPOR	1.203711	0.268412	4.485	0.0001	0.268217	0 294483	0.911	0.3627
SOUTHAFR	-1.543387	0.275718	-5.598	0.0001	1.203355	0.302727	3.975	0.0001
SPAIN	1.829358	0.298475	6.129	0.0001	1.383631	0.303678	4.556	0.0001
SRILANKA	-1.125085	0.281025	-4.004	0.0001	0.592191	0.409658	1 446	0.1487
SUDAN	-1.736941	0 305531	-5.685	0.0001	0.367470	0.352681	1.042	0.2977
SWAZILAN	-1 347769	0 280041	-4 813	0.0001	0.662423	0.412551	1 606	0.1087
SWEDEN	-0.845518	0.334246	-2.530	0.0116	1.786883	0.370329	4.825	0.0001
SWITZERL	0.240603	0.305695	0 787	0.4315	1.199288	0 408995	2.932	0.0035
SYRIA	-2.551247	0.292704	-8.716	0.0001	-0.462129	0.329618	-1.402	0.1613
TANZANIA	-2.087999	0.319031	-6.545	0.0001	0.942474	0.517298	1.822	0.0688
THAILAND	0.198391	0.269875	0.735	0.4625	1.127371	0.333250	3.383	0.0008
TRINIDAD	-1.006982	0.276557	-3.641	0.0003	-0.460186	0.291680	-1.578	0.1150
TUNISIA	-0.675642	0.263894	-2.560	0.0106	-0.433394	0.306326	-1.415	0.1575
TURKEY	-0.466307	0.278426	-1.675	0.0943	0.164595	0.323319	0.509	0.6108
UK	0.145349	0.437243	0.332	0.7397	3.162130	0.370070	8 545	0.0001
USA	1.881913	0.422944	4 450	0.0001	3.572333	0.448397	7.967	0.0001
URUGUAY	-1.683043	0.284561	-5.915	0.0001	-0.727668	0.299657	-2.428	0.0154
VENEZUEL	-1.454647	0.265720	-5 474	0.0001	-0.369985	0.281882	-1.313	0.1897
YUGOSLAV	-3.314092	0.283112	-11.706	0.0001	-1.406545	0.282431	-4.980	0.0001
ZAIRE	-2.271918	0.322168	-7.052	0.0001	0.719708	0.479236	1.502	0.1335
ZAMBIA	-1.280315	0.308685	-4.148	0.0001	0.793909	0.465883	1.704	0.0887
ZIMBABWE	-2.416235	0.296266	-8.156	0.0001	0.575555	0.372409	1.545	0.1226
YR1981	0.276314	0.091376	3.024	0.0026	0.016945	0.096364	0.176	0.8605
YR1982	0.180497	0.093644	1 927	0.0543	-0 015913	0.098504	-0 162	0.8717
YR1983	0.094319	0.095893	0.984	0.3256	-0.045977	0.100995	-0.455	0.6491
YR1984	0.115587	0.100098	1.155	0.2485	0.121008	0.105203	1 150	0.2504
YR1985	0.151148	0.103222	1.464	0.1435	0.097154	0.109024	0.891	0.3731
YR1986	0.165207	0.101697	1.625	0.1046	0.173727	0.108163	1.606	0.1086
YR1987	0 294207	0.101728	2.892	0.0039	0.270956	0.108907	2.488	0.0130
YR1988	0.410449	0.104259	3.937	0.0001	0.271474	0.113374	2.395	0.0169
YR1989	0.465477	0.108151	4.304	0.0001	0.350880	0.118453	2.962	0.0031
YR1990	0.503291	0.108649	4.632	0.0001	0.298948	0.120844	2.474	0.0136
System weighted R-sq: 0.9303		N = 946				Degree of freedom = 1685		

Note

Portugal and Year 1980 omitted as base dummies.

D–8 In-outflows of four financial items in one system with 3SLS simultaneous estimation (dummy coefficients reported)

IK type / DV / Ind. var.	Portfolio Inflow (PORTI) Par est	(t-stat)	Portfolio Outflow(PORTO) Par est	(t-stat)	Bank capital Inflow (BANKI) Par est	(t-stat)	Bank capital Outflow (BANKO) Par est	(t-stat)	Other-sector capital Inflow (OTHI) Par est	(t-stat)	Other-sector capital Outflow (OTHO) Par est	(t-stat)	FDI Inflow (FDII) Par est	(t-Stat)	FDI Outflow (FDIO) Par est	(t-stat)
INTERCEPT	2.1114	(4.457) ***	0.454	(.425)	3.3347	(6.512) ***	3.7446	(2.667) ***	5.4539	(13.82) ***	1.649	(1.416)	3.738	(9.435) ***	-2.9591	(-2.764) ***
IGOVTD	3.3E-06	(1.292)	-0.0015	(-.619)												
IDEPD					0.0005	(.171)	-0.0105	(-3.544) ***								
IMKTD									0.0008	(.312)	-0.0007	(-.301)				
PPPR													-0.1812	(-3.235) ***	-0.1365	(-2.474) **
RISKD	0.019	(3.07) ***			0.0166	(2.737) ***			0.0187	(3.797) ***			0.0146	(3.263) ***		
RISKCP			-3.E-05	(-.016)											-0.004	(-1.991) **
RISKDC							-0.0356	(-3.378) ***			-0.0278	(-3.297) ***				
GNYPC			0.3169	(2.24) **	0.2335	(1.32)					0.5111	(3.512) ***			0.7138	(5.439) ***
CAB	-0.0039	(-1.147)	0.0082	(3.236) **	0.0016	(.45)	0.0122	(3.789) ***	-0.0059	(-2.048) **	0.0074	(2.75) ***	-0.0033	(-1.308)	0.0089	(3.622) ***
EXCHCONT			0.1221	(1.366)			-0.2523	(-2.146) **			-0.1219	(-1.25)			-0.1977	(-2.243) **
TFDIVD	-0.0138	(-2.276) **	0.0026	(.604)												
TFINTD					-0.0046	(-.724)	-0.006	(-1.042)	-0.0023	(-0.456)	0.0062	(1.235)				
TFCORD													0.0064	(1.205)	-0.0009	(-1.289)
TREATY	7.3E-05	(1.228)			8.2E-05	(1.412)			8.1E-05	(1.684) *			0.0001	(3.217) ***		
CD	0.4277	(2.504) **							0.5616	(4.2) ***						
INDSTP					0.0014	(.22)							0.0238	(4.897) ***		
TELECOMM			0.1461	(3.668) ***			0.1594	(2.963) ***			0.0813	(1.829) *			0.0099	(.25)
PORTI			0.1699	(3.81) ***	0.1315	(1.808) *	0.0185	(.276)	0.1256	(2.075) **	-0.092	(-1.633)	0.306	(5.96) ***	0.0165	(.331)
PORTO	0.273	(4.246) ***			0.1844	(2.347) **	0.2494	(3.32) ***	-0.3693	(-6.113) ***	0.1829	(2.966) ***	-0.1664	(-2.865) ***	0.1244	(2.23) **
BANKI	0.0891	(1.032)	0.0909	(1.438)			0.2561	(4.397) ***	0.2675	(3.909) ***	-0.1921	(-2.884) ***	0.2244	(3.515) ***	0.101	(1.623)
BANKO	0.0634	(.806)	0.0563	(.965)	0.1475	(2.639) ***			-0.1155	(-1.767) *	0.0953	(1.567)	0.1467	(2.55) **	0.0289	(.516)
OTHI	-0.0259	(-.281)	-0.4719	(-8.011) ***	0.5722	(6.928) ***	-0.1117	(-1.353)			0.2171	(4.509) ***	-0.0684	(-1.008)	0.2756	(4.375) ***
OTHO	0.0285	(.314)	0.3155	(4.966) ***	-0.4673	(-5.514) ***	0.0199	(.238)	0.2267	(4.534) ***			0.027	(.415)	0.2912	(4.645) ***
FDII	0.2103	(2.603) ***	-0.0024	(-.04)	0.038	(.461)	0.1024	(1.306)	0.2305	(3.278) ***	0.0559	(.856)			0.269	(5.459) ***
FDIO	0.0742	(.802)	0.2268	(3.36) ***	0.22572	(2.498) **	0.0774	(.891)	0.3167	(4.135) ***	-0.073	(-1.015)	0.263	(4.728) ***		
ALGERIA	-2.3903	(-6.342) ***	-0.3668	(-1.313)	-1.4819	(-3.86) ***	-2.0098	(-5.646) ***	0.3756	(1.162)	0.9945	(3.318) ***	-2.9255	(-10.64) ***	-0.6	(-2.252) **
ARGENTIN	1.0019	(2.609) ***	2.2558	(7.348) ***	-0.4559	(-1.196)	-1.194	(-3.031) ***	0.5255	(1.618)	0.8538	(2.609) ***	0.4256	(1.543)	0.1666	(0.574)
AUSTRALI	1.1145	(2.65) **	1.7433	(5.229) ***	0.6586	(1.504)	0.1245	(.283)	1.6651	(4.517) ***	1.3507	(3.626) ***	1.267	(4.064) ***	1.527	(4.831) ***
AUSTRIA	1.1729	(2.798) ***	2.0476	(6.01) ***	0.4853	(1.136)	0.6928	(1.547)	-1.3952	(-3.848) ***	-1.6445	(-4.359) ***	-0.7716	(-2.516)	-0.2605	(-.795)
BAHRAIN	-1.9976	(-5.634) ***	-0.8713	(-3.016) **	-1.7103	(-4.708) ***	-1.0258	(-2.779) ***	-3.2648	(-10.71) ***	-3.3747	(-10.87) ***	-2.6283	(-9.84) ***	-1.3575	(-4.807) ***
BANGLADE	-1.3592	(-3.419) ***	0.1788	(.386)	-0.9304	(-2.23) **	-0.61878	(-1.024)	-2.7198	(-7.972) ***	-1.8543	(-3.684) ***	-2.2706	(-7.22) ***	0.8242	(1.794) *
BARBADOS	-1.4048	(-3.41) ***	-0.4192	(-1.295)	-1.968	(-4.739) ***	-3.6347	(-8.928) ***	-2.257	(-6.529) ***	-2.5098	(-7.242) ***	-1.8943	(-6.194) ***	-1.3007	(-4.264) ***
BELGIUML	0.5131	(1.171)	3.1956	(9.338) ***	2.2929	(5.018) ***	2.4285	(5.27) ***	-0.4828	(-1.255)	-0.6381	(-1.637)	0.8334	(2.517) **	1.1685	(3.516) ***
BOLIVIA	-1.5056	(-3.84) ***	-0.2421	(-.722)	-1.6589	(-4.193) ***	-2.055	(-4.764) ***	-1.897	(-5.665) ***	-1.3739	(-3.823) ***	-1.2009	(-4.053) ***	0.1107	(.333)
BRAZIL	-0.8083	(-2.12) **	1.2875	(4.496) ***	1.2963	(3.356) ***	1.5569	(4.271) ***	0.9336	(2.837) ***	1.5837	(5.19) ***	1.5121	(5.329) ***	2.0206	(7.412) ***
CANADA	1.5163	(3.128) ***	2.6107	(6.908) ***	-0.1524	(-.312)	0.1556	(.32)	-0.768	(-1.864) *	-1.4941	(-3.669) ***	-0.4958	(-1.382)	1.739	(4.884) ***
CHILE	-0.2307	(-.628)	0.2564	(.864)	0.8785	(2.351) **	0.6299	(1.679) *	0.0907	(.286)	0.2828	(.892)	-0.4103	(-1.529)	-0.0628	(-.224)
COLOMBIA	-2.0933	(-5.861) ***	-0.5671	(-1.866) *	-1.4771	(-4.064) ***	-1.7968	(-4.639) ***	-0.3316	(-1.077)	-0.0439	(-.135)	0.252	(.939)	1.0726	(3.622) ***

DV / Ind. var.	Inflow (PORTI) Par est	(t-stat)	Outflow(PORTO) Par est	(t-stat)	Inflow (BANKI) Par est	(t-stat)	Outflow (BANKO) Par est	(t-stat)	Inflow (OTHI) Par est	(t-stat)	Outflow (OTHO) Par est	(t-stat)	Inflow (FDII) Par est	(t-Stat)	Outflow (FDIO) Par est	(t-stat)
CONGO	-1.5227	(-3.94) ***	-0.3464	(-1.147)	-2.3604	(-6.043) ***	-2.8805	(-7.468) ***	-0.8504	(-2.571) **	-0.5787	(-1.787) *	-1.8773	(-6.43) ***	-0.4108	(-1.398)
COSTARIC	-1.5288	(-3.976) ***	-0.2553	(-.878)	-1.9114	(-4.864) ***	-2.6584	(-7.189) ***	-1.3117	(-3.951) ***	-1.199	(-3.828) ***	-0.6022	(-2.038) **	-0.1057	(-.37)
COTEIVOR	-1.6002	(-4.264) ***	0.0057	(.018)	-0.0226	(-.059)	-1.5629	(-3.925) ***	-1.425	(-4.41) ***	-0.8196	(-2.449) **	-0.7941	(-2.821) ***	-0.0138	(-.046)
CYPRUS	-0.7765	(-1.608)	-0.6929	(-2.274)	-0.1048	(-.22)	-2.4286	(-6.33) ***	-1.2224	(-2.999) ***	-2.5831	(-8.002) ***	-0.2156	(-.627)	-1.3733	(-4.825) ***
DENMARK	0.3123	(.631)	1.8352	(4.785) ***	-0.3040	(-.609)	0.268	(.52)	-0.1195	(-.284)	-2.7881	(-6.717) ***	-1.2617	(-3.494) ***	-0.1423	(-.386)
DOMINIRP	-1.434	(-3.641) ***	-0.2002	(-.602)	-1.6492	(-4.173) ***	-2.12	(-5) ***	-3.112	(-9.246) ***	-2.4645	(-6.908) ***	-0.5773	(-1.935) *	0.264	(.805)
ECUADOR	-1.9385	(-5.168) ***	-0.0906	(-.292)	-2.2679	(-5.971) ***	-2.679	(-6.757) ***	-0.9803	(-3.035) ***	-0.6973	(-2.091) **	-1.0923	(-3.943) ***	-0.4706	(-1.579)
EGYPT	-1.5561	(-4.153) ***	-0.0751	(-.219)	-0.2823	(-.73)	-0.1394	(-.316)	-1.0321	(-3.175) ***	0.2344	(.636)	1.3651	(4.817) ***	1.8904	(5.788) ***
ELSALVAD	-1.0541	(-2.462) **	-0.5855	(-1.79) *	-1.3076	(-2.951) ***	-2.3638(	-5.704 ***	-2.535	(-6.953) ***	-2.1676	(-6.171) ***	-0.7322	(-2.308) **	0.0422	(.134)
ETHIOPIA	-1.315	(-3.228) ***	0.2054	(.401)	-2.3102	(-5.428) ***	-2.3893(	-3.563) ***	-1.371	(-3.935) ***	-0.6177	(-1.107)	-2.2606	(-7.039) ***	1.0375	(2.043) **
FINLAND	1.2413	(4.489) ***	1.4979	(4.393) ***	0.7298	(1.906) *	-0.6342	(-1.445)	-0.3486	(-1.052)	-0.7508	(-2.037) **	-1.0039	(-3.495) ***	0.7778	(2.373) **
FRANCE	1.3793	(2.741) ***	2.2214	(6.086) ***	1.5351	(3.088) ***	2.0898	(4.482) ***	0.5326	(1.255)	0.7609	(1.939) *	0.6328	(1.686) *	2.2566	(6.594) ***
GABON	-1.6681	(-4.413) ***	-0.7693	(-2.669) ***	-1.9091	(-4.881) ***	-2.6359	(-7.212) ***	-1.1689	(-3.613) ***	-1.4219	(-4.613) ***	-1.0896	(-3.743) ***	-0.2417	(-.874)
GERMANY	1.1587	(2.575) **	2.654	(6.803) ***	1.4206	(2.693) ***	2.2481	(4.552) ***	0.2016	(.444)	0.6095	(1.463)	-0.4243	(-1.088)	2.4697	(6.848) ***
GREECE	-2.1706	(-5.339) ***	-1.122	(-3.593) ***	-0.2299	(-.555)	-2.7489	(-6.912) ***	-0.2545	(-.718)	-0.7262	(-2.14) **	1.1314	(3.875) ***	-0.19	(-.645)
GUATEMAL	-0.3455	(-.842)	0.6081	(1.857) *	-1.8651	(-4.402) ***	-2.9462	(-7.095) ***	-1.1313	(-3.249) ***	-1.4744	(-4.211) ***	-0.0189	(-.06)	0.221	(.696)
HAITI	-1.3358	(-3.196) ****	0.0335	(.072)	-2.1321	(-4.785) ***	-2.186	(-3.587) ***	-2.2215	(-6.202) ***	-2.0366	(-4.017) ***	-1.678	(-5.023) ***	0.8349	(1.81) *
HONDURAS	-1.4888	(-3.789) ***	-0.3826	(-1.176)	-2.1372	(-5.306) ***	-2.7099	(-6.482) ***	-1.4446	(-4.273) ***	-1.1493	(-3.266) ***	-1.2816	(-4.309) ***	0.0166	(.053)
ICELAND	-1.3562	(-3.082) ****	-1.0843	(-2.751) ***	-0.968	(-2.224) **	-2.9018	(-5.638) ***	-2.2516	(-6.068) ***	-2.9385	(-6.843) ***	-2.0219	(-6.136) ***	-1.9199	(-5.025) ***
INDIA	-2.3299	(-5.836) ***	0.3356	(.821)	-1.9406	(-4.869) ***	-0.7813	(-1.466)	-1.0294	(-3.039) ***	-0.2706	(-.609)	-3.2657	(-11.36) ***	0.1276	(.32)
INDONESI	-1.4346	(-3.663) ***	1.2387	(3.237) ***	-3.9931	(-10.31) ***	-3.1437	(-6.305) ***	-0.2602	(-.779)	0.5433	(1.305)	-0.3654	(-1.273)	0.8176	(2.169) **
IRELAND	1.1305	(2.447) **	0.6219	(1.752) *	2.3948	(5.333) ***	-0.4877	(-1.115)	-2.821	(-7.946) ***	-1.5852	(-4.313) ***	-0.5739	(-1.68) *	-1.1146	(-3.457) ***
ISRAEL	1.2679	(3.88) ***	1.4108	(4.717) ***	0.0299	(.051)	-0.1044	(-.273)	0.4586	(1.138)	-0.9831	(-3.03) ***	-2.2715	(-5.011) ***	-0.4767	(-1.666) *
ITALY	0.2438	(.536)	2.299	(6.59) ***	0.9915	(2.143) **	1.0105	(2.204) **	1.3306	(3.359) ***	1.1614	(3.006) ***	0.7548	(2.245) **	1.8374	(5.564) ***
JAMAICA	-1.4991	(-3.804) ****	-0.4604	(-1.495)	-2.381	(-6.104) ***	-2.7198	(-7.045) ***	-1.8093	(-5.473) ***	-1.8295	(-5.634) ***	-1.6429	(-5.615) ***	0.462	(1.564)
JAPAN	2.1261	(4.023) ***	3.6727	(8.746) ***	1.9903	(3.759) ***	2.5356	(4.725) ***	0.532	(1.18)	0.5249	(1.162)	-0.2401	(-.65)	2.5749	(6.631) ***
KENYA	-1.9841	(-5.293) ***	-0.1691	(-.438)	-2.6652	(-6.791) ***	-2.7446	(-5.49) ***	-1.8663	(-5.783) ***	-1.09	(-2.605) ***	-1.1932	(-4.095) ***	0.7966	(2.103) **
KOREA	-0.5403	(-1.522)	0.0135	(.05)	0.2986	(.835)	0.0151	(0.044)	-0.2429	(-.797)	0.0196	(.068)	-1.0033	(-3.845) ***	0.5256	(2.057) **
LIBYA	-0.7645	(-2.013) **	1.4058	(4.679) ***	-1.1571	(-2.872) ***	-2.158	(-5.59) ***	-0.4646	(-1.431)	-1.8216	(-5.614) ***	-1.3805	(-4.649) ***	0.7728	(2.715) ***
MADAGASC	-1.8295	(-4.363) ***	-0.1252	(-.288)	-1.716	(-3.874) ***	-2.0758	(-3.659) ***	-4.0251	(-11.34) ***	-2.6342	(-5.579) ***	-2.396	(-7.343) ***	0.6428	(1.503)
MALAYSIA	-0.1399	(-.346)	1.01	(3.234) ***	-1.0048	(-2.399) **	-0.528	(-1.339)	-1.1562	(-3.379) ***	-0.535	(-1.617)	0.1381	(.46)	0.3337	(1.136)
MAURITIU	-1.6397	(-4.329) ***	-0.3547	(-1.213)	-2.6874	(-7.026) ***	-2.6529	(-7.129) ***	-2.6294	(-8.088) ***	-2.601	(-8.336) ***	-2.0343	(-7.205) ***	-0.65283	(-2.319) **
MEXICO	0.9683	(2.592) **	2.8797	(10.21) ***	2.3903	(6.444) ***	1.1409	(3.212) **	0.8513	(2.691) ***	1.7392	(5.787) ***	1.8904	(6.793) ***	0.6447	(2.37) **
MOROCCO	-1.722	(-4.582) ***	-0.2033	(-.627)	-2.0908	(-5.421) ***	-1.8417	(-4.367) ***	-0.7113	(-2.167) **	-0.1907	(-.54)	-1.1214	(-3.871) ***	0.3051	(.944)
MOZAMBIQ	-1.374	(-3.329) ***	0.1839	(.358)	-2.5264	(-5.997) ***	-2.9018	(-4.328) ***	-3.9307	(-11.19) ***	-2.4542	(-4.396) ***	-2.4092	(-7.481) ***	1.1322	(2.212) **
NEPAL	-1.5251	(-3.897) ***	0.3013	(0.565)	-2.5025	(-6.018) ***	-2.533	(-3.625) ***	-3.0604	(-9.115) ***	-1.6969	(-2.922) ***	-2.4412	(-7.787) ***	1.2891	(2.43) **
NETHERLA	1.155	(2.574) **	2.3923	(6.609) ***	2.0423	(4.606) ***	2.1009	(4.548) ***	-0.3923	(-1.038)	-0.157	(-.404)	0.7437	(2.253) **	2.5439	(7.535) ***
NEWZEALA	-2.1732	(-5.809) ***	-1.5921	(-5.188) ***	-1.7028	(-4.482) ***	-3.382	(-8.425) ***	-1.4693	(-4.593) ***	-2.9011	(-8.6) ***	0.3733	(1.321)	0.711	(2.395) **
NIGERIA	0.1191	(.323)	1.3833	(3.479) ***	-1.5355	(-4.124) **	-1.0818	(-2.103) **	-0.8192	(-2.586) ***	0.3476	(.81)	0.4426	(1.538)	1.965	(4.962) ***
NORWAY	0.4641	(1.077)	1.8975	(5.118) ***	-0.2975	(-.666)	-0.2005	(-.409)	-0.2807	(-.747)	-0.2463	(-.596)	-1.0672	(-3.373) ***	0.5576	(1.587)
OMAN	-2.4194	(-5.867) ***	-0.9761	(-3.095) ***	-1.6371	(-3.742) ***	-1.9226	(-4.741) ***	-3.3238	(-9.459) ***	-3.0838	(-8.968) ***	-1.3188	(-4.264) ***	-1.0719	(-3.675) ***
PAKISTAN	-0.4762	(-1.266)	0.2686	(.669)	-0.4332	(-1.125)	-1.1379	(-2.189) **	-1.2133	(-3.762) ***	-0.8806	(-2.029) **	-0.352	(-1.213)	1.14867	(2.893) ***
PAPUANEW	-2.0975	(-5.373) ***	-0.3176	(-.957)	-2.101	(-4.935) ***	-2.9551	(-6.732) ***	-1.5215	(-4.298) ***	-1.3294	(-3.525) ***	-0.1732	(-.594)	0.1827	(.569)
PARAGUAY	-1.8936	(-4.955) ***	-0.2843	(-.935)	-1.6303	(-4.209) ***	-2.2744	(-5.905) ***	-1.6382	(-5.026) ***	-1.4134	(-4.325) ***	-1.837	(-6.441) ***	-0.7363	(-2.509) **

DV / Ind. var.	Inflow (PORTI)		Outflow(PORTO)		Inflow (BANKI)		Outflow (BANKO)		Inflow (OTHI)		Outflow (OTHO)		Inflow (FDII)		Outflow (FDIO)	
	Par est	(t-stat)	Par est	(t-stat)	Par est	(t-stat)	Par est	(t-stat)	Par est	(t-stat)	Par est	(t-stat)	Par est	(t-Stat)	Par est	(t-stat)
NERU	-1.5504	(-4.025) ***	-0.7192	(-2.308) **	-2.3125	(-6.069) ***	-3.3124	(-8.605) ***	-1.2552	(-3.889) ***	-0.7793	(-2.422) **	-1.4836	(-5.293) ***	0.0538	(.185)
PHILIPPI	-1.4362	(-3.947) ***	-0.669	(-1.92) *	-0.4076	(-1.125)	-1.5276	(-3.437) ***	-0.3815	(-1.241)	0.4804	(1.297)	-0.3577	(-1.331)	1.3319	(3.928) ***
SAUDIARA	1.3058	(3.086) ***	3.284	(10.51) ***	-1.0945	(-2.589) ***	1.2242	(3.083) ***	0.1486	(.421)	-1.9682	(-6.001) ***	-0.6815	(-2.224) **	0.2061	(.698)
SENEGAL	-1.5403	(-3.766) ***	-0.1019	(-.289)	-1.6147	(-3.795) ***	-1.9648	(-4.324) ***	-2.0001	(-5.698) ***	-1.5745	(-4.157) ***	-1.2528	(-4.124) ***	0.6333	(1.917) *
SEYCHELL	-1.0088	(-2.219) **	-0.7434	(-2.378) **	-1.9542	(-4.177) ***	-3.3093	(-8.485) ***	-3.3045	(-8.563) ***	-4.0984	(12.47) ***	-1.132	(-3.27) ***	-0.7597	(-2.552) **
SIERRALE	-1.3193	(-3.272) ***	0.1004	(.207)	-2.2817	(-5.265) ***	-2.6775	(-4.238) ***	-2.5187	(-7.188) ***	-1.871	(-3.58) ***	-1.4621	(-4.484) ***	1.6594	(3.453) ***
SINGAPOR	0.5479	(1.211)	0.5187	(1.68) *	0.7837	(1.997) **	-0.1207	(-.306)	-1.4837	(-4.333) ***	-1.4351	(-4.327) ***	1.606	(5.619) ***	0.0347	(.119)
SOUTHAFR	-0.7593	(-1.991) *	1.0079	(3.394) ***	-0.2498	(-.62)	-2.1324	(-5.45) ***	-0.9373	(-2.766) ***	-0.2749	(-.829)	-1.2797	(-4.434) ***	1.4244	(4.912) ***
SPAIN	0.4279	(1.065)	0.3991	(1.337)	0.623	(1.555)	-1.017	(-2.713) ***	0.7615	(2.273) **	0.4582	(1.445)	2.001	(6.747) ***	1.5391	(5.504) ***
SRILANKA	-1.6332	(-4.341) ***	-0.0169	(-.045)	-1.4085	(-3.69) ***	-1.7302	(-3.542) ***	-1.3178	(-4.075) ***	-0.5683	(-1.39)	-1.1348	(-3.962) ***	0.5978	(1.607)
SUDAN	-1.1329	(-2.648) **	-0.4382	(-1.242)	-0.7532	(-1.685) *	-1.3737	(-3.064) ***	-3.5124	(-9.686) ***	-3.0279	(-8.108) ***	-1.8244	(-5.495) ***	0.2035	(.604)
SWAZILAN	-1.3108	(-3.406) ***	-0.0532	(-.139)	-2.3379	(-6.063) ***	-2.842	(-5.717) ***	-3.6089	(-10.95) ***	-2.3134	(-5.581) ***	-1.3384	(-4.656) ***	0.8175	(2.157) **
SWEDEN	0.6626	(1.378)	1.4865	(4.009) ***	0.8066	(1.621)	0.4338	(.864)	-0.3571	(-.84)	-0.1172	(-.276)	-0.534	(-1.565)	1.831	(5.324) ***
SWITZERL	0.6705	(1.508)	3.006	(7.524) ***	1.0794	(2.415) **	1.0058	(1.931) *	-1.2303	(-3.286) ***	-1.1824	(-2.718) ***	0.4958	(1.511)	1.0262	(2.641) ***
SYRIA	-1.4332	(-3.662) ***	-0.2582	(-.84)	-0.3329	(.829)	-1.7969	(-4.583) ***	-1.5472	(-4.6) ***	-1.6175	(-4.946) ***	-2.4185	(-8.034) ***	-0.5444	(-1.803) *
TANZANIA	-1.1508	(-2.802) **	0.0367	(.077)	-2.1728	(-4.938) ***	-2.7599	(-4.452) ***	-2.5643	(-7.275) ***	-1.799	(-3.496) ***	-2.2227	(-6.75) ***	0.946	(2.01) *
THAILAND	0.4572	(1.233)	1.201	(3.77) ***	-1.1771	(-3.049) ***	-1.1303	(-2.725) ***	0.1945	(.593)	0.9341	(2.673) ***	0.0376	(.137)	1.1919	(3.847) ***
TRINIDAD	-2.0804	(-5.715) ***	-1.0202	(-3.666) ***	-2.4709	(-6.658) ***	-3.1793	(-9.01) ***	-1.9137	(-6.126) ***	-1.7033	(-5.706) ***	-0.8865	(-3.126) ***	-0.3745	(-1.386)
TUNISIA	-1.3075	(-3.628) ***	-0.0992	(-.341)	-1.668	(-4.587) ***	-1.7324	(-4.656) ***	-1.227	(-3.955) ***	-0.707	(-2.263) **	-0.6689	(-2.515) **	-0.3945	(-1.401)
TURKEY	-0.4569	(-1.179)	0.5531	(1.797) *	0.038	(.101)	-0.3044	(-.785)	0.0997	(.309)	-0.0431	(-.133)	-0.3399	(-1.194)	0.2659	(.896)
UK	1.6365	(3.441) ***	3.3227	(8.446) ***	2.6625	(5.571) ***	2.8829	(6.087) ***	0.0112	(.028)	0.234	(.586)	1.1199	(3.193) ***	3.2079	(9.243) ***
USA	1.8115	(3.094) ***	3.6888	(8.002) ***	2.0472	(3.468) ***	3.0126	(5.124) ***	-0.267	(-.537)	0.5989	(1.212)	1.935	(4.456) ***	3.315	(7.737) ***
URUGUAY	-0.4803	(-1.244)	-0.0512	(-.177)	0.3265	(.844)	-0.8349	(-2.286) **	-1.6122	(-4.879) ***	-1.7645	(-5.693) ***	-1.6862	(-5.844) ***	-0.81	(-2.912) ***
VENEZUEL	-1.9253	(-5.098) ***	-0.6099	(-2.144) *	-0.6905	(-1.807) *	-1.683	(-4.632) ***	-0.1963	(-.612)	0.5503	(1.807) *	-1.2918	(-4.778) ***	-0.0756	(-.289)
YUGOSLAV	-1.6147	(-4.21) ***	-0.6148	(-2.221) **	1.5509	(3.977) ***	0.4518	(1.281)	0.4794	(1.46)	0.673	(2.29) **	-2.9857	(-10.17) ***	-1.1196	(-4.165) ***
ZAIRE	-1.3521	(-3.244) ***	-0.332	(-.757)	-0.8662	(-2.063) **	-2.4979	(-4.415) ***	-3.1611	(-8.855) ***	-2.6096	(-5.531) ***	-2.4288	(-7.421) ***	0.6844	(1.569)
ZAMBIA	-1.6281	(-4.181) ***	-0.0477	(-.113)	-1.5809	(-4.024) ***	-1.4658	(-2.665) ***	-0.696	(-2.087) **	-0.3781	(-.824)	-1.5208	(-4.999) ***	0.6819	(1.615)
ZIMBABWE	-0.8035	(-2.089) *	1.1587	(3.412) ***	-1.8102	(-4.701) ***	-2.3212	(-5.324) ***	-2.5721	(-7.812) ***	-2.384	(-6.51) ***	-2.4809	(-8.267) ***	0.6393	(1.851) *
YR1981	0.0661	(.526)	0.093	(.998)	0.0899	(.711)	-0.0553	(-.468)	0.2192	(2.036) **	0.1256	(1.262)	0.2625	(2.837) ***	0.0124	(.14)
YR1982	0.0616	(.488)	0.1184	(1.258)	-0.0772	(-.605)	-0.068	(-.572)	0.1828	(1.691) **	0.1038	(1.036)	0.1753	(1.846) *	-0.028	(-.309)
YR1983	0.1345	(1.059)	0.1496	(1.572)	-0.0637	(-.498)	-0.0114	(-.095)	-0.0215	(-.197)	-0.0582	(-.576)	0.0582	(.598)	-0.0835	(-.896)
YR1984	0.2983	(2.296) **	0.1419	(1.455)	0.0765	(.587)	0.1933	(1.576)	0.1254	(1.126)	0.1616	(1.564)	0.0463	(.46)	0.0923	(.953)
YR1985	0.4961	(3.802) ***	0.2344	(2.355) **	0.1952	(1.486)	0.2374	(1.915) *	0.1045	(.934)	0.2109	(2.02) **	0.0735	(.714)	0.0861	(.858)
YR1986	0.3961	(3.032) ***	0.3189	(3.136) ***	0.0258	(.194)	0.3023	(2.398) **	0.1151	(1.03)	0.2243	(2.117) **	0.1074	(1.065)	0.1766	(1.778) *
YR1987	0.4051	(3.048) ***	0.316	(3.106) ***	0.1641	(1.222)	0.2714	(2.114) **	0.1546	(1.362)	0.2317	(2.151) **	0.2538	(2.517) **	0.2664	(2.703) ***
YR1988	0.4284	(3.198) ***	0.4179	(3.954) ***	0.091	(.669)	0.3117	(2.353) **	0.0356	(.311)	0.2044	(1.836) *	0.3488	(3.378) ***	0.2343	(2.261) **
YR1989	0.3427	(2.49) **	0.3843	(3.538) ***	0.06	(.433)	0.255	(1.866) *	0.089	(.759)	0.1116	(.973)	0.3938	(3.665) ***	0.299	(2.778) ***
YR1990	0.2269	(1.637)	0.3951	(3.513) ***	0.0304	(.217)	0.2325	(1.655) *	0.3268	(2.762) ***	0.1073	(.909)	0.42939	(3.964) ***	0.2481	(2.234) **
System weighted R-sq: 0.9008							N = 946						Degree of freedom = 6692			

Notes

1 Portugal and Year 1980 omitted as base dummies.

2 *** = significant at 1% level; ** = significant at 5% level; * = significant at 10% level.

D–9 Four types of short-term capital flows with 3SLS simultaneous estimation (dummy coefficients reported)

Equation / DV / Ind. var.	Type 1 inflow		Type 2 inflow		Type 1 outflow		Type 2 outflow	
	STKI1 (log of type 1 inf.)		STKI2 (log of type 2 inf.)		STKO1 (log of type 1 outf.)		STKO2(log of type 2 outf.)	
	Par est	(t-stat)	Par est	(t-stat)	Par est	(t-stat)	Par est	(t-stat)
INTERCEPT	3 820176	(6 031) ***	4 566011	(6 954) ***	1 691478	(819)	3.469412	(1 491)
PPPR	-0 31764	(-3 018) ***	-0.42317	(-3 673) ***	0.089503	(867)	-0.0907	(- 731)
RISKD	0.027106	(3.332) ***			0 011706	(1.477)		
RISKDC			0 00333	(205)			-0 06904	(-4 197) ***
GNYPC					0.512782	(2 06) **	0 165827	(.568)
CAB	-0.00353	(- 78)	-0.008	(-1 648) *	0.013129	(3.113) ***	0.009434	(1.839) *
EXCHCONT	-0.37472	(-2.157) **					-0 27917	(-1 42)
TFINTD	-0 01022	(-1.229)					0.002241	(237)
TDINTD			0 011014	(1 513)	0.001792	(.274)		
TREATY			7.97E-05	(94)	2.55E-05	(.32)		
CD	0 46625	(2 102) **			0.40759	(1.845) *		
TELECOMM	0.118301	(1.722) *	0.218942	(2.975) ***				
STKI1			0 205628	(2.239) **	0.057	(.801)	-0 22065	(-2 313) **
STKI2	0.310501	(3 436) ***			-0 18846	(-2 227) **	0 145364	(1 532)
STKO1	0 109286	(1 51)	-0 50546	(-5.805) ***			-0 20651	(-2 263) **
STKO2	-0.21434	(-3.049) ***	0.10526	(1.391)	0.022045	(.343)		
ALGERIA	0 270568	(519)	0 04893	(091)	-2 33264	(-5.007) ***	-0 88384	(-1.625)
ARGENTIN	1 281109	(2 349) **	0 793863	(1.456)	-0 29335	(-.625)	3.118331	(5 293) ***
AUSTRALI	-0 04209	(-.075)	-0.84123	(-1 426)	0.017557	(031)	0 297328	(443)
AUSTRIA	2 861664	(5 283) ***	0 860715	(1 424)	0 947632	(1 494)	2 888476	(4 006) ***
BAHRAIN	-0 42722	(- 823)	-0 4545	(- 843)	-1 05823	(-2 151) **	0.846235	(1.429)
BANGLADE	0 588766	(1 101)	-1 69005	(-3 058) ***	0 525641	(619)	-0 40316	(- 402)
BARBADOS	0 007369	(013)	-1 21461	(-2 223) **	-2 25647	(-4 475) ***	-1 12887	(-1 853) *
BELGIUML	4 419287	(7 252) ***	0.785767	(1 235)	3 036918	(4 674) ***	3 607827	(4 891) ***
BOLIVIA	-0 13827	(- 248)	-1 00612	(-1 82) *	-0 87631	(-1 455)	-0 10779	(-.153)
BRAZIL	2 214823	(4.322) ***	-0.41121	(-.79)	0.316592	(645)	1 940984	(3 432) ***
CANADA	1 789063	(2 75) ***	0.95622	(1.35)	1.423992	(2 148) **	4 013686	(5 419) ***
CHILE	1 759337	(3.396) ***	0 362952	(.658)	0.033442	(.063)	0 651307	(1.055)
COLOMBIA	0.48739	(99)	-1 56807	(-2.974) ***	0.404998	(.74)	1.307634	(2 074) **
CONGO	0 713489	(1.31)	-0 866467	(-1.585)	-0 58444	(-1 102)	-0.55704	(- 895)
COSTARIC	1.162225	(2 254) **	-1.70314	(-3.275) ***	-1 44812	(-2.951) ***	-0 15146	(- 261)
COTEIVOR	1 547321	(2.986) ***	-0 79171	(-1 46)	-1 58419	(-2 923) ***	0 028963	(.045)
CYPRUS	2.36201	(3 688) ***	-1 66961	(-3 127) ***	-1.50584	(-2 464) **	-1 0145	(-1.773) *
DENMARK	2.918323	(5 091) ***	-1 23029	(-1.9) *	0.806087	(1 109)	0 090237	(114)
DOMINIRP	0 117841	(216)	-1.51933	(-2 743) ***	-1.58329	(-2.694) ***	-0 41738	(-.6)
ECUADOR	1.295725	(2.396) **	-1 24301	(-2 232) **	-1 35737	(-2.574) **	-0 33927	(- 538)
EGYPT	-0 68692	(-1.297)	0 286344	(498)	-0.47104	(- 74)	0.930309	(1.272)
ELSALVAD	0 322998	(.546)	-1 6047	(-2 695) ***	-1 61514	(-2.671) ***	-0 64442	(-.951)
ETHIOPIA	-0.21543	(- 392)	-0 90812	(-1.627)	-0 99083	(-1 058)	-0 841	(-.756)
FINLAND	3 547992	(6 64) ***	0 172196	(297)	0 185073	(.281)	2 43462	(3 485) ***
FRANCE	4 319113	(7 284) ***	0 366948	(.572)	3 090682	(4 753) ***	2.565519	(3 471) ***
GABON	0 339359	(626)	-1.04812	(-1.952)	-0.55211	(-1.123)	-0.6105	(-1 062)
GERMANY	2 912046	(4.504) ***	2 989836	(4.127) ***	2 936924	(4.275) ***	4 67841	(6.13) ***
GREECE	2 055612	(3 973) ***	-2 48058	(-4 639) ***	-3 19342	(-6.777) ***	-0 80887	(-1 384)
GUATEMAL	1 643169	(2.989) ***	-1.65713	(-3 013) ***	-1 82251	(-3.241) ***	-0 04879	(-.073)
HAITI	-0 551558	(-1 016)	-1 54159	(-2 795) ***	-1 15937	(-1.38)	-0 79593	(- 799)
HONDURAS	-0 23701	(- 452)	-1 50523	(-2 837) ***	-2.1576	(-3 885) ***	-0 33619	(- 504)
ICELAND	0.744224	(1 293)	-1 15638	(-1 999) **	-2.66601	(-3.651) ***	-0.89905	(-1 13)
INDIA	-0.61377	(-1.185)	-0 28796	(- 531)	-0.98678	(-1 226)	0 545301	(.629)
INDONESI	0.128303	(.242)	-2 61994	(-4 962) ***	-2 59072	(-3 451) ***	0.658482	(821)
IRELAND	3.087061	(5 777) ***	-1 8222	(-3 437) ***	0 261714	(.471)	-0 6896	(-1 135)
ISRAEL	2 313486	(3.585) ***	-0.5191	(- 993)	0 445865	(.654)	1 222568	(2.008) **
ITALY	3.762625	(6 428) ***	0.845009	(1.332)	2.043817	(3 221) ***	2 025729	(2 889) ***
JAMAICA	0 893485	(1.656) *	-1.65556	(-3.033) ***	-2.17228	(-4.003) ***	-0 49974	(- 795)
JAPAN	4 672989	(7.135) ***	1.400321	(2 548) **	2.486159	(3.541) ***	2 159351	(2.624) ***
KENYA	-0.129389	(- 254)	-1 84976	(-3.49) ***	-1.53088	(-2 149) **	-0 71629	(- 869)
KOREA	1.92598	(3 906) ***	-1 20538	(-2 311) **	-0 48247	(-1.04)	2.123723	(3 896) ***
LIBYA	2 090974	(3.791) ***	1 084076	(1 984) **	-1.1643	(-2 215) **	-0 18042	(-.304)
MADAGASC	-0.99181	(-1.77) *	-1.326	(-2 345) **	-1 42988	(-1.832) *	-0 43888	(-.472)
MALAYSIA	-0 82166	(-1 501)	0 310601	(57)	0 762178	(1.296)	-0 19642	(-.317)
MAURITIU	-0 65493	(-1.249)	-1 2632	(-2.331) **	-1 71374	(-3 423) ***	-0 68165	(-1.146)
MEXICO	3.032629	(5 752) ***	-1 40011	(-2 564) **	1 93757	(3.849) **	3.012782	(5 222) ***
MOROCCO	1.032415	(1 98) **	-1 00718	(-1 862) *	-0 03861	(-.067)	-0 04181	(-.061)
MOZAMBIQ	-1.00388	(-1.8) *	-2.06031	(-3.59) ***	-1.25181	(-1.305)	-1.09263	(-.976)

Equation / Ind. var.	Type 1 inflow		Type 2 inflow		Type 1 outflow		Type 2 outflow	
	Par est	(t-stat)	Par est	(t-stat)	Par est	(t-stat)	Par est	(t-stat)
NEPAL	-0.8988	(-1 703) *	-1.16386	(-2 1) **	-0.92485	(- 921)	-0 78693	(-.676)
NETHERLA	2 887726	(5.305) ***	-0.43759	(-.728)	1.499133	(2 449) **	1.130546	(1.608)
NEWZEALA	0 35308	(.697)	-0 60778	(-1.183)	-2.93659	(-5.313) ***	-0.35799	(-.576)
NIGERIA	1 600291	(3.053) ***	-0.86575	(-1 532)	1.654776	(2.202) **	0 252525	(29)
NORWAY	0 560081	(1 014)	2 190438	(3 586) ***	-0 15804	(-.237)	2 276229	(2 991) ***
OMAN	-1 11699	(-2 035) **	-0 60751	(-1.107)	-1 16938	(-2.431) **	-0 33356	(-.554)
PAKISTAN	1.558611	(3 033) ***	-2 00389	(-3 748) ***	-0.39919	(-.54)	0.131156	(.151)
PAPUANEW	-0 52827	(- 915)	-2.74524	(-4 597) ***	-2 68442	(-4.315) ***	-1 55195	(-2 112) **
PARAGUAY	-0 35528	(- 655)	0 072338	(131)	-2 11235	(-4 141) ***	-0.02045	(- 033)
PERU	1 299805	(2 542) **	-1 45923	(-2.799) ***	-2 70543	(-5 24) ***	0.573269	(.931)
PHILIPPI	1 930804	(3 709) ***	-2.72943	(-5.075) ***	-1.52049	(-2.468) **	1.951574	(2.72) ***
SAUDIARA	-0 86893	(-1.519)	1 42305	(2.141) **	2 130419	(4.232) ***	0.041409	(.063)
SENEGAL	0 301596	(.557)	-0 7518	(-1 384)	-1 40145	(-2 363) **	-0 28959	(- 402)
SEYCHELL	-0 46964	(-.782)	-1.35329	(-2.454) **	-2 78882	(-5.07) ***	-1 52044	(-2.677) ***
SIERRALE	-0 17652	(- 309)	-1.77009	(-3 114) ***	-0 80091	(-.911)	-0.94822	(-.91)
SINGAPOR	2 193863	(4.083) ***	-0.42379	(-.756)	0.37308	(.697)	0.823101	(1.387)
SOUTHAFR	1 314742	(2 429) **	-1.66379	(-2 995) ***	-0.42954	(-.895)	1.57868	(2 702) ***
SPAIN	2 916418	(5.363) ***	-0.48744	(-.872)	-1 3559	(-2 526) **	0.764733	(1.304)
SRILANKA	1 626813	(3 122) ***	-1.68989	(-3.098) ***	-0 87822	(-1 27)	0.894474	(1.105)
SUDAN	0.48185	(.869)	-0 11071	(- 199)	-0.70619	-1 203	-0.80688	(-1.168)
SWAZILAN	-0.39759	(- 748)	-1.63944	(-2.992) ***	-1 23171	(-1.777) *	-0.91771	(-1 117)
SWEDEN	2.53324	(4 46) ***	-1.60943	(-2.435) **	-0 07297	(- 103)	0.316417	(403)
SWITZERL	2 62359	(4 552) ***	1 158353	(1 923) *	1.825622	(2.687) ***	-0.34731	(-.423)
SYRIA	1.901003	(3.536) ***	-1.0648	(-1 94) *	-1 51544	(-2 862) ***	-0 27866	(- 445)
TANZANIA	0 031903	(059)	-1 69783	(-3.1)	-1 39441	(-1 624)	-0 43735	(-.428)
THAILAND	2 133109	(4.055) ***	-2 0508	(-3 941) ***	-1 72315	(-2 873) ***	0.808055	(1.208)
TRINIDAD	-0 58984	(-1.156)	-1.15337	(-2 106) **	-2 15042	(-4.508) ***	-0 07006	(- 126)
TUNISIA	0 860543	(1 704) *	-1.45608	(-2 775) ***	-0.73893	(-1.413)	-0 55039	(- 902)
TURKEY	2 044058	(3 98) ***	-1 39091	(-2 616) ***	-0.61277	(-1 169)	1 733619	(2 766) ***
UK	4.416733	(6 466) ***	1 873446	(2 259) **	4.525482	(6 12) ***	3 788172	(4 982) ***
USA	3 805306	(4 784) ***	1 702998	(1.99) **	4 851299	(6.217) ***	6 651895	(7.387) ***
URUGUAY	1 605879	(2.894) ***	-0 69517	(-1.265)	-0 5742	(-1.177)	-0 33151	(-.581)
VENEZUEL	0 90567	(1.677) *	0 130526	(.235)	1 585199	(3 339) ***	2.366825	(3.9) ***
YUGOSLAV	1.945167	(3 657) ***	-0.18538	(- 35)	-1.07436	(-2.248) **	1.859781	(3.352) ***
ZAIRE	0 729088	(1.327)	-2.09902	(-3.788) ***	-1 69676	(-2 168) **	-0.80518	(- 87)
ZAMBIA	1.38633	(2.538) **	-1 03232	(-1 837) *	0.09482	(.123)	0 189831	(.205)
ZIMBABWE	-0.17341	(-.339)	-1.12223	(-2.111) **	-2.35741	(-3.919) ***	-0.18005	(-.255)
YR1981	0 01167	(075)	0 238144	(1 302)	0.200505	(1.294)	0 198342	(1 04)
YR1982	-0 09232	(-.592)	0.739977	(3.974) ***	-0 0043	(-.028)	0.539394	(2 784) ***
YR1983	-0 07067	(- 453)	0.861104	(4.522) ***	-0 00819	(-.053)	0.348217	(1 763) *
YR1984	0 174028	(1 116)	0.488768	(2 446) **	0 228345	(1.473)	0.319318	(1.559)
YR1985	0 17808	(1 142)	0 948053	(4.564) ***	0.234505	(1 513)	0 688599	(3.264) ***
YR1986	0 15318	(982)	0 55993	(2 743) ***	0.25486	(1 644)	0.692693	(3 407) ***
YR1987	0 29589	(1 898) *	0 46855	(2.272) **	0 12965	(836)	0 465431	(2 307) **
YR1988	0 30089	(1 93) *	0 437995	(2 027) **	0 29369	(1.895) *	0 536321	(2 595) ***
YR1989	0 26756	(1 726) *	0.399247	(1 771) *	0.32158	(2 075) **	0 412979	(1 942) *
YR1990	0.38128	(2.445) **	0.582853	(2.524) **	0.411108	(2.652) ***	0.556489	(2.623) **
System weighted R-sq: 7028			N = 946			Degree of fıeedom = 3362		

Notes

1 Portugal and Year 1980 omitted as base dummies.

2 *** = significant at 1% level; ** = significant at 5% level; * = significant at 10% level.

Bibliography

Abel, A.B. (1979), *Investment and the Value of Capital*, New York: Garland.

Abel, A.B. (1980), 'Empirical Investment Equations: An Integrative Framework', *Carnegie-Rochester Series on Public Policy*, pp. 39–91.

Abel, A.B. and Blanchard, O.J. (1986), 'The Present Value of Profits and Cyclical Movements in Investments', *Econometrica*, pp. 249–73.

Adler, M. and Dumas, B. (1983), 'International Portfolio Choice and Corporation Finance: A Synthesis', *Journal of Finance*, 38, pp. 925–84.

Anderson, R.W. and Harris, C.J. (1986), 'A Model of Innovation with Application to New Financial Products', *Oxford Economic Papers*, 38, pp. 203–18.

Bagehot, W. (1880), *Economic Studies* in R.H. Hutton (ed.), London: Longmans, reprinted in 1976, *The Collected Works of Walter Bagehot*, Volume 11, Norman St John Stevas (ed.), London: The Economist.

Barry, C.B. and Brown, S.J. (1985), 'Differential Information and Security Market Equilibrium', *Journal of Financial and Quantitative Analysis*, 20, pp. 407–22.

Bawa, V.S., Brown, S.J. and Klein, R.W. (1979), *Estimation Risk and Optimal Portfolio Choice*, Amsterdam: North Holland.

Bayoumi, T. (1990), 'Saving-Investment Correlations: Immobile Capital, Government Policy, or Endogenous Behavior?', *IMF Staff Paper*, 37, pp. 101–10.

Bean, D.L. (1978), 'International Reserve Flows and Money Market Equilibrium: The Japanese Case' in J.A. Frankel and H.G. Johnson (eds.), *The Monetary Approach to the Balance of Payments*, London: Allen and Unwin.

Bental, B. (1985), 'Is Capital Mobility Always Desirable?: A Welfare Analysis of Portfolio Autarky in a Growing Economy', *International Economic Review*, 26, pp. 203–12.

Bischoff, C.W. (1971), 'The Effects of Alternative Lag Distributions' in G. Fromm (ed.), *Tax Incentives and Capital Spending*, Washington, DC: Brookings Institute.

Black, F. (1974), 'International Capital Market Equilibrium with Investment Barriers', *Journal of Financial Economics*, 1, pp. 337–52.

Branson, W.H. (1968), *Financial Capital Flows in the United States Balance of Payments*, Amsterdam: North-Holland.

Branson, W.H., Halttunen, H. and Masson, P. (1977), 'Exchange Rates in the Short-Run: The Dollar-Deutsche Mark Rate', *European Economic Review*, 10.

Branson, William H. and Henderson, D.W. (1985), 'The Specification and Influence of Asset Markets' in Ronald W. Jones and Peter B. Kenen (eds.), *Handbook of International Economics*, Vol. II, Amsterdam: North-Holland.

Branson, W.H. and Hill, R.D. Jr. (1971), 'Capital Movements in the OECD Area: An Econometric Analysis', *OECD Economic Outlook: Occasional Studies*, December, OECD Publications.

Branson, W.H. and Jaffee, D.M. (1991), 'The Globalization of Information and Capital Mobility' in J. Ronen and J. Livinat (eds.), *Accounting and Financial Globalization*, New York: Quorum Books.

Branson, W.H. and Willet, T.D. (1972), Policy Toward Short-Term Capital Movements: Some Implications of the Portfolio Approach' in F. Machlup, W.S. Salant and L. Tarshis (eds.), *International Mobility and Movement of Capital: A Conference of the Universities*, National Bureau Committee for Economic Research: Columbia University Press.

Brown, B. (1987), *The Flight of International Capital: A contemporary history*, London: Croom Helm.

Brown, S.J. (1979), 'The Effect of estimation Risk on Capital Market Equilibrium', *Journal of Financial and Quantitative Analysis*, 14, pp. 215–20.

Bruno, M. (1986), 'Aggregate Supply and Demand Factors in OECD Unemployment: An Update', *Econometrica* supplement, pp. 35–53.

Bryant, R.C. (1975), 'Empirical Research on Financial Capital Flows' in P. Kenen (ed.), *International Trade and Finance: Frontier for Research*, Cambridge: Cambridge University Press.

Bryant, R.C. and Hendershott, P.H. (1970), 'Financial Capital Flows in the Balance of Payments of the United States: An Exploratory Empirical Study', *Princeton Studies in International Finance*, No. 25.

Cairnes, J.E. (1874), *Some Leading Principles of Political Economy: Newly Expounded*, reprinted in 1967, New York: Augustus M. Kelley.

Casson, M.C. and associates (1986), *Multinationals and World Trade*, London: Allen and Unwin.

Chappell, H.W. and Cheng, D.C. (1982), 'Expectations, Tobin's Q, and Investment: A Note', *Journal of Finance*, pp. 231–6.

Chirinko, R.S. (1987), 'Tobin's Q and Financial Policy', *Journal of Monetary Economics*, 19, pp. 69–87.

Cumby, R.E. and Mishkin, F.S. (1985), 'The International Linkage of Interest Rates: The European–U.S. Connection', *Journal of International Money and Finance*, No. 4.

Cumby, R.E. and Obstfeld, M. (1984), 'International Interest Rate and Price Level Linkages under Flexible Exchange Rates: A Review of Recent Evidence' in J.F.O. Bilson and R C. Marston (eds.), *Exchange Rate Theory and Practice*, Chicago: University of Chicago Press.

Datapro Information Services Group (1992), *SWIFT – The International Banking Network*, (November), Delran, NJ: McGraw-Hill.

Datapro Information Services Group (1992), *Overview of Network Service*, (August), Delran, NJ: McGraw-Hill.

Datapro Information Services Group (1993), *International Switched Services: Overview*, (September), Delran, NJ: McGraw-Hill.

Deardorff, A.V. (1984), 'An Exposition and Exploration of Kruger's Trade Model', *Canadian Journal of Economics*, 17, pp. 731–46.

Dinenis, E. (1985), 'Q, Gestation Lags and Investment: Is the Flexible Accelerator a Mirage?', *Discussion Paper: Center for Labour Economics*, No. 236, London: London School of Economics.

Dooley, M., Frankel, J. and Mathieson, D. (1987), 'International Capital Mobility: What Do Saving-Investment Correlation Tell Us?', *IMF Staff Papers*, 34, pp. 503–30.

Dornbusch, R. (1975), 'A Portfolio Balance Model of the Open Economy', *Journal of Monetary Economics*, 1.

Dornbusch, R. (1980), 'Exchange Rate Economics: Where Do We Stand?', *Brookings Papers on Economic Activity*, 1.

Driskill, R.A. (1981), 'Exchange Rate Dynamics: An Empirical investigation', *Journal of Political Economy*, 89, No. 2.

Dunning, J.H. (1988), *Multinationals, Technology and Competitiveness*, London: the Academic Division of Union Hyman Ltd.

Dunning, J.H. and Cantwell, J. (1987), *IRM Directory of Statistics of International Investment and Production*, New York: New York University Press.

Eaton, J. and Gersovitz, M. (1980), 'LDC Participation in International Financial Markets', *Journal of Development Economics*, 7, pp. 2–21.

Eaton, J. and Gersovitz, M. (1984), 'A Theory of Expropriation and Derivations from Perfect Capital Mobility', *Economic Journal*, 94, pp. 16–40.

Farber, A., Roll, R. and Solnik, B. (1977), 'An Empirical Study of Risk Under Fixed and Flexible Exchange Rates' in K. Brunner and A.H. Meltzer (eds.), *Stabilization of the Domestic and International Economy*, Amsterdam: North Holland.

Feldstein, M. (1983), 'Domestic Savings and International Capital Mobility in the Long Run and the Short Run', *European Economic Review*, 21, pp. 139–51.

Feldstein, M. and Bachaetta, P. (1991), 'National Savings and International Investment' in D. Bernheim and J. Shoven (eds.), *National Saving and Economic Performance*, Chicago: University of Chicago Press.

Feldstein, M. and Horioka, C. (1980), 'Domestic Saving and International Capital Flows', *Economic Journal*, 90, pp. 314–29.

Financing Foreign Operations (FFO) (various years), *Business International Corporations*, New York: FFO.

Finnerty, J.D. (1988), 'Financial Engineering in Corporate Finance: Overview', *Financial Management*, Winter 1988, pp. 14–39.

Fischer, S. and Merton, R.C. (1984), 'Macroeconomics and Finance: The Role of the Stock Market' in K. Brunner and A.H. Meltzer (eds.), *Essays on Macroeconomic Implications of Financial and Labor Markets and Political Processes*, Amsterdam: North-Holland.

Floyd, J.E. (1985), *World Monetary Equilibrium: International monetary theory in an historical-institutional context*, Philadelphia: University of Pennsylvania Press.

Fleming, J.M. (1962), 'Domestic Financial Policies under Fixed and Floating Exchange Rates', *International Monetary Fund Staff Papers*, 9, pp. 369–79.

Frankel, J.A. (1971), 'A Theory of Money Trade and Balance of Payments in a Model of Accumulation', *Journal of International Economics*, May, pp. 159–87.

Frankel, J.A. (1989), 'Quantifying International Capital Mobility in the 1980s', *NBER Working Paper Series*, No. 2856, National Bureau of Economic Research.

Frankel, J.A. (1992), 'Measuring International Capital Mobility: A Review', *AEA Papers and Proceedings*, May, pp. 197–202.

Frankel, J.A. and Johnson, H.G. (eds.) (1976), *The Monetary Approach to the Balance of Payments*, London: Allen and Unwin.

Frankel, J.A. and Razin, A. (1987), *Fiscal Policies and the World Economy: An Intertemporal Approach*, Cambridge, MA: MIT Press.

Frankel, J.A., Gylfason, T. and Heilliwell, J.E. (1980), 'Synthesis of Money and Keynesian Approaches to Short-Run Balance-of-Payments Theory', *Economic Journal*, 90, pp. 582–92.

Froot, K.A. and Stein, J.C. (1991), 'Exchange Rates and Foreign Direct Investment: An Imperfect Capital Markets Approach', *Quarterly Journal of Economics*, 106, pp. 1191–217.

Garbade, K. and Silber, W.L. (1978), 'Technology, Communication, and the Performance of Financial Markets: 1840–1975', *Journal of Finance*, 33, pp. 819–31.

Genberg, A.H. (1978), 'Aspect of the Monetary Approach to Balance-of-Payments Theory: An Empirical Study of Sweden' in J.A. Frankel and H.G. Johnson (eds.), op. cit.

Gill, S. and Law, D. (1988), *The Global Political Economy: Perspectives, Problems and Policies*, Baltimore: Johns Hopkins University Press.

Gilman, M.G. (1981), *The Financing of Foreign Direct Investment: A study of the determinants of capital flows in multinational enterprises*, New York: St. Martin's Press.

Green, Robert T. (1972), *Political Instability as a Determinant of U.S. Foreign Investment*, Studies in Marketing No. 17, Bureau of Business Research, Austin: University of Texas Press.

Haque, N.U. and Montiel, P.J. (1991), 'How Mobile is Capital in Developing Countries?', *Finance and Development*, September, pp. 38–9.

Harrod, R.F. (1951), *The Life of John Maynard Keynes*, London: Macmillan.

Hayashi, F. and Inoue, T. (1987), *Implementing the Q-Theory of Investment in Microdata: Japanese Manufacturing 1977–1985*, mimeo, Osaka: Osaka University Press.

Haynes, S.E. (1988), 'Identification of Interest Rates and International Capital Flows', *Review of Economics and Statistics*, pp. 103–11.

Haynes, S.E. and Pippenger, J. (1979), 'International Capital Markets: A Synthesis of Alternative Models', *Economics Letters*, 3, pp. 179–85.

Haynes, S.E. and Pippenger, J. (1982), 'Discrimination Among Alternative Models of International Capital Markets', *Journal of Macroeconomics*, Winter, pp. 23–46.

Heckscher, E.F. and Ohlin, B. (1991), *Heckscher – Ohlin Trade Theory*, a translated version of *Utrikeshandelns verkan pa inkomstfordelningen. Nagra teoretiska grundlinjer* (Heckscher, 1919) and *Hendelns Teori* (Ohlin, 1924) tr. and ed. H. Flam and M.J. Flanders, Cambridge, MA: MIT Press.

Herring, R.J. and Marston, R.C. (1977), 'Sterilization Policy: The Trade-Off Between Monetary Autonomy and Control over Foreign Exchange Reserves', *European Economic Review*, 10, pp. 325–43.

Hirschleifer, J. (1973), 'Exchange Theory: The Missing Chapter', *Western Economic Journal*, 11, pp. 129–46.

Hodrick, R.J. (1979), *Some Evidence on the Equality of Expected Real Interest Rates across Countries*, mimeo, Pittsburg, PA: Carnegie-Mellon.

Hood, N. and Young, S. (1979), *The Economics of Multinational Enterprise*, London: Longman.

Howard, D.H. (1979), 'The Real Rate of Interest on International Financial Markets', *International Finance Discussion Papers*, No. 136, Board of Governors of the Federal Reserve System.

Hume, D. (1955), 'Of the Balance of Trade' in E. Rotwein (ed.), *David Hume: Writings on Economics*, London: Nelson.

Huizinga, Harry (1991), 'Foreign Investment Incentives and International Cross-Hauling of Capital', *Canadian Journal of Economics*, 24, pp. 710–6.

Institutional Investor (1980–1990), *Rating Country Risk*, every September issue.

International Finance Corporation (1989–1992), 'Emerging Stock Markets', Washington, DC: IFC.

International Monetary Fund (Research Department) (1983–1993), *Balance of Payments Statistics Yearbook*, Washington, DC: IMF.

International Monetary Fund (Research Department) (1985–1992), *International Financial Statistics Yearbook*, Washington, DC: IMF.

International Monetary Fund (Research Department) (1991), 'Determinants and Systemic Consequences of International Capital Flows', *Occasional Paper*, March 1991, Washington, DC: IMF.

International Research Group (1981–1992), *International Country Risk Guide*, New York: International Country Report Co.

International Telecommunication Union (1980–1992), *Yearbook of Common Carrier Telecommunication Statistics*, Geneva: ITU.

Iversen, C. (1936), *Aspect of the Theory of International Capital Movement*, Copenhagen: Oxford University Press.

Johnson, H.G. (1972), *Further Essays in Monetary Economics*, London: Allen and Unwin, reprinted in J.A. Frankel and H.G. Johnson (eds.), op. cit.

Johnson, P.D., McKibbin, W.J. and Trevor, R.G. (1982), 'Exchange Rates and Capital Flows: A Sensitivity Analysis', *Canadian Journal of Economics*, 15, pp. 669–92.

Jorgenson, D.W. (1963), 'Capital Theory and Investment Behavior', *American Economic Review*, May.

Kane, E.J. (1988), 'Interaction of Financial and Regulatory Innovation', *American Economic Review*, 78, pp. 328–34.

Kauri, J., Pentti, J.K and Porter, M.G. (1974), 'International Capital Flows and Portfolio Equilibrium', *Journal of Political Economy*, 82, pp. 443–67.

Kelly, T.R. (1987), 'Financial Innovation and Social Benefits' in R. Barre and Lord Roll (eds.), *Finance and the International Economy: The AMEX Bank Review Prize Essays*, New York: Oxford University Press.

Keynes, J.M. (1929), 'The German Transfer Problem', *Economic Journal*, 39, pp. 1–7.

Keynes, J.M. (1930), *A Treatise on Money*, London: Macmillan, reprinted 1971 in *The Collected Writings of John Maynard Keynes*, London: Macmillan.

Keynes, J.M. (1936), *The General Theory of Employment, Interest and Money*, London: Macmillan; New York: Harcourt, Brace and World.

Kock, K. (1929), *A Study of Interest Rates*, Stockholm.

Kravis, I.B. and Lipsey, R.E. (1978), 'Price Behavior in the Light of Balance of Payments Theories', *Journal of Political Economy*, 80, pp. 48–62.

Khayenbuehl, T.E. (1985), *Country Risk: Assessment and Monitoring*, Lexington, MA: Lexington Books.

Krugman, P.R. (1989), 'Private Capital Flows to Problem Debtors' in J. Sachs (ed.), *Developing Country Debt. Vol 1: The International Financial System*, Chicago: University of Chicago Press.

Lehfeldt, R.A. (1912), 'The Rate of Interest on British and Foreign Investments', *Journal of the Royal Statistics Society*, 14, pp. 196–415.

Leff, N.H. (1984), 'Externalities, Information Costs, and Social Benefit-Cost Analysis for Economic Development: An Example from Telecommunications', *Economic Development and Cultural Change*, 32, pp. 255–76.

Lensink, R. and Van Bergeijk, P.A.G. (1991), 'The Determinants of Developing Countries' Access to the International Capital Market', *Journal of Development Studies*, 28, pp. 86–103.

Longman Group Ltd. (1984, 1986), *International Directory of Telecommunications: Market Trends, Companies, and Personnel*, 1st and 2nd edns, Essex: Longman.

Lopez-Claros (1987), 'The Community: One Road to Integration', *Finance and Development*, pp. 35–38.

MacDougall, G.D.A. (1960), 'The Benefits and Costs of Private Investment from Abroad: A Theoretical Approach', *Economic Record*, Special Issue (March), reprinted in R.E. Caves and H.G. Johnson (eds.) (1968), *Readings in International Economics*, Homewood, Ill.: Irwin.

Machlup, F. (1932), *Die Theorie der Kapitalflucht*, Welteirtschaftliches, Arch. II.

Machlup, F. (1943), *International Trade and the National Income Multiplier*, Philadelphia: Blakiston.

Maddala, G.S. (1988), *Introduction to Econometrics*, New York: Macmillan Publishing Co.

Madansky, A. (1964), 'On Efficiency of Three-Stage Least Squares Estimation', *Econometrica*, 32, p. 55.

Mairesse, J. and Dermont, B. (1985), 'Labor and Investment Demand at Firm Level: A Comparison of French, Germany, and U.S. manufacturing, 1970–1979', *European Economic Review*, pp. 201–32.

Markowitz, H. (1952), 'Portfolio Selection', *Journal of Finance*, 7, pp. 77–91.

Marshall, A. (1923), *Money, Credit and Commerce*, reprinted in 1965, New York: Augustus M. Kelly.

Marwah, K. and Bodkin, R.G. (1984), 'A Model of the Canadian Global Exchange Rate: A Test of the 1970s', *Journal of Policy Modeling*, 6, No. 4.

Marwah, K. and Klein, L.R. (1983), 'A Model of Foreign Exchange Markets: Endogenizing Capital Flows and Exchange Rates', *Journal of Economics*, Supplementum, 3.

Marwah, K., Klein, L.R. and Bodkin, R.G. (1985), 'Bilateral Capital Flows and the Exchange Rate: the case of the U.S.A. vis-à-vis Canada, France, West Germany, and the U.K.', *European Economic Review*, 29, pp. 89–110.

Meade, J.E. (1951), *The Theory of International Economic Policy, Vol 1: The Balance of Payments*, London: Oxford University Press.

Meese, R. (1980), 'Dynamic Factor Demand Schedules for Labor and Capital under Rational Expectation', *Journal of Econometrics*, pp. 141–58.

Mill, J.S. (1909), *Principles of Political Economy*, Ashley edition, London: Longmans (reprinted in 1976 by Augustus M. Kelly Publishers (Fairfield, NJ)).

Miller, N. and Whitman, M.V.N. (1973), 'Alternative Theories and Tests of U.S. Short-Term Foreign Investment', *Journal of Finance*, 28, pp. 1131–50.

Mishikin, F. S. (1984), 'Are Interest Rates Equal Across Countries? An Empirical Investigation of International Parity Conditions', *Journal of Finance*, 39, pp. 1345–58.

Mundell, R.A. (1960), 'The Monetary Dynamics of International Adjustment under Fixed and Flexible Exchange Rates', *Quarterly Journal of Economics*, 74, pp. 227–57.

Mundell, R.A . (1962), 'The Appropriate Use of Monetary and Fiscal Policy under Fixed Exchange Rate', *International Monetary Fund Staff Papers*, March, pp. 70–9.

Murphy, R.G. (1986), 'Productivity Shocks, Nontraded Goods and Optimal Capital Accumulation', *European Economic Review*, 30, pp. 1081–95.

Mussa, M. (1974), 'Trade and the Balance of Payments: a Two-Country Monetary Model', paper delivered at the *Fourth Konstanz Conference on Monetary Theory and Policy 1973*, reprinted in J.A. Frankel and H.G. Johnson (eds.), op. cit.

Mussa, M. (1977), 'External and Internal Adjustment Costs and the Theory of Aggregated Firm Investment', *Economica*, 44, pp. 163–78.

Niho, Y. and Musacchio, R.A. (1983), 'Effects of Regulation and Capital Market Imperfections on the Dynamic Behavior of a Firm', *Southern Economic Journal*, 49, pp. 625–36.

Nunnenkamp, P. (1990), 'Determinants of Voluntary and Involuntary Bank Lending to Developing Countries in the 1980s', *Kyklos*, 43, pp. 555–77.

Obstfeld, M. (1986), 'Capital Mobility in the World Economy: Theory and Measurement', *Carnegie-Rochester Conference Series on Public Policy*, 24, pp. 55–104.

O'Brien, R. (1992), *Global Financial Integration: The end of geography*, London and New York: Royal Institute of International Affairs.

Organization for Economic Cooperation and Development (1989), *Telecommunication Network-Based Services: Policy implication*, Information Computer Communications Policy No. 18, Paris: OECD.

Organization for Economic Cooperation and Development (1992), *Financial Market Trends*, No. 51 (February), Paris: OECD.

Ohlin, B. (1924), *Handelns Teori*, PhD dissertation, Stockholm: A.B. Nordiska Bokhandeln.

Ohlin, B. (1929), 'Mr. Keynes' Views on the Transfer Problem: Part II. A Rejoinder from Professor Ohlin', *Economic Journal*, 39, pp. 400–4.

Ohlin, B. (1967), *Interregional and International Trade*, rev. edn, Cambridge, MA: Harvard University Press.

Omae, K. (1985), *Triad Power: The Coming Shape of Global Competition*, New York: Free Press.

Persson, T. and Tabellini, G. (1992), 'The Politics of 1992: Fiscal Policy and European Integration', *Review of Economic Studies*, 89, pp. 689–701.

Podolski, T.M. (1986), *Financial Innovation and the Money Supply*, London and New York: Basil Blackwell.

Price Waterhouse (1992), *Doing Business in Foreign Countries. A Guide Book for International Investments in Foreign Countries*, New York: Price Waterhouse.

Ricardo, D. (1973), *Principle of Political Economy and Taxation*, Donald Winch edition, London: Dent; New York: Dutton.

Ruffin, R.J. and Rassekh, F. (1986), 'The Role of Foreign Direct Investment in U.S. Capital Outflows', *American Economic Review*, 76, pp. 1126–30.

Salinger, M.and Summers, L.H. (1983), 'Tax reform and Corporate Finance: A Microeconomic Simulation Study', in M.S. Feldstein (ed.), *Behavioral Simulation Methods in Tax Policy Analysis*, Chicago: University of Chicago Press.

Shafer, J.R. and Loopesko, B.E. (1983), 'Floating Exchange Rates after Ten Years', *Brooking Papers on Economic Activity*, 1.

Sinn, S. (1992), 'Saving-Investment Correlations and Capital Mobility: On the Evidence from Annual Data', *Economic Journal*, 102, pp. 1162–70.

Smith, A. (1991), *Wealth of Nations*, Campbell edition, New York: Alfred A Knopf.

Stekler, L. (1988), 'Adequacy of International Transactions and Position Data for Policy Consideration', *International Finance Discussion Paper*, No. 337, November, Washington, DC: Board of Governors of the Federal Reserve System.

Stevens, G.V.G. et al. (1984), *The U.S. Economy in an Interdependent World: A Multicountry Model*, Washington, DC: Board of Governors of the Federal Reserve System.

Stiglitz, J.E. (1982), 'Information and Capital Markets' in W.F. Sharpe and C.M. Cootner (eds.), *Financial Economics: Essays in Honor of Paul Cootner*, Englewood Cliffs, New Jersey: Prentice-Hall (revised version of Part II of a paper presented at the New Orleans meetings of the Economic Society, 1971).

Stiglitz, J.E. (1987), 'Technological Changes, Sunk Costs, and Competition', *Brookings Papers on Economic Activity*, 3, pp. 883–973.

Stiglitz, J.E. (1992), 'Capital Markets and Economic Fluctuations in Capital Economies', *European Economic Review*, 36, pp. 269–306.

Stiglitz, J.E. and Weiss, A. (1981), 'Credit Rationing in Markets with Imperfect Information', *American Economic Review*, 71, pp. 393–410.

Stockman, A. and Svensson, L.E.O. (1987), 'Capital Flows, Investment, and Exchange Rates', *Journal of Monetary Economics*, 19, pp. 171–201.

Stulz, R.M. (1981), 'On the Effects of Barriers to International Investment', *Journal of Finance*, 36, pp. 923–34.

Tesar, L.L. (1991), 'Savings, Investment and International Capital Flows', *Journal of International Economics*, 31, pp. 55–78.

Tobin, J. (1958), 'Liquidity Preference as Behavior Towards Risk', *Review of Economic Studies*, 25, pp. 65–85.

Tobin, J. (1969), 'A General Equilibrium Approach to Monetary Theory', *Journal of Money, Credit, and Banking*, 1, pp. 15–29.

United Nations (1991), *World Investment Directory: Foreign Direct Investment Legal Framework and Corporate Data*, New York: United Nations.

United Nations (1992), *Foreign Direct Investments: The Service Sector and International Banking*, U.N. Center on Transnational Corporations, New York: United Nations.

United Nations (1992), *World Investment Directory 1992: Foreign Direct Investment Legal Framework and Corporate Data*, Vols I, II, and III, New York: United Nations.

Vos, R. (1988), 'Savings, Investment and Foreign Capital Flows: Have Capital Market Become Integrates?', *Journal of Development Studies*, 88, pp. 310–34.

Vinals, J. and Berges, A. (1988), 'Financial Innovation and Capital Formation' in A. Heertje (ed.), *Innovation, Technology, and Finance*, Oxford: Basil Blackwell, pp. 158–202.

Viner, J. (1929), *Political Aspects of International Finance*, Cambridge, MA: Harvard University Press.

Walter, N. (1989), 'Implication of EC Financial Integration', *Business Economics*, pp. 18–22.

Webb, M.A. (1982), 'The Effect of Customs Unions Among Specialized Countries on International Capital Flows', *Economic Record*, pp. 352–6.

Webb, M.A. (1990), 'Preferential Trading Agreements and Capital Flows', *Journal of Development Economics*, 32, pp. 181–90.

White, H.D. (1933), *The French International Accounts 1880–1913*, Cambridge, MA: Harvard University Press.

Williams, J.H. (1929), 'The Theory of International Trade Reconsidered', *Economic Journal*, 39, pp. 195–209.

Williamson, O. (1981), 'The Economics of Organization: The Transaction Cost Approach', *American Journal of Sociology*, 97, pp. 548–77.

Wong, D. (1990), 'What do Saving-Investment Relations Tell Us about Capital Mobility?', *Journal of International Money and Finance*, 9, pp. 60–74.

World Bank (1982–1993), *World Tables*, Baltimore: Johns Hopkins University Press.

World Bank (1992), *World Debt Tables*, Baltimore: Johns Hopkins University Press.

Yumoto, M., Shima, K., Koike, H. and Taguch, H. (1986), 'Financial innovation in Major Industrial Countries' in Y. Suzuki and H. Yomo (eds.), *Financial Innovation and Monetary Policy: Asia and West*, Tokyo: University of Tokyo Press.

Zecher, J. R. (1978), 'Monetary Equilibrium and International Reserve Flows in Australia' in J.A. Frankel and H.G. Johnson (eds.), op. cit.

For Product Safety Concerns and Information please contact our EU representative GPSR@taylorandfrancis.com Taylor & Francis Verlag GmbH, Kaufingerstraße 24, 80331 München, Germany

Printed and bound by CPI Group (UK) Ltd, Croydon, CR0 4YY
08/05/2025
01864437-0001